THE ANTHROPOLOGY
OF SLAVERY

The Anthropology of Slavery

The Womb of Iron and Gold

CLAUDE MEILLASSOUX

Translated by Alide Dasnois

The University of Chicago Press

To Quentin

The University of Chicago Press, Chicago 60637
The Athlone Press, London
Translation © 1991 The Athlone Press and
The University of Chicago
All rights reserved. Published 1991
Printed in Great Britain

00 99 98 97 96 95 94 93 92 91   6 5 4 3 2 1

ISBN: 0-226-51911-2 (cloth); 0-226-51912-0 (paper)

First published in France 1986
by Presses Universitaires de France, Paris as
Anthropologie de l'esclavage: Le ventre de fer et d'argent
© 1986 Presses Universitaires de France

The Publishers wish to record their thanks to the
French Ministry of Culture for a grant
towards the cost of translation.

Library of Congress Cataloging-in-Publication Data

Meillassoux, Claude.
[Anthropologie de l'esclavage, English]
The anthropology of slavery: the womb of iron and gold / Claude
Meillassoux; translated by Alide Dasnois.
p.   cm.
Translation of: Anthropologie de l'esclavage.
Includes bibliographical references and index.
ISBN 0-226-51911-2.   –   ISBN 0-226-51912-0 (pbk.)
1. Slavery – Africa – Conditions of slaves – History.   2. Slavery –
Economic aspects – Africa – History.   3. Slave trade – Africa –
History.   4. Social structure – Africa – History.
HT1321.M4513   1991
306.3'62'096 – dc20

LCN: 91-18852

This book is printed on acid-free paper

Contents

Note on Glossary

In an attempt to make this study more readable, I have included a Glossary at the end of the text in order to define certain terms and phrases in the sense in which I have used them – or, more correctly, in which I have done my best to use them. Some of these definitions do not correspond exactly to those given either in dictionaries or in the specialized literature. Other entries are an attempt to restore to the words a meaning which has been lost or has become less clear. Finally, some, particularly those which have to do with kinship, are bound up with a methodological perspective which I have not been able to elaborate here; I hope, nevertheless, that these definitions will help to make this perspective more comprehensible.

C.M.

Publisher's Note on Translation

The Publisher wishes to acknowledge the help of Dr Felicity Edholm and Elizabeth Lebas in advising on the translation of this work.

Foreword

The study of slavery has focused on the Americas and, to a lesser extent, classical antiquity. The most common image is most certainly the black slave of the American South, and for good reason. In 1860, there were four million slaves in the United States. The vision of slave studies broadened to include the rest of the Americas, and for those interested in Claude Meillassoux's anthropology of slavery it will be essential to keep in mind that these slaves, too, traced their origin to Africa. African slaves – how they got from Africa to the Americas and what happened to them and their descendants in the Americas – are a major subject of modern history, not only because of the scale of the oppression and its bitter legacy but also because the interaction among continents and peoples over several centuries represents the pain and suffering that gave birth to the modern world.

Meillassoux is concerned about African slaves, but in this book he does not focus on those who went to the Americas. His concern is for those who stayed in Africa, and he draws on their experience to construct a theoretical framework for the study of slavery as a concept and as an institution. It is perhaps common sense, however often overlooked, that the African slaves who were brought from Africa were slaves before they left Africa. The scholarship of the last twenty years has demonstrated that the variety and intensity of servile relationships and methods of oppression that can be equated with slavery were probably more developed in Africa than anywhere else in the world at any period in history. Furthermore, there were certainly more slaves in Africa in the nineteenth century than there were in the Americas at any time. The study of Africa's slaves, therefore, cannot only focus on the Americas.

Claude Meillassoux has contributed to the study of slavery in Africa for over twenty years. This book represents the

7

theoretical vision that has resulted from his scholarship. His thesis is both simple and complex; he begins with the premise that slavery arises from an economy of theft, in which people are stolen through acts of violence and are then converted into commodities. For Meillassoux, the slave is the most fundamental form of property. Besides being a major contribution to the study of slavery, this insight fleshes out the theory of Marx and Engels, who did not think through the logic of slavery in its entirety. Furthermore, the oppression associated with African slavery on both sides of the Atlantic becomes clearer. Meillassoux's vision is not a pleasing picture because slavery was oppressive, whether in the Americas or in Africa.

Paul E. Lovejoy
York University
Ontario

Introduction

Current research seems to be concerned less with slavery as a social system than with the definition of the slave. While the convergence of semantics and law helps to identify the phenomenon, it is unable to characterize slavery as an institution. In African societies, as in ancient societies (Vidal-Naquet, 1965–7) the words translated as 'slave' can also be applied to wider categories, sometimes to all those who are or have been in any sort of temporal or religious subjugation, in relation to an elder, a sovereign, a protector or a spiritual guide. These words may mean, variously, subservient, submissive, dependent, subject to, and may even refer to a disciple. Conversely, most slave societies have a wide vocabulary covering different conditions of subjugation which no longer have any equivalent in our language and are uniformly translated by the word 'slave'.

In legal terms, the slave is described as an object,[1] a possession, therefore alienable and subject to his or her master.

But given the nature of his or her exploitation, the assimilation of a human being to an object, or even to an animal, is an untenable and contradictory fiction. If the slave were in practice treated in this way, slavery would present no advantages over the use of material tools or over the breeding of cattle; and in fact, slaves are not used as the objects or animals to which the ideological fiction tends to reduce them. All their tasks, even porterage, call for the use of reason, if only to a limited extent, and their utility and productivity grow in proportion to the use of their intelligence. Efficient slave management implies a greater or lesser recognition of the slave's capacities as *Homo sapiens*, and thus a constant shift towards notions of obedience and duty which renders the slave indistinguishable, in strictly legal terms, from other categories of dependants. Pubescent girls, cadets, wives and pawned people are, like the slave, subject to the absolute power of the head of the family. They can be beaten, sold and even killed. The obligation to work weighs on all those, freeborn or subservient, who are dependent on a master, a 'patriarch' or a sovereign. On the other hand, certain slaves enjoy privileges – wealth, rank, office – which put them in what appears to be a superior position; and of these, it is said that they are 'kin'. The soldier–slave, the henchman, the rich slave, who benefit indirectly from the labour of other slaves or even of free men, or who themselves own slaves, are not expected to work. In terms of the slave–object fiction, as in the situations described above, the only institutional relationship relevant to the slave which is recognized by law is his relationship with his master. The legal definition of the slave therefore applies to this – strictly individual – relationship.

In these circumstances, the law both ratifies and conceals social relations, sanctioning them in the form most suited to preserve the interests of those for whom the law is conceived and worded. It cannot, therefore, be seen as the objective expression of social reality; nor can it contain an explanation of this reality. In expressing the slave relation as individual, the law fixes the limits within which the authority of the master over the slave can be exercised; thus the individual relation masks and neutralizes the class relation. The individual relation merely reflects a personalized and individualized conception of authority, based on patriarchal ideology. In fact, in strictly legal – that is, individual – terms, the definition of the slave necessarily depends to some extent on that of the free man or woman, because of this implicit ideological reference. This explains the apparently infinite variety of the conditions of individual slaves – a variety which cannot be explained by the legal principle, which is itself indeterminate.

Even the most pertinent and most widely applicable criterion – that of the legal alienability of the slave, irrespective of his or her condition – lacks precision. Certain individuals who are not slaves can be alienated, and not all slaves are, in fact, alienable.

The weakness of the legalistic approach is that it considers alienability as a characteristic specific to slaves. Yet alienability has meaning only in the context of institutions which make alienation possible: wars of capture or 'slave markets' – that is, the set of mechanisms and operations through which a set of individuals can be deprived of social personality, transformed into livestock, sold as merchandise and exploited or employed in such a way that the cost of capture or purchase can be covered. But alienation merely represents the transcendental state of the slave. It takes place only when the slave cannot perform productive or functional tasks, for whatever reason, in the society in which he finds himself. Alienation is merely the effect and confirmation of a process of depersonalization which has already been inflicted on the slave through capture. Final alienation takes place on the 'sacrificial' altar as well as on the market – that is, in religious rites as well as in commercial transactions. The state of the slave is expressed in his relation to these institutional social frameworks, not in his individual relation to his master.

All the African societies examined in this study are linked, directly or indirectly, to the market. Some supply it, others are supplied from it. In the final analysis, the real or potential fate of the slaves – their *state* [see Glossary], in other words – is necessarily defined with respect to the market, even if all slaves are not necessarily directly subject to the market at all times. It is through the market that the common *state* of slaves, as a social class, is defined, and it is with respect to the market that the different, changing and individual *condition* of each slave is defined according to the mode of insertion of the slave in each slave society. The individual relation of the slave to his or her master cannot be explained outside this context.

The distinction between the *state* and the *condition* of the slave, inherent in this process, is one of the keys to understanding the problem. Because of the importance of this distinction, this study is divided into three parts: the first covers the whole of the economic space of slavery which structures the *state* of the slave; the other two are devoted to the political and economic forms which slavery takes in the two main types of African societies in which it is present, military aristocracies and merchant societies.

In an important collaborative work on African slavery, Miers and Kopytoff (1977) take a very different approach. They offer in their introduction a genetic explanation of slavery which seems to me to take legalism, functionalism and economism to extremes.

Miers and Kopytoff consider that what they call 'minors' (children, young people, women) are in a dependent position in the family and that, on the other hand, the kinship system allows for the transfer of dependency; and they see slavery as the extension of this double phenomenon to aliens. As a result, the thrust of their argument turns around what they call the 'slavery–kinship continuum' and their theory of 'the transfer of rights-in-persons'. In the first place, they discover that ownership has a peculiar meaning in Africa in that it entails not only 'rights-in-things', but a set of 'rights-in-things-and-in-persons'. Next they discover what they consider to be another feature peculiar to African culture, though they do not specify to which type of society they refer: the fact that 'the concept of rights-in-persons and transactions in them . . . constitute some of the basic elements on which kinship systems are constructed'. Such transactions, they write,

> are a formal part of African concepts of kinship. . . . The transactability of such rights, as discrete and separate items, is also remarkable. Moreover, transfers of such rights are normally made in exchange for goods and money, and the transfer may cover the total rights-in-a-person. As a result, such phenomena as kinship, adoption, the acquisition of wives and children, are all inextricably bound up with exchanges that involve precise equivalence in goods and money. . . . Consequently, to say that what makes a person a slave is the fact that he is 'property', is in fact to say 'a slave is a person over whom certain [un-

specified] rights are exercised'. (1977:11)

This theory, according to Miers and Kopytoff, is likely to surprise 'the Westerner', who cannot conceive that rights can be divided up and applied to individuals as well as to things. What surprises me personally is that Miers and Kopytoff do not see that their explanation rests on the strict application of Western notions of law and of liberal economics. In our society, property is a set of rights, *usus, fructus* and *abusus*, which can, indeed, be attributed separately to different parties or persons. What is more, in domestic society it is not property which is in question but patrimony, which is governed by completely different rules of transfer.

It is no longer possible today to defend the 'vulgar' materialist thesis that bridewealth is 'an acquisition of rights' over children or wives 'in exchange for a precise equivalent in goods or in money' – a purchase, in other words. Not only do Miers and Kopytoff forget that the matrimonial transaction can take place, and did in fact take place, in numerous African societies without bridewealth, but the notion of equivalence of individuals with goods is not relevant to domestic societies. What is correct in Miers and Kopytoff's theory is that kinship relations are constantly manipulated. What is false is that they are manipulated against currency through purchase. In matrimonial relations, the only equivalent to a pubescent woman is another pubescent woman, with the same potential fertility. The concept of bridewealth does not bear children. When the two terms of a transaction are identical, intermediate goods (if they exist) have no intrinsic value and cannot be exchanged for themselves. Only when these goods enter the commercial circuit outside the community and are produced for exchange can they acquire an intrinsic value and communicate their saleability to the matrimonial circuits, resulting in the transformation of individuals into commodities. The effect of this transformation cannot be attributed to 'kinship'. There is no 'continuum' between the two levels, but rather a qualitative change. Miers and Kopytoff believe that 'rights-in-persons' are communicated to the slave system; in fact, the reverse is true: the saleability of slavery contaminates and reifies kinship relations.

The theory of rights-in-persons yet again introduces the principles of conservative classical economics into historical situations for which they are even less suited than in our days. Miers and Kopytoff see 'the roots of the servile institution in the need for wives and children, the wish to enlarge one's group . . . to have clients, servants and retainers' (p.67). This need grows with 'the infinite urge to absorb more consumer goods . . . much in the same way [as in our] modern consumer societies'. These needs and wishes are satisfied, as Adam Smith would have us believe, thanks to 'the human propensity for truck and barter' (p.67).

It would be difficult to go further than Miers and Kopytoff in using economic motivations to interpret social phenomena! Why, in these circumstances, would certain populations wish to 'sell' their children? If the desire of peoples is to 'enlarge their group', why would the majority be prepared to alienate their dependants, and thus to impoverish themselves in absolute terms for the benefit of a small fraction? And where is it possible to find examples of this? It is true that there are parents, driven by hunger, who are forced to sell their children, but this takes place in a context where saleability is already active as a direct or indirect result of trade. Within the original domestic economy, nothing, as has been noted above, can replace a human being as a producer or reproducer except another, identical, human being. If the 'propensity to barter' is the motor of exchange, it can allow only for the barter of one man for another man or of one woman for another woman. How can this explain the accumulation of human beings for the benefit of a few? In return for what 'riches' would one be tempted to give up the greatest of all riches? The sale of kin is neither 'traditional' nor compatible with the organization of kinship.

This weakness in Miers and Kopytoff's approach results in the assimilation of slavery to kinship, when in fact the two institutions are strictly antinomic. If, *by the purely ideological extension of kinship*, the slave is sometimes assimilated to a sort of perpetual cadet, with the obligations of a dependant in terms of customary notions of morality, he still never acquires the essential prerogatives – those bound up with paternity. His status of non-kin stems from the specificity of slave exploitation and its mode of reproduction. Ignorance of this point blinds one to the contours of slavery, for it is in fact slavery which highlights its opposite, franchise. The free man is defined only in relation to the slave. Society is transformed by the very fact of the introduction of slaves within its midst. It becomes a class society, if it was not one already. New rules are established and the old rules remain only in order to perpetuate the domination of the free classes and their reproduction as such. The presentation of slavery as an extension of kinship implies approval of the old paternalistic idea which has always been used as moral backing for slavery. It means falling into the trap of an apologist ideology in which the slave-owner tries to pass off those he exploits as his beloved children.

Although Miers and Kopytoff lean heavily on economism and naive materialism in their interpretation of servitude and its transformations, they declare: 'we don't need to appeal to an economic *raison d'être* for the existence of slavery'! Perhaps what they mean is that slaves are not necessarily used as producers, which is true. However, the economic scope of slavery is not limited to the productive use of slaves, nor to the profit which it can generate. Whatever their employment, slaves are imported at a cost: that of war or that of export goods. Putting slaves to work involves a choice between commercial and natural reproduction. Those slaves who are not assigned to agricultural labour must be fed, and at low levels of productivity this is a domestic problem which is difficult to resolve. It implies – assuming that the masters do not work for their own slaves! – the exploitation of a different fraction of free men or of other slaves, as well as institutions which can extract their surplus-product and transfer it. When they are used in political activity or in war, slaves take part in the establishment of the political class and act as the means of its economic domination – which becomes even more necessary, since idle slaves must be provided for.

In merchant society, the condition of slaves, who can be manipulated at will, changes further in terms of their relation (and that of their products) to the market, through the articulation of their food production and profits, through their entry as a stolen means of production into the general

economy, through the nature of the product which enables
them to be replaced, and so on. Because they do not consider
the practical aspects of slave management, Miers and Kopytoff are blind to its economic implications. It seems clear –
though they do not explicitly say so – that Miers and Kopytoff imagine that by dismissing 'the economic *raison d'être* of
slavery' they can also dismiss the 'Marxist' interpretation, in
the commonly held belief that historical materialism can be
reduced to the same economistic causality which they themselves use, apparently unwittingly.

What, then, does historical materialism – and particularly
what do Marx and Engels – contribute to an understanding
of slavery?

The contributions of the two authors vary in quality in
their different works. Engels in particular worked on the
conditions leading to the emergence of slavery (1884/1954:
145–63). He sees slavery as the effect (following the dissolution of the gentle order) of three main divisions of labour:

a. The division between agriculture and pastoralism,
which gives rise to regular exchange, the emergence of
money, and an increase both in production and in the productivity of labour. With an increase in work there is an
increasing demand for the producers that war provides.[2]

b. The separation of craftwork from agriculture. The
value of labour-power increases and men are themselves
introduced into exchange as objects of exchange. Slavery
becomes an essential component of the social system and
war becomes a permanent sector of industry.

c. The separation of town and country which favours the
development of a merchant class, the differential accumulation of wealth and its concentration in the hands of a class
which takes over the producers by increasing the number
of slaves: slavery becomes the dominant form of production.

Marx writes of slavery as such even less than Engels does. He
deals with it only in comparison with other modes of pro-

duction. In order to understand the thrust of his ideas on the subject, his writings in the *Formen*[3] need to be distinguished from those in *Capital*.

In the *Formen*, Marx almost always associates slavery with serfdom. His remarks are more suggestive than workable, and are often confused. Sometimes he sees slavery as 'the development of property based on tribalism';[4] sometimes as the result of the extension of the family, in which case slavery is 'latent' (ibid. 122–3).[5] Sometimes he seeks the origins of slavery in the appropriation of the means of subsistence (ibid. 101); sometimes in conquest (ibid. 93). Marx does not resolve the question of the possible endogenous development of slavery, nor of its historical emergence through contact between civilizations. He does not make clear the organic link between slaves as a *class* and their masters, in spite of a pertinent comment (ibid. 95) on the historical nature of the individualization of class relations;[6] he does not distinguish clearly between the systems of subordination which are set up between kin in the relations of agricultural production and those which result from capture. Some of his comments help us to understand the 'juridical' confusion between subjects, family dependants and slaves (ibid. 92), but they do not resolve the problem of the specificity of the slave relation.

Marx's observations in *Capital* (Marx, 1867/1970), while they are less dense and do not constitute a theoretical corpus which would lead to the classification of slavery as a mode of production, are characterized by a rigour which is not to be found in the *Formen*. Marx broadly distinguishes two main forms of slavery: in the first, so-called 'patriarchal' slavery, ownership of an individual may be an 'accident' and in any case the labour of the slave is directed towards the direct production of the means of subsistence (*Capital* III, ch. XX: 332) – in other words, use-value. With the effects of trade, patriarchal slavery can develop into a system geared to the production of surplus-value (*Capital* I, ch. X: 236) in which the slave is subject to fiercer and fiercer exploitation, as exchange-value develops (*Capital* I, ch. X: 236). It is this form of slavery, which produces exchange-value, to which Marx most often refers.

Although Marx still, in *Capital*, often associates slavery

with 'serfdom', he characterizes the former by the fact that it requires an initial outlay of money which he assimilates to fixed capital (*Capital* II, ch. XX: 483). The benefit gained by the owner is seen as interest on the capital advanced, or as anticipated, capitalized surplus-value, or as profits (if capitalist concepts are dominant), or as rent: 'Whatever it may be called, the available surplus-product appropriated . . . is here the normal and prevailing form' (*Capital* III, ch. XLVII: 804). But the advance on fixed capital invested in the purchase of the slave forces the owner to invest further capital in exploitation of the slave. Thus, there is necessarily a choice to be made between the purchase of more slaves and that of the means of production which would increase their productivity. In the first case (that of slavery in ancient times), as Engels states (1884: 111), the number of slaves may be considerable: up to eighteen times the number of free men. The relation between masters and slaves, 'which appears as the motor of production', would still exclude the reification of the relations of production (*Capital* III, ch. XLVIII: 831). Because of the inequality of these social relations, Marx notes *à propos* of Aristotle, slavery obscures the equality of tasks and thus the conception of value in the minds of men (*Capital* I, ch. I: 59).

When, as in American slavery, the labour of the slave is mediated by investments (however limited, as Marx notes), domination over men tends once again to be achieved through domination over things (Engels, 1884: 208). The surplus-labour of the slave increases as soon as it 'is no longer a question of obtaining from him a certain quantity of useful products' (*Capital* I, ch. X: 236). The slave trade enables the easy replacement of slaves by 'foreign Negroes' whose life-span is less important than their productivity (*Capital* I, ch. X: 266). Marx touches on the problem of reproduction, emphasizing that in America natural growth was insufficient and the slave trade was necessary to meet the needs of the market (*Capital* II, ch. XX: 483). Engels similarly notes that the slaves of Rome reproduced themselves to a very limited extent and that colossal supplies of slaves ensured by war were a precondition for the development of the great landed estates. The continual wars the Germans waged among themselves, like those between the Saxons and the Normans, were also designed to supply the slave market (1884: 200). In fact, Roman slavery disappeared with the decline of trade and of the towns, and the development of colonies and of serfdom (ibid. 1398; 1877: 362). It should be noted that Marx, and especially Engels, referring to slaves in ancient Europe, point to the social role of certain slaves – because they did not belong to any *gens* – as favourite slaves, with access to wealth, honours and high rank; these slaves constituted the basis for a new nobility among the Franks and the Germans. This nobility was doubtless associated with those military suites who waged war on their own account and through wars of plunder supplied the slave market.

Despite the absence of a systematic study of the phenomenon of slavery, many of these reflections are still relevant. A few points should, however, be corrected.

So-called 'patriarchal' slavery should not – because of its 'accidental' character – be identified as a class relation and does not in itself lead to a slave system of production. As I see it, this is not, strictly speaking, slavery, but rather an isolated phenomenon of subservience.

The distinction between subsistence slavery, which produces a rent in food, and slavery which generates profit must be retained, but the two are not always mutually exclusive. While subsistence slavery does dominate military and ancillary slavery in aristocratic and military societies, it still continues to be an indispensable basis for the creation of profit in merchant slavery.

Marx and Engels suggest, as a general economic condition for the emergence of slavery, an increase in productivity such that labour-energy is able to supply more than what is necessary for the subsistence of the producer.[7] But in any society adults always produce more than they themselves need, in order to feed younger generations. It is this share, reserved for reproduction, which is appropriated by the slave-owner when he tears the adult out of his milieu to produce for him and finally when he replaces him, once he is no longer productive, with another slave. Slavery is thus the only mode of production which allows the human surplus-product to be appropriated independently of increases in the productivity of labour over the level of 'simple reproduction'. Serfdom, on the contrary, necessitates higher productivity, since the serf has to ensure, at the very least, both his own 'simple reproduction' and that of his masters.

The weakness of Marx and Engels's reasoning lies in their repeated confusion of slavery with serfdom – a confusion which also affects their arguments on the problem of value[8] and on the relationship between slavery and kinship.

On the other hand, as Engels suggests, it is possible that relations between wide-ranging nomads and sedentary agriculturalists favoured slavery. Cattle-raising nomads are, at one and the same time, economically dependent on sedentary agriculturalists who cultivate the subsistence goods they need, and militarily and logistically dominant through their control over animal energy. This energy – which enables the herds to feed themselves on the move – also provides a means of transport for long-distance trade or can be offered as a service in exchange for agricultural goods. It also provides speedy mounts which are efficient instruments of plunder and abduction. Not all cattle-raisers are involved in pillage, but wide-ranging nomads, better mounted and in contact with other sedentary peoples beyond the desert, can combine plunder with abduction and transport their surplus booty to distant clients.

In this way the contact between pastoralists and sedentary peoples provides the opportunity for subservience, and nomadism supplies its logistics. But this contact still does not explain the demand for slaves from the client populations – in other words, the 'genesis' of slavery.

The underlying cause of this mode of exploitation and of the confrontations between peoples which result from it is probably to be found in a centuries-long historical process. Slavery is a period in universal history which has affected all continents, sometimes simultaneously, sometimes successively. Its 'genesis' is the sum of all that happened during an indeterminate period in many places. African trade in slaves to the Maghreb, then to Europe, which is the origin of slavery in black Africa, merely took over from the trade in slaves which had lasted for centuries in Asia, on the European continent and around the Mediterranean. The Slavs supplied their contingent of 'slaves', the Esclavons theirs of 'esclaves'; our ancestors the Gauls regularly sold their English captives to the Romans; the Vikings took captives and sold them while carrying on their coastal trade. Muslim and Christian pirates took each other captive. The process of enslavement had been under way for a long time, and in order to explain it in Africa it is necessary to explain its emergence on the Euro-Asian continent. Yet paradoxically it is in Africa, the last of the continents to supply the slave trade, that some seek an explanation for the origins of slavery, on the basis of an endogenous development of societies which are still suspected of primitivism and isolation and which are, therefore, laboratories for retarded fantasies.

It is not possible in this study to reconstitute a history of the emergence of slavery in the world. This work is not a general theory of slavery, but a theoretical essay on slavery based on my knowledge of a small part of Africa. But the history of slavery in Africa is indispensable to any understanding of the facts which accompany it: it is this history which reveals the specificity of the slave mode of production, gives an economic meaning to war and provides a means of interpreting certain forms of power. It shows that the phenomenon of slavery is embedded in a social and political complex with considerable geographical scope. The anthropological dimension is significant only in the context of the economy and the demography of all the people concerned, both the plundered and the plundering. This perspective offers a constantly widening dimension to research on slavery, a dimension which I have not, in this study, exhausted.

In the regions of Africa where I have worked, slavery is within the reach of living memory. However, it is not present in all its variants. It is therefore tempting to seek data elsewhere. In some of my examples I have succumbed to this temptation, but I have tried to stop short of unruly comparisons. This study has shown me that the notion of slavery in Africa covers such a wide variety of situations that a similar heterogeneity can be suspected elsewhere – in ancient times or in the Americas, for example. Slavery, rigorously defined, may have universal characteristics, but its definition, which is the main object of this study, must be generally accepted if a real discussion is to take place. I have, therefore, decided not to undertake a criticism of the classical works on slavery in other periods or in other regions: first because their authors' criteria for differentiation are not the same as mine, and secondly because, not being on my own ground, I would not have been able to locate areas of agreement and disagreement with any certainty.

At a number of points, this work refers to my previous writing and I have reproduced parts of the argument for the sake of clarity. In order to make the exposition more readable, I have also compiled an alphabetical glossary of the notions and concepts used in the body of the text (see p. 335). This exercise has shown me how easy it is to drift away from one's own vocabulary, and has forced me to take up the work again several times to steer it back to coherence. I am not sure that I have succeeded.

Finally, I would like to emphasize that, in their essentials, my information and my analysis have been fed by the very rich contributions of my colleagues in a previous collaborative work.[9]

Introductory Chapter

Kin and Aliens

1 'TO BE BORN AND GROW UP TOGETHER'

In a penetrating and masterly work, E. Benveniste (1969) reveals 'the social origins of the concept "free"' on the basis of a semantic analysis. 'The primary meaning', he writes, 'is not, as we might be tempted to imagine, "released from something"; it refers to membership of an ethnic stock described by a metaphor taken from plant growth. This membership confers a privilege which is unknown to the alien and the slave' (1969, I: 324). Free men (the free-born, the gentles) are those 'who were born and have developed together' (ibid. 323, emphasis added).[1] The alien, *a contrario*, is he who did not grow up in the interstices of the social and economic networks which situate a man with respect to others.

Benveniste's discovery conforms to analysis of the development of the domestic agricultural economy in its double process of production and reproduction and of the place which the (male) individual acquires in this society through *his double participation in the productive and reproductive cycles*. The Maninka, using terms which are nearly identical to those of Benveniste, in fact say, when referring to their congeners, those with whom they can identify themselves, '*ka wolo nyoronka, ka mo nyoronka*': to be born together, to

23

mature together. This does not express 'consanguinity' but rather 'congeneration': the growing-up of individuals together and in relation to each other.

As I have tried to show elsewhere (1981: 1–1 and 1–3), in the domestic community, social organization is built around constraints linked to the agricultural use of the land as a means of labour: the labour invested in the land gives rise to delayed production which compels the members of the community to stick together, not only during the fallow season but also from one agricultural cycle to the next, since the means of subsistence produced during one cycle are used for the reproduction of the labour-energy to be applied to production in the following cycle. Thus constantly renewed relations, which are lifelong and based on anteriority, are formed between productive and non-productive individuals in the social context and between producers of different ages in the work context, through which successive generations ensure their future.

'We dig a well today for tomorrow's thirst', say the Maninka. This linking together of generations is also expressed in the Mossi dictum: 'Somebody looked after you until your teeth grew, look after him when his teeth fall out' (according to J.M. Kohler, 1972: 49). This is a more elegant way of saying what Aristotle expressed painstakingly: 'If they have children, it is in order to draw advantage from this, since all the trouble they have while in full possession of their strength in bringing up children who are still lacking in vigour, they will be compensated for when the latter have in turn become strong and they themselves feel the impotence of old age' (*Economics* [1958]: 22). Since merchant exchange is unknown in self-sustenance society, its product has no external outlets and circulates according to a redistributive system which ensures the satisfaction of the needs of the whole community through the production of its active members.

Domestic society is not a class society. Relations of production are, it is true, established between productive and unproductive individuals, as in any mode of production. However, unlike class society, in domestic society the attribute of productive or unproductive refers only to physical and intellectual capacity and not to social insertion. In domestic society, all adults who can work are productive; those who are unproductive are children, old people and the disabled. Each person's share, over his or her lifetime, depends not on rank but on the relative lengths of the active and unproductive periods of his or her life. Like other goods in this type of society, the surplus-product is distributed through exchange which is free but deferred (Meillassoux, 1981, I, 3: 4). In a patrilineal system, the needs of demographic and social reproduction force the productive community to open out to other similar communities, in order to organize the distribution and allocation of pubescent women. *The precedence of the male individual in the productive cycle normally corresponds to the sequence of access to wives, and thus to the rank of elder or cadet in the reproductive cycle.* Social paternity inserts individuals in this reproductive cycle and completes its correspondence with the productive cycle, whether anterior or posterior, since the growth of children depends on the productive capacities of the 'fathers' who supply food, and is thus linked to their productive cycle. In domestic communities the two cycles are always closely linked, complete in themselves but subordinated one to the other. Rank and status are expressed in kinship, *a codified expression of the common development of men relative to each other*, congruently with the lifelong evolution of each individual in the double cycle of material production and human reproduction. Thus it is in principle a closed system, which can be penetrated only through birth or its equivalent, adoption.

In this way, the closing up of the commuunity around the *men* who have grown up together in its midst – the *congeners* (in the precise sense of the word) – is the distant and immanent condition for the slave relation. This relation is made possible by the latent distinction *which can be organically established between gentles and aliens.* The individual who has not been brought up in this double productive and reproductive cycle is thus an alien. On this basis he is distinguished from the *gentle*, who was born and has grown up within the community.[2]

The economic basis of this distinction between gentles and aliens highlights one of the objective conditions for the emergence of the exploitation of labour in domestic society. It must be noted, in order to avoid confusion later, that the functioning of the domestic community merely generates the distinction between gentle and alien. The relation of exploitation which can develop from this base is an aberrant phenomenon. It can evolve towards slavery only when, simultaneously, the conditions of existence of the domestic economy change and disappear as a result of insertion into the market.

exogenous exchange

2 KIN

The *productivity* of agricultural subsistence labour determines a society's capacities for reproduction and demographic growth.

The physical existence of a society and its perpetuation necessitate a minimal productivity to ensure, at the very least, the renewal of the generations; that is, the 'simple reproduction' (one for one) of the producers. Each active labourer must be able to supply a *surplus-product*[3] of food sufficient to feed a replacement up to productive age, taking into account mortality at each age. Demographic growth further necessitates the stocking of food so as to reduce mortality rates during periods of scarcity or famine. Thus productivity determines the proportion of individuals who can be fed from the production of others.

The productivity of subsistence farming in sub-Saharan Africa has until the present been limited by the use of manual techniques based on individual tools rather than the social means of production. In most cases subsistence agriculture is still at the stage of the hoe.

In the domestic self-sustenance economy, the whole of the surplus-product (after deduction for the care of post-productive individuals) is reinvested in the community's capacity for reproduction. This explains the concern with the renewal of the generations and the close link between the process of reproduction and the social structure.

The transfer of an individual's surplus-product to his elders or his descendants is the material content of the filiation relation. As long as an active adult is unmarried, his surplus-product goes to his elders. Once he is married and 'the father of a family', his link with his progeny is materialized in his contribution to their growth. Exploitation of cadets by their elders could take place only through the imposition of a limit on the progeny of the cadets, or, rather, through the indefinite prolongation of their unmarried state. But the economic effects of the exploitation of labour through the maintenance of the cadets' unmarried state are limited and threaten the bases of physical, structural and ideological reproduction of the domestic community. The 'value' of subsistence goods, in an economy without exchange, is realized only through their internal investment in the formation and care of future producers. If exploitation is accompanied by a reduction in the birth rate, it immediately has negative effects. Further, the man who is denied a wife – that is, the means of social reproduction – is also denied the possibility of investing his product in dependants who, through their future labour, will in their turn free him from his dependence on his elders and possibly give him the rank of elder. Thus he is not treated as *kin*. He is excluded from the prerogatives attached to this status.[4]

This exclusion can be applied only to cadets whose kinship links are weak or non-existent: that is, to individuals who are exceptions in a domestic society under normal conditions. Poor relatives could constitute an exploited *social class* only if their total surplus-product were sufficient to ensure the permanent and regular reproduction of the exploiting class. But since their existence is uncertain and the result of the dysfunction of the society rather than of its organic function, this continuity cannot be ensured.

In fact, the social assimilation of poor relatives is so difficult that, among the Dogon, bastards who might have swelled the ranks of exploited persons were rather sold as slaves to slave-traders. D. Paulme (1940: 433–4) reports that the colonial prohibition of slave-trading, far from giving rise to internal slavery, provoked an increase in infanticides and abortions. Exploitation could be systematic and continuous only if a fraction of the members of the community were arbitrarily denied access to wives – that is, if a 'class' of unmarried individuals were constituted. But if it were doomed

to celibacy, this class could only be reproduced institutionally. It would not be the result of 'status-creating' marriage.
Its members would therefore not be 'born'. Thus while it is
possible, in the domestic community, to reduce poor relatives to occasional and individual subservience, the hypothesis of systematic, *sui generis* slavery, born of the normal functioning of domestic society, seems improbable. The
argument below will in fact demonstrate that the slave is
above all, as Benveniste implies, the alien *par excellence*, if not
the alien in an absolute sense.

3 ALIENS

It seems difficult, in the domestic context, to transform relatives into a class of slaves. But neither is the fact of not being
born into the domestic community sufficient to make an individual into an absolute alien and reduce him to subservience and exploitation. This is clear from the modes of insertion into domestic societies of individuals without kinship
links.

The domestic community can never be effectively closed.
We know that the hazards of natural reproduction in small
demographic units make the maintenance of an efficient proportion of producers to unproductive individuals at all times
impossible. It is this practical necessity which leads to the
manipulation of social relations in order to control production, since it cannot be left, as in our densely populated societies, to the law of probabilities. The community is driven to
outside recruitment to reconstitute its numbers and its structures – through war, matrimonial or political strategies. For
these reasons, the community is never completely closed. It
must be able to open out in spite of its constitution. The
needs of reproduction compel it to define modes of insertion
for aliens, alongside matrimonial institutions, and these
modes differ according to whether the alien is a man or a
woman.

The insertion of a woman into a community proportion-
ally increases its reproductive capacity. A male individual, on
the other hand, increases this capacity very little or not at all,

since a few men or even a single man can impregnate all the pubescent women in a community. One adult man could probably regularly impregnate between fifteen and thirty women. Thus the ratio does not favour men in terms of reproduction, since more than 90 per cent of them (for a sex ratio of 1:1) are superfluous to the natural fulfilment of the reproductive function. If all the men are to be admitted, they must be accepted and acknowledged, *by convention* or institutionally, as reproducers, and each must be granted a place in the sequence of access to women. It is not so much as a 'natural' reproducer that the man has his place in the social system, but as a social reproducer, recognized by convention as such.[5]

In domestic kinship society, the potential fertility of the women is mediated socially by the man, whose social insertion as a reproducer goes along with a specifically masculine attribute: that of generating relations of filiation. The man's capacity for occasional impregnation has social effect only in the strict and legitimized framework of accepted matrimonial relations. In the final analysis this legitimization replaces the act of fertilization, since the conjugal tie suffices, in patrilineal society, to ensure that the husband is acknowledged as the father of his wife's children. In matrilineal society, the man establishes a filiation relation with his sister's children, *independently of any capacity for natural fertilization*. Although the woman is the irreplaceable producer of her progeny, she is dispossessed of the juridical right to socialize her children. Since her progeny is a sort of gross contribution to the community, the social position of the woman herself is of little importance in the establishment of relations of filiation. Only that of her husband or her brother is decisive. Thus in domestic society the birth of a (legitimate) boy is seen as more valuable than that of a girl, since the boy will be able to attract or to keep the progeny of a woman within the community.

Now, male aliens who are not inserted into these kinship relations contribute nothing in terms of physical or social reproduction which cannot be accomplished by a man who already belongs to the community. *A priori* it is thus not as a sire, strictly speaking, that the insertion of an alien man can be evaluated, since this position can be filled by any other male in the community. The alien man can fill the reproductive *function* only if he is himself linked by kinship and accepted as a 'social father': that is, if his hosts formally allow him to reproduce or to extend the structures – rather than the numbers – of the host community. But the descendants of an alien man belong to the host community only in two cases: if he marries a daughter of the community whose progeny, lacking a paternal family, would thus remain within the community; or if, having been *adopted*, the man is married to a woman from an affine community. The first solution, giving a daughter in marriage to an alien, is very widely practised. It enables the unequivocal integration of the alien into the host community, since relations of affinity are constituted on the basis of which all other relations can be founded, in particular those which define the newcomer's access to the life-giving land and those which regulate the devolution of his wife's progeny. In this case, the insertion of the alien is easier if he has already taken part for some time in the productive cycle, if, inserted as a young man, he grew up with his adoptive brothers, or if, as a prisoner of war, he was held by the community as a replacement for a lost warrior whose social personality he takes over (cf. Héritier, 1975; P.P. Rey, 1975).

The insertion of an alien through his marriage to a daughter of the community gives the doyen the advantage of maintaining under his sole authority a wife, a male dependant and all his progeny during the first generation. But it has the disadvantage of depriving the community of a bride in return for the daughter given to the alien, and this at the expense of a cadet. In other words, the alien usurps the place of a cadet in the reproductive cycle without necessarily having contributed equally to the productive cycle.

If an alien accepted into a group is to have access to a woman from another community (that is, if he is to be married as an affiliated cadet), his kinship in the host community must first be established: he must be adopted. Now, this adoption will be accepted by the cadets born into the community only if the marriage of the adopted individual reinforces the lineage without depriving his adoptive 'brothers' of the wives to whom the community has a right in the general cycle of circulation of women. The insertion of the alien into the reproductive cycle thus takes place, as a rule, when there are comparatively few cadets in the community or when the balance of the sexes or the ratio between productive and unproductive individuals is unsatisfactory.

Whatever the case, the alien is socialized through the connections which bind him to the other members of the community, either as a cadet (if he is married to the daughter of an allied clan) or as an affine (if he marries a daughter of the host clan). These ties give him and his descendants progressive access to the prerogatives which make up the social person, and in particular to paternity. The family he builds is promised to posterity; all it lacks is a paternal ancestry which his progeny is called upon to acquire with time.

Nevertheless, the insertion of the male alien into the community as a social reproducer is, as we have seen, limited in frequency and in scope. Although it is sometimes necessary to re-establish a certain balance, this mode of integration usually concerns a few men only, even if they are cases in point. It does not constitute a regular process of constant renewal of the alien group; nor for that matter, is it conceived for this purpose.

The integration of a pubescent woman has greater advantages and is much simpler. We know that domestic societies prefer the abduction of women to the capture of men. When abduction is not followed by marriage, the abducted woman, withdrawn from her native milieu, deprived of arbitration through the intervention of her family, without rights over her progeny, and, furthermore, assigned to hard argricultural labour and household tasks, might seem to be the forerunner of the slave. Whatever the filiation system of the society into which the abducted woman is inserted, her progeny is attributed to the family of the man to whom she is married. In this way elements of patrifiliation are introduced into matrilineal societies.

In all filiation systems, the children of a union with an alien, man or woman, will always be socially weakened in that they will belong only to a single lineage, where membership of two lineages is an essential element of *civilization* (that is, of insertion into 'civil' society). Through his or her double parentage, the gentle can call on a maternal relative to intervene against a paternal decision, or conversely. Young people frequently resort to this when, for example, they are faced with an unwanted marriage or when they have committed some fault. Membership of two lineages thus gives individuals access to *arbitration*, which is a form of justice in such societies. Conversely, membership of a single lineage weighs heavily on the child of an alien man or woman married to a gentle. Lacking the resources of free-born children who have a double ascendance, the children of the alien man or woman are less well protected and more often victims of harassment and injustice.

Among the Bamana, the Maninka, the Fulbe and the Soninke, and among neighbouring patrilineal populations, the *fadenya* (as it is called in Bamana) expresses rivalry between half-brothers (born of the same father but of different mothers). Each evokes the merits of his maternal lineage to distinguish himself as a rival to the others. This way of asserting himself is not available to the son of the alien man or woman. His situation is similar to that of the 'bastard' (an individual who has no paternal kin) and he is – sometimes cruelly – despised. On the other hand, children of two relatives from the same clan, bearing the same patronymic, are held in esteem among the Soninke, the Wolof, and so on, and given a specific name (*Niyame* among the Soninke).

In domestic non-slave society, the line is extended with the passage of generations and the position of children of alien origin gradually becomes comparable to that of the children of other families whose genealogical roots rarely go back further than five generations. At the end of this period, reabsorption has been completed, as numerous populations demonstrate.

Thus the alien, man or woman, who is inserted into the domestic community as a social reproducer, does not reproduce his or her original alien status. His or her descendants are gentles, even if for a time their lack of paternal or maternal ascendance makes them vulnerable. Because of this process of amalgamation, aliens do not reproduce in domestic society as a distinct social body.

4 THE DENIAL OF KINSHIP

Another possibility is that men of alien origin (that is, those who do not belong to the matrimonial set of which the community is part) are taken into the community without being integrated as sons-in-law or as affines. In this case their insertion raises a number of difficulties concerning the redistribution of their material and perhaps also their human production: difficulties which illustrate the incompatibility of the domestic economy with slavery while revealing the conditions for its emergence.

The men who are not integrated into the domestic community are generally those who, having no relations of kinship, affinity or vicinity, are vulnerable to capture. Through vicinal wars, snatches of vagabonds or of travellers caught by surprise in the village surroundings, the shelter of starving persons during periods of famine, individuals are introduced into the community who are likely to remain 'aliens'. *war b/w neighbours*

Vicinal wars which take place within the same matrimonial area cannot be assimilated to wars of capture fought by military states or pillaging bands. In vicinal war, a few individuals only are engaged in fighting. Compensation is paid for the few deaths which take place. Prisoners are held as hostages for ransom or used to replace a man killed in combat; only those men whose families refuse to redeem them are held. These men are liable to become and to remain 'aliens'. But this type of war in no way contributes to the regular supply of aliens to the community. As to the snatch, it affects only isolated individuals who happen to have strayed on to the land of the domestic community and whose own social base is too distant for them to be reclaimed. Sometimes (as among the Samo – Héritier, 1975) some of these wanderers – merchants, marabouts and others who through their functions maintain peaceful relations with the outside world – are spared. Finally, the community may acquire an individual in a deal, a transaction which does not express organic commercial relations and therefore does not alter the characteristics of the domestic economy.

Neither vicinal war, nor snatches, nor exchange ensure a

steady and *continuous* source of captives, and as a result the supply of aliens is always random and occasional rather than organized. Since the renewal of the supply of unmarried aliens is not regular, neither is their production; thus *it cannot permanently free from labour a stable class of masters*. The number of these aliens or captives who are not absorbed into gentle society is thus generally small. Held in inorganic relations at the social level, if not at the individual level, they do not constitute a social class.

If the alien is not inserted into the reproductive cycle but only into production, he is not re-socialized into the host society since he builds no kinship links within it. As a direct result of this, as we have seen, his objective situation is, immediately, that of the exploited. But does this mean, in a domestic society, that he is a slave?

Several authors (Rey, 1975; Olivier de Sardan, 1975) consider that in this context the alien is like a 'permanent cadet', assigned, alongside the other members of the community, to productive tasks in which he takes part as an equal, eating from the same plate and benefiting, like all the other members of the community and according to his individual needs, from the common product.

But the notion of 'permanent cadet' is *a priori* a contradiction in terms, since the social vocation of the 'cadet', in the domestic community, is to become an elder, if only as regards his own descendants. To be relegated permanently to the condition of 'cadet' is to be excluded from the reproductive cycle and thus deprived of the attributes of the social person; to be excluded, therefore, from the class of 'persons', of 'kin'. In economic terms, the *affiliated relative* is in fact the relative who, inserted into the productive cycle, is simultaneously in debt for the means of subsistence which enabled him or her to grow and a creditor as regards the means of subsistence which he or she supplies to future and post-producers. If a man has no access to a wife and to progeny, he can never reclaim his product; as a result he is neither an affiliated relative nor a free man, nor, therefore, a 'cadet'.

In the domestic economy, where the conditions of production exclude individual gain, where the interweaving of tasks makes it impossible to assess each person's product, where labour-time is measured on the scale of a lifetime and where, in particular, access to the land is possible only through insertion into the *totality* of domestic social relations, *a gross surplus-product can be created only through the limitation of demographic growth and the social allocation of children.*

Thus, contrary to what might be concluded from an analysis limited to the working conditions of the domestic 'captive', which appear to be the same as those of all the other members of the community, he is indeed exploited, in that *limitations* are imposed on his *physical and social reproduction* through the rules of access to wives and of devolution of paternity.

This brings us to the discovery, in its latent form, of *a characteristic which appears in all forms of slavery* and is its very essence: *the social incapacity of the slave to reproduce socially* that is, the slave's juridical inability to become 'kin'. This inability, which is the organic condition for the potential exploitation of labour in the domestic community, makes slavery *the antithesis of kinship*[6] and is the *legal* means of subordination of the slave in *all* forms of enslavement, even where the slave is not exploited as a productive labourer. But, unlike domestic society, in a slave economy this condition pertains to a class reproduced by institutional means and not to a few occasionally exploited individuals.

5 ONE CAPTIVE DOES NOT MAKE SLAVERY

If the alien who is unmarried – or frustrated of possible progeny – can be considered to be in the objective situation of a slave, it does not, nevertheless, follow that the host society can be seen as a 'slave' society.

In the historical conditions in which the domestic society exists, the exploitation of the alien or the captive results from the restricted capacity of the community to integrate him or her as a genetic or social reproducer, rather than from a desire to employ him or her as a producer. The exploitation which nevertheless does take place, as we have seen, is not directly visible. The mechanisms of production and reproduction do not create a physically *separate* surplus-product. Since its only outlet is the community itself, the communal product, to which the captive contributes is distributed according to prevailing norms: to each according to his needs. Since there is no outlet outside the community, the surplus-product of exploitation has no use either as a possible tribute or as an exchange-value.

It is not possible, either, to use the captives to free an exploiting *class* from productive labour. If exploitation is not systematically renewed and if it does not give rise to a category of individuals who are institutionally kept subordinate (*de facto* or *de jure*), it cannot be seen as a system. Slavery, *as a mode of exploitation*, exists only where *there is a distinct class of individuals*, with the same social state and *renewed constantly and institutionally*, so that, since this class fills its functions permanently, the relations of exploitation and the exploiting class which benefits from them can also be regularly and continually reconstituted. But we have seen that the conditions for the renewal of unmarried aliens in domestic society are incompatible with its constitution. The reproduction of slaves through genetic growth comes up against organic and practical impossibilities. The organic impossibility stems from the fact that, in order to be exploited, the 'alien' is rendered incapable of reproducing socially as a distinct social category; the practical impossibility stems from the fact that such reproduction presupposes, demographically, a minimum number of subjugated persons which is considerably higher than the usual membership of the domestic community. The community cannot assemble and subjugate so many people without deeply, if not radically, changing its structures.

Apart from integration into the community, snatches or vicinal wars, which cannot ensure a continuous supply of subjugated persons, the other means of renewing this supply would be permanent raids, organized periodic wars and regular purchase, all of which are outside the reach of the self-sustenance economy and which, once again, can take place only after the transformation of the economy into another form of society, in different historical conditions.

Thus, since the captive alien cannot be integrated into a lasting and renewable institutional framework, his or her intrusion presents difficulties of assimilation which are illustrated in various sociocultural practices.[7] The case of the Samo reported by Françoise Héritier (1975) is an example. The Samo are a segment of the population of what is now Burkina-Faso, living in autonomous and largely endogamous villages. Like many similar populations, the Samo often engaged in vicinal war. However, these wars were not used as an opportunity for capture. Prisoners were not taken and the wounded were killed. When the Samo seized a Mossi horseman who had come to raid them, they emasculated him and put him to death. If they sometimes organized commandos to capture a few victims, it was not in order to hold them but rather to exchange them with *jula* merchants for cowrie shells, which were mainly used for prestige.

Although they lived in a slave-trading zone, although they were visited by merchants who enjoyed immunity from attack, the Samo did not buy slaves. Aliens introduced into Samo villages came mainly from the snatching of wandering individuals, especially women and children driven from their villages by famine. The insertion of these aliens into the community was achieved through the intervention of a specific individual, the *lamutyiri* (master of the rains), whose function seems to have been to polarize around his own person, and thus to neutralize, situations incompatible with the functioning of domestic relations. In this case the insertion of the alien took place according to complex rules which prevented any lineage, even that of the *lamutyiri*, from gaining influence over others. The product of the captive's labour was reintegrated into the social circuits but never used to produce commodities for the external market. As for the captive's children, various prohibitions prevented them from contributing to the growth of the *lamutyiri's* lineage or of any other. It would thus seem clear that among the Samo, the concern to preserve the sociocultural framework prevailed over concerns relating to exploitation, and that the institutions described above were designed to neutralize the economic and social effects of the alien's insertion.

As regards the populations described by P.P. Rey (1975), although they were under heavy pressure from the slave trade on the coast of equatorial Africa, the changes to which they were subject remained within the framework of domestic relations. Among these populations, an individual rejected by his own lineage and received into another community could be assigned to production only if he were integrated as a 'cadet'; his tasks, his functions, his participation in collective labour and the collective product were not differentiated from those of other members of the community. It was not subjugation so much as a transfer of filiation which operated here. But the main difference between this dependent (called a *mutere*) and the cadet was that the *mutere* could be sold in slave-trading, which his original lineage had previously prohibited. If, on the other hand, he was retained in the host lineage and married, if he was allowed to become the father of a family in the same way as the other cadets in the community, he was objectively not subject to exploitation. Thus Rey is correct in asserting that, *in this type of society*, enslavement could not develop.[8]

Transformations in the societies described by Rey took place not through the constitution of new relations of production but through the misuse of customary rules as a result of the slave trade. Two successive operations (the transfer of dependence which created the *mutere* and then the sale of the *mutere* by the lineage which received him) made possible the metamorphosis of cadets from producers into commodities and of elders from patriarchs into shameful dealers.

Finally, the similar case of the Kukuya (Bonnafé, 1975) reveals a double process at work: on the one hand, the integration of aliens (especially women) as reproducers in subordinated lineages where domestic relations prevailed; on the other, the constitution of these lineages as a group exploited by the dominant lineages. These latter began to sell goods on the market in exchange for captives. The aliens, the *kibaki*, were not only dispossessed of a fraction of their product, but were also dispossessed (logically) of their prerogatives as 'fathers' to the benefit of the master (p.551). In the context of slave-trading, some of the characteristics of slavery show up clearly in the dominant fraction constituted as a class with respect to the lineages subordinated to it.

6 IMMOLATIONS

In many cases, the insertion of a male alien into the domestic community and the impossibility of reproducing him are a mild inducement to preserve his life. But if a captive is used neither in social reproduction nor in production, he is reduced to an object deprived of all active functions, easily assimilated, because of the glorious circumstances of his capture, to a prestige good. Like other similar goods, he can be destroyed (immolated) – for example during funerals or religious ceremonies.

The immolations which are fairly frequent in this type of segmented society generally involve the alien men whose integration into the community's structures presents difficulties. Their execution, even when they were of working age, was not a 'sacrifice' in the sense of a renunciation. It is not surprising that the immolation of captured men is more frequent than that of women, since the latter's economic and social value, as procreators, is not subordinated to the difficult process of integration. Immolations of women, when they take place, are always associated with rare and important moments, such as the settlement of a village: a young, virgin and pubescent woman is offered in order to underline the *sacrifice* – that of a reproducer – involved in her death and, for the same reason, a gentle woman rather than an alien or a captive is chosen. Her execution implies a real loss, a renunciation of her posterity and of the relations of filiation which would have been constituted through her marriage – a 'sacrifice' in the fullest sense of the word.

7 PAWNED PEOPLE

The existence of individuals given in pawn by their families to a creditor who can employ them freely until the clearing of the debt is reported in many African societies. Some see this as a form of slavery, if not as its origin. In the first place, in my opinion, this institution is not inherent to domestic society. The existence of a debt presupposes a hierarchization of lineages based on the acquisition of wealth, and thus the disappearance of the principles of equality and solidarity between families; this can take place only through contamination by the merchant economy, if not by slavery itself. Far from being at the origin of slavery, pawning may be a corollary of the merchant economy. Furthermore, the pawned person, although in a position of submission, never loses the quality of kin, nor any of the prerogatives attached to it. He lives within his family and his condition, unlike the state of the slave, is reversible, since in principle it is linked to the clearing of the debt.

Thus slavery, in that it involves class relations, can emerge only (1) through the dislocation of the productive and reproductive cycles on which kinship is based, and thus through the emergence of the absolute alien, the non-kin; (2) through the incessant renewal of this social category excluded from kinship reproduction relations and thus through the creation of substitute apparatuses.

Slavery is not the extension of kinship, as some authors suggest (Miers and Kopytoff, 1977). Its genesis is not to be found in domestic society. Its origins must be sought elsewhere. Far from being isolated, these societies have for centuries, almost throughout the world, been involved, closely or from a distance, in world-scale upheavals and in particular in merchant revolutions, often against their will. If there is a genesis of slavery in Africa, it must be sought in a history which extends beyond the African continent.

Part I

THE WOMB:

The Dialectic of Slavery

1

The Historical Dimension of Slavery in West Africa

A previous study suggested the hypothesis that contradictions within domestic society led to a hierarchization of lineages and to political domination by some lineages over others, rather than to the emergence of slavery. Slavery developed in Africa, probably as it did everywhere else, as a result of contact between different civilizations. The history of the peoples concerned and of the encounters between them is determinant. This study[1], which is limited to the Sahelo-Sudanese region, shows that from its beginnings slavery developed in an intercontintal context, and that the institutions of war and trade were the necessary conditions for its existence.

The geographical focus of this work is the Sahelo-Sudanese region, where slavery developed early; it therefore provides a point of reference. Those aspects of the region's history which are relevant to the problem under consideration (the object and the scope of wars, the development of exchange, the functioning of States) will be described. Again with reference to this region I shall attempt briefly to define the objective conditions for the emergence of slavery in other areas. The aim of this rather summary and arbitrary procedure is merely to suggest a few sociohistorical frameworks within which an examination of the differing evolution of slavery in other parts of Africa can be attempted.

1 FROM EMPIRES TO MERCHANTS

The earliest written accounts of the slave trade in the Sahel refer to Fezzan and date from the seventh century,[2] but from the ninth century onwards the effects of this trade are noted in West Africa.[3] Al-Yakubi (872) refers to the export of *sudan* (black) slaves from Awdaghust and from Zawila, further to the south. 'It has been reported to me', he adds, 'that the kings of the Sudan sell *sudan* [Blacks] in this way, for no reason and not because of war.'[4]

Kawar, a fifteen–day walk from Zawila, had a Muslim population of various origins, mostly Berber, which carried out the trade in Sudan[5] (in Cuoq, 1975: 48–9). It seems that this trade was already well organized in the tenth century and centred on Zawila, which the authors of the period situate 'on the frontiers of the Maghreb. . . . It is a medium–sized town with a large district bordering on the territory of the Sudan', where the slaves 'sold in the Islamic countries' came from. 'They are a race of a pure black colour' (Al-Istakhri, in the year 951, in Cuoq, 1975: 65). Most eunuchs, according to Hudud al-Alam (982–3 in Cuoq, 1975: 69), also came from this Sudan, described as lying between the ocean to the west and the desert to the north: 'Merchants from Egypt come to this region . . . they steal children . . . they castrate them and import them to Europe, where they sell them. Among [the Sudanese] there are people who steal other people's children to sell them to the merchants when they come' (ibid.: 70). Edrissi (about 1154) repeatedly notes that the populations of the desert and of the Sudanic States (Barisa, Silla, Tekrur, Ghana, Ghiyaro) reduced the Lam-Lam[6] inhabitants to captivity, 'transporting them to their own countries and selling them to merchants who come there and who take them elsewhere' (Edrissi, in Mauny, 1961: 337). The Lam-Lam, he explains,

> are continually the victims of incursions[7] by the peoples of neighbouring countries who capture them, using various tricks, and carry them off to their own countries to sell them by the dozen to merchants; at the moment a con-

siderable number are being carried off, destined for the western Maghreb. (ibid.)

Elsewhere, al-Idrisi (1154)[8] explains the tactics of the slave-raiders of Ghiyaro: 'These people ride excellent camels; they take a supply of water, travel by night, arrive by day and then, having taken their booty, they return to their country with the number of Lam-Lam slaves which, with the permission of God, fall to their lot' (in Mauny, 1961: 337). He adds that the town of Tekrur was a market where the Moors exchanged wool, glass and copper for slaves and gold (in Cuoq, 1975: 129).

These exports of slaves are mentioned at various times in the history of the Maghreb: by al-Biruni towards 1050, al-Zuhri towards 1154–61, al-Sharishi towards 1223, Ibn Khaldun towards 1375. In 1416 al-Makrisi further reports that 'a caravan from Takrur arrived for the pilgrimage [to Mecca] with 1,700 head of slaves, men and women, and a great quantity of gold' to be sold on arrival. It is possible that these writers merely reiterate what others have written, but they would not do so if events did not also repeat themselves.

These short extracts contain all the features of the history of the slave trade in this region: the formation of military States, the pillage of black populations, apparently particularist and pagan, by these States; the organization of merchant networks stretching from the Sudan to the Maghreb.

How powerful were these States? What, in this context, was the purpose of the wars in which, from all accounts, they were constantly involved?

In the Middle Ages in Africa, these States were first and foremost instruments for the supply of slaves. In the eleventh century, Ghana (a Sahelian State) had large armies and cavalry at its disposal. El-Bekri (1068/1965: 332) claims that the king could put 200,000 warriors into the field, 'of whom more than 40,000 are armed with bows and arrows' as well as his cavalry.[9] 'The people of Ghana', writes al-Zuhri (1154–61), 'fight in the lands of the Barbara, the Amima and seize the inhabitants as others seized them in the past, when they themselves were pagan. . . . The inhabitants of Ghana *raid them every year*' (Cuoq, 1975: 120).[10] In other areas war was continuous and was held to be holy: 'The king of Silla [in the valley of the Senegal River] *always* wages war against the Blacks who are infidels (El-Bekri: 324). In this respect he rivals Ghana, just as the king of Ambara, himself once a victim, became a raider. The Beni-Lemtuna waged a holy war against the Blacks (El-Bekri: 311). The role of the Almoravids in the eleventh century in supplying the slave markets is not made explicit, but indications are that these holy men did not neglect this activity: Yaya ben Umar, one of Ibn Yacin's warriors,[11] made an alliance with the Lemtuna to attack a non-Muslim Berber tribe. 'The Lemtuna raided them and took captives whom they distributed among themselves, having passed on a fifth of their booty to their emir' (reported by Ibn Idhari, much later, in the fifteenth century – in Cuoq, 1975: 223). At the sack of Awdaghost (1054–5) the town numbered thousands of slaves and the Almoravids seized every one they found (El-Bekri: 317); no mention is made of any emancipation of the captives. Ibn Yacin is also known to have taken a third of the goods owned by those who rallied to his cause: goods which probably included a certain number of slaves.

In the fourteenth century, Al-Omari's description of Mali is similar to that given by El-Bekri of Ghana: the Mali army numbered '100,000 men', including '10,000 horsemen' (pp.66–7) and its sovereigns *'constantly* wage holy war and are *continually* on expeditions against the pagan Negroes' (Al-Omari: 81). According to the *Tarikh es-Sudan* [*TES*]: 20), 'the king of Mali conquered Sonxai, Timbuktu, Zagha, Mima, Baghena and the surrounding country as far as the ocean'.[12] Only the merchant city of Jenne was able to resist his repeated attacks. It is certain that from this time onwards slave-trading was one of the main activities and one of the principal resources of the political and military formations in the Sahelo-Sudanese region: Tekrur, Ghana, Mali, Ghiroy, Silla. During the following centuries, war was a permanent feature of the history of Sonxai. The *chi* (sovereign) Suleyman Dama 'spent *his whole reign* on warlike expeditions' (*TES*: 85). Soni Ali 'was engaged on warlike expeditions and on the conquest of countries' (*TES*: 104). He conquered the Baram, the Nunu

Sanbadja, Timbuktu, Jenne, the country of the Kunta, Borgu and Gurma (*TES*: 104–5) as well as tangling with the Mossi (see below) (Rouch, 1953: 182). *Askia* Mohammed conquered Bagana, Air (*Tarikh el-Fettach* [*TEF*]: 135), Kingi (*TEF*: 145) and Kusata (*TEF*: 214). The sovereign Mohammed Benkan had such an appetite for warlike expeditions that he is said to have exhausted the patience of the people of Sonxai. Thus the chroniclers chant on the interminable list of expeditions and wars, right up to the disappearance of the *askias*[13] (Rouch, 1953: 195).

The narrators do not always explain the causes or consequences of these wars. However, Edrissi reports that they contributed to the supply of slaves. The chronicles relate that booty was taken, but do not always describe what that booty was. When details are given, slaves are almost always mentioned. According to Rouch (1953: 182–3), some of the wars waged by Soni Ali against the Dendi or the Tuareg 'had no other purpose than to supply soldiers for Sonxai'. Sometimes the information is more precise: in 1501 the *askia* supplied himself with slaves during a campaign against Mali (Rouch, 1953: 195). In 1558 *Askia* Daud 'made a victorious incursion against Mali during which he took many slaves', including the daughter of the king (C. Monteil, 1932/1971: 43). The inhabitants of three towns 'have their origin in the remainder of the booty collected in the country of the Mossi by El-Hadj'. Others were brought as whole villages during the expeditions of *Askia* Mohammed into the distant Kusata country (*TEF*: 214). After an incursion by *Askia* Ismail into Gurma (a region which constantly attracted Sonxai attacks) 'the booty was such that a slave sold at Kagho for 300 cowries' (*TES*: 157). In 1550 *Askia* Daud brought back from Baxana a large number of *mabi* praise-singers[14] (*TES*: 60).

Following the Moroccan invasion, which contributed to the disintegration of Sonxai political structures, internal security collapsed and the people 'ravaged each other' to the extent that 'free men' began to be reduced to slavery (*TES*: 223), which deeply troubled the narrator. The Bambara seized Sonxai women, Qadi Mansur defeated *Askia* Nuh and reduced all the Sonxai with him to captivity: 'men and women, young and old, praise-singers of both sexes'.

Towards 1591–2, Qadi Mami, 'setting off against the Zaghrani who lived in Yaroua, . . . swooped down on them, killed their men and took their women and their children as captives to Timbuktu, where they were sold at a price ranging from 200 to 400 cowries' (*TES*: 243). At Chenenkou, the Moroccans 'took a large number of persons, men and women, men trained in the law and great believers'. Some of these conquerors released their prisoners, but others sold them (*TES*: 275).

The slaves' countries of origin – Wangara, Kaniaga, Bitu, Mali, Jafunu (*TES*: 174), and so on – and the patronymics of the populations brought back or subordinated by the Sonxai show a tremendous intermixing. Indeed, from the ninth century onwards these wars were characterized by their extended scope. Distance seems to have been no obstacle to armies which often operated 1,000 kilometres or more from their base. As we have seen, according to the first early narrators, these armies often numbered as many as 100,000 men. Some were horsemen, though the majority were foot-soldiers. We know little about the organization and tactics of these armies. Some hypotheses are necessary. First, these wars were not all of the same nature. In the eighteenth and nineteenth centuries, Mungo Park and the Bambara (Bazin, 1975; Meillassoux and Niaré, 1963) distinguished two types of armed action: one consisted of raids carried out by a restricted number of individuals, the other of mounted expeditions in which a large number of soldiers took part. In both cases the object was the capture of slaves. I think one must also distinguish between, on the one hand, battles which were the bloody expression of a settling of accounts between kingdoms, armies against armies, of rivalries for the seizure of certain strongholds or for the control of merchant cities – battles which retained a certain degree of formality – and, on the other, the great expeditions against peasant populations which involved thousands of men in the pillage of far-off lands and during which no quarter was given. Where the capture of slaves necessitated long journeys, the effective superiority of a kingdom over 'pagan and rural' populations depended on its ability to mobilize large numbers of men and to organize, move and supply its troops, as much as on the use of warhorses.[15]

These wars were self-perpetuating. They created the condition for their own development by stimulating improvements in tactics and armaments. A simple ambush or a foray, which had earlier been sufficient to capture slaves from inadequately defended populations, led these populations to develop more efficient defences[16] through the building of fortifications and the establishment of military organizations capable of fighting back. This escalation of the means of defence encouraged the emergence of other warrior aristocracies whose purpose was to defend the vulnerable village communities and later to attack and capture in their turn. As a result military expeditions were forced either to move further and further afield towards populations which were still poorly protected, or to become more and more powerful in order to attack nearer populations which were better defended. These large armies, composed mostly of ill-armed foot-soldiers, were, no doubt, quite undisciplined.[17] Their movements probably resembled an exodus, ravaging the villages in their path, more than an ordered march. Battles were probably no more than the sum of single combats. In spite of their numbers, these troops were not very effective against soldiers with experience of war, as the encounter between the Sonxai armies and the Moroccan troops in 1591 shows (*TES*: 219–20).[18] There is no doubt that the military organization of the Moroccans and their use of firearms[19] enabled them, from the sixteenth century onwards, to reduce the numbers of men deployed; the number of Moroccan soldiers who conquered Sonxai did not exceed 3,000 (*TES*: 217).

The Mossi kingdoms, in the savannah to the south, separated from the Sahara by the States described above, were established in a different context. Mossi armies made several attempts to break through to the north and the Saharan slave markets; with the invasion of Timbuktu in 1337, of Walata in 1480 – if not earlier, in 1447 (Person, 1958: 46, in Izard, 1970: 51) – of Masina in 1465 (Izard, 1970). In each of these attempts they clashed with the States of the Sahel, and in particular with Sonxai (Izard, 1970: 34–70). The failure of these attempts was followed by reprisals by the Sonxai sovereigns. *Askia* Mohammed organized a holy war against the Mossi, 'carrying off their children into captivity' (*TES*: 121–2). Cut off from outlets towards the Sahara, victims of wars and pillage, the Mossi fell back and established powerful States aimed rather at defence.[20]

As protector of the populations against capture by the people of the Sahel, the Mossi military aristocracy achieved an exceptional degree of social and political integration of these populations. This aristocracy was not subject to the competing thrust of the merchants and of Islam. The *naba* were never Muslims and had no reason to wage a holy war. Their foreign wars, after the attempts to break through to the north, were not on the same scale as those waged by their northern neighbours. Slavery, instead of gravitating around the need to export, tended to be concentrated around the Crown. Demand from the court increased its aristocratic character and polarized its development. The royal slaves described by Izard (1975) were the descendants of captives taken on expeditions to the remote Bamana.

It was only later, in the nineteenth century, that *Naba* Baongo or Baogho (1855–94) (Izard, 1970: 353), twenty-sixth successor to the founder of the dynasty, 'had the idea of selling prisoners taken in war' (Delobsom, 1933: 85). Before him, however, Mossi warriors had already associated themselves with Sonxai bandits to supply the demand for slaves (Héritier, 1975), but it was only in the nineteenth century that the Mossi kingdom emerged as a supplier of slaves to the European slave trade.

The opportune conversion of the Sahelian princes to Islam – a conversion which did not affect the population as a whole at the same time – gave them a moral justification for fighting and subjugating the 'pagans'.[21] It was in the interests of the Muslim marabouts, whose close link with commerce is well known, to encourage their sovereigns to supply the slave market in this way.

The capture of prisoners and the permanent military deployment which it necessitated provide a more satisfactory explanation of the constitution of aristocratic and military States than the exploitation of gold and the gold trade.[22] The importance of gold resources for the States which controlled the circulation of gold and were able to consolidate their strength and the prestige of their princes through purchase of horses and other goods must not, of course, be underestimated (Levtzion, 1973: 115–16; Kaba, 1981). But the gold trade does not explain the *nature* of the medieval States. The failure of attempts by the Mali sovereigns to take over the gold mines by *military* force is well known; as soon as force was used, the miners deserted the deposits and production was brought to a halt for lack of producers (Al-Omari: 58, 70).[23] The enormous apparatus of war was not suited to the establishment of permanent, organized productive activity, nor to its control. In Bure, in Bambouk and in Tambura, gold was usually extracted not by slaves belonging to the sovereign but by independent populations. The merchants who maintained peaceful contact with these gold-panners were better suited to preserving the social conditions of production than the destructive warriors. Warriors and brigands, on the other hand, were efficient when it came to seizing goods and men by the destruction of the groups which produced them – that is, by pillage and abduction.

The grandeur and the ruin of the Sudanese 'empires' and the shift of the great political formations from west to east – a shift which is generally attributed to the exhaustion of the gold deposits after each had successively made its fortune[24] – is equally well, if not better, explained by a double phenomenon: on one hand, depopulation following the flight of populations subject to incursions;[25] on the other, the conquest and progressive 'civilization' of the remaining pagan populations. In the first case, the human material was exhausted; in the second, it was the *social* material supplying slaves in large numbers which disappeared. In fact, military expansion led to the gradual extension of the conquered territories and to the transformation of zones for incursion into administrated zones – that is, to the political subjection of populations which were no longer alien (and thus vulnerable to capture) but subject and thus vulnerable to exploitation.[26] Furthermore, wars in this region were always accompanied by the

extension of organized and *professional* trade, with the in-
filtration and installation of Islamized merchants – which was
not the case in the regions further to the south. The simultaneous spread of military conquest, of State administrations,
of trade and of Islam favoured the civilizing of the conquered
populations and thus their statutory incorporation as subjects
of the political formation. As a result of this process, the
source of supply of slaves dried up. Territorial conquest thus
opened up two possibilities: either the State changed its mode
of exploitation and partly or completely abandoned the
seizure of its 'subjects' in favour of the exploitation of their
labour or the appropriation of their product – in which case
the producer acquired a 'civilized' status which protected him
from capture by his own sovereign in the same way as from
capture by alien sovereigns – or the sovereign continued to
draw human material from the inhabitants of the occupied
territories but could no longer justify his civil authority over
them and saw his power decline.

The protection of their subjects from subjugation is
generally a characteristic of strong States. This was true of
the Mossi. The *Tarikh es-Sudan* illustrates, in the case of Sonxai, the elaboration of a status which protected the free man
against subjugation and made provision for the redemption
of those who had been wrongfully subjugated. As regards
lower classes, *Askia* Mohammed had established a com-
promise: only certain 'tribes' could have their children taken
away and exchanged for horses.[27]

The Sahelo-Sudanese region, containing the great States
which supplied slaves to the Mediterranean and the Sahara,
with its long history of war, conquest and trade, was also the
centre of the development of an African slavery. El-Bekri refers briefly to its existence in the eleventh century. In the
fourteenth century, Ibn Battuta remarks on it in the Sudanese
States, and particularly in Mali. He notes slaves of both
sexes, children and adults; especially palace servants (Battuta:
53, 62), royal soldiers (ibid.: 53) and concubines (ibid.: 59).
Some were employed as porters (ibid.: 46), others in the copper mines (ibid.: 76). They were subjected to corporal
punishment and could be given as presents (ibid.: 64). Some
references provide evidence of a trade in slaves involving

women and young men (ibid.: 76) and of a trans-Saharan trade (600 young women were brought by caravan across the desert – ibid.: 78). The court of Mali is also known to have contained a certain number of Turkish slaves of good quality (Al-Omari: 66).

The *Tarikhs el-Fettach* and *es-Sudan* gave clearer information about the dominant forms of slavery in the kingdom of Gao.[28] In the sixteenth century, slavery as described in the *Tarikhs* was essentially limited to the court, to the provision of its material needs, on the one hand, and to its administration on the other. The documents refer to slaves on the land organized in plantations for the production of the material needs of the king, his followers and his army, and of 'the poor'. Slaves at court seem to have been extremely numerous.[29] Some of the female captives were earmarked for the reproduction of the clan; all the *askias* but one were the sons of concubines.

The king drew his supply of slaves from distant regions, but no description is given of the slave trade. We know indirectly that the merchants of Gao were involved in it (*TEF*: 191s.). As for the king, when he traded his captives it was less as producers than as objects of exchange. According to manuscript C of the *Tarikh el-Fettach* (p. 109), the *askia* had at his disposal the children of three 'tribes' which he could exchange for horses. Much is also made of presents of slaves, sometimes accompanied by donations of land, attributed to the generosity of a king seen as very devout and thus highly esteemed by the authors of the chronicles.

Thus the period of domination by the medieval Sahelian States corresponded to the constitution and domination of an aristocratic class founded on wars of abduction. The evidence describes a slavery linked to these aristocratic forms of society: slavery at court, military slavery, slaves on the land; all intended for the maintenance of the dominant class and the reproduction of its means of domination – war and the administration of war.

Although the captives' product was intended to be sold, it would be wrong to conclude that the structures and destiny of this military class were based on trade. Its main activity was war; war shaped its social organization and the modes of

domination of the aristocracy, as it shaped the nature of the
slavery which grew up around this aristocracy. In fact the pillaging aristocrats, unlike the merchants, did not sell in order
to buy other goods intended for sale. Their involvement in
trade was usually limited to the purchase of use-goods. They
were not in any sense intermediaries in the circuit of commodities. The African aristocracy, like most others, considered it beneath them to take part in venal activities. They
merely transformed free individuals into commodities,
through capture. It was the merchants who took over the
products, lived by and profited from trade, and were
organized socially in terms of this activity.

2 FROM MERCHANT CITIES TO MUSLIM ARISTOCRACIES

The merchant economy in fact developed parallel to the
building of empires, although it is less often mentioned in the
written sources. The presence of merchants, markets, cities
or quarters populated by merchants, organized networks,
commercial circuits, 'money' (cowries, pieces of copper or
commodity-standards) is noted throughout the Sahel. (El-
Bekri; Al-Omari: 75; Battuta: 72; Bovill, 1968; Mauny, 1961;
M. Johnson, 1970). The gold trade alone cannot explain this
organization. *Merchant* trade was established and penetrated
everywhere, following and sometimes preceding the progress of the armies.[30]

The emergence of Sahelian and Saharan cities (almost entirely dependent on supplies from outside), the development
of Islam and of the use of clothing (C. Monteil, 1927), the
acquisition of wealth by the nomads who transported goods,
all created a growing demand for the *products of agricultural
and craft labour* in the Sudan. The *dura* (millet) consumed in
Awdaghost was imported from the Sudan. Timbuktu,
according to the *Tarikh es-Sudan* (p.36), was from the beginning a warehouse for grain. Jenne was a huge market, particularly for subsistence goods (fish, millet, onions, rice, bao-
bab leaves, spices) and for craft goods, cotton, cotton fabrics
and woollen goods [*kasse*] bound for the northern markets
(Research trip, 1965). The city's stocks of food enabled it to

hold out for 'seven years, seven months and seven days', according to the *TES* (p.26) (in other words, for a long time) against Soni Ali's siege.

Confined at first to the cities of the Sahara, then to those of the Sahel, or to the merchant quarters of the capitals, the traders gradually established themselves further and further south under the ideological protection of Islam, settling in the villages under the protection of local sovereigns. In this way Islamo-Sahelian civilization penetrated the savannah and drew the local populations into a more and more complex social and political framework. Little is known about the rhythm of penetration of the merchants, the cities and the markets into the savannah. Mauny estimates that it began in the fourteenth century and that by 1500 the main features of interregional trade within West Africa were well established (Mauny, 1961: 389).[31] Wadan and Singetti date from the fifteenth century (Mauny, ibid.: 430). In the sixteenth century the frontier towns of Walata, Timbuktu, Jenne and Gao, among others, were established and their activity continued in spite of the Moroccan invasion in 1590.[32] However, limited settlement by Islamized merchant families should not be confused with the Islamization of the populations, which often came later.[33] This slow and gradual installation of the merchants was accompanied by the establishment of organized commercial networks, which formed the substratum of later political organization.

The States, relying on their military organization which enabled the marketing of slave-commodities, benefited from the existence of trade, but they did not control it. The sale of captives, the import of horses (which for a long time came from North Africa – Doutressoulle, 1940; McCall, 1967) and of prestige goods depended on the organization of merchants. In this way the merchants emerged as a class associated with the military class but in competition with it and tending to erode its power. The development of trade, which was often associated with the prosperity of States, could also lead to their downfall if they were not able to exercise political control over it.[34]

While slave-based production developed, as I believe it did, slavery ceased to be the privilege of sovereigns and the

court. It spread into the population, and each community became liable to employ slaves and sell their production on the
market. Along with the weakening of the empires, one can
see the development of a mosaic of chiefdoms and merchant
towns varying in size, the spread of productive slavery
within peasant communities, the replacement of trade in men
by trade in products.

The classical historians – and in particular Delafosse (1912)
– have tended to see the emergence of a merchant class in this
region as an effect of the dispersal of the Soninke populations
of Wagadu (ancient Ghana); a dispersal which, it seems, practically never stopped after the conquest and destruction of
this State by the Almoravids in the eleventh century. According to this interpretation, these 'Soninke', all of whom were
destined to become merchants, were responsible for the
spread of trade to the Sudan, independently of all other factors. This is a rather simplistic view of history; furthermore,
it leads. to the confusion – for which Delafosse is also responsible – of Soninke and 'Maraka'.[35] In fact, neither the
maraka nor the *jula* (when the term describes families who
were professionally engaged in trade) had a single ethnic origin. Moreover, ethnic identity was in no way determinant.
The 'foreign' origin of most of the merchants can be satis-
factorily explained by socioeconomic factors (Meillassoux,
1971a: 32). The proliferation of the *jula* and the *maraka*, their
spread and their growing influence were the results of an economic conjuncture and not of an accident of history or of an
innate predisposition in certain 'races' for trade.

Behind the political organization of the States, therefore,
grew the power of the cities, merchant strongholds which
tried throughout their history to break away from the imperial administration – sometimes, like Jenne, with lasting
success. In this way the power of the merchants, backed up
by Islam, was established everywhere beneath the surface of
the power of the warrior aristocracies, and ready to take over
at any time. Wagadu (Ghana) broke up, Mali crumbled,
while the merchant towns which had grown up within their
orbit – Awdaghost, Walata, Jara, Tishit, Wadan – survived
and continued their trade along the same routes as before, enjoying a prosperity based perhaps less on the slave trade than

C in place of imperial?)

on the trade in commodities produced by the labour of
slaves. By the sixteenth century the merchant economy had
already taken shape. In addition to the trade in slaves to the
north – whose importance is still difficult to assess[36] – and the
gold trade, there was now a real trade in commodities almost
throughout the Sahel, involving craft and agricultural goods
and creating a local demand for slaves as producers. The last
empire, that of Gao, disintegrated after the Moroccan conquest; little by little the sultan's proconsuls lost control over
the pashas and qadis under their authority. The decentral-
ization of power seems also to have been an index of a relative decline in sales of slaves with respect to trade in commodities and of the relative decline of the Sahelian slave trade
with respect to the sub-Saharan slave trade. Political
organization was transformed. Centralized power was replaced by federations of fortified villages under the authority
of families who were responsible for the organization of
defence (sometimes in rotation); by fiefdoms dominated by a
local dynasty ruling over a few towns or by merchant cities
which, to protect themselves, organized a militia or hired
mercenary clans.

The chronicles, which are devoted mainly to the military
prowess of the warrior aristocracies, have little to say about
the history of these social formations. Unlike their predecessors, they did not engage in spectacular exploits. The absence
of chronicles comparable to the *Tarikhs* and the discreet
silence of historians during the first half of the seventeenth
century are an index of weakening of the great military aristocracies and the probable emergence in their place of prosaic
bourgeois societies concerned more with routine production
than with feats of arms.[37]

The traditions described by C. Monteil (1924: 20–21) in the
Segu and Karata regions testify to the existence of these
towns in the seventeenth century and the use of slaves as producers by their *jula* or *maraka* inhabitants. These villages,
which in Bamana circles were known as *maraka* villages,
'were remarkable for their affluence and sometimes their
great wealth, which gave them a sort of pre-eminence over
the Bambara *dugu* [villages]: this prosperity was based on the

labour of a servile population which the Soninke[38] had
acquired through commercial practices'. According to the
same author, these villages enjoyed considerable political independence.[39] The appearance of the *jula* traders, according
to C. Monteil, dates from Soni Ali's reign over the Sonxai
empire. The importance of Kong, a merchant city *par excellence*, whose position in the savannah was comparable to
that of Jenne in the loop of the Niger, dates, if Binger is correct, from the fourteenth century (1892, II: 393), though it
acquired political independence only in 1790.[40]

The European slave trade was to challenge – although not
to halt – the rise of the merchants, and to provide the warriors with the opportunity of winning back their place in the
political arena. The emergence of Segu as a political formation in the heart of the savannah, from the middle of the
seventeenth century, was a result of this conjuncture of
events. The demand for slaves from the coast led to a new insecurity. Villagers captured each other's women and children; bands were formed; federations of the *tegere* (bandits)
were organized. Bamana tales related how the Kulibali,
members of a warrior clan from Kaarta, acting as mercenaries for a merchant town, seized power after conflict with
the civil authorities (J. Bazin, oral communication). The
birth of the State of Segu, under the authority of Biton Kulibali, was marked by armed conflict with the surrounding
merchant towns (C. Monteil, 1924: 44) and in particular with
the city of Kong which twice attacked Segu, without success
(ibid.: 40–44). One can in fact easily imagine the merchants'
concern at the emergence of a rival force built on war. Later a
modus vivendi was established between Segu and some of the
merchant communities, notably those of the Maraka, which
were seen as the necessary complement to the military
economy (Bazin, 1972; Roberts, 1978). The organization of
Segu is an example of the formation of a 'military democracy', originally composed of leaders of associated bands, all
equal to one another, who appointed one among themselves
as *primus inter pares* but allowed him only limited power.[41]

Two methods of appointment were used among the
Bamana warriors, as among the Malinke or among hunters:
election and the drawing of lots. At the time of Biton Kuli-

bali, the leaders of Bamana raids were chosen by lot, each warrior or bandit considering himself equal to the others. However, this egalitarian form of power did not eliminate rivalries between warriors; it led fairly quickly to the dominance of a single warrior who, claiming hereditary power, replaced the elections with a dynastic order through a *coup d'état*. These barons were not all noble, any more than the king was. Many of them were recruited through capture. Booty was 'the price of their heads'; they were all lives 'in reprieve from death'. 'They have no children, they have only captives.' This warrior – almost ruffian – status was imposed on all the citizens of Segu, because it was in fact the condition of citizenship and not even the sovereign was exempt.[42] Segu's function was war and the capture of men. In a single expedition, one of the sovereigns of Segu brought back so many slaves that he received 10,000 for himself alone (Sauvageot, 1965: 135). Social organization reflected military organization. Villages were peopled by prisoners who were set together as pseudo-clans (Bazin, 1972, 1975). War-fellowship competed with kinship. During this period Segu was an important supplier of captives of both sexes. Some were sent to the coast of Guinea or Gambia in exchange for guns and goods from Europe; others were sold to the *maraka*, traders and employers of slaves, who lived within the kingdom's sphere of influence but preserved their autonomy (Bazin, ibid.; Roberts, 1978). These slaves produced commodities and means of subsistence which were exported or used by the court. The rest of the captives were retained by the soldiers, either for exchange or to work the land. In this way the human booty was divided into two categories, each with its own market: the men were destined for the European slave trade, the women and young people for the local slave trade, for agricultural or domestic labour, or for sale to the *maraka*. However, trade with the *maraka*, as a means both of marketing slaves and of obtaining part of their means of subsistence, limited the use of slaves on the land by the Bamana of Segu. (The captives retained by the Bamana were more often drafted into the army or used in raids.) The Segu warriors could maintain their domination only through the periodic use of violence. Da Monson, one of the Segu sovereigns, described the *maraka* as ears of millet which had to be harvested from time to time to encourage denser growth.

Unlike the sovereigns of the medieval States and of Sonxai, the Bamana kings never made use of religious pretexts in order to reduce men to captivity. The State of Masina, on the other hand, which was established towards 1818 as a means of defence against Bamana raids and attacks, proclaimed itself Muslim. Masina was peopled mainly by herdsmen, organized under the authority of rival warrior chiefs, the *ardo-en*, each of whom had a limited and poorly administrated area under his power. As a result the populations were prey to frequent incursions by troops from Segu, sometimes with the connivance of the *ardo-en* themselves. To counter the military organization of the Bamana, Masina, on the initiative of Sheku Amadu, also developed a constitution, but a theocratic one; government was exercised by a college of marabouts recruited by co-optation, who brought the military chiefs under their civil authority, organized the economy and defence efficiently, and soon became capable of conquest and of slave-trading in their turn. This political construction became the refuge of a class of merchants who enjoyed a degree of protection without precedent in any Sudanese State: personal protection – war was waged with neighbouring Kaarta to save a rich trader from exactions (Ba and Daget, 1962: 173) and protection of goods. Commodities were protected by law, even against requisition by the army in time of war (ibid.: 46, 164).

Masina was a base from which the merchant class could invest the merchant towns, like Jenne, which was cleared of Sonxai animist elements in this way (ibid.: 151s.) – that is, withdrawn from the rival military power of the *askia*. Nevertheless, Sheku Amadu and his marabouts professed asceticism. They themselves were strangers to trade. They represented a clerical class which asserted itself politically as bearer of a powerful and coherent ideology able to offer, in a world in the process of economic transformation, an alternative to the power of the aristocracy. Indeed they, more than the aristocratic class, respected and listened to the demands of the wealthy. But social inequalities did not disappear in this clerical State. It was the declared wish of Sheku Amadu that castes and slavery should continue; he considered free men, people of caste and slaves to be of different species and impossible to amalgamate (Ba and Daget, 1962: 67).

The principal document in our possession (Ba and Daget, 1962) gives little information on slavery. In contrast to the centralized military States, it seems that there was State slavery and private slavery. Prisoners of war, who belonged to the State and did not practise Islam, were assigned to agricultural production on public land until their conversion or religious education permitted their emancipation and their eventual integration into society. Such at least was the doctrine, in conformity with the precepts of Islam (ibid.: 67). We do not, however, know how many slaves were in fact emancipated, nor to what extent the balance between the number of captives and the needs of the State allowed for emancipation. Private slaves were in principle expected to take part in war as foot-soldiers (ibid.: 151) unless their masters paid a tax on all those who stayed behind. Certain slaves were assigned to the craft castes to work on the manufacture of arms. We know nothing more about their activities.

While Masina was a political construction born of an alliance between trade and Islam, it is clear that the Omarian tempest which broke upon the whole Sudan in the mid-nineteenth century, in the name of Tijanism, was based less on religion than on wars of capture. In spite of his piety, El Haj Umar was first and foremost a warrior, who did indeed use the means supplied by Islam to rally the *talibe*,[43] but only in order to submit them to efficient military discipline; did invoke orthodoxy, but only in order to transform all other Muslims into infidels who became justifiable prey for his attacks and could be put to death if legitimately taken captive; did indeed use Arabic writing, but as much as a tool of administration as of learning.

El Haj Umar indiscriminately attacked the pagan Bambara of Segu and the devout administrators of Masina,[44] the Muslim towns and the lords who drank *dolo*.[45] The most obvious result of his military action was the marketing of a considerable number of slaves, especially women and children. The men, more difficult to sell since the Atlantic slave trade had slowed down, were massacred, if they were not already slaves (see below, Part III, Chapter 2).

These wars have been given an ideological interpretation ('fanaticism', 'holy war') but in fact they were based on very slender religious pretexts: one bead more or less in the rosary; one position of the arms during prayer rather than another. . . . Were these wars really so disinterested? Their results suggest the contrary. During these wars, more goods and property, particularly slaves, were shifted than ever before. They led to the provision of slave-producers to nearly all the populations of the Sahel, at the expense of those peoples who were still particularist and poorly protected.

The reason why these slave-supplying wars broke out with such ferocity at a time when the Atlantic slave outlets were closed was no doubt that *the economic development of the large Sudanese zone could already support a market for these commodities in abundance.* The development of productive and merchant slavery had reached a point where it fanned the flames of war, but the growth of production does not itself explain the scope of the wars of capture fought by El Haj Umar, Samori and their like. Another factor contributed, by reducing the returns from war, to its intensification. During the Atlantic slave trade there were outlets for all the captives, because there were two distinct slave markets. The first, the European market, absorbed *adult* men whatever their social condition, free men or recaptured slaves, but the demand for women and children from this market was low. The other, the continental African market, provided an outlet mostly for women and children and had little use for adult men except recaptured slaves.[46] In this way all the captives could be sold.

When the American markets were closed off and the Atlantic slave trade disappeared, there was no longer any outlet for male captives of free-born origin; from this time onwards they were generally massacred on the battlefield. Only recaptured male slaves and women and children seized in raids on conquered villages were held. But profits from war fell as a result, since the costs remained the same whether all or only part of the spoils were sold. For war to remain profitable, it had to be intensified: bigger populations had to be attacked, military operations had to be more frequent. But in spite of population growth, the African continent could not absorb such large numbers of slaves, since some of them (the men) were not much in demand. It is known that during the second half of the nineteenth century the price of slaves dropped, and with it the returns from war; this stimulated an increase in the supply of captives and an extension of the conquered territories. On the part of the users, this drop in prices encouraged the employment of slaves in production, especially since the armies provided an outlet for the sale of agricultural goods. While the productivity of war dropped, the profitability of slaves increased. The merchants and peasants who exploited slaves profited from an unprecedented supply of labour-power on the market, at prices which enabled such rapid amortization that the conditions of slave reproduction were transformed.

On the other hand, merchants lost political power to a new dominant political class, a Muslim warrior aristocracy which, from El Haj Umar onwards, clashed both with the class of pagan military aristocracies and with the class of clerical marabouts described above in Masina. Thus, as soon as Islam became the dominant ideology, the social group to which it spread diversified and formed an opposition, and at the same time took over the functions previously carried out by the lay aristocracies. From then on control of the army tended to be confused with control of ideology, with one dominating the other and vice versa. Masina and Qadiriya Muslims had succeeded in subordinating the warriors to the clerical marabouts; the Tijaniya subordinated the marabouts and the Islamized merchants to a Muslim warrior aristocracy.

At the end of the nineteenth century, the wars of El Haj Umar, like those of Samori, completed the profound inter-mixing of populations which had begun ten centuries earlier in this zone. The prophet carried along with him large numbers of Futanke, and Bunduke who settled the Kaarta villages emptied of their inhabitants and spread as far as Masina and Seeno. In the same way Samori carried with him the troops recruited on the way, deporting whole populations, waging scattered wars of capture from the Sahel and the savannah as

far as the forest. The intermixing which followed the movements of captives, the deportation of populations, the movement of soldiers, the flight of harassed populations, the
movement of merchants; the constant threat which weighed
on so many human beings while at the same time each tried
to benefit from the servitude of others – all these factors contributed to a closely interwoven society, spread over thousands of kilometres. Its component clans, castes and classes
acknowledged each other, clashed and gradually united over
vast areas. Among them, and one against the other,
numerous differing and often compulsive alliances were
built, woven into a 'symplectic'[47] social fabric, forming a
new society where ethnic particularisms tended to disappear
in favour of the extension of a sphere of diffused socialization
which reached the very heart of each State and each clan. This
society was open to complex forms of power, but averse to
absolutism. It was a society steeped in intrigue where each
element – anxious to retain its freedom and its self-respect
but afraid, for the same reasons, of betrayal which would
lead to subordination and disgrace – sought the alliance
which could provide security within which to develop, to act
and to progress in this world of cunning and haughtiness.[48]

3 SLAVERY AND THE FRENCH COLONIZATION

The French conquest came at a time when war, trade and
slavery were all at their height. The ruin caused by war, frequently described by travellers and soldiers, could not conceal the intense productive and merchant activity in the
region (cf. Aubin-Sugy, 1975).

The reports of the colonial administrators on slavery,
drawn up in 1894 and 1902,[49] albeit biased, provide un-
equalled descriptions of the situation.

Two main outlets are distinguishable from the sources: the
former continental market which continued to absorb slave-
producers to meet the demand for grain and cotton from the
cities and the Sahara; and the new coastal market which now,
instead of re-exporting slaves, employed them near the trading posts in producing goods to be sold in authorized trade

(the trade in products). As Klein (1971) and Fage (1969) correctly note, the reconversion of the economy based on the slave trade encouraged slavery in regions where, for the reasons given above (lack of a market for products), it had previously been limited to the court. This was the marabout revolution! It led to an organized trade in slaves with its own staff, its markets, its price lists, covering a large part of West Africa and involving a high number of productive units.[50]

As a result of war and the consequent deportations of individuals from supplier areas to consumer areas, slavery was unevenly spread during the nineteenth century. Where it existed, the proportion of subjugated people to free men was variable. The figures provided by the colonial surveys referred to above have no more than indicative value, because of the methods used for their collection (estimates, censuses which were incomplete and not standardized between regions, changing definitions of social categories, and so on). Between one report and another on the same district, the figures sometimes double. Deherme (1908: 383), who has tried to collate this information, estimates that a quarter of the population of West Africa had been subjugated: 200,000 in Senegal, 600,000 in Upper Senegal-Niger, 250,000 in Dahomey, the same in the Ivory Coast, 450,000 in Guinea (see also Klein, 1983; Boutillier, 1968: 528, and M. Diop, 1971–2: 22s.). Analysis of the colonial reports by administrative area shows an uneven distribution of the slave population: less than 10 per cent of the population in eight of the sixty-five districts; 10–20 per cent in eight others; about 25 per cent in six districts; about a third in seven districts – in all, eighteen districts account for about 50 per cent of slaves and eleven for more than two-thirds. Furthermore, the nomads, the *jula* of Kong (and certain other districts) seem to have had more than 100 per cent slaves, slaves numbering up to four times the free-born population. Thus slaves accounted for more than 50 per cent of the population in more than half the districts.

These figures must be substantially corrected. Totals, especially by region, conceal differences between social groups living in the same area. Boutillier (1975), in his triple study of the populations of Buna, clearly shows the important variations between *jula* merchants, Kulango peasants and the old aristocracies. These large variations in the proportion of slaves reveal differing capacities to make use of a distinct class of producers and to establish appropriate relations of production.

This quick historical overview, limited to aspects relevant to slavery, leads to the conclusion that slavery as an institution – whether it fed the slave trade or production, whether it contributed to the building of great empires or of towns – played a major role in the economic and political development of the Sahelo-Sudanese region.

Slavery has left deep scars, persistent prejudices and the after-effects of exploitation which have lasted up to the present and testify to the foundations and functions of this institution in pre-colonial society. Even today, marriages between gentles and the descendants of slaves, even in the most progressive circles, come up against bitter resistance; even among immigrant workers from these regions, the descendants of slaves still sometimes have to rebel against the duties imposed by their former masters, in spite of the fact that they are all subject to the same conditions (Samuel, 1977).

Slavery was by no means a superficial aspect of the organization of these societies. Their history cannot be understood unless it is taken into account.

2

Extraneousness

Capture and the slave trade set in motion a process through which the captive was rendered extraneous and thus prepared for his or her state as absolute alien in the society into which he or she was delivered.

1 CONDITIONING TO EXTRANEOUSNESS

The slave always came from far away. His or her extraneousness started with exoticism.[1] The distances which the armies of the medieval African States covered to bring back captives were considerable. The distance between Kumbi, capital of Wagadu, and the 'Lam–Lam' country situated (roughly) to the south of the Niger River was on average 500 kilometres. The troops of the *askia* of Sonxai raided Kusata which, at the time, was situated near Diema, more than 1,000 kilometres west of Gao. The value of the captives increased with distance, which was an unsurmountable barrier to escape.

Before the Atlantic slave trade, black slaves were sent as far as the Maghreb, the Near and Middle East, to Turkey and even to India (Deschamps, 1971). We find traces of them in mainland Europe and in Sicily (Verlinden, 1955, 1966). With the emergence of the European slave trade they were flung over the whole of the American continent, as far as the West

Indies, as well as into Europe.[2] When the trade within tropical Africa developed in the nineteenth century, captives were still sent over long distances, despite the fact that there were no longer any outlets outside the African continent. To the distances which the merchants forced their human cattle to travel must be added the ever-increasing distances which the warriors had to cover in order to find new sources of supply. Bonte (1975: 55) shows that the catchment areas of the Kel Kreff Tuareg, for example, were as far away as Kebbi, Menaka, Djerma, and so on. Among the Abron, the slaves were of Moshi (Mossi) and Gurunsi origin (Terray, 1975b: 392). Busansi, Konkonba and Tyokosi were veritable reservoirs of slaves for the Asante and for most of the Akan peoples (ibid.: 392). Most of the Anyi captives originated from the savannah to the north and from Kong (Perrot, 1975: 363, 366). But Kong was also a market to which came slaves from even more distant regions. All the examples show that the slave came from areas which were far away and difficult to reach. When it was not the merchant who covered these distances, it was the warrior. The slave was never a neighbour. It was common practice to resell captured slaves in order to buy others who came from further away (Balde, 1975: 193s.).

If we bear in mind the final destination of the slaves exported from Africa, the area covered takes on worldwide dimensions. Thus the slave economy was contained in a very extended area, and this gave rise not only to means of capture but also to a complex and organized set of mechanisms of deportation, commercialization, transport, markets and conditioning of the 'merchandise' (training, various sorts of care, presentation, castration). Distance was itself a means of conditioning. Various reports (Daumas, 1857; Mercadier, 1971) show its importance as an element in the alienation of captives: beyond a certain point in the journey, where flight became unlikely, the physical and moral treatment of the slaves was deliberately changed, and their own behaviour changed also:

> Griga, the Mawri slave captured near Sokoto, tells that after one and a half days of forced march with their abduc-

tors, deprived of food and water, the captives in the caravan lost all hope of being saved and at the same time became 'almost grateful' to be given something to drink. When they stopped to share out the slaves, at a water hole in Dallol Basso, the caravaneers slit the throats of four women who seemed too faded, and emasculated two children, one of whom died during the night, so as to lighten the load by getting rid of useless mouths and to decide on routes according to the nature of the human merchandise which had been prepared in this way. (from Mercadier, 1971)

Geographical distance laid the basis for the social distance – almost absolute, in spite of appearances to the contrary – through which the slave was to be separated from his or her master and fixed, irreversibly, in the state of an alien. This geographical space of slavery – extending over thousands of kilometres – within which human beings were moulded into living merchandise was structured, organized and articulated for this purpose.

2 THE CONSTITUTION OF THE SPACE OF SLAVERY

Facts about the origin of slave relations between such distant populations are rare, but we do have one example from the beginnings of the European trade in African slaves. The first captives were taken from the Mauritanian coast by Portuguese explorers, more as a curiosity than as merchandise. One of these prisoners, a Moor of high rank, offered to deliver ten other captives to King Henry in exchange for himself. This was in about 1442. In this way the first transaction took place through an African intermediary, encouraging the Portuguese first to raid the coast and then to delegate the organization of capture to local chiefs from whom they bought the booty (Deschamps, 1971: 38–40). It seems that this pattern was generalized and organized as early as the Middle Ages: external demand led to the formation of local bands, then of pillaging States which sporadically or constantly abducted individuals from ever more distant popu-

trade creates more complex social orgs. - finally states

lations which were considered 'savage'. Almost all the peoples who were victim to these raids had a common feature: they functioned according to the domestic mode of production. These were agricultural, sedentary, pagan societies, with a self-sustenance economy.[3]

The cells which made up these societies were 'houses': organic groups of producers and commensals (those who shared the same cooking pot). Among themselves they tolerated arbitration but not sovereignty. These farming populations were vulnerable. The tilling of the fields obliged them to spread out during the cultivating season. Extensive farming limited the possibilities of regrouping into big villages. Their members, once dispersed, could not rapidly be reassembled. Unlike their attackers, who were supplied with arms and horses by their customers in the rich slave-buying areas, these domestic societies had at their disposal only light arms (bows, poisoned arrows and sometimes agricultural implements) and rarely had horses.[4] Collective defence depended on alliances which were fragile because of conflict between clans.[5]

The peasants hid or regrouped in spite of the distance between fields; they took shelter behind stronger and stronger defences (ranging from log ramparts to the solid *tata* of the Bamana and the Maninka);[6] they took refuge in sites which were difficult to reach, like the so-called palaeonegritic populations of the mountains of north Togo or of Adamawa; they clung to cliffs like the Telem and later the Dogon. In spite of the transformations imposed on their agriculture by these new conditions of farming (intensive cultivation on smaller pieces of land or mobilization of labour for the construction of defences) they preserved their cellular and domestic forms of social and political organization to a remarkable extent.

The accounts describe these raids as surprise attacks. The attackers would keep the villages under observation and as soon as the population dropped its guard, the warriors would swoop down on the fields or on the wells where the women were assembled, or would ambush isolated individuals. Captives were immediately sorted and those who had no value – old people or young children who would slow down escape – were immediately killed. Some accounts suggest that when the same village was repeatedly raided, a way out was left so that part of the population could escape. Was this so that this population could reproduce itself, or was it designed merely to flush the villagers from their hiding places into open country where they could be more easily captured? Was it to avoid bloody and desperate battles? It is reported that the Trarza Moors were careful not to raid the same villages so often as to endanger the reproduction of the population. But these methods of conservation were neither generalized nor very systematic, and in many other cases whole regions were devastated and depopulated by raids and slaving wars (cf. Binger, 1892).

As Barth (quoted by Aubin-Sugy, 1976: 136) reports, other populations which had been pillaged and brought into submission were made to pay an annual tribute in slaves. This tribute did not consist only of members of the peoples under submission, and sometimes these peoples had to become raiders in their turn in order to pay. It seems that a number of warrior chiefdoms were established in this way, on the edges of the most important slave-owning empires or States. Thus in the nineteenth century the Vute of Cameroon, having been victims of raids by the armies of the *lamido* of Adamawa, became his suppliers, hunting slaves among their own neighbours on his behalf and inventing new forms of war, new arms and new tactics (J.-L. Siran, 1980; below, Part II, B, 1, 5). These pillaging societies constituted the outer reaches of the slave economy.

The general state of insecurity which prevailed in these hunting-groups also favoured the formation of bands of young men within the pillaged societies, who grouped together both to protect themselves against capture and to benefit from it.[7] Some of these bands, militarily organized, succeeded in imposing their authority on peasant populations who accepted their domination in exchange for 'protection' (M. Piault, 1982). The political formations constituted in this way, with new structures, captured slaves both for the market and for their own use.

Thus slavery set up an economic and political system over a large area, within which several structured elements can be distinguished. Slavery established a direct relation between a military slave-owning society and the raided populations from which it constantly drained off captives. The economic and social growth of the warrior or military (aristocratic) society was based on this relation and on its perpetuation. Here the cost of the slave was equivalent to the cost of his or her capture: the slave in the military slave-owning society had only use-value. His or her reproduction depended on an apparatus of war or brigandage.

Still, some of the captives were sold to traders who brought them to merchant slave-owning societies. In this way the master-slave relation which developed was mediated twice: once by the society which supplied captives, first abducting and then selling them; and once by the commercial apparatus which ensured the transport and sale of captives. In this extended economic space the captive acquired exchange-value. His or her reproduction took place through the double operation of capture and sale on the market. Thus slavery brought into play:

– the societies within which slaves were captured, which represent the milieu in which they were 'produced', demographically and economically;

– the aristocratic slave-owning societies which made use of a military apparatus to tear these human beings from the milieu in which they were produced and reproduced;

– the merchant societies which controlled the commercial apparatus necessary for the sale of captives;

– the merchant societies which were consumers of slaves.

As a social system of production, slavery cannot be dissociated from this set of elements, which is essentially founded on the constant and permanent transfer of human beings within this organic and organized economic space.

3 PRIMARY RELATIONS OF SLAVERY

Most studies of slavery take the master-slave relation, expressed in terms of 'ownership', as their starting point. This relation is established as necessary and sufficient to contain the totality of the phenomenon of slavery (Hindess and Hirst, 1975). But if slavery is to be conceived of as a system, perhaps a mode of production, there must be *continuity* of slave relations; thus these relations must be *reproduced organically and institutionally* in such a way as to preserve the sociopolitical organization of slavery, and thus there must be a specific and constantly renewed relation of exploitation and domination between social groups.

Historical analysis has shown that the master-slave relation is the by-product of a relation which is established within the framework of the total economic space of slavery – that is, between slave-owning societies (employers of slaves) and those societies which produce human beings. This relation, moreover, is established through the workings of a complex set of apparatuses which ensure the economic organization of this space (the military and commercial apparatuses by means of which human beings are captured and transferred from one society to another).[8]

There is no doubt that the relations between raiding peoples and those who were raided were in practice unequal, brutal, discontinuous and circumstantial. They hardly evoke an ordered and institutionalized economic system. On one side were societies which were historically identifiable and geographically defined, politically, militarily and commercially organized, producing on the basis of class relations which provided a hierarchical structure into which slaves, once admitted, were inserted organically. On the other side were nameless and distant populations, scattered, often little known to the above societies and seen as part of a vague and unorganized set of 'savages'. There was no formal relation between the two, no link other than the raw violence imposed by one of the parties where neither war nor peace was ever declared or concluded.

The apparatuses established to link slave-owning societies

and societies which produced slaves – the army or the pillaging band – did not, by their very nature, allow mutual political recognition. When these relations were relayed by trade, they became so distant, so frequently mediated and broken up into so many stages that the parties no longer had any sense of their respective existence as a people or a nation. Relations were maintained on the basis of lack of recognition, of exoticism, and of an implacable 'otherness'. The images which the slave-owning populations had of the peoples among whom they captured slaves – images which they transmitted to those who approached or studied them – clearly express the reality and the nature of the political relations between them.

In order to mark out social distance, the slave-owning societies generally gave pillaged peoples a name which did not belong to them: for the Sudanese of the Middle Ages, these savage peoples, sources of captives, were the Lam-Lam or the Nyam-Nyam, said to live in the little-explored southern regions; for the Peul Muslims of Fuuta-Jallo they were the *Keeseero*, an undifferentiated term used to describe the black pagans of the South (the 'Kissi' of the colonial administrators) (Balde, 1975: 181). 'In the dialects of the Tuarga and the Berbers of the Sahara, Djanawen, Ganawn (singular: Ganaw) means "black slaves"' (J. Lanfry, 1966). The same term [*genewa*] was used in Timbuktu to describe Blacks (Cuoq, 1975: 119, p.1). Djawanen was to become Guinean for the Europeans. For the nineteenth-century Soninke, 'Bambara' was still practically synonymous with slave.

In reality these terms did not apply to specific ethnic groups or political formations, but to a confused set of diverse populations from which the suppliers of slaves, warriors or merchants, drew their stock. The slavers used these vague and badly defined names to describe populations which in their view had a common characteristic: a hardiness which came close to bestiality and manifested itself in coarseness, ignorance, intellectual inferiority, amorality and savage practices (cannibalism, generally): character traits which thus predisposed these populations to capture and exploitation similar to that undergone by animals[9] – predisposed or even predestined them, according to the Peul of Fuuta Jallo, who gave thanks to God for having created 'pagans with hard heads but with strong arms destined to serve believers' (Vieillard, in Balde, 1975: 198).

Above all, these undifferentiated peoples were seen as having no social or political existence – proof of which, in the eyes of their captors, was the absence of chiefs. Added to their supposed inability to understand, this political vacuum made communication impossible. Now, however crude these images may seem, they did correctly reflect the nature of the political relation which the slave-raiders had to maintain with the raided societies in order to preserve the slave relation. For this relation of otherness, maintained both by practice and by ideology, determines all other relations. It is the basis of slave relations of production and of the specific exploitation of labour associated with them. It is in fact the ideological expression of a relation between dominant and dominated which divides the set of free-born citizens in the slave-owning societies from the set of populations destined to be raided and plundered in the past, the present and the future. It is expressed in negative terms but is in fact the positive means of maintaining that social distance which is the necessary condition for slavery.[10]

Otherness, combined with the class relation which developed with exploitation within the slave-owning society, provoked a racist reaction to slaves. This is because both somatic traits (ugliness, heaviness) and character traits (stupidity, laziness, shiftiness) were always associated with the state of the slave. Because of their alien origin, slaves were permanently relegated to the category of beings of a different and naturally inferior *species*: tolerated if they kept their distance, rejected if they showed the slightest desire to identify themselves with 'humans'.

Thus pillage represented a permanent relation of extortion accompanied by an ideology which supplied its justification and by institutions which facilitated its perpetuation.[11] Raiders and raided were linked in a relationship which was necessary to the reproduction of the slave social system as a whole. I shall call this relationship the 'primary class relation', since it is a relationship not of exploitation but of extortion; it is not organic but necessary; it is a relationship not between master and slave but between two social sets. One of these sets was composed of slave-owning societies, the other of societies subject to the constant plunder of part of their demographic increase and their labour-energy. The fact that pillaging and pillaged populations did not each belong to a single political set does not affect the nature of this relation.[12] I shall show that this primary relation represents a necessary stage in the process of exploitation which develops within the slave-owning society between the class of masters and that of slaves; and that the former (extortion) must be repeated if the latter (exploitation) is to take place.

The plunder by the predatory society of the pillaged societies is, in its continuous or periodic nature, characteristic of slavery. Whatever the intensity or frequency of raids on a particular village or population, on a global scale where pillaging societies enter into conflict with the set of populations in which they operate, this plunder creates a permanent and continuous flow of human riches at the expense of the pillaged societies as a whole. There is abundant historical proof that this relation tended to be regular. The evidence shows unequivocally that slavery was always associated with war, abduction or brigandage, which were the principal means of direct or indirect supply. Slaving wars were characterized by their repetitive or seasonal nature. In Senegambia, in Dahomey, in Segu, in the Mawri country, in Anzourou, and so on, or wherever such wars were waged, the armies went into the field every year (sometimes more often) to capture the 'two-legged cattle' (Piault, 1975: 325) which was to supply the kingdoms, the markets or the dealers.

C. Aubin-Sugy (1975), who finds a tendency towards political centralization in nineteenth-century Sahelian Africa as a result of these wars of capture, notes this rhythm of war: 'Every year, the armies bring back an abundant harvest of cattle and of slaves.' Seasonal expeditions became characteristic of slave wars, revealing their permanently organic nature. In contrast, the raids by bands which complemented supplies from war or were the main means of capture are often described as continuous, although they – unlike military campaigns – generally took place during the cultivating season so that the peasants could be taken by surprise in the fields.

Do the continuity and institutionalized regularity of the supply of captives and the concern, at times, with the reproduction of the pillaged populations[13] reflect a constant rise in demand (the reproduction of slaves being ensured by their natural increase), or do they reflect the organic need of the slave economy to ensure its reproduction through the incessant draining of other populations? The question is important, because the way in which slavery is to be characterized depends on the answer.

[handwritten annotations:]

imp.

— demand, or social reproduction, key to organic nature of slave system?

"harvest cycles" in slave-acquisition wars.

3

Sterility

What we know about the demography of slaves suggests that a continual inflow of captives was necessary, as much to renew the slave population as to increase it. The demographic reproduction of slaves does not seem to have been a concern of the slave-owners.

In the Bamoum kingdom, where two-thirds of the population was enslaved, 'thousands of slaves remain single' (Tardits, 1980a: 466). Those who had distinguished themselves through their behaviour or their exploits had preferential access to women, but their families 'remained small' (ibid.: 467). In 1819 Bowdich found that in Asante most of the slaves were single. Barth was surprised that so few slaves were born in the Sudan (1857–8, II: 151–2). He noted that 'domestic slaves' were rarely allowed to marry, and he correctly concluded that this absence of reproduction was a major factor in the perpetuation of slave raids. Terray (1975a: 437) also notes that in the country of the Abron there was no natural reproduction of relations of captivity.[1] Slaves of both sexes assigned to production, to transport or to agriculture – the vast majority – were in fact rarely 'married' in the social sense of the word – that is, capable of having progeny and establishing filiation relations. Soldier-slaves, who were permitted to reproduce themselves, had a fairly short life expectancy: the Dahomeyan and Sonxai armies regularly had to replace men killed in combat through the capture of new slaves (Herskovits, 1938, II: 96–7; Le Hérissé, 1911: 375s.).

These general findings regarding the celibacy of slaves seem, however, to be contradicted by another phenomenon: there were more female than male slaves in most slave-owning African societies, and the demand for and price of female slaves were higher on all the markets (M. Klein, 1983).

We know from Arab witnesses that the slave trade in the Maghreb involved women and children particularly. The same was true of the inter-African slave trade in the Middle Ages (cf. ch.1) as in more contemporary periods (Nadel, 1942: 9; Malowist, 1966; Goody, 1980; Piault, 1975: 18; Archives d'OM, K14/K18 Kouroussa; especially Lovejoy, 1983 and Fisher and Fisher, 1970). We know that male prisoners of war were executed as soon as the demand for male captives dropped with the prohibition of the Atlantic slave trade (Kouroubari, 1959: 546–9; Archives d'OM, K14).[2] Demand on the internal African market was primarily for women. In Gumbu (Mali), a big town whose inhabitants before colonization numbered some 5,200, of whom nearly 40 per cent were slaves, it seems that there were three female slaves to each male and each child. A count made in 1965 showed that nearly sixty years after the abolition of slavery by the French, families of slave origin still had smaller numbers of children than those of free-born origin (1965 Mission).

Censuses undertaken in fifty-two districts in West Africa by the French colonial administration, collected by M. Klein (1983: 68–9) show that the number of male slaves was higher than that of female in only eight districts, and in seven others numbers of the two sexes were almost equal. In thirty-seven other cases, women represented between 60 per cent and more than 200 per cent of slaves. Although such statistics are not completely reliable, their repetition illustrates the imbalance of the sex ratio observed throughout.

Some have argued that if women were more in demand than men, and if they were worth more, this could only have been because of the one natural advantage women had over men – that is, their capacity for procreation (Goody, 1980). In this view, a bigger female slave population indicates a policy of reproduction of slaves through natural increase. The authors who follow this reasoning sometimes confuse slaves bought as concubines, whose progeny was free-born – and who thus did not contribute to the renewal of the slave population – with women bought as workers.

But in fact the hypothesis which suggests that female slaves (more numerous and more expensive than male slaves) were preferred because they ensured slave reproduction has no objective basis. There are no statistics or evidence to demonstrate the demographic reproduction of the slave classes. On the contrary, at a general level it is clear that in slave-owning societies where female slaves were preponderant, in black Africa as well as in the Maghreb, slaves were constantly imported, in the same way as in slave-owning societies where men predominated – in the West Indies, for example.

Thanks to the studies presented in *Women and Slavery in Africa* (Robertson and Klein, eds, 1983) we have a few precise and precious examples of the fertility of women slaves in some African societies. Such information is still rare and cannot be generalized, but it is clear that in each of the situations described in this work, women slaves had few children and, contrary to what might have been expected if female slaves had been preferred because of their procreative capacity, there is no sign even of simple reproduction of the servile population. The figures from the French censuses quoted above (M. Klein, 1983: 69) show that the average number of children per woman counted was 0·94, which would give a gross rate of reproduction well below 0·5 per cent. M. Strobel (1983: 121) found that in a group of fifteen adult slaves which she studied in Mombasa at the beginning of the nineteenth century there were ten women but only eleven living children of both sexes. Many of these women, adds M. Strobel, 'as several other slaves, never married' (ibid.: 120). Elsewhere the author remarks that 'there is no evidence that slaves who had children[3] were favoured over those who did not' (ibid.: 121). M. Strobel nevertheless considers that this low fertility must have been a disappointment to the masters (ibid.: 120), but the frequency of this situation in other slave-owning societies casts doubt on this interpretation.

The case of the merchant towns of Upper Zaïre in the

nineteenth century is even more patent (Harms, 1983). Although it seems that these towns numbered on average 140 female slaves to 100 male, natural reproduction did not take place. Travellers were struck by the lack of children in the streets; a survey in 1889 counted 384 adults in the slave population (of whom 204·8 would have been women in terms of the proportion quoted above) for fifty children, or 0·24 children per woman, a fertility rate of less than 0·12. Harms also sees this sterility as counter to the wishes of the class of masters, but for two distinct reasons which he seems to confuse. Was it because their slave *concubines* did not give them descendants (who would in any case not have had slave status): 'They were angry at individual women for failing *to bear them* children' (ibid.: 108)? Or was it rather because the slaves did not reproduce among themselves? 'The traders were forced to continually buy new slaves *in order* to keep up the population of their villages' (ibid.: 109).

This last remark shows that in practice slave reproduction took place through purchase, independently of any supposed intention on the part of the masters: 'The Bobangi didn't bear many children, they just bought people' (ibid.: 109). In merchant societies, the principal means of reproduction was money: 'If you had no money, the people were finished for good' (Harms, 1983), as a merchant from Bolobo (Upper Zaïre) expressed it. Harms sees the sterility of the women as a form of resistance against their condition, but this explanation is not founded on any evidence or testimony. It is in contradiction to the behaviour reported by other authors which rather suggests the resignation of these women to their condition, if not their alienation.

Accounts of female slaves' way of life show more clearly why it was not propitious to motherhood. The story of Adukwe, for example, as related by C. Robertson (1983), is a story of wanderings, of instability, of a succession of poor living conditions. Her relationships with men were fragile and often illegitimate. Her children were usually not acknowledged or maintained by their fathers; she herself was never maintained by any of her lovers. She had several abortions. With the exception of a daughter, her children did not live beyond the age of five. The case of Bwanikwa, related by

M. Wright (1983), also illustrates these poor living conditions which did not favour motherhood.

R. Maugham (1961: 200) tells the contemporary story of a woman enslaved by the Tuareg: captured by the Regeibat, she fell pregnant twice, one of her children died and she abandoned the other in order to escape. The Saharan slave–owners claimed that venereal disease could be cured by sexual relations with a young virgin slave (Mercadier, 1971: 91). This particularly ignoble custom revealed a complete lack of concern for the fertility of the young slaves or for their future partners. [4]

The fragility of relations between slaves in the Nzakara region is also emphasized by A. Laurentin (1960: 164): 'Marital ties between two slaves did not prevent the master from taking away one of the two partners to use in exchange or to endow a relative or a client with a spouse.' This way of life did not favour either motherhood or the rearing of children. Since they had no dowry, women slaves were in practice never 'married'. When they were under the power of a master to whom the children would belong, he was not the children's father; any more than the man whose children they had borne (and who, as a result, had little or no interest in the children).

When the master tolerated or even imposed the union of two slaves, the general rule was that it was not a 'marriage' in the proper sense of the term (otherwise the genitor, rather than the woman's master, would have had the paternity of the children). The union could be dissolved at any time. Among the Anyi, union between slaves took place without any ceremony 'since they are like chickens and cocks who keep each other warm', according to their masters (C. H. Perrot, 1983: 164). Women slaves were tempted to have abortions so as not to become attached to children who could be taken away from them or not to have to look after the children if they were separated from their partners.

Neither did the attitude of the masters to the children of slaves suggest any real concern for reproduction. Hogendorn (1977: 377) reports that while the women slaves were working on the plantations of Sokoto, the young children were grouped together under a tree and their mothers could go to breastfeed them only with the guard's permission. At Gumbu, slave babies were buried up to their necks in sand to keep them quiet. A witness questioned by R. Maugham (1961: 176) reports that the Tuareg abandoned children who cried too much in the desert. The Islamic Code of slavery (in Daumas, 1857: 322) assimilated pregnancy to an ailment 'which had a damning effect, when Negresses who had been sold were in this condition'. Like those who were considered mad or were suffering from a hidden illness, pregnant slaves could be returned to their owners.[5]

Motherhood was not as desirable a state for the woman slave as for the free-born woman. In societies where the lineage ethic predominated, the free-born woman's fertility was a source of pride, and it seems unlikely that these societies would have accepted that women slaves (even or particularly the masters' concubines) could be superior in this respect to the wives of the dominant class. The fertility of women slaves was more easily acknowledged once their condition had been transformed, once they enjoyed some form of emancipation and their unions were stabilized by becoming more similar to 'marriages', either with men of their own class who had also been emancipated or with their master. In the latter case, the woman was often enfranchised through the conception or birth of a child. In this case it was no longer a question of slavery as such. These women were then slaves only in terms of their origin: their progeny, even if still in a position of dependence, acquired free-born status. Thus generative reproduction of slaves did not take place here.[6]

The low fertility of female slaves is also apparent in the royal courts in aristocratic societies. The palace of the sovereign of Dahomey, where large numbers of women lived – including a high proportion of captives – cannot be seen as fertile ground. The progeny of the kings, although remarkable in each case, was low in terms of the high number of women to whom they had access. Glele had 129 children and Gbehanzin 77 (Bay, 1983; 16–17) from a total of 5,000 to 8,000 *ahosi* (wives or female dependants), many of whom were in principle forbidden other sexual relations. Njoya, one of the

Bamoum sovereigns with the largest number of descendants, had 1,200 wives. He fathered 350 children, of whom only 163 were still living at his death (Tardits, 1980a: 602, 631). In some courts the fertility of the royal wives was sometimes cut short by the custom of executing them on the death of their husband the sovereign. At Porto Novo, between 1688 and 1908, there were nineteen reigns which lasted on average eleven and a half years, some of which lasted two, four or six years. Each king had numerous young wives who died with him (Akindele, 1953: 65). Thus in fact, whatever the intentions imputed to the class of masters and whether the dominant mode was slave, aristocratic or merchant, the class of slaves did not renew itself by natural increase.

In this respect African slavery is no different from slavery as it is known elsewhere. In contrast to the free woman, the primary value of the female slave stemmed not from her reproductive capacity but from other factors linked to the nature of slavery which affected human beings even in those essentials which seem the most 'natural'.

4

Profits and Accumulation

The coherence which links the history of slavery, the demography of slavery and the analysis of the domestic community reveals a very particular 'mode of production'.

Slavery as a *social system* – as distinguished from individual enslavement – is not the *sui generis* product of the domestic community. The exploitation of slaves necessitates the establishment of social relations which are the social and juridical antithesis of kinship relations. It can be imposed only on an 'alien' social category which is distinct from the categories of kin. Indeed, slavery was accompanied by constant raids and wars of capture; it led to the development of a large-scale commercial network and a market system which were necessary for the transfer of captives from one social system to another. Wars of capture and markets had their counterpart in the sterility of the women slaves who, despite their sex and their numbers, were deprived of reproductive functions. The specificity of the slave economy rests on this set of factors.

Labour-power was produced outside the economy in which it was employed. It was not bought from the producer but withdrawn through plunder which made the slave into a commodity whose commercial value was dissociated from his or her cost of production. Slavery involves two social classes, depending on the form of acquisition: the aristocratic class which captured for its own use and the merchant class which bought slaves from the aristocrats. Slavery functioned in each case according to distinct models of exploitation.

But, above all, it is clear from all this that the mode of reproduction shaped the functioning of slavery: profits from slavery, relations of production and the accumulation process were all subordinated to the mode of reproduction.

Before embarking on case studies to demonstrate this point and its implications, it is necessary at this stage, in order to clarify the argument, briefly to list some of the principal characteristics of slavery as they emerge from this work. These characteristics will be discussed more fully later in the book.

1 SUBSISTENCE SLAVERY

Since by definition slaves were not maintained by their masters, they had to produce at least their own subsistence and in some cases that of other slaves assigned to non-agricultural tasks. Food production was essentially the primary task of slaves, all the more so to the extent that they were designed to free the class of masters from labour. The state of the slave resulted from his or her mode of exploitation in food production; even if a slave was withdrawn from agricultural production and his or her condition was transformed, this primary state did not change.

In order to demonstrate the particularities and the diversity of slavery, its primary objective, the exploitation of male or female slaves as producers of subsistence goods, must first be examined. The introduction of slaves was first and foremost a response to this need, even if – as we shall see – the social and political effects of slavery could at times result in the exploitation of free peasants for the profit of a dominant class. In the same way, we shall *assume* here that the slave class did not produce for the market, that their masters tried to make them work as hard as possible, and that there were no costs attached to their acquisition.[1] I shall call this form of exploitation, under which the slave produced only use-value, subsistence slavery.

When captives were introduced into the community, they

brought with them the fraction of the social product which had been invested in their formation by their community of origin.[2] In rustic societies, where active participation started very young, an individual's production equalled his or her consumption at between twelve and sixteen years of age before overtaking it. (T. Brun and C. Layrac, 1979; Elwert, 1973). In practice, capture as a means of procuring productive agents made possible the selection of those subjects who were most desirable in this respect, through the physical elimination of those who were too young or too old to be productive. (Examples of this practice are to be found in Lacroix, 1967: 146; Mercadier, 1971: 11, 17, 36, 39; Daumas, 1857.)

In order to maximize profits from the labour of the slave-owning society, the whole of his or her surplus-product had to be abstracted, and thus the slave's social capacity for reproduction had to be reduced to zero: he or she could not be allowed to have children to feed. This was possible because of the mode of renewal of slaves through acquisition or plunder. In this way slave-owning societies could draw a twofold benefit from slaves:

a. the society acquired accumulated energy (αK) in the physical person of the labourer abducted from his or her society of origin;

b. the society retained the whole surplus-product of the slave's labour, equivalent to the difference between the slave's production during his or her active life and his or her consumption during the time the slave survived within the slave-owning society.[3]

The essential part of profit from slaves is not αK (the volume of food absorbed by the slave before his or her capture) but the surplus-product which could be seized in its entirety since the slave was replaced by abduction.

The plunder of the raided populations and the seizure of the whole of the slave's surplus-product cannot be dissociated from each other. Since the masters did not leave any part of the surplus food product to the slaves to feed their progeny, these slaves could be replaced only through the capture of other slaves. Capture and exploitation are organically linked, since the renewal of profits from the exploitation of the production capacities of the slaves presupposes the continual introduction into the slave-owning society of ready-made new producers who are also economically incapable of reproducing themselves as slaves. Plunder or extortion took place at the expense of an alien society, exploitation at the expense of the class of slaves constituted in this way.

Thus the productive and reproductive cycles were separated. Their unity had been the basis of kinship and had prevented the *sui generis* formation of a slave class. Slave exploitation both affected and identified the real alien: he or she who had been born and had grown up outside the community and who could be replaced only by an individual with exactly the same characteristics, *de jure* or *de facto*.

The exploitation of slaves necessarily excluded the exploited individual from the social relations of kinship, and thus also from citizenship. It locked him or her into the state of alien. The seizure of the total surplus produced by slaves condemned them to permanent extraneousness, since it meant that they had to be denied any progeny who might absorb even the smallest part of that surplus. This explains the restrictions on the physical reproduction of slaves, the prohibition of marriages among them, the confiscation of the children of women slaves by their master and, more generally, the refusal to grant them rights to paternity or maternity.[4]

De-socialized, de-personalized, de-sexualized, slaves could be condemned to an exploitation which was not tempered by any desire to preserve their physical and social capacities for reproduction. Thus, in terms of this logic, maximum profit could be obtained by reducing the maintenance costs of the slave to the length of his or her active life, through manumission or immolation as soon as he or she was no longer productive. In terms of the same logic, the slave could be fed the minimum necessary for the reproduction of his or her labour-energy, while at the same time being subjected to punishments or given rewards which increased the intensity of labour. However, these measures were not essential to the exploitation of slaves.[5] Slaves who were well fed and lived to old age were still exploited and alienated because of their mode of reproduction. The characterization of a social system does not depend only on relations of production between individuals.

2 THE DIFFERENCE BETWEEN SERFDOM AND SLAVERY

It is therefore useful at this point to distinguish between the slave mode of production and serfdom. This distinction is all the more necessary in that Marx and Engels – and many other authors – tend to assimilate one to the other.

The preceding analysis shows that the difference stems from the mode of reproduction: serfs were not bought on the market but reproduced themselves through demographic increase. They therefore had to be able to use part of their agricultural surplus-product to feed the next generation. For simple reproduction to take place (where each producer is replaced by another as soon as he or she is no longer productive) the surplus-product of the active population had at least to equal the consumption of an equal number of pre-productive individuals (without taking into account mortality at each age). If in addition the masters were to receive a rent, productivity had to be high enough to ensure that the means of subsistence needed for the reproduction of the young serfs did not absorb the whole product. Thus, whatever the case, productivity under serfdom had to be higher than under slavery.[6] On the other hand, serfdom did not involve the costs of acquisition of slaves.

The exploitation of the serf was based on his settlement on a strip of land which was conventionally defined as 'that piece of land necessary to support a man and his family'.[7] Under serfdom (unlike sharecropping) rents were extracted on the basis of fixed dues: the serf had to deliver the same quantity of products each year, whatever the volume of his production. He had to supply the same number of working days. He could be exempted from part of these payments only through the indulgence of his master. Caught between limited means of production and labour-time, on one hand, and irreducible dues on the other, the serf was obliged to limit the size of his family – that is, the number of non-productive individuals to be fed – in terms of what was left of his surplus-product. Under these conditions abortion was practised and children were abandoned, while old non-productive individuals were not allowed to live long. Unless agricultural productivity was very high or the lord was lenient (which was unlikely), serfdom as a mode of production did not *a priori* favour demographic growth.

A further effect of fixed dues – which were usually calculated on the basis of good harvests – was to prevent the serf from building up reserves. This meant that he was periodically in debt to the lord. Only the lord was in a position to accumulate stocks, on the basis of the dues paid by the serfs to tide him over during periods of shortage. Thus when the harvest was poor the serf was obliged to ask the lord for aid in order to survive and to start the agricultural cycle over again; the nobles were able to appear generous when in fact they were only giving the serfs back the minimum necessary for their survival and their continued production. Under serfdom the labourer was neither bought nor sold individually; he was not a commodity, but he was nevertheless part of a patrimony and could – with his household – be given away as a donation, an inheritance, a privilege or any other form of free transfer, handed over with the land he cultivated.[8] Unlike the slave, the serf lived in a household, since this was the necessary condition for his reproduction. As we shall see, conditions analogous to serfdom were granted to certain categories of slaves who were given a partner and authorized to live in a household, and had to pay fixed dues. The condition of these slaves (for reasons which will be discussed below) was a forerunner within slavery for the emergence of serfdom.

3 HOW MANY SLAVES? HOW MANY SERFS?

For any given level of consumption, the number of food-producing slaves necessary to feed the class of masters depends on two factors: the agricultural productivity of the slave and the length of his or her active life.

For a given population of free individuals, the number of slaves is determined at any time by the ratio of their annual surplus-product to the annual consumption of the class of masters, who are assumed to be idle. A calculation (see appendix) which has only comparative value, based on the estimated productivity of sorghum cultivation with hoes, shows that in this example slaves of productive age had to constitute 29·8 per cent of the total population (or 42·5 per cent of the free-born population) in order to feed the class of masters.

Since the *active* lifespan of the slave was, naturally, shorter than the *total* lifespan of the master, slaves had to be renewed in proportion to these two lifespans. If, for example, a slave's active life was half as long as the lifespan of a master, the total number of slaves had to be renewed twice in each free-born generation. In the hypothetical example above, 85 slaves would have been necessary for each generation of 100 free-born individuals.[9]

The figure of 85 slaves abstracts from the mortality of the servile producers before 'retirement' age and assumes that the slave dies on reaching this age (that is, as soon as his or her surplus-product drops below his or her consumption). It is also assumed that food stocks are zero and that no demographic growth takes place either in the free-born or in the servile population. Thus the figures which result from these estimates are minima. As regards the land under cultivation, it is assumed that returns are the same everywhere. The assumption that members of the free-born class do not share in the production of food corresponds to behaviour which was frequent, if not general: 'The Itsekiri now term agriculture "slave work" and are loath to lower their status by performing it themselves' (Bradbury, 1967: 175).[10]

Under serfdom, where the whole servile population reproduced itself through demographic increase, with the same productivity and assuming one replacement for each serf, an active population of both sexes of 61 would have been necessary for 100 idle individuals, instead of 42·5. The difference is necessary to feed the new generation of servile individuals. The total number of servile individuals would have been at least 122 in order to ensure simple reproduction, and the land area necessary for their subsistence would have been 123·8 per cent of the land assigned to the masters. Thus the total numbers of servile individuals are always nearly three times as high as under slavery, and the land area necessary to feed the whole population increases to the same extent. These calculations do not take into account either demographic growth or the building-up of reserves.

4 ADVANTAGES OF SLAVERY

The most visible immediate advantage of slavery is that it spares the slave-owning class the presence and supervision of a total serf population which provides the demographic infrastructure necessary to ensure the existence of an active population which renews itself but does not increase. Under serfdom, faced with an exploited class integrated into society, the seigneurial class had to exercise greater repression for the same economic results. Now, the lord did not have at his disposal the same means of social control over the serfs as the master over the slaves. The heterogeneity of the slave class, because of its origins and its constant renewal, made possible a number of different forms of social advancement (including access to the 'privileges' of serfdom) which created divisions within it. In contrast, the stability of the serf population, its territorially settled and peasant nature and its restructuring along the lines of the family provided possibilities of resistance of which the serfs made use. Serf revolts are a constant feature of feudal history; but slave revolts were rare. Even more than the slave-owning class, the seigneurial class had to turn to repression and force of arms, and to confront the people. In the same way, serfdom, by increasing the areas of land necessary for the settlement of the active population, tended more than slavery towards territorial conquest.

But the decisive advantages of slavery over serfdom lie elsewhere. Slavery made possible *immediate increases in production*, through the immediate addition of active labourers. While the numbers of serfs of productive age depended on the number of pubescent women in the serf population and on the time their progeny needed to become productive, slavery meant that productive workers were available at once. Slavery enabled, through the transfer of individuals, an accumulation process which was not possible under serfdom. Accumulation and growth under slavery depended on capacities for capture and purchase – that is, on variables (warfare and commerce) which made possible a more flexible and faster rate of reproduction and increase in numbers than demographic growth.

Finally, and above all, as long as this process of accumulation lasted, *production could increase independently of the productivity of labour through the mere addition of other producers*, who could constantly be acquired outside the society where they were employed.

5 CONSTRAINTS AND COSTS OF SLAVERY

Corresponding to the advantages of slavery are constraints and limits imposed by its mode of reproduction. These differ according to whether the slave is assigned to the production of a use-good (the means of subsistence) or a commodity.

In the first case, the reproduction of the slave who produces subsistence goods can take place only through capture, since by definition he or she does not produce anything which would make possible the purchase of a replacement. These replacements must thus be captured either by the slave-owning class itself or by its armed retainers, who either feed themselves or are fed by their captives. Subsistence slavery tends to be found particularly in military and aristocratic societies devoted to wars of abduction. The cost of the slave for the capturing societies is reduced to the cost of capture, which is dissociated from the slave's cost of production. If, as a number of authors argue (Curtin, 1975; Person, 1968–75; Terray, 1982a), capture was the by-product of wars which the princes would have fought anyway, the cost of capture would be zero. But even when the purpose of these wars was capture – which in my opinion was generally the case in this historical context – the mobilization by the aristocracy of a fighting peasantry which produced its own means of subsistence and its own arms, the use of soldier-slaves of servile origin who lived on the production of an exploited peasantry, in addition to the unequal distribution of the human booty in favour of the masters – all these factors reduced the cost of capture to the benefit of the slave-owning aristocracy (see Part II, B below). The slave came into the hands of this aristocracy invested both with the intrinsic value extorted in his or her person and with the labour of the combatants involved in his or her capture.

Because of this double relation of exploitation, the aristocratic class did not pay the cost of 'production' of the slave, and paid only a small part of his or her capture. Moreover, the exchange of captives for imported instruments of abduction (arms and horses, in particular) contributed to the renewal of wars of capture. Thus, once in the hands of the aristocrat, the slave did not represent a large investment. The slave could be assigned to the production of subsistence goods (in spite of his or her low productivity), subjected to lifelong exploitation, or immolated for prestige.

The situation was different in merchant slave-owning society, where the slave was bought for use in the production of commodities. Access to slaves took place through the market, and commodities had to be provided in exchange. The market was necessarily the site both of the sale of slaves and of the purchase of their production. In this economy, the cost of reproduction of the slave employed for profit can be calculated in terms of *the ratio of the purchase price of the slave to the selling price of his or her production.* The slave's rate of reproduction was his or her rate of amortization, and we shall see that at times this was as little as a few months. The slave represented an investment, an immobilization of capital. This investment had to be amortized as fast as possible so as to reinvest the capital it represented in production. If the amortization of the slave took less time than the time needed by an equivalent servile population to bring an individual up to productive age, a demand of this size had to be met through the draining of larger and larger populations whose total demographic increase was equal at any given moment to the demand for individuals of productive age. Unlike the subsistence slave, the slave employed for profit (profit-slave) could be found only in the context of an extended market where the capturing societies could provide supplies of slaves in quantities determined by price ratios on the market.

However, to the extent that slavery immobilized capital in the purchase of labourers, it reduced the possibilities for investment in the means of production which could increase *US* the productivity of labour. Since accumulation took place through increases in the number of producers, it had little effect on rises in productivity. Productivity of labour was *But not* almost constant under slavery, both because growth could *case in* take place through the addition of labourers and through their accelerated renewal and because as a result the capital *sugar* necessary for the transformation of working conditions was *system.* immobilized.[11] On the other hand, since this accumulation took no account of the needs of demographic reproduction under conditions of low productivity, it could only be destructive and take place at the expense of other populations. It was limited in the final analysis by the spread of the devastated areas and by the demographic resources of the populations on which it fed.

The economic logic of slavery confirms the observation of its historical functioning. Exploitation of slaves took place on the basis of a reserve of manpower outside the exploiting society. It necessitated a military and commercial apparatus capable of draining the eco-demographic increment in alien populations and of transferring this already existing manpower ('ready-made', as Marx put it) from the milieu in which it had been formed into the milieu in which it was to be exploited, at a faster rate than any demographic growth which might take place in the servile population within the exploiting society.

Because of the organic nature of this transfer, it is the mode of reproduction rather than the mode of production which determines the nature of profits from slavery and of the accumulation process. It is also the mode of reproduction which renders the slave's social state permanent, notwithstanding the various uses to which he or she might be assigned. For if capture and the market are the conditions for the slave's economic existence, they are also the conditions for his or her social non-existence.

Comparative estimates of the number of slaves and of serfs necessary to maintain a given non-productive population

The calculations below have only comparative value. They are in fact based on very approximate estimates made in the field from observation of the cultivation of sorghum with hoes in the Sahelo-Sudanese region.

I assume that the agricultural production and consumption of active women – who had onerous household tasks – were lower than those of men. Consumption by non-productive individuals is an average figure for both sexes for the age group 0 to 15 years, assuming that at 15 an individual's production equals his or her consumption. I have abstracted from the need for seed and for reserves (and thus from bad years) so as to calculate only a gross annual product. I have not taken into account mortality by age, which would increase the consumption of non-productive individuals in proportion to the number among them who did not reach productive age and cut down the production of active individuals who died before the age at which their production would have dropped to equal their consumption (45 years).

I assume that the free-born population does not produce, that the sex ratio within it is in balance, and that it is distributed by age as follows:

Under 15	50%
15 to 45	40%
over 45	10%

Annual consumption of a free-born population of 100 individuals:

Consumption of an adult man   300 kg
Consumption of all other categories   180 kg
Total consumption:

$$50 \times 180 = 9{,}000 \text{ (young people)}$$
$$20 \times 300 = 6{,}000 \text{ (adult men)}$$
$$20 \times 180 = 3{,}600 \text{ (adult women)}$$
$$10 \times 180 = \underline{1{,}800} \text{ (old people)}$$
$$\text{Total} = 20{,}400$$

a. Exploitation of a slave population

I assume here that the sex ratio in the slave population favours women in the proportion of 60:40, and that slaves die at forty-five:

Annual production of an active man   1,000 kg
Annual production of an active woman   500 kg

Consumption is the same as for the free-born population.
Annual surplus-product:

Man: 1,000 − 300 = 700 kg
Woman: 500 − 180 = 320 kg

Corrected for the sex ratio, the average individual production is 480 kg.

Number of slaves necessary for the year under consideration:

$$\frac{20,400}{480} = 42 \cdot 5 \text{ for a free-born population of } 100$$

If the active life of these slaves is half as long as the total lifespan of a free-born individual, the slave population has to be renewed twice for each generation of free-born individuals.

b. Exploitation of a serf population

I assume here that the sex ratio is in balance, that all the serfs live in households, and that they reproduce themselves at the rate of one replacement per active man or woman. Thus the consumption of two minors (360 kg) must be subtracted from the serfs' gross surplus-product of 1,020 kg per couple, leaving a net surplus-product of 660 kg per couple. The number of serfs necessary for the maintenance of the same free-born population as before is:

$$\frac{20,400}{330} = 61 \text{ active individuals of both sexes}$$

The total serf population (active and pre-productive individuals) – if old people die at forty-five – necessary to maintain a free-born population of 100 is 122.
The total consumption of this serf population is:

30·3 × 300 =   9,150 kg (active men)
89·5 × 180 = 16,110 kg (active women and pre-productive individuals)
                 25,260 kg

or 123 per cent of the consumption of the free-born class, necessitating the same proportion of the land for its subsistence.

The number of active serfs represents 135 per cent of the slave population in the first example and the total serf population 271 per cent.

(See Part III, Chapter 5 on demographic implications.)

5

Unborn and Reprieved from Death

Slavery exists as a social system only if a distinct class of individuals with the same *state* is constituted and renewed continually and institutionally so that, since its functions are permanently ensured, the relations of exploitation and the class which benefits from them are also renewed as such, regularly and continually.

If, in the final analysis, profit from slavery is realized through the constant plunder of human beings from an alien society, slavery must always be associated with the appropriate institutions: capture and slave markets.

Slaves acquire, through their transfer, two properties which cannot be dissociated form one another. Through the first, an economic property, slaves bring with them an accumulated quantity of labour-power which represents, depending on their ages, the whole or part of the cost of producing them or 'breeding' them as producers; through the second, a social property, the slaves are inserted as *absolute aliens* in the slave-owning host society.

Their mode of exploitation is linked to this twofold genesis, and *they reproduce themselves as slaves only to the extent that this double condition is reproduced*. The very nature of the profit made from the acquisition of slaves – in other words, the cost of reproduction of labour-energy – leads to the specific form of exploitation in which the slaves must be denied the use of their (physical or social) capacities for reproduction if they are to be renewed as such. This denial excludes them from the organic relations through which a slave class could reproduce itself through natural increase, and thus maintains the original alien state of the slaves and the specific characteristics determined by their mode of exploitation.

Now, through a dialectical detour, the social characteristics of the slaves (in particular the fact that they are not gentle) which result from their mode of exploitation sometimes take precedence over their economic capacities for production as an indirect means of accumulation or as a means of political domination by the dominant class. Slavery, which is the antithesis of kinship, can also be a complement to or even a substitute for it; it can be used as an instrument by dynasties, and it can be a threat to them.

How is the social situation of the slaves formed, transformed and transmitted, given the economic conditions of exploitation?

As a result of the slave mode of production, it is a characteristic of slaves that they are first necessarily removed from the society where they were originally conceived and bred, to be introduced and reproduced as aliens in the slave-owning society. This necessity, which is economic in origin, is met through processes of de-personalization and de-socialization of the slaves which follow their capture.

The state of slaves is the outcome of a succession of metamorphoses which make them into individuals without links of kinship, affinity, or neighbourhood, and thus suitable for exploitation.

Through capture they are torn from their original societies and *de-socialized*; through their mode of insertion into the receiving society and their univocal relationship with their masters they are *de-civilized*[1] and even *de-personalized*. Through these processes their *state* is defined. This state is original and thus permanent, unalterably attached to the captive. Because of this original and indelible stigma, slaves, once in the hands of a master, could be assigned to any task, irrespective of their sex or age, and without being granted a status corresponding to the *condition* defined by their employment. Slaves of either sex could perform men's or women's work. They could also carry out social or political duties without the original stigma being rubbed out by this promotion. The *state* and *condition* of the slave were distinct and did not affect each other.

1 DE-SOCIALIZATION

Captured individuals withdrawn from their native social milieu were not yet 'slaves'. At first they were only 'prisoners', 'captured' or 'captive'.[2] Their final condition and state of slave became apparent only with their insertion into the host society: their *state* was linked to their situation of de-socialized 'aliens' in this new milieu, and their *condition* to the position they were to occupy in the general process of production and reproduction of the system.

The slave relation must therefore be analysed on two successive levels, in terms of:

1. the circumstances in which an individual emerged as an 'alien' in a society;

2. the way in which the alien was inserted into the organic relations within the different slave systems which can be observed.

The societies which concern us are status societies in which social position and rank are acquired through *birth* (or its equivalent, adoption) and lost through *death* (or its equivalent, *forfeiture*). Benveniste (1969, I: 321s.) shows the association in Indo-European languages between the *freedom* of the citizen and birth (but also growth), where *free* individuals were *'those who were born and have grown up together'*. We have seen that this idea of *growing up together* is based on a fundamental economic reality in terms of which the rank and status of individuals are precisely ordered in the agricultural domestic community (Introductory Chapter, section 1).

The societies which were confronted with slavery

necessarily overflowed the domestic institutional framework, since faced with the slave (the absolute alien) the native had to be able to define himself juridically as a 'gentle', claim his privileges as such and base his superiority on an ideology. The (negative) *state* of the slave contrasts with the (positive) *status* of the gentle. Societies which had not conceived and elaborated conservative notions to define the social norms of reproduction were obliged to do so when confronted with slavery in order to distinguish their own members from slaves. Kinship was strengthened, developed and refined in opposition to non-kin. Like all forms of servitude which exclude individuals from the community and from gentle status, slavery doubtless contributed to the invention by contrast, of so-called 'blood' kinship. In the same way, *status* probably appeared with the development of the capacities for exploitation and domination of one class over another as a means of distinguishing their respective members. Thus slavery necessarily leads back to status and class societies.

If for the moment we limit ourselves to an empirical approach, we find that in status societies man's socialization, his position and his rank within society, are established through the following successive relations:

– affiliative (or ancestral) relations in terms of which an individual belongs *through birth and upbringing* to a community of individuals with a common patrimony which gives access to the means of subsistence;

– *conjugal relations and relations of affinity* which establish rights over junior dependants and thus give access to the means of social reproduction;

– relations of ascendance or of *elderhood* which establish authority over these descendants and over the product of their labour;

– relations of *alliance* with neighbouring communities which are mediated by the individual's belonging to his or her own community.

This socialization is considerably weaker in the case of free-born women. The free-born woman did not necessarily have access through affiliation to the patrimony of her paternal group; her rights over her progeny established through conjugal relations were not equal to those of the man. In marrying she lost her condition of gentle in her affine community. She had only secondary authority[3] with respect to her female kin and female affine cadets. Her protection against capture was physical more than social: women left the village less often and for shorter periods of time, sometimes guarded by armed men. The danger of abduction even from societies which did not own slaves was permanent.

Protected and thus in a position of submission in her own community, alien and exiled among her affines, assigned to servant's work, the woman's situation in domestic society was a forerunner of slavery. 'Do not lose touch with your family unless you want to become the slave of your husband,' warns a Mungo fable (from Jewsiewicki, 1981: 74).

The rupture or the dissolution of the relations listed above led to the de-socialization which turned an individual into an alien.[4] In contrast, de-socialization was unlikely if one of these relations was maintained, since if a rupture took place a kin, an affine or an ally would intervene to testify to the status of the captive or to pay the ransom.

In sociogeographic terms these relations functioned within an *area of socialization* inside which an individual acknowledged as a gentle was protected against captivity, if not against abduction.

Thus in spite of appearances which are sometimes to the contrary, villages and tribes which were hostile to one another and between which war was frequent, if not endemic, can be considered to belong to the same society, to the extent that ransom or the exchange of prisoners was admitted and practised between them. This was the case with the Kissi,[5] for example, or the Alladian (Augé, 1975). In contrast, according to the same criterion, groups which were culturally or linguistically linked but captured each other without practising redemption – like the Samo, according to

F. Héritier (1975) – belonged to different societies.

In the first case, the prisoner's position in the society of his or her abductors was generally that of a *hostage* who was held for purposes of ransom, exchange for another prisoner, or replacement of a kin killed in fighting (Augé, 1975). The prisoner retained the attributes of the social person in that he could still be re-socialized – either in his original milieu, if he was bought back, or in the new milieu if he was kept in exchange for a lost member, with the latter's attributes.

The prisoner of war could become a captive if he was not bought back or exchanged by his own community. In this case the social ties of which he could have taken advantage had been broken, and as a result he was de-socialized through the indifference of his co-citizens or his kin (Piault, 1975).

These areas of socialization varied in size and content. The Guro villages which were part of a single matrimonial set (Meillassoux, 1964, ch. 9), within which conciliation procedures were recognized, constituted an area of socialization which contrasted with other areas where conciliation was not practised (1964: 227). The same was true of a kingdom whose subjects were expressly protected against capture by their own sovereign, such as Dahomey at one time, Sonxai or the Mossi States, whose subjects were identified by scarification and preserved from capture or sale throughout the kingdom (Tiendrebeogo, 1963: 11). For the same reasons, Fuuta Tooro, according to Oumar Kane (unpublished manuscript), did not provide a satisfactory source of supply for the slave-traders, since 'the inhabitants do not subjugate each other. They organize the repurchase of captives taken in their territory'.

In the Sahelo-Sudanese regions of West Africa, the intermixing of populations through war and the fortunes and misfortunes of States led to a specific situation. Clans were patronymic – at least from the Wolof country as far as Masina – and spread over huge areas. People of caste knew each person's status even far from his or her region of origin. These clans and castes were linked by alliances at all levels of the social hierarchy, which protected individuals against 'betrayal' and possible enslavement. Within this area, which spread over thousands of kilometres, an individual could not be captured by his kin, his affines or his allies; moreover, they were expected to buy him back if they found him in servitude. Here the patronymic was more often used as a means of identification than scarification. Certain social groups, such as aristocrats, enjoyed even wider protection as a result of their fame, their extended alliances and the class solidarity which operated among them (Piault, 1975). Among the Bamana, for example, although their conquerors did not always show clemency towards vanquished nobles, they did adopt the latters' uncircumcised sons as their own children (Niaré, oral communication).

In this region, members of castes, whose status was considered to be different from that of free-born individuals, could become part of the conqueror's entourage without being enslaved by making known their status of praise-singers (hagiographers), smiths or leatherworkers.[6] Thus in order to defend themselves against servitude, the free-born populations exiled by the Peul of Wasulu claimed to be smiths so as to benefit from the traditional alliance between these two populations (Amselle, 1977).

The spread of such alliances partly explains why wars of capture spread so far in this area and involved such huge military operations. It also explains the usefulness of the merchants as a means of removing the captives from their areas of socialization.

The absence of all these social ties in the host society made the prisoner into an 'alien'.

The notion of 'alien' is common to all African populations. It is generally contrasted with the notion of 'man' – that is, of 'citizen' or 'gentle', of a person with social prerogatives within the milieu in question. The 'man' (the gentle) was defined by his insertion in the social relations defined above (p.102) – an insertion which gave him access, through his position in the community, to civil and economic prerogatives and to a corresponding rank, by virtue of the ties which linked him to others or of their common submission to the same authority.

The alien, on the other hand, had to bind himself to a protector who could act as his referee and his 'witness' in the society which he entered. This initial link was necessary for the establishment of all other links. In the absence of this security, alone, the alien was doomed to subjugation. Slaves were *absolute aliens*, as Benveniste points out. In Indo-European languages the word slave is either a foreign word or the word for 'alien'.

The word *'zenj'* used in the *Tarikhs es-Sudan* and *el-Fettach* to designate subjugated persons in general is of Arab origin,[7] like many of the words which are used among the Sahelo-Sudanese populations to designate social categories.[8]

The alien tribe from which certain slaves originated gave its name to all slaves, like the *kangame* of the Anyi and the Baule, the *dunko* of the Abron or the *jon* of the Bamana.[9]

Once he had been finally removed from his own milieu through capture the slave was considered as socially dead, just as if he had been vanquished and killed in combat. Among the Mande, at one time, prisoners of war brought home by the conquerors were offered *dege* (millet and milk porridge) – because it was held that a man should not die on an empty stomach – and then presented with their arms so that they could kill themselves. Anyone who refused was slapped in the face by his abductor and kept as a captive:[10] he had accepted the contempt which deprived him of personality. There could be no better way to illustrate the fact that the captive *had been reprieved from death*, that he was socially dead, as M. Izard (1975) points out with regard to the Mossi royal slaves.[11]

The slave had indeed been reprieved from death, either because he had not been killed on the battlefield or because he had not been put to death for his crimes. The prisoner of war owed his life to the leniency of the conqueror, the master, or whoever took charge of him, and he could lose it at their hands at any moment. He was 'socially dead' and his only prerogatives were those – always of a precarious nature – which were granted to him.

The same applied to the individual who had been *repudiated*. Here again it was because he had not been put to death for his crimes that an individual was subjugated by the person whom he had wronged, handed over to 'comrades in the trade' or sold (P.-P. Rey, 1975). In slave society the captive was put beyond social death and seen as *not-born*.[12] Logically, since he had not been born, the captive could not make sacrifices to his ancestors; he had no access to the institutions which made possible the creation of ties of marriage, of affinity, even less of paternity, for how can a person who has never been brought into the world pass on 'life'? Birth is, much more than a biological fact, a social fact ruled by human laws.[13] Paul Riesman (1974: 88) suggests that the etymology of the Fula term *rimaïbe*, slaves, is 'those who have not given birth'. Thus capture (or purchase, which presupposes capture) marked slaves with an indelible stigma.

The fundamental juridical situation of the captive in the host society thus stemmed from his de-socialization: as a person who was 'socially dead', 'not-born', he was absolutely without rights. For this reason he was also without status, since status was linked to birth. The intrusion of individuals without status meant that in contrast the members of the host society took on the status of 'born', thus of 'kin' and of 'citizens'.

Status, as a positive notion, is thus contrasted here with *state*, which I define in terms of negative or privative criteria.[14] Now, this state was the same in all slave societies, since it resulted from the same original situation, de-socialization, which was itself a result of capture or, in the final analysis, of the mode of reproduction of these societies, itself linked to the slave mode of exploitation.

2 DE-PERSONALIZATION

If de-socialization deprived individuals of the social relations which constituted them as persons, it did not necessarily deprive them of the *capacity* to build such links.

The individual lost this capacity through *de-personalization* within the slave society.

The distinction between de-socialization and de-personalization can be seen in the ways in which captives were received and inserted both in societies in the forest regions and in the patrilineal societies of the West African savannah.

In these circumstances avuncularity or patrilinearity were

not decisive in the integration of the slave: kinship relations could be and were manipulated in terms of social needs. Each structural framework led to different procedures, but their effects were comparable.

Avuncularity had effects at the level of ideology in particular, as a means of insertion and alienation of slaves. Through the creation of fictitious, incomplete and degraded kinship links, slaves were associated both with the class of masters and with that of their congeners. C.-H. Perrot's description (1975) of the reception of slaves in Anyi society is a remarkable illustration of this. Their heads were shaved in simulation of a fictitious birth;[15] their purchaser was known as their 'father' and his sister or wife as their 'mother'. Through ceremonial libations the slaves were placed under the protection of the ancestors of the lineage which received them. These two *fictitious* relations of filiation, which implied only the obligation to obey, attached the slaves to the class of gentles. But they were not the collaterals of their 'father's' children; they were the 'brothers' or 'sisters' of other captives integrated at the same time and in the same way, with the same fictitious 'father' and 'mother'. Their age with respect to other captives, and thus their 'elderness', was linked not to their birth but to the beginning of their new lives when they entered their master's house. In reality, the creation of these new kinship ties had no positive effects on their state. They were seen as having no real maternal or paternal lineage. They were therefore not persons: their social negation emerges clearly from the fact that they often had no name. They were sometimes addressed by the first part of a distich to which they replied with the second.[16]

The privileges which they might enjoy did not differ in any way from those which would have existed in a society where the slave was not subjected to this use of the kinship idiom. The kinship code was used as an ideological means of alienation, domination, repression and control: insertion as minors and dependants with no rights inflicted on slaves duties of respect and obedience which were identical to those of dependent kin within the same house, while at the same time they were excluded from the rights granted to cadets within the community.

De-personalization was completed through the *reification* of the slave. This was more frequent in regions where trade was intense, like the Sahelo-Sudanese regions, where captives were sold on the market. They were, successively, *commodities* in the hands of the merchants (the so-called 'slave-trade captives'), then *use-goods* and *patrimony* in the hands of the buyers. In all these cases, they were *objects*. Since they were seen as livestock, and thus de-personalized, their re-socialization, in juridical terms, was improbable and in fact unknown, since it presupposed not only the rebuilding of links with other, similarly de-personalized captives, but also permission to build links with gentles of the sort which constitute the social person.

In the patrilineal societies of the savannah, slaves who had been acquired were introduced like living livestock,[17] without any of the pretences resorted to in avuncular societies. Slaves had no rights; they were entirely at the mercy of their masters, on whose arbitrary decisions depended any privileges the slaves might enjoy. These privileges might be identical to those granted to slaves who had only been de-socialized. But, unlike the latter, re-socialization or complete integration into the receiving society was impossible for de-personalized slaves, just as it was impossible for their progeny, who would always bear an indelible mark. In fact no amalgamation was possible between the two different 'species' of free-born individuals and slaves.[18]

3 DE-SEXUALIZATION

De-socialization led to de-sexualization. In any social system, to be a man or a woman means to be acknowledged as having certain functions and prerogatives linked to cultural notions of femininity or masculinity. Some are purely conventional or circumstantial, as the distribution of tasks shows: nothing in nature predisposes women, for example, to household tasks or men to military activities. Sex is determinant only in relation to pregnancy. But this function must be authorized and socially acknowledged. If, like most slave women, some women are excluded from it, or if they are denied motherhood, they lose their only sexual characteristic.

If she was not one of the master's concubines but was assigned to labour, the female slave's fate was analogous to the male's, since it was labour, not sex, which determined her fate.

For some time anthropologists have used women's ability to work to explain their condition in domestic societies, or to describe institutions like dowry,[19] but it is their reproductive function which is usually used to explain the high demand for women on the African slave markets and their higher value relative to men.[20] In my opinion, these arguments should be reversed.

On the first point, it was her capacity for procreation which was valued in the free woman taken as a wife. Her submission as a reproducer led to her submission as a labourer (Meillassoux, 1981). Under slavery, by contrast, it was her qualities as a labourer and her qualifications for the performance of certain tasks which gave the woman the greatest value. Slave women were used deliberately as reproducers only to the advantage of the dominant classes, because of the particular social character of their progeny, which was in general differentiated from that of free-born origin.[21] In contrast, progeny of two slaves was only a by-product of slavery, with no significant effects on reproduction.

The use of free women in labour was widespread in Africa. Apart from the nomad civilizations of the Sahara, there were relatively few societies in which free women were exempted from heavy physical labour. Yet the image of the fragile woman, even if it is valid only in the restricted context of the dominant classes in the West, leads us to think that the use of women for heavy work, and particularly for warfare, is incongruous or incompatible with their 'nature'. This is no doubt why the preference for women shown by the African slave-owners has usually been explained by Western anthropologists in terms of specifically feminine qualities, in particular that of procreator. Yet such a hypothesis is in contradiction with the economic logic of slavery as I have tried to explain it.

If the work she could do was the main source of a woman's value, demand must have been dominated by factors bound up with the sexual distribution of tasks – or, in other words, with the specific ability of women to perform certain tasks which were particularly in demand. C. Robertson (1983: 223) points this out with respect to pawns, but it is true of all servile labour: the higher demand for girls relative to boys 'had to do with the sexual division of labour'. In African societies as a whole, in fact, women performed a larger number of tasks than men and worked longer hours. They performed many agricultural tasks, which they shared with men, and all domestic tasks (Keim, 1983).[22] If slave-owning societies, whose economy was based on a sexual distribution of tasks analogous to that in the societies which supplied slaves, used them for the same tasks, the demand for women would immediately be higher than the demand for men.

But since the sexual distribution of tasks was mostly established by convention, certain tasks which were usually performed by women and needed no training could also be performed by male slaves. Examples are carrying water or wood (though this was seen as humiliating). The same was not true of cooking, bringing up children (independently of breast-feeding) or some crafts. It was not that male slaves could not perform these tasks, since they had no derogatory connotation, but the skills involved were handed down from one woman to another and it was difficult for women to train men.

While men could sometimes replace women, it was still more frequent for women to replace men, even in the hardest tasks. J. Duncan noted in about 1840 in Dahomey that 'women were usually preferred as porters, because it was agreed that they could carry heavier loads of merchandise for longer distances than men, who were notorious for desertion' (in Obichere, 1978: 9).[23] Not only were women considered physically superior to men, but they had the additional advantage of being more docile. There is therefore no reason to think that the demand for women to perform these tasks (which nevertheless were seen as masculine) was lower than the demand for men: on the contrary.

In slave society, since the slave class was reproduced through the plundering of alien societies and through purchase on the market, *the 'procreative' function was in the hands of men*, whether warriors or merchants: it was they who, by force of arms or by payment, 'procreated' the individuals who were to reconstitute the exploited class. They, better than women, could decide on the age and sex distributon of this class and speed up its rate of reproduction. Conversely, the reproductive role of the woman was weakened relative to those functions which were linked to or derived from her slave state, such as the function of labourer or neutral agent of authority.[24] The woman was further and further removed from her role of *mother.* In domestic society this role had already been subordinated to that of *wife:* the woman's husband or brother claimed the filiation of her children, and this right meant that the organization of society depended on its masculine elements. However, since the woman was still the means of production of living beings which made up kinship, the future of the community depended on her fertility. As a result, even if she was frustrated in her experience of maternal filiation, the free-born woman was judged and gauged as a mother, honoured and even revered as such in terms of the expectations of the community.

By contrast, women under slavery were in no way seen as sacred. The facts and accounts which we have analysed show that since the slave was the anti-kin, the female slave could not be a 'mother'. She was recruited not for procreation but for work on feminine tasks; if she formed a couple, she did not marry; if she bore children, she was reduced to the role of child-bearer; her children belonged to her master and could be torn from her at any moment. In her old age, she had no recognized rights or ties which could hold out the hope that her children would meet her needs. On the contrary: the example of the Tyokosi (Rey-Hulman, 1975: 319) shows that

the master could use witchcraft as a subterfuge in order to
banish old female slaves to other forms of hard labour for the
rest of their lives. The case of the master's concubines or that
of women used as supervisors for household control cannot
be considered the norm of feminine slavery. Their condition
of wife or concubine was accompanied by an alienation unknown in domestic society; to the extent that, unprotected
by their own lineages, they fell under the unrestrained
authority of their husbands. If they were married to a king,
their children entered a class of which they themselves were
not in fact members and became dependent on the sovereign,
who used them as he liked. Where women slaves were pro-
moted to administrative functions or even functions of prestige (cf. Part II, A, Chapter 3 below) it was not because of
their own qualities but because of (the social neutrality con-
ferred on them by enslavement.) Their alienation as women
was added to their class alienation. The de-personalization
and de-socialization of the slave was accompanied by de-
sexualization.

A. Laurentin (1960: 138) reports that among the Nzakara a
girl slave who stole a few scraps of meat – food which was
forbidden to slaves – had her hand cut off at her mistress's
orders. Her condition as a woman (and a child) did not
cleanse her of the stain of slavery, or protect her from class
repression on the part of another woman.

4 DE-CIVILIZATION

Slaves were inserted into free-born society by the establishment of a *univocal* institutional link which bound them to
their master. This was the only relation granted to them.
Their (exclusive dependence on a single individual) distinguished slaves from all other members of the collectivity.[25]
They were hence 'de-civilized'. They did not identify themselves socially with respect to the collectivity as a whole, in
the sense that they could not resort to the arbitration of a
third party to settle any claims they might have on their
master.

The 'civilization' of an individual is the juridical recognition of socialization, of belonging to civil society, to the city; it is the capacity to resort, in the case of disagreement with the person on whom one directly depends, to the arbitration of an authority which is superior or equal to the parties in question.

In domestic societies, this arbitration took place through the individual's links to both paternal and maternal lineages, which meant that an uncle or an aunt could intervene as mediator or arbitrator in conflicts between a cadet and a doyen. In matrimonial relations, the wife's family retained the same ability to intervene if there was conflict between the wife and her husband. Beyond the domestic community, the recognition of a conciliator acceptable to both parties marked the beginning of a process of *civil* justice. In societies where power was centralized, civilization was incarnated by the juridical decisions of the sovereign.

None of these possibilities was open to slaves. They depended only on the will of their master. They were completely at his disposal. He could punish them and even put them to death without facing any consequences. There could be no arbitration. The fact that they were forbidden any possessions – since they were not persons – put them at the mercy of the laws of the free-born: since they could not pay fines, they could only be corporally punished.[26] Thus slaves were permanently de-civilized by the fact of being aliens without any kinship links.

The beginnings of re-civilization can be observed in some Sahelo-Sudanese societies with the custom of 'the slit ear'. The slave who wished to change masters inflicted symbolic bodily harm on a man, his child or his horse, in the hope of being handed over in damages to the victim.[27] But in offering himself as material compensation the slave identified himself, once again, as an object. Furthermore, the master could deliver another (male or female) slave instead and take his revenge on the guilty party. The slave might desire arbitration, but he was not entitled to it.

Further steps were taken towards re-civilization when the sovereign or the representatives of Islam granted slaves legal guarantees and the right to claim their justice in limited and clearly defined cases, in an attempt to make public law applicable even to private relationships. Finally, royal slaves often fell under common law, since they depended on a master who was the source of all law.

At the juridical level, there was therefore a logical continuum between the state of the alien, de-socialized through removal from and abandonment by his or her own milieu, his or her isolation, and the state of the slave, de-civilized through the concentration of all his or her social ties in the person of the master. The de-socialization of slaves, originally linked to the mode of exploitation which doomed them to celibacy, was confirmed in law as their 'natural' state. De-socialization made them completely available, not only economically but socially and politically. Their inability to penetrate the network of social relations which made up the person, the kin or the citizen rendered them 'neutral' in all these respects. Apart from functions related to power,[28] they could be assigned to any employment, depending on the multiple and varied needs of the slave-owning society, and still remain slaves. Their state as individuals deprived of rights, resulting from their original and inalterable situation of aliens, was seen as inherent and thus distinct from their condition, whatever the nature of their labour or their functions. This state persisted as long as their availability met the needs of the class of masters. The diversity of these needs with respect to slaves explains the diversity of the conditions of slaves, while their state reflects the unalterability of their fate.

6

Promotion of Slaves

The single mode of production which defines the slave class by the uniformity of its state contrasts with the differing modes of exploitation which determine its condition. These distinctions are essential to an understanding of the aristocratic and merchant systems which will be described later in this book. Possible links between them and the social and political characteristics of each will be analysed.

1 DRUDGE–SLAVES

The most frequent form of exploitation, which I shall call full exploitation, obliged the slaves to cultivate their master's land and to perform all the tasks – domestic, construction, transport, and so forth – assigned to them, with no limit on time worked and at any time of the day or night. 'You have no fields other than those of the master, and your needs are his', said one slave (in Olivier de Sardan 1976: 140). And the cultivation of another's land was seen by the Kusa Soninke as the height of shame. The slaves produced nothing for themselves. The master provided them with what he considered to be their necessary food, and sometimes clothing. They built their own huts. They received no wages and owned nothing of their own. This was the lowest class of slaves. We

116

no longer know what proportion of slaves were subjected to
this form of exploitation since this type of slave disappeared
with the slave trade and, as a result of the mode of exploitation, did not leave any progeny. In my opinion drudge-slaves
represented the great majority of slaves.

2 ALLOTMENT SLAVES

Allotment slaves existed alongside the drudge-slaves. They
were allowed to cultivate a strip of land to meet all or part of
their basic needs. These slaves worked on their master's land
for a fixed part of the day. They also performed daily
services, but in principle they were left free for a few hours
each day to work on their strip of land; although the product
of this labour belonged by right not to them but to the master
who could allow them to use it. In this case the master's rent
in labour was lower, but he no longer had to supply the
slaves with all their basic needs.

3 SETTLED SLAVES

A third form of slavery functioned when the slave was exempted from cultivating his master's fields and assigned to
the cultivation of a piece of land and the payment of a fixed
and invariable part of the annual product to the master. These
dues were seen as the redemption of labour in the master's
fields. In this form of exploitation, the slaves provided a rent
in products, and no longer in labour. This qualitative change
in exploitation generally involved a change in the social condition of slaves through access to a hut, which enabled them
to live in a couple and to bring up progeny.
   This way of life had the appearance of conjugality and
family life. However, unlike true kinship, the links between
these slaves were determined by conditions imposed by the
master for his own benefit. The slaves were not fathers or
mothers; neither were they married in the same way as the
free-born. In order to build the economic links between them
which are the infrastructure of kinship, they had to fulfil their

obligations to the master. Thus among the Soninke of Gumbu, the man, who was seen as the 'husband', had to pay dues if he was to be allowed to create and maintain these protofamilial links. In order to live 'in a family' and to have joint use of the product of the woman's labour and possibly that of the children (from productive age until they themselves were settled by the master) the man had to agree to pay annual dues for the woman and for those of her children who had reached maturity. If this redemption did not take place, those who were not redeemed reverted to the condition of drudge-slaves in the service of their respective masters. The protofamilial links were broken. These arrangements subordinated the woman slave living in a couple with a man slave who had marital prerogatives to the man: the advantages and constraints of redemption fell to the man. The woman knew of them and suffered them through him. Her relative redemption was diminished by her protoconjugal dependence.

Settled slaves were recruited mainly among slaves born in captivity, but could also be recruited among bought slaves if the master so desired. In contrast, not all those who were born slaves obtained this privilege: it was arbitrarily granted. Settled slaves were allowed to keep whatever they could produce over and above their dues, but this privilege could be withdrawn at any time.

It was through such savings that settled slaves could redeem their own persons – as opposed to their labour – and manumit themselves.

4 MANUMITTED SLAVES

This next level was reached when – usually through the ceremony designed to make it public – a hut-slave was allowed by his master to deliver himself from all dues in kind or in labour, by paying cattle or slaves in exchange for himself and for all those in his household whom he wanted to emancipate, if he could afford it.[1] He could then benefit from the product of these dependants and sometimes also of their future progeny, as well as their goods, while still being liable for services and in some cases for gifts such as horses or slaves, according to my Soninke informants.

Certain manumitted families, generally the oldest, could enter the master's family circle and provide him with domestic workers, factotums, intendants and even regents if the heir to a house was too young to take charge. In Gumbu, their children were circumcised at the same time as those of the master, and at his expense. Some young slave-born men became the chosen and faithful companions of young free-born men. The story of Sillamaxan and Pulori, told by the Peul of Niger, is a literary and almost mythical description of this type of relationship (C. Seydou, 1972).

The Zerma Sonxai liked to talk of their *horso*[2] as 'kin' (Olivier de Sardan, 1982: '*horso*'). The fate of these favoured slaves is often evoked by certain authors as if it were that of all slaves: certainly this was the category of slaves most willingly described by the masters, and at the same time manumitted slaves themselves exaggerated their privileges and built them up so as to rise in the social scale. Nevertheless, masters and slaves remained separate. The condition of the slaves was changed, but not their state. In Gumbu, for example, the *kome-xoore*[3] did not have access to free-born women, although his own wives and daughters could be taken as concubines by the masters or merely used for their pleasure. In this respect he could never be 'integrated' into the master's family, however 'familiar' the relations between them seemed to be. He did not have access to hereditary or elective power except by proxy. He had to live in the master's village and could not move without the master's permission. He had to wage war at the master's side and hand over his booty, even if part of it was returned. His possessions were mixed up with those of the master, even if he was allowed to do what he liked with them. Unless the master gave an undertaking to the contrary, his children could be sold, given away or pawned if he committed a serious offence or if his master was ruined; he himself could be put to death by his master. These extreme measures were rare, it is true, but were never ruled out. The seven *kome-xoore* families of Gumbu married among themselves according to the matrimonial model of the *hooro* (free-born) and paid bride-wealth to the fiancée's family, not to the master, as in the previous cases. But the master had to be informed of the choice of wife. When the *kome-xoore* married a slave he himself had bought, he had to give a present to his master in order to redeem his wife. The manumitted slave could own slaves in his turn: all the *kome-xoore* of Gumbu owned one or two.

Manumission could be graciously granted by the master to any slave of his choice, irrespective of the slave's condition or generation. Slaves of old stock whose masters died without direct heirs were considered to have been manumitted; they then came under the other houses in the clan. Manumitted slaves were never more than a small fraction of the enslaved population. In Gumbu in 1965 there were 1,040 *saarido* (slaves born in captivity) and 53 manumitted slaves (Meillassoux, 1972d).[4] Although the condition of slaves has been abolished today, their state is the same: they still wear the stain of servitude, the masters still claim the right to inspect their possessions, the same prejudices weigh on them and the men are still refused access to free women. They are still excluded from kinship, the kinship of the free-born, which alone can lead to citizenship.

5 ENFRANCHISEMENT

The term enfranchisement is frequently used in the specialized literature to mean manumission in the sense in which I have used the word above. The true meaning of the term 'enfranchisement', as a process through which the slave acquires *all* the prerogatives of the free-born – including the *honour* attached to his status – and thus the *obliteration* and the effacement of his origins, is thus lost.[5]

The 'enfranchisement' offered by Islam was really only manumission – sometimes expensive, sometimes free, granted in such a way as to highlight the master's generosity or repentance. In reality such manumissions were, once again, designed to serve the master's own interests. A slave was redeemed to make of him a devoted servant, whose privileges attached him to his master; or he was redeemed because he was too old to be kept on. A young slave girl had to be redeemed when the repudiation of a wife was reversed, and a converted slave when one had killed a Muslim. In reality slaves who had been converted to Islam, who should have been enfranchised, were more frequently merely manumitted. The alleged enfranchisement of concubines was not disinterested, and was limited and sometimes reversible. In particular it made possible the opportune enfranchisement of their progeny. The woman still had the inferior condition of a concubine, rarely of a wife. These (so-called) enfranchised men and women stayed close to their masters and had no freedom of movement.

Among the populations I have studied, the truly enfranchised – that is, slaves who have recovered all the prerogatives and honour of the free-born – cannot be named or even referred to as such, otherwise they immediately lose all the benefits of enfranchisement, which is aimed at the obliteration of the original stigma of capture or slave birth.[6] Such families exist. Scandalmongers raise doubts about the slave origin of certain families, who defend themselves vigorously. The cases reported to me always involve families or clans rather than individuals, singled out for the bravery of the men or for certain services rendered to the masters' families. These enfranchised families had the right to leave their former masters and usually settled on new land to raise new stock far from those who would not have been prepared to forget their origins.

Enfranchisement was a secret which, in the Sahelo-Sudanese milieu, could be used as security in an alliance between the family of the former master and that of the enfranchised.

6 BORN OUTSIDE BIRTH

IN SPARTA, LIBERTY IS BOUNDLESS; SO IS SLAVERY.
(PROVERB, IN BARTHÉLEMY, *Anarchasis*, Paris, 1790)

The process of emancipation described above, which was fairly common in Africa, is often seen in the ethnographic literature as taking place automatically with the passage of generations. Olivier de Sardan, for example, writes as follows about emancipated slaves [*horso*] among the Zerma Sonxai: 'As for the conditions of accession to *horso* status, they are, officially, simple: after three generations in the same family, vulgar captives become *horso*' (1982: 216).[7] But this accession could not have been generalized, since it could take place only if the genitors of the *horso* had been privileged to form a couple and to have recognized progeny. Olivier de Sardan admits that this was not the case for all slaves, and particularly not for the *cire bannya*, who were neither allotment nor settled slaves (and who were perhaps in the majority): 'The son and the grandson of the *cire bannya* are for ever *cire bannya* and never become *horso*', his informant explains (1982: 94). Thus the condition of *horso* stemmed from an arbitrary act on the part of the master: it was he who decided which slaves would remain *cire bannya* and which would be granted the privilege of being settled.[8] In all known cases, it was the masters who decided on unions between their slaves.[9] This intervention, which depended on the masters alone, excludes *a priori* any 'automatic' content (and any rights) in the process of promoting slaves.

In all slave societies, unless they were enfranchised in the full sense of the word, slaves were always slaves, as were any of their progeny, irrespective of the passage of generations. Enslavement left an indelible mark[10] which was the only thing the slaves could transmit to their descendants. This was as true of patrilineal as of avuncular societies. Meyer Fortes (1969: 263) shows this for the avuncular Ashanti society: the 'stigma of slavery was never extinguishable'. The same seems to have been true for the royal slaves of the Abron, whose descendants are in a servile state even today (Terray, seminar on social classes, 1972–3). This stain was even more marked in patrilineal societies. In the Aboh country (present-day Nigeria), according to a study by Nwachukwu-Ogedengbe (1977: 149), which is very rigorous and contains no trace of romanticism, 'the slaves never acquired the status of free men. . . . The line of demarcation was fixed and rigid and mobility, in the purely political and social sense, was confined within the limits of the slave's own social stratum.'

The permanent nature of the slaves' state is still visible today in Bamana, Soninke, Maninka, Tamasheq, Moorish,

Fula, Futanke and other societies in the Sahelo-Sudanese region.[11] Many observers are of the opposite opinion, because information gathered in the field can effectively be interpreted in terms of an automatic progression of the slaves' status. It is true that the 'children' of trade-slaves are said to be 'slave-born' and that their own 'children' are said to be emancipated slaves. But this discourse contains two ambiguities. In many African languages there is no precise kinship term for the category of 'son' or 'daughter' as the direct descendant of a genitor or genitrix. The term used to describe progeny has the most general sense of 'offspring', 'little one', 'kid', without any direct filiative content. It includes grandchildren as well as nephews/nieces and grand-nephews/nieces. In genealogy, it refers to descendants in general, irrespective of the number of generations. Secondly, this discourse describes a practice but not a norm. Emancipation or redemption was not an obligation for the master, and slaves born in captivity were the principal but not the only category of slaves affected. These statuses could be granted without restriction to favourite slaves who had been acquired by the master. There was no necessary relation between birth and redemption, or between genealogical seniority and emancipation. Since slaves were not socially born, their essential state could not be modified by their birth. They could not claim birth to alter their state.

It is true that with time and the passage of generations the fate of the slaves tended to improve, but this was the result of circumstances, not of rights. Slaves who had grown up within the host group, and who since childhood had performed functions and tasks comparable to those of gentles, were likely to form emotional links within the community. Unlike slaves who had been captured as adults, they would not have had memories of their former condition or been tempted to return to their former status through flight. They would have been conditioned to their fate while still young and trained in the functions which they were expected to fulfil. They were likely to be trusted. In particular, the slave-born were better integrated into family riches than slaves who had been acquired. In the hands of the head of the family, these slaves were not commodities bought to be sold at a profit; they were a *patrimony*, an indivisible possession which belonged to the community as a whole and of which the head of the family had only custody and management. The sale of slaves was an admission of the ruin of one's house, just like the sale of cattle or family treasures. 'It is quite possible to sell a *horso*', Olivier de Sardan (1976: 56) was told by a *horso* who immediately went on to emphasize the risks attached to such sales, 'but if you sell him so as to marry off your son, or because of a famine, or because you are in tatters, *if you take the son of your own "horso" to sell him*, the son you wanted to marry off will not marry, your captive himself will die; or the famine will not spare you.'

It is nevertheless true that the inalienability of slaves was not based on any 'right' acquired by them, since *the sale even of settled slaves, although humiliating or even dangerous for the owner, was always possible in cases of need.* Bazin (1975: 159, n.36) notes this with respect to the Bamana of Segu: 'Contrary to what is generally claimed in the "coutumiers" [collections of local customs made by the colonial administration – C.M.], it was not, strictly speaking, forbidden to sell *woloso-jon* [the slave-born – C.M.]. It was just very unlikely . . .' Further on, he confirms that slaves, even those of the second generation, could be sold.

The denial of rights is clearly expressed by Olivier de Sardan's informant. In response to the question 'didn't the *horso* ask their master not to sell them?', he replied, 'What they said did not count' (1976: 56). Terray (1982b: 126), who supports the thesis that slaves from birth were 'integrated into the lineage', nevertheless admits that among the Abron they could be sold 'for serious offences' – 'like other dependants', he adds, forgetting that the offender was sold by his master and not by his own kin. If the circumstances mentioned above helped to improve the lot of those who were born into slavery, they did not make this promotion automatic.

Certain slaves, in spite of their seniority, were to languish for generations[12] in miserable conditions, while a few benefited from the benevolence of the master if they had managed to please him. On the other hand, other slaves, although they had been bought, would enjoy the condition of settled slaves during their own lifetime. Examples of this were reported to me by the Soninke of Gumbu. Tautain (1884: 349) also notes: 'The trade captive [that is, the bought slave – C.M.] could become a hut captive [*woroso* – C.M.] through the master's favour.' The same applied to their descendants, whose condition and possible emancipation depended entirely on the master's pleasure.[13] Thus slaves of the same generation lived side by side in different situations. It was also possible to settle slaves without granting them the privilege of having progeny: in the Segu kingdom, whole villages were peopled by captured slaves, reconstituted into fictitious lineages and renewed through inflows of new captives. It is true that distant categories of slaves existed, but *this was because of their real situation, which depended on the arbitrary decisions of the master and was not based on any rights.*

The slave-born cannot be identified with settled or manumitted slaves. All slaves had the same state, irrespective of their origin, whether their enslavement had taken place through birth or acquisition (capture or purchase). The decision of the master made them into settled or manumitted slaves whose situation seemed less uncertain, but they were never assimilated to the free-born. Their material privileges were precarious and could be taken away: their possessions were by law part of those of the master. The man was not allowed matrimonial relations with free-born women. He could never testify against a free-born individual. Above all, the slave-born individual was always alienable, as were his children. This is indisputably true of those who were not settled slaves. It was still true of those who had committed a serious offence or whose master was ruined. The slave could always be put to death by his master, 'just as the "father" could kill his children'. Furthermore, the very fact that an individual's servile origins were known showed that he or she had not been integrated into free-born society. Only silence on the subject of these origins could prove enfranchisement in the full sense of the term.

7 ALWAYS SLAVES

Settled slaves, whether or not they were slave-born, who reproduced themselves through their own production were
involved in relations of production and reproduction which
were different from those of the slave who was not settled. In
practice, as we have seen, this difference was reflected in the
way they were treated.

If they nevertheless remained slaves by law, it was because
this form of exploitation, while it resembled serfdom, was
inserted into an economic context which enabled its perpetuation: warfare and markets. Even if for some slaves sale was
unlikely, while it was still allowed this latent but real – and
useful – possibility decisively affected the state of all slaves.
The general slave mode of reproduction (and not, here, the
mode of production) prevailed over their juridical state and
made them all, potentially or in reality, into objects.

Since the market replaced birth, the effects of birth, both in
its biological form and in terms of its social implications,
were secondary.

While the dominant modes of reproduction were still capture and purchase, as long as it was still possible to buy and
sell human beings, alienation in all senses of the word
weighed on everyone in law as well as in practice. They were
all alienable, therefore they were all slaves,[14] even when some
of them took part in different relations of production. A man
who, even after several generations, can still be rendered incapable of becoming a 'father' by the master's decision to refuse him a partner – a decision which stems from the mode of
exploitation which is characteristic of slavery – is still a slave.

Thus the coexistence of two modes of reproduction, one
typical of slavery and the other resembling serfdom, is
possible within slave society and can frequently be observed.
But the instruments of the first – warfare and the market
– by their very existence define the social state of those
who take part in the second. Serfdom as a form, though it
affects only a fraction of slaves, nevertheless heralds the
transformation of slave society; but this transformation
is possible only in determinate historical circumstances,

once the supply of captives dries up.

8 ALIENATION

Thus the slave, irrespective of his condition, could have a partner but not a wife; progeny but not descendants; sometimes forebears but never ancestors. The relationships which he built with his congeners, even when they took on the appearance of kinship, were all mediated by the master, who concentrated all these social relations and was still the only vector linking the slave to his own 'family' and to other slaves. It was not in fact in the interests of the class of masters to create, of its own free will, a social class with rights which could be used in opposition to it. On the contrary, the numerical importance of the slaves forced the master to contain them through his own arbitrary decisions and to justify this through an inegalitarian ideology.

Through their univocal link with the master, on whom their lot was entirely dependent, and because of the permanent nature of their state,[15] irrespective of their condition, slaves were particularly vulnerable to alienation and sensitive to ideological pressure. The stereotype of slaves (sometimes supplied by the slaves themselves) is of persons who are ugly, strong-limbed, lying, lewd, coarse, dirty and lazy. Deschamps (1971: 22) reports that the Arabs of Iraq described their Zandj slaves as smelly, stupid, nasty, stealing, aggressive, anthropophagous, naked and gay for no reason; but they were strong and able to undertake heavy work, which no doubt made all the rest bearable.

J.-P. Olivier de Sardan (1973, 1984: 37) analyses Sonxai images of slaves as inferior by nature – images which were stronger than even the most obvious realities: slaves were seen as coarse featured, even when objectively they were handsome. In the story of the relationship between Silla-maxan and Pulori (reported by C. Seydou, 1972), which tells of the close friendship between the former, a noble, and the latter, his slave, the social distinction is still manifest: the slave's foot is too big to fit his master's slipper. Furthermore, whatever his exploits, the slave who aspired to a wife of superior condition was cruelly called to order. Whatever his capabilities or his exploits, he never reached the level of a free man. In a Soninke epic which also tells of an association between a noble and his slave, the former kills 100 men when the latter only kills 99; the former's horse knocks over 100 warriors, the slave's horse only 99 (Jiri Silla, Yerere, 1965).

For the Peul Djelgobe (Riesman, 1974) the slave was also an individual who could not master his own needs, who was a 'slave' to them: slave to hunger, to thirst, to sexual desire, while the nobleman could resist the demands of his body.

Among the Bamana or the Soninke, as among the Sonxai, slaves were seen as being without shame; men and women of all ages performed obscene dances, used lewd language, did not conform to the prohibitions which good manners imposed on the free-born and, in so doing, made them laugh.[16] The slaves themselves assumed this image, partly because they had been conditioned to this sort of behaviour, partly because in so doing, without fooling themselves, they knew they could please the master by doing what was expected of them.[17]

Slaves who had been captured young or born in captivity learned from childhood that they were not of the same species as free men; that if a free man 'is ten, a slave is never more than nine' (Soninke dictum); that the Creator had wished things to be so, since 'just as the fingers of the hand were created of unequal lengths, so people are of unequal value' (ibid.). Even when the boy slave was circumcised at the same time as the young master and at the expense of those to whom he belonged, even when he took part like free young people in the same associations of people of his age, he was always the one who undertook the chores and tasks which necessitated physical effort, for his companions. As soon as a free man, whoever he might be, expressed a desire, irrespective of the time of day or night, or of the place, the slave rose and set to work to satisfy him. With respect to the free-born class he always behaved like an obliging minor, whatever the respective ages of master and slave.

Since all the slaves' social relationships were mediated by

the master, slaves were incapable of building up active relationships with their congeners. The master discouraged
them.[18] If they formed a couple, it was through the master's
intervention, since the two partners could belong to different
individuals and the children would then belong to the
mother's master. Only slaves of the same rank were admitted
to celebrations affecting a slave. There was a hierarchy
among slaves according to their master's status, their ethnic
origin, their religion or the length of time they had been enslaved. Since improvements in their lot depended only on
their master, they refused solidarity which would link them
to the least privileged in their midst. Alienation was not only
the objective effect of their exploitation. Slaves were conditioned to it by the ideology with which they were incul-
cated, which was shown to be frighteningly effective.[19]

There are examples of the revolt of peoples subject to
raids, or subjugated by conquest or occupation, of captives
held in barracks waiting to be sold; there are examples of the
flight of slaves; but rarely of *slave revolts* in the proper sense.
E. Terray explains this in terms of the process of automatic
emancipation which he considers existed among the Abron
and which would have resulted in a reduction of the numbers
of slaves. But in the Sahelo-Sudanese region, where this was
not the case, more than half the population was often slaves,
and this does not seem to have been a cause of concern for
their masters. In Africa as it was then, the slave class might
just as well not have been part of history.

7

Half-Breed Slaves

The ambiguous status of half-breeds born of slaves and masters makes them appear similar to manumitted slaves, with whom they sometimes shared certain functions and obligations with respect to the class of masters. Yet they were distinct from manumitted slaves in that they had a filiative relation with a free-born lineage. Nevertheless, the filiative relation was immediately corrected by class considerations: marriage between free-born and slave was forbidden if it introduced a filiative relation between a male slave and the woman's progeny. Only in avuncular societies, therefore, was it authorized for both sexes. In patrilineal societies it was authorized – in the form of concubinage rather than marriage – for free-born men.

The Anyi-Ndenye, where such a case has been documented by C. H. Perrot (1983), provide an introductory example. In this avuncular society, the descendants of a union between a free-born father and a slave woman were the *auloba* (ibid.). Among common people, these children did not have all the advantages of free birth, since, having no maternal lineage, they could neither inherit nor reach the position of doyen. Yet they were not considered to be *kangaba* (born of two slaves). In fact it seems that their lot and their status depended fairly arbitrarily on their father's decisions. It was convenient to keep these descendants in an inferior position, since, having no maternal uncle with whom they would otherwise have had to live, they could be kept in their father's house. Boys born of such unions were doubly useful in that they increased the numbers of the masculine house (instead of that of the maternal uncle) and ensured its continuity. During genealogical ruptures they could be temporarily entrusted with the management of the patrimony, without fear of a diversion of power, since their status did not give them access to the position of doyen or to chieftainship within the paternal lineage (although cases of usurpation from similar positions do exist). In royal families, the dependent social position of these half-breeds led to the constitution of 'dependent but distinct lineages' (ibid.: 166) whose members married only among themselves and were given administrative or ritual duties.

Thus the *aulaba* constituted a distinct social 'species'. Nevertheless, C.-H. Perrot also notes that the children of a sovereign and a slave could be assimilated to other *famyeba* (sons of the king), since one of the royal privileges in terms of common law in this matrilineal society was apparently to 'make his own [paternal – C.M.] blood prevail over that of "maternal" relatives among his descendants' (ibid.: 164). 'The "grandson of the king" was given the title *ehenenana*, whatever the social origin of his mother or his grandmother' (ibid.). In such cases it was said that 'the penis prevails over the cord'. In other words, the king, through marriage to a slave, had the power to impose mono-patrilineal succession, which enabled him to exclude other aspirant families from power. It is to be noted that in these examples filiation and status are dissociated. One could be recognized without the other.

In the case of a marriage between a free-born woman and a slave, the status of the mother always prevailed over that of the genitor, in conformity with the principles of avuncular kinship. Since filiation through the father was not determinant in such societies, the slave genitor, like the free-born father, did not transmit his status. Since he had no sister, being without kin, the slave could not exercise the rights of a maternal uncle. Thus this sort of mixed marriage did not challenge the system of avuncular filiation. Filiation and the transmission of status were congruent. In this case the progeny was considered to be free-born, like the mother. The marriage of a free-born woman and a slave enabled the matrilineage to exclude affines and to concentrate avuncular succession in the progeny, which was more privileged than progeny with only a paternal branch.

Thus in all cases the state of slave was not transmitted by the genitor; it was transmitted by the genitrix, but in conditions arbitrarily defined by the paternal lineage. Franchise was always transmitted by the mother and if necessary by the father. But even in the latter case, the issue of a marriage between a free-born man and a slave woman would always be weakened by the absence of a maternal lineage.

In patrilineal Sahelo-Sudanese societies, all sexual relations, whether real or merely symbolic, between free-born women and slaves were strictly forbidden. Men slaves were even forbidden to sit on the same mat as a free-born woman and, still more, to touch her.

Captain Peroz (1896: 418–19) tells of the atrocious punishment dealt out by Samori to two of his daughters, aged thirteen and fourteen, and to their young slave lovers:

> . . . a few tender words, a few furtive squeezings of hands, such was their crime. But the pages were not of the race of free men.
>
> Some wicked spy . . . denounced them to the almamy . . .
>
> The offence was soon admitted to and, forthwith, the executioner tore off the hands of the pages which had pressed those of the sovereign's daughters and hung them, bleeding, to the door of the palace. Then Fatima and Aïssa, stripped quite naked, their hands tied behind their backs, were exhibited on the pillory in the marketplace.
>
> The following morning, the sword had expunged for ever the very slight offence of the two pages: their heads were flung in front of the pillory where the two daughters of the emir were panting with shame and thirst.
>
> Near the marketplace, between the palace and the town

of Bissandougou, huge ditches have been dug to hold the refuse of the two towns which are the capital of the Almamy.

In the evening, at five o'clock, the fanatical brutes who guard Samory untied the two unhappy children and flung them, still alive, into these sewers; then they buried them under a heap of ferruginous stones the colour of blood collected in the nearby field.

The strangled cries of the young martyrs could be heard all through the night.

The following morning, all was quiet: knowing nothing of this horrible drama and passing by this ignoble tomb, we saw, caught between two huge stones, a small fist, stiffened and bloody, encircled by a gold bracelet.[1]

Thus for Samori his own daughters, barely touched by slaves, were no more than refuse.

Sexual relations between a gentle woman and a slave were, then, a calamity and a source of shame for her family, who tried to cleanse the stain by all the means at their disposal, including abortion and sometimes death. If the birth of a child took place in these conditions, it had no social or juridical effects. Since the free-born woman was not the vector of filiation, she could not transmit her status to her progeny. And since the male slave was in the same situation, their union could only produce totally asocialized beings, slaves by definition.

In contrast, unions between free-born men and female slaves were common. In this case it was said that 'the womb colours the skin', since masculine filiation did not operate in the same way as among the free-born. In fact, it was the genitrix's lack of status which was transmitted to the child. The link between the child and his or her genitrix was acknowledged only through the patrimonial relations which existed between master and slave: the progeny of the woman slave, herself the property of the master, belonged to the master. The progeny of the woman slave was itself enslaved, whatever the status of the genitor.[2] In practice this was the case for children born after the master had used a slave for his pleasure. If the master wished to establish filiation with the progeny of a slave (his mistress or his concubine) he could do so by the 'enfranchisement' of the woman *before the birth* of the child. As a result slave women were sometimes considered to have been 'enfranchised' either by their marriage to a free-born man or, if they were merely concubines, by pregnancy or by giving birth, depending on the case.[3] Acknowledged to have been born of a free-born woman, the child was then indisputably free-born. If, however, the child died very young (before weaning), the woman could be relegated to the condition of slave.[4] Once again it must be remembered that this progeny, although free-born, was weakened by the absence of a maternal lineage. But here, as in avuncular society, this weakness made these children the favourites of the doyen or the king. Since they had no other protector, they were completely subordinated to him. At the Sonxai court the *askias* were often the sons of an 'enfranchised' mother. Here again mono-lineal succession is imposed through mixed unions.

As in avuncular society, marriages between free-born and slaves could also be a means of constituting a dependent social corps, neither free-born nor slave, to whom functions of trust could be given. This was the case of the *mangu* among the Soninke of Gajaga (a valley in eastern Senegal), from whom warriors in the service of the dominant Bacili house were mainly recruited. The *mangu* apparently lived under the same conditions as the free-born lineages. Nevertheless, *vis-à-vis* the aristocratic house of the Bacili, their position was that of hereditary obligors. Locally they were said to be *wanukunke*, individuals of alien origin who had come to put themselves under the protection of the Bacili and had been given slave women as wives. Since these women had not been enfranchised by the Bacili and were still their property, their progeny belonged to the Bacili. . . . As a result, generation after generation, the *mangu* belonged to their hosts.[5] This was doubtless less a juridical situation than the expression of a subordination whose ideological justification was the stigma of an original and unalterable servitude. Within the hierarchy of obligors, clients and slaves, the *mangu* assumed the position of seniors. Their condition resembled that of the *kome-xooro*, manumitted slaves of old stock, with whom they are sometimes confused, but they had not been bought or captured and they did not number among their ascendants slaves who had been forced to work, so that they had a certain dignity. In principle they, like the masters, could expect signs of respect and symbolic dues from slaves of all categories. On the other hand the slaves did not beg from them, which shows that they were not considered the equals of the masters.

Thus mixed unions brought into play two forms of social weakening of progeny. The first existed when the progeny was free-born, either because the mother was herself free-born (in avuncular societies) or because she had been enfranchised, since this progeny (as in the case of marriage between a gentle woman and an alien) came from a single lineage. The second form of weakening existed when franchise was not transmitted through the union. The progeny could juridically be slave, but this was not the case of the *aulaba* among the Anyi, nor of the *wanukunke* among the Gajaga: their ambiguous status exposed them to manipulation. They were subordinated to a greater extent than the free-born, but since they were nevertheless bearers of franchise, their master could set them up as rivals to free-born individuals.

In the examples above, then, the status of the half-breeds did not conform to the rules of kinship. These rules only applied within the limits of the class relation, which was determinant. This can only be understood with reference to the conditions of filiation in domestic societies where neither classes nor slavery existed. Where patrilineal filiation prevailed, the child belonged to the family of the publicly acknowledged husband of the genitrix. In many societies the personality of the genitor, if he was not the husband, did not come into play. Once bridewealth had been paid for a woman by her husband's family or once the marriage ceremonies had taken place, the child was attributed to his or her paternal family. In avuncular societies filiation was established, according to the same principle, with the maternal family, through the genitrix's eldest brother. The husband's family had only limited rights over the wife's progeny. In both cases filiation could be or was independent of conception. There was no difference in status between husband and wife which might have changed the direction of filiation. The rules of filiation conformed to those of the transmission of clan prerogatives, if they existed.

In class society notions of adultery and bastardy come into play, necessitating the coincidence of 'conception' and 'paternity'. These notions seem to be justified only when they preserve social hierarchy through a mode of reproduction specific to each class: nobles reproduce through birth and slaves through acquisition. For this purpose two rules, which are social in nature and do not stem from kinship, take precedence over all others: a free-born man could, at will, ensure that the progeny of a slave woman was free-born; a male slave could not establish filiative relations, in conformity with the general rule of slavery. In practice it can be observed that if in avuncular society it is the woman's status which always takes precedence, this is because since filiation takes place through her, her progeny cannot have a different status from that of the parents. The rule 'the penis prevails over the cord' is opportunely added here, *in contradiction* to the avuncular principle, and the reproduction of dynastic lineages is thus encouraged.

In patrilineal slave society, only the woman of slave origin transmits her state or her status if she is enfranchised. Here the rule 'the womb colours the skin' is restrictively applied, since the free-born woman cannot transmit her status to the children of a slave, because hypogamy is prohibited. Thus the transmission of status in this case is *counter to all the apparent rules of patrilineality*: it takes place through a woman (in spite of the fact that filiation is masculine) and only if this woman is of slave origin (in spite of the fact that slaves have no kinship relations). These paradoxical rules are in fact the application of the principles of social kinship across the class line: biological links cannot transmit any status or position which is not socially recognized. These contradictions stem from the application of the kinship idiom to the class idiom, and vice versa.

Thus enslavement, even when inherited long before, even when diluted by the 'blood' of the free-born, fed a powerful ideology of discrimination and arbitrariness. 'Kinship relations' allowed the half-breed to languish at the level of man-servant or to be born into the world of the free, depending on the needs of the master.

Transition

Revenge of the Anti-Kin

It is clear from the above that the slave was characterized, in kinship society, by exclusion from the prerogatives associated with 'birth', where birth was a social event which defined an individual's position and status. The same exclusion applied to the slave born in captivity through the denial of his genitors' capacities for paternity: the slave deprived of all personality could not create social links through the mere act of biological creation. The state of the slave clearly proclaimed his or her origins – alien to gentle society – and the real and/or juridical conditions of his or her reproduction.

The fiction of an individual who was not-born – which, let me repeat, was supported by the slave's mode of exploitation – thus created within kinship society an individual who was antithetical, a non-kin, whose social virtues could in many cases take precedence over his or her productive capacities, so that slavery took on an aberrant appearance. Since slaves were not kin, they had no right to the benefits of kinship or franchise: fields, wives, descendants, ancestors. But these deprivations which helped to exclude the slaves from civil society were also at the origin of their progress in the circles of power. There are two reasons for this: first, the slave owed what he was to his master. It was his master who gave birth to him each day, by letting him live another day. Only his master could grant him the attributes of a person, albeit fictitious and precarious. The slave owed his master everything, including his loyalty.

Second, since the slave was naturally excluded from inheritance and from succession within the master's lineage, he had no possible claim to possessions or titles. He was thus not involved in rivalries between collaterals or other pretenders to power occasioned by kinship and particularly by dynastic societies. When the question of succession became urgent, any relative became a dangerous rival since he could claim to be the legitimate heir. The trust the doyen, the dynastic head or the king put in his relatives was tempered by his fear of being removed from authority and perhaps murdered. He would tend to distance them from positions too close to power and to entrust these positions rather to neutral, subjugated individuals, whose functions depended on his own will and not on their birth. The slave was not the only agent who was neutral in terms of kinship (people of caste afflicted with endogamy, celibate priests and women were also neutral in this respect) but, stripped of ideology, of faith and of parental loyalty, the slave was a more docile associate. We shall also see that the exclusion of kin to the benefit of slaves, at the level of authority, had its counterpart in the replacement of free men by slaves for productive purposes.

In addition, in some societies, the absence of progeny gave the slaves an advantage which their masters dreaded: they were not vulnerable to the curses which could strike the descendants of those who gave themselves over to the manipulation of potions or talismans. This is why some of them acquired the reputation of dangerous miracle-workers.

Thus slaves, once fully exploited agricultural workers with a resulting absence of status, took on, because of their social and political non-existence, administrative, policing and ancillary functions and even positions of trust. It was because of the permanent nature of their state that their condition could be changed and they could even be placed close to power at minimal risk to its holder.

In societies ruled by kinship, the anti-kin could be an

effective agent of social and political manipulation. By re-placing free men with slaves, the masters could protect them-selves from ambitious relatives or rebellious subjects; and at the same time they could protect themselves from these henchmen, by granting them differentiated privileges which divided them among themselves and further attached them to their master.

Although this dialectic – which, as we shall see, could be used against the masters – did not affect all slave societies or all slaves to the same extent, it was particularly present in aristocratic societies, where it gave slavery, as an institution, an image which was at times paradoxical and which cannot be explained in terms of the logic of hierarchy or naive materialism.

Part II

IRON:

Aristocratic Slavery

A

Slavery and Power

1

The Coming of the Brigands

The *Hudud al Alam* (a tenth-century Persian document) describes the Sudan (the land south of the desert separating it from the Maghreb) as follows:

> no region is more populated than this. The merchants steal children there and take them away. They castrate them and take them to Egypt, where they sell them. *Among them [the Sudanese] there are people who steal each other's children to sell them to the merchants* when they come. (in Cuoq, 1975: 69)

This quotation demonstrates the existence of what I shall call *brigandage* – that is, the practice of abducting captives *from within the same community*, among relatives and neighbours.[1]

This internal brigandage seems to have been practised among village populations who did not necessarily fall within the military orbit of plundering States or alien raiders, but lived in the collection areas of the slaver merchants or were drawn by the attraction of nearby slave markets.

In brigandage, the abduction and sale of captives were undertaken not by aliens but by the members of the community itself, acting anonymously. No one was safe from those who were supposedly the protectors of the community: 'The sister is threatened by the brother, the wife by the husband, the child by the father or the uncle' (A.-C. Niaré,

1964 Mission). The danger of social decomposition was serious, since brigandage benefited one fraction of society only: the young adult warriors organized in small bands. Through the sale of their relatives and neighbours, especially women and children, they could acquire arms and horses to attack neighbouring societies. By kidnapping the women for their own use they competed with the authority of their elders, who were increasingly incapable of marrying them because of these abductions.

Brigandage seems to have had one of two effects on political power: either the clans organized themselves to resist it, like the Mande in the thirteenth century, or the warrior class used it as the basis of its power, as in Segu at the end of the sixteenth century.

1 THE KING AND THE BRIGANDS

Mande tradition tells, in various accounts (M.-M. Diabaté, 1970a and b; Innes, 1974; Niane, 1960; Wa Kamissoko, 1975) of the historical legend of Sunjata, said to have lived in about the thirteenth century in the upper Niger valley.[2] Sunjata was one of those Sudanese heroes destined from birth to resolve a crisis, usually political in nature, by means which were magical rather than tactical and usually not exemplary.[3] The legend tells mainly of the combat in which he engaged Suma-wuru Kante, who at the time was a military threat to Mande. Wa Kamissoko adds elements which directly concern the problem of slavery. 'At this time, complained the praise-singer [Kamissoko, 1975] endemic brigandage raged, "brother against brother". . . . The strongest captured the weakest and carried them off by treachery to sell them . . .' (ibid.: 38). 'Can the population grow if people capture each other all the time to sell some to others?' (ibid.: 49). 'Behind what village', asked Wa Kamissoko, 'does the path of treachery not pass?' (ibid.: 11) – referring to the paths which led to the Sahelian bush, along which the brigands led their captured congeners by night. 'There was not one of those who reigned in the land who did not put the bit in the mouth of the Malinke to sell him to the *maraka* (merchants)' (ibid.: 6).

('If today there are so many Malinke in the Sahel or in the Sosso, it is the Malinke themselves who are the main cause') (ibid.: 9). The heroes of Mande legend, like Tiramaxan or Fakoli, seem to have been such hunters of men.[4]

By placing slavery at the centre of the political problem of Mande in the thirteenth century, Wa Kamissoko's account has the merit of making intelligible an event which had previously been interpreted as the sudden and inexplicable emergence of an 'empire' – the Mali empire – at the initiative of a mythological personage, Sunjata, whose exceptional personality was seen as the only cause.

Kamissoko explains that when these events took place Mande was divided into more than thirty small chiefdoms (ibid.: 60), whose *masa* (chiefs) could be compared to ordinary village chiefs.[5] The authority of these chiefs, who were Sunjata's peers and rivals, stemmed, like his own, from their membership of a clan. They struggled among themselves for a fragile pre-eminence which they tried to impose on their peers through hunting or warlike feats (Diabaté, 1970a). They fought each other, seized each other's villages, hunted each other and made peace with each other. They were not chiefs of bands. It was clear that they belonged to a clan. They bore a *jamu* (patronym) which linked them to a house and was proof of their lineage. This was also true of Sunjata, whose father is known and who is sometimes said to have been *masa* of Mande for a time (Innes, 1974: 27–8). From birth he was surrounded by smiths and praise-singers of caste. He was poor, which was the true quality of gentlemen. But Sunjata was not capable, any more than the other warlords, of protecting himself with his clan alone against alien plunderers who came to seize captives, or against bands of local brigands. Faced with these two threats, legend attributes to Sunjata two feats. The first is the better known and the most famous. He succeeded in federating a dozen Mande clans (Innes, 1974: 61) and in defeating the terrible Sumawuru.

But Sunjata's most important achievement, according to Wa Kamissoko, seems to have been the elimination of the internal threat of brigandage, in the following way.

It appears that after his victory over Sumawuru, Sunjata asked his peers to elect him sovereign of the federation of

Mande (Kamissoko, 1975: 42): 'Since thou hast driven war
from our door, we renounce [power] and we invest thee as
niyamoko' (ibid.: 61).[6] 'If you put me on the throne of Mande,
promised Sunjata in return, no one will ever be sold again'
(ibid.: 42). He kept his word: 'He reigned without ever putting an iron in anyone's mouth to take him to be sold' (ibid.:
36). 'Everyone agreed not to sell their people' (ibid.: 44). 'He
was mostly known', explains Wa Kamissoko, 'for having
stopped the sale of the people of Mande' (ibid.: 46).[7] Thus
with him the Maninka were no longer 'aliens' to each other.
In this account of events, whether mythical or real, Sunjata is
credited with having invented locally both the *natio* (the set of
those who acknowledge each other as having prerogatives
which stem from being well born) and *royalty*, the power
which, in these turbulent times, guaranteed the franchise of
those who accepted authority.[8]

Faced with brigands who exercised their power by attack-
ing indiscriminately and thus undermined the effectiveness of
the bonds linking those who belonged to the same society,
Sunjata restored the sociopolitical structures of the clans and
regenerated the organic relations between congeners: relatives, affines, allies or neighbours. It is true that in order to
do so he challenged certain rules of elderhood and equality
between clans, by imposing himself in spite of his youth –
which in any case is characteristic of this type of hero – and
by demanding pre-eminence over his peers. But he did not
attack the elders or their authority in the same way as Biton
Kulibali in Segu, as we shall see. He did not act against clan
institutions; on the contrary, he preserved them, since in fact
conflict between clans had not been eliminated and unity was
achieved by consensus as much as by constraint (Kamissoko,
1975: 75).

All the historians of the region, following Delafosse (1912),
attribute to Sunjata the foundation of an empire which they
identify with the Melli empire visited in the fourteenth
century by Ibn Battuta.[9] Yet the praise-singers do not tell of
any State which survived Sunjata. The political formation
which he dominated was merely a federation of clans with no
future. No lasting State was likely to emerge from this
assembly of chiefs of rival clans: in Mande tradition, the

power of a hero cannot be preserved against the wishes of his peers and must be handed over once he has achieved what he needed to accomplish.[10] It is more likely that Mande became a land of farmers and merchants. 'He who has chosen farming, and only farming, will farm. Sunjata is no more. He who has chosen trade, and nothing but trade, will give himself over to trade. Suba has lived' (M.M. Diabaté, 1970: 89–90).[11]

2 THE BRIGAND-KING

Unlike Mande, the powerful Segu State of the seventeenth to eighteenth century developed as a result of the slave wars (see Part I, Chapter 1). It emerged from the political development of brigandage and not from struggles against this practice. It asserted itself not through the preservation of the social order but through its destruction. It built a new society which tore up clan society.

Its founder, Biton Kulibali, was different in several respects from Sunjata. Tradition emphasizes his 'alien' quality and is not concerned with his father (praise-singers Taïru and Sangare, in Kesteloot, 1978: 580, 582). The legend does not credit him with any ancestors, any royal precedent or any of the marks of predestination for power (ibid.: 601).[12] Biton belonged to a different class. He had no 'birth' – or at least, he did not claim any. He did not set himself up as a protector against brigandage. He practised it.

Towards the seventeenth century, demand for slaves created by the European slave trade reached the Niger basin, where a village civilization, dotted with small political formations without much power, predominated. In this context, bands reappeared. Some were led by small clan aristocrats, others by individuals without birth. Biton was one of the latter. He drew to himself men of various origins thrown up by the disordered times: escaped slaves, rebellious cadets or *miskin* who had been humiliated.[13]

The institution which predominated at the time was thus the *armed band*. Changes took place in opposition to it or on the basis of it. The band grouped together men of 'virile' age,

among whom kinship relations were secondary or non-existent; it recruited through co-optation; hierarchies were set
up, on each expedition, on the basis of feats and military prowess. Each was master of his own means of action, arms and
sometimes horses. Solidarity depended on strength through
unity, since numbers were necessary in order to attack successfully and to minimize risks. Expeditions were decided on
together and the booty was divided among the participants.
Neither the composition of the band nor the rules of precedence within it were fixed.[14] In Bamana or Maninka bands,
for example, the leader of each expedition could traditionally
be drawn by lots from among the warriors (Kamissoko,
1975: 53, 57; Niaré, Missions, 1963–4; Leynaud, n.d. [1961], I:
24). The band was a true mode of sociopolitical organization
which, when consolidated, threatened domestic gentle
society – not only because it plundered, but also because their
respective structures were incompatible. Within the band,
the power of the young warriors threatened that of the
elders. When the former had the upper hand, the older members could even be assassinated.

'Men who were disapproved of or disliked in their village
joined these bands', which were not of a permanent nature.
'In groups of thirty or forty they settle in the bush in straw
huts which they abandon as soon as they have been spotted
or as soon as they have captured enough women and children
to go and sell them further away.' These bands also attacked
merchant caravans, but kidnapping was their main activity.
A woman could not go from one village to another without
running the risk of disappearing. Some of these brigands,
who lived in the village, pretended to be setting out on a
journey and went to meet their accomplices. They were
masked so that they would not be recognized. It seems that in
the Wasolon they did not kidnap only the children and
women of their neighbours but also the children of their 'sisters' (from A.-C. Niaré, Mission, 1963, II: R9).[15]

　　Class opposition between bands was very marked. Biton,
who had allied himself with a band led by a Soninke aristocrat from Doua, was told by an elder: 'Stay among people

of the same class, keep your distance from the nobles of Doua' (C. Monteil, 1924: 30).

The military-political organization of the band left lasting traces on the constitution of the regime which grew from it: 'The band had no chief and there was no distribution of the booty: each man kept what he had managed to seize', explained the praise-singer S. Jala (Bazin, 1982: 42–3). In the absence of a permanent chief, the band might choose a leader for each expedition, by election or by drawing lots. Collective decisions were taken by the assembly [*ton*] of the bandits, according to a fairly strict procedure. Biton's 'reign' was marked by raids and capture in the villages of the region (in Kesteloot, 1978: 596, 597). He massacred and sowed terror in the population (ibid.: 597; Sauvageot, 1965: 165). As was frequently the case, he soon set himself up as 'protector' against his own plunder, as a solution to the insecurity caused by himself and his band. He demanded tributes from the villages which rallied to him in order to escape plunder: exactions which were so heavy that the people had to sell 'their own kind' and 'even their mothers' in order to pay (in Kesteloot, 1978: 597). If from then on Biton set himself up as a 'protector' comparable to Sunjata, this was merely an appearance. His power was not based on the reinforcement of domestic and patriarchal institutions in defence against an alien threat. On the contrary, he tended to destroy these institutions and impose his own rules. 'In order to remove the barriers which the tribes[16] and the families tried to maintain among themselves, they displaced whole populations and took them sometimes here, sometimes there' (Monteil, 1924: 50).

Biton, as in any warrior society of this sort, attacked the hierarchy of age. He transgressed the rules of respect due to the old: 'He had 100 old people slapped, he had them tied and sent back to their families' (praise-singers Taïru and Sangare, quoted in Kesteloot, 1978: 596). He challenged their authority even more radically by substituting his own, when he had 740 of his warriors' fathers killed and then forced the warriors to shave their heads – that is, to be 'reborn' as his own dependants (Monteil, 1924: 40).[17] This social reconstruction took place for as long as the Segu kingdom existed, even after Biton's death. Pseudo-lineages were reconstituted from captives who had been regrouped (Bazin, 1975).[18] Pseudo-villages were repopulated with individuals in the same age group, with the exception of children and old people (Sauvageot, 1965). The state of *jon*, of dependant, of slave, tended to be generalized (Bazin, 1975). No one was to base his position on birth, on age, or on links and degrees of kinship, as did the free-born. Social reproduction depended on the warrior more than on the 'father': the members of Biton's *ton* were single men (Sauvageot, 1965: 155).

This differs from what happened in Mande, in that a new society was being formed. This new society gave precedence to associations rather than clans, to adhesion and co-optation as forms of recruitment rather than kinship and birth, to prowess and feats rather than age. The *ton-jon* formed the dominant class, made up of rival warriors who were jealous of their autonomy and were often of captured origin themselves. They were loyal to the institutional corps which they had created (the *ton*), not to a master or to a dynasty. This was therefore a military class, but it was distinct from the clan aristocracies which dominated the region at a local level: it was in opposition to these aristocracies and imposed itself on them (Meillassoux and Silla, 1978; Aubin-Sugy, 1975: 493s.). The *ton-jon* of Segu replaced the code of war between these rival aristocracies with tactics which had no place for honour but were efficient, like mass attacks or sieges, and did not rely on the war apparatuses which 'born' nobility generally used.

The general assembly was the mode of government which usually emerged from the band (Monteil, 1924: 29, 31, 57–60, etc.). The principle of parity operated between members of the *ton*. Since plunder was their main activity, courage and feats were the most important criteria for the selection of a leader. The *ton* was conceived as an institution which gave each man the chance to speak, although often opinions were expressed in tense conditions. For previous norms did not completely disappear. The point of reference was the inherited ancestral order of kinship relations which still dominated individual relationships and private hierarchies. In conflicts and rivalries between *ton-jon* each man appealed to those values which gave him an advantage. Each time a leader was chosen – perhaps for traditional reasons and certainly for reasons of opportunism – principles of filiation and age were evoked as criteria for selection, in competition with fighting prowess.

As the band increased its domination and extended its sovereignty, its founder tried to escape the control of his peers. Bids for power were often attempted, against all the rules: Biton violated the principle of equality and governed without the *ton*; his sons, in order to ensure their succession, sought the support of the *ton* but tried to influence it by magic or violence; the second of these sons, after a reign of terror, was assassinated by the *ton masa* (the president of the assembly), who invoked *age* in order to claim power; he gave himself the title of doyen [*ton koroba*; great old one of the *ton*] (Monteil, 1924: 59). When he died, aspirants to the succession were told to prove their value with bow and arrow, but the elected leader was, once again, the eldest; as was his successor, who was nevertheless obliged to declare war as soon as he took power to prove his pugnacity (ibid.: 46). Later this declaration of war became the rule at each new enthronement (Bazin, 1982).

Finally it was by the use of force, under the pretext of the re-establishment of the warrior values which had dominated at the origin of the *ton*, that Ngolo Jara (who was possibly originally a captive) seized power and transformed it, through a new contradiction, into a dynastic system. But notwithstanding this, the principle of succession was still not established. Age and feats still competed in decisions as to which of Ngolo's sons would take his place. Choices were justified by the 'discovery' in the elected successor of the marks of the legendary hero (Bazin, 1979), but within the context of dynastic permanence which was quite foreign to the transitory power of the symplectic society [see Glossary].

Until the coming of the Jara, the political history of Segu was therefore marked by the social origin of its members and by the activities of brigandage which originally impregnated its institutions.

Yet very soon, the conditions in which brigandage had developed were to disappear. In dominating rather than raiding the population, in replacing booty with tribute, the band constituted its own political space and its own subjects, with whom its relations, once based on hostility, came to be based on authority (and later on exploitation), and from being sporadic became continuous. The band took on tasks of management, administration and protection from the very brigandage out of which it had emerged.

Alongside protection, sovereign in essence, the band gradually took on another regular function, that of arbitration between rival clans, villages or chiefdoms which sought the support of this military corps, which alone had the use of decisive armed force (Bazin, 1982). Protection and arbitration are the two pillars of *sovereignty*; they favour the emergence of a king and of a territorially based State, On the basis of the creation of a zone within which this sovereignty was exercised, another, contrasting, zone was defined within which 'aliens' were captured. From then on, brigandage had to cease within the 'civilized' or sovereign zone, to be diverted to the exterior in the form of raids or wars.[19] This transformation was not without effects on political relations within the military State, and raids and war ceased to be no longer merely an expression of foreign policy or a means of supplying the slave-trade economy and became the decisive extension of the internal policy of the kingdoms.

'When a band of *tegere* [brigands] was discovered by the villagers, they alerted the *faama* [sovereign] so that he could exterminate them.[20] Captives who originated from the area were released and the others were handed over to the *faama*' (Niaré, 1967 Mission). This intervention by the sovereign and this differentiation between captives underlined the distinction made above between the status of alien and that of subject, a distinction which was not made under brigandage. In contrast, the State of Segu granted its subjects the political virtue of citizenship, which protected them against capture. Only those without citizenship were the prey of the slaving State of Segu. In this way slavery and the slave trade contributed to shape citizenship as a means of identification and safety, and to reinforce royalty in opposition to brigandage.

State- building

The spread and success of the band created the conditions for its disappearance. The distinction beween those who were to be protected against capture and aliens led to the emergence of four principles which were to dominate social organization: the principles of *gentleness* and of *citizenship* in terms of which those who had formerly been threatened by the band came under its protection; the principle of *sovereignty* which guaranteed this protection; and the principle of *civil society*, whose internal conflicts had to be arbitrated.

Within the band, relations between its members were transformed to the extent that relations between the band and the population were themselves transformed. The man who set himself up as leader of the band usually also became the leader of the subject populations. The sovereignty with which he was invested reinforced in its turn his position of authority within the band. A hierarchy of a permanent nature was established in contradiction to the principle of parity which had been applied among its members. From then on power no longer fell to the bravest man of the moment. Succession was fixed in the hands of a man who was seen as sovereign by the people and around whom a court or house tended to be constituted, in opposition to the rival houses of his companions.[21]

In this situation, brigandage, the organizational foundation of the band, also disappeared. Once a zone of political membership had been constituted within which the citizenship or subjection of its members was recognized, the authority could no longer capture people without abolishing itself. Capture had to take place outside the area of sovereignty, and thus involved new military practices like raids or war, each of which led to distinct structures of power.

3 COMPANIONS ON RAIDS

Raids took place in almost all the parts of Africa which were affected by the slave trade. It is not possible to determine the relative contributions of raids and warfare in the supply of slaves (Curtin, 1975: 154–5, 186–7), but numerous accounts point to the existence of raids or describe the way they were organized. They were characterized by surprise attacks, ruses, rapid interventions and withdrawals and attacks on poorly protected village populations, especially women and children.

Lamiral (in Walckenaer, 1842, V: 216–17) tells how the Moors went about raiding the populations of northern Senegal between 1779 and 1789:

> One cannot imagine the ruses and the skill which these Moors use to surprise the Negroes. Fifteen or twenty of them set off and stop a league from the village they wish to plunder. They leave their horses in the wood and lie in wait near a spring, at the entrance to the village, or in the fields of sorghum guarded by the children. They are able to wait patiently there for whole days and nights, lying flat on their stomachs and crawling from one place to another. As soon as they see someone, they leap on him, close his mouth and take him away. This is all the easier for them since the young girls and the children go in a group to the springs or the fields[22] which are often far from the villages. A multitude of examples have not made the Negroes more suspicious or more careful; the Moors always use the same ruses and they always succeed. This sort of hunt supplies them with many more children than women or men. When they take their captives to the merchants, these poor children who have been carried behind, bareback, are covered with deep sores, faint with hunger and fatigue and subject to the most cruel fears. The Europeans choose the prettiest and the most alert to make into domestic servants. Few Whites do not have one of these little girls, who often later become great 'signares' [women of captive origin, who have become rich through the slave trade, often the mistresses of slave-traders] (from the travels of Lamiral, 1779–89).

Raids necessitated small numbers of troops and summary weapons with respect, as we shall see, to war. Guns were not indispensable: they were too noisy to use in the abduction of women and children in open country without alerting the villagers. In contrast, rapid means of transport were necessary (horses, dromedaries or pirogues) so that the captives could be taken beyond the reach of possible pursuit.[23]

According to Daumas (1858: 246) the Tuareg knew of different forms of raid whose main object was capture: the *khrofeta*, an abduction expedition which was carried out late in the afternoon; the *terbige*, the *kriana* or the *tehha* which could involve up to 500 or 600 horses. These activities seem to have brought high returns, judging by the numbers captured: Daumas mentions successively a caravan which arrived at Timimoun 'of 200 Negroes and Negresses' (ibid.: 71), a convoy of 400 slaves (of whom 300 were women) and another, the same day, of 1,500 persons (ibid.: 221). Bernus (unpublished, Seminar on War, 1975–6) also points out the richness of the Tamasheq vocabulary which not only describes different types of raid but also distinguishes between the plunder of cattle or slaves and the kidnapping of free individuals. Surprise was doubtless the essential ingredient of success, but the use of writing was perhaps as important, since it enabled the Tuareg from Teneka to assemble their men in one day (Olivier de Sardan, 1976: 66). Knowledge of the desert and the use of fast animals like the dromedary made possible raids at considerable distances from base, without fear of reprisals.

Along the Niger, the Kurtey, themselves victims of Tuareg raids, became robbers of men, regularly taking captives from among the populations living alongside the Tilaberi archipelago:

> Up to fifteen pirogues could sail up the river. But these raids were in no way epic: the Kurtey encountered no opposition on the river itself, which they sailed up by day, and they hid their pirogues when night fell. Then they paddled silently until they saw the tents of the cultivators on the edge of the water. . . . The Kurtey encircled the huts in silence, then tied the unfortunate sleepers up in their own mat and took the whole lot away in their pirogues. (Olivier de Sardan, 1969: 32)

These techniques, which were still those of brigandage,

illustrate the continuity between brigandage and raids in two respects.

The raid allowed the free recruitment of participants, who sometimes chose the leader and decided on the operation: it ensured the appropriation of the booty by the plunderers, who were always masters of the undertaking and of its results. When part of the booty was due to the sovereign under whose authority the plunderers fell, it was as free owners of their captives that they paid these dues, not as dependants acting for the benefit of a superior. The booty of which they had the use was not the product of a 'redistribution'. The ruffians of Segu expressed this when they said that the booty taken in a raid was 'the price of their lives' and that it was theirs without division.

Thus raids which took place from a State blocked the centralization of power by encouraging the constitution and maintenance of an independent warrior class which could appropriate resources and riches and enter into competition with the sovereign. Now, the sovereign had to draw from this class the military and civil staff through whom he could protect the people and exercise his authority over them. In this balance of forces, the sovereign's power over the warrior class could not be complete.[24] Examples can be found in most nomad societies which went in for raiding: the emir of the Moor fractions studied by P. Bonte (in Seminar on War, 1975–6) had only moral authority over the clans which depended on him, with none of the attributes of sovereignty. The emir had no control over the raids undertaken by his subjects. He could fill only conciliatory functions with the agreement of the parties involved.

Thus two political forces were at work under the influence of raids. The first, a centralizing force, was in contradiction to companionship; it favoured the emergence of a 'king' who represented the power of the band with respect to populations which had been subjugated by frequent raids; the second was a threat to this same power, in that the warrior raiders were allowed to keep their independence, their resources and their arms. The rising importance of war relative to raids as a means of seizing slaves was a sign of the king's victory over his companions.

2

The Great Task of the Kings

1 'OUR HOE IS OUR GUN'

A thesis in which conflict and violence are assimilated, inspired by ethological determinism,[1] holds that war is no more than the product of an 'aggressive instinct' of animal origin.[2] This thesis is never made explicit, nor is it universally applied by modern historians to conflicts as a whole, but it is implicitly present whenever no attempt is made to analyse the historical and sociopolitical circumstances of these conflicts. The lack of exposure given to the forces behind war seems to be an admission that it is the result of primary urges and not of historical and cultural circumstances. This thesis is a regression from Clausewitz, who saw war not as the spilling over of instincts but as an instrument of the policy of nations and the assertion of power. It confuses violence in general with the *premediated organization of force* and is thus blind to the functions of this organization. In fact, warfare implies the establishment of an apparatus which seems always to have been costly for the economy of the various military societies; it is not a spontaneous reflex of individual aggression during a moment of emotion. The pecking of a goose which feels threatened has nothing in common with the entry into campaign of an army which has taken

157

months or years to prepare, organize, staff, maintain, feed, and so on.

This thesis is paralleled by an ideology which tends to present aggression, and by assimilation warfare, as the supreme expression of masculine values (virility) and the source of all hierarchy. I have tried to show elsewhere (1979e; 1981) how wars of abduction, in societies which did not practise an ordered exchange of wives, made men into the effective agents of social reproduction, and how this function came politically to conceal natural procreation by women; how the man, disadvantaged at the level of procreation, magnified his function of social reproducer and imposed it, even at the risk of his life. I have tried to show how the man, whose role as abductor made him a threat to the woman, came to protect her against himself. Finally, I have tried to show how, in the context of slavery, he asserted himself, through warfare or raids, as the provider of all wealth, including human beings. In these circumstances all armed conflict necessarily provided an opportunity to assert the superiority of the man as an individual capable, through his 'valour', of conquering, accumulating, protecting and reproducing society. To the extent that, independently of other more immediate goals, the ideological function of warfare was also to assert masculine domination, warfare, whatever its purpose, was justified in terms of 'honour'; a pretext for war was always found which glorified the warrior and became the official cause of the conflict: the defence of honour, the political subordination of neighbours, victory over a rival, the punishment of the impudent – pretexts which can be found for any war. It was on the basis of this sort of pretext that forms of behaviour associated with war were encouraged up to the point where aggression was seen both as inherent to human nature and as the expression of masculine virtue.

In the historical context of the slave trade, it was in the moral interests of the merchants and the sovereigns who supplied slaves to adhere to the thesis, long-standing even then, of war as a 'natural phenomenon'. This enabled them to claim that the lives of prisoners who would otherwise have been massacred had been saved thanks to the slave trade (Snelgrave, 1734: 169). It was assumed that these wars would have taken place in any case, independently of the existence of the slave trade or even of internal slavery. However, even if all sorts of armed conflicts took place before the slave trade, its emergence cannot be ignored as a cause of war. Capture was not only a strong economic motive for war; it was also, for the States which had been constituted around it, the condition of their existence and their survival. Wars waged on other pretexts were usually a response to these concerns and in practice always resulted in capture.

Yet the idea that wars waged by the slaving States were disinterested or strictly political exists among contemporary historians. According to Person (1968), for example, Samori's strategic and political objectives were more important than his desire to take slaves.[3] Curtin (1975: 123) doubts that the slaving kingdoms waged war with the deliberate intention of capture.

This opinion is shared by Terray (1982a: 123), who generalizes from the case of the Abron (1975a: 121–2). He admits that captives constituted the most important part of the booty from warfare and that most of them went to the Abron sovereign; but he sees other causes as the origin of most of these wars – the subjugation of neighbouring peoples, the rebellion against the powerful Ashanti rivals of the Abron, and so forth. The only exceptions were the military expeditions against the Djimini, the Gyamala and the Tagwana after the 1818 disaster: 'In this case the purpose was to repopulate the devastated kingdom' (p.122). Still, documents concerning the Ashanti (Rattray, 1929: 218) show that capture was more important than territorial conquest.[4] Le Hérissé (1911: 246–7) reports that the Dahomey wars resulted in territorial expansion only when 'the enlargement of the kingdom was possible in continuity', and Bradbury (1957: 75) reports that in Benin 'the main purpose of warfare seems to have been the capture of slaves rather than territory'. It must in fact be remembered that the extension of sovereignty over new populations transformed them from potential captives into subjects and to this extent reduced the benefits of war. For purposes of conquest, wars should have been aimed at threatening kingdoms rather than at hunting-grounds. But it was the raided peoples in these hunting-grounds who were brought into the orbit of the kingdom through frequent raids on them.

It is true that slaving States fought wars to gain access to the sea, to crush a rebellion, to protect their territory or to drive off a competitor, but these wars were induced by the politics of the slave trade and were part of a set of activities designed to create or preserve the conditions for the capture and sale of captives. These strategic wars were conjunctural, not periodic. They were fought with a certain splendour which the seasonal wars (aimed at capture) did not have.

For the Bamoum kingdom, whose economy was based on subsistence slavery, 'the objectives seem to be unchanging: to take prisoners to work on the kingdom's lands' (Tardits, 1980: 192). Under one of the Bamoum kings, only raids for capture took place, and no territorial conquest (ibid.: 177). In Dahomey, Le Hérissé points out, 'many wars were only slave-hunts' (1911: 246) and Skertchly (1874: 447) notes that 'the wars are merely slave-taking expeditions or head hunts ... Every man, woman and child [is] captured if possible. None are killed save in self-defense, as the object is to capture, not to butcher' (ibid.). In the same way, the soldiers of Kayor (present-day Senegal) 'spare their enemies so as to make more slaves' (in Walckenaer, 1842, 4: 131–2). De Marchais explains that 'all the attention of the victor is focused on taking a large number of prisoners' (Labat, 1730, in Walckenaer, 1842, 10: 60).

Bademba, master of Sikasso and a contemporary of Samori, fought wars only 'to increase his wealth in slaves and in women' (Kouroubari, 1959: 547). In the ancient kingdom of Kongo, writes G. Balandier (1965: 110s.), the causes of many wars were economic: 'raids of possessions and of young men destined for deportation by the slave-traders or for domestic slavery'. The alliance described by Mollien (1818/1967: 155) between the States of Bundu, Fuuta Tooro and Fuuta Jallo, 'in order to put an end to idolatry', made it possible to wage a 'holy' war which 'more than any other cause supplied innumerable slaves which the Negro merchants sold to the Moors'. Dunbar (1977: 160) holds that the political rivalries in Damagaram[5] were a 'pretext' for capture. As regards the Aboh wars,[6] although they contained, according to Nwachukwu–Ogedengbe (1977: 139), 'diplomatic and economic undercurrents', their frequency and intensity were increased by 'the insatiable demand for slaves'.

Numerous other declarations and testimonies of the same sort show that capture as undertaken by the slaving military States was not the by-product of wars fought for other reasons: it was the main purpose of the construction and use of the military apparatus, even if this apparatus could be used for other sorts of conflict.[7] A few statistics highlight the purpose of these wars. In Damagaram, 'seven thousand slaves' were brought back from a single campaign in Kano (Dunbar, 1977: 160). Manson, king of Segu, took 900 prisoners in one day in Kaarta (Mungo Park, 1960: 22). Under Gezo (Dahomey) 4,000 slaves were taken in a campaign conducted almost expressly to meet the needs of a slave-ship anchored at Whyda (Herskovits, 1978, I: 324). The Nupe of the Sudan took 2,000 captives in an attack on a single village (Nadel, 1942: 113), and so on. Not all wars were so fruitful, but this merely increased the number of military undertakings.

Wars of capture and political wars were not of the same order and did not take place in parallel. Capture necessitated specific techniques, arms and organization, particularly when it was aimed at catching *living* men and women. Could this strategy be made to conform to the needs of a military (and political) 'victory' which would rather have entailed the physical suppression of enemy resistance, whatever the cost? It seems not, from the little that is known of the way these wars were fought. According to Dalzel (1793), when King Adahoonzan II of Dahomey (1774–86) fought wars of vengeance (or political wars) against his rivals, he gave no quarter and took no slaves, massacring all the men, women and children. Among the Arab nomads, wars of vengeance were waged in order to massacre the vanquished, irrespective of their age or sex. These wars had a specific name, *tehha*, which clearly distinguished them from wars in which captives were taken (Daumas, 1858: 246).

If all these wars had been merely political, the booty taken would have been meagre, too small to supply the demand for slaves on the market. On the contrary: the annual and seasonal character of the wars of capture and their timing at fixed intervals indicate that they were in fact functional.[8] Wars of capture were fought in the same way that fields were cultivated. 'Our hoe is our gun', said the Jawara of Kingi.[9] These periodic wars cannot be seen as having been provoked by incidents. Their explicit and systematic purpose was capture.

The demand for slaves in merchant slave societies is determinant in this respect. While aristocratic societies needed slaves only for their own use, in the context of the prestative economy, the number would be limited by the size of the free-born population and, in the absence of an external outlet, would probably have shown irregular variations: renewal could take place through occasional capture or demographic growth, and any excess could be sacrificed. If these aristocratic societies were called on to supply demand from the merchant slaving societies, there was a multiplier effect on internal demand: additional soldier-slaves were needed to fight wars, additional slaves to produce food for these soldiers, additional captives to be used in exchange for military goods. The increase in capture led in turn to friction with other, competing, capturing societies and thus to military and economic reinforcement which further increased the need for captives. At a certain level of investment in war, the mechanism was set in motion. The military societies were forced to sell more and more captives in order to preserve their military potential and thus their warlike and political structures. The effects of supply and demand were reversed: it was the capturing societies which turned to the market to sell their captives. This is why these wars seem to have been fought for their own sake and without any lucrative purpose. But, in spite of the reciprocal effect of supply on the part of the captors and demand on the part of the merchant slavers, the dynamic of the capturing society was strongly influenced by the pull from merchant societies, since it was among the latter that the tendency to increase the demand for slaves was inherent. Not only was the market area continuously extended (as more and more societies entered the orbit of the slave market), but each slaving economy tended to increase its production of commodities. Indeed, if slavery was to continue to be more advantageous than serfdom, *supplies on the market* had to be sufficiently abundant for the reproduction of slaves through trade to top their eco-demographic increase at all times: this was possible only if demand from the merchant society was permanent, inducing the capturing societies to fight wars until the provision of slaves became their very reason for being (see Part III, Chapter 5).

But this regularity was an expensive matter for the States which captured slaves. War necessitated a permanent infrastructure and resources. Capture should have covered these costs and the dominant class should have profited from it, but this profit was also the result of the exploitation of the population which supplied the men and food needed for warfare. The repetition of wars of capture, their dimensions, the constraints they imposed on the people, set in motion a process through which the slaves became no longer only victims but also instruments of war.

2 SOLDIER–SLAVES

Unlike the raid, which concerned only a fraction of professional warriors, war involved the whole of civil society. It directly or indirectly mobilized the entire population. It was directed by the highest political authorities. It was an 'affair of State' (Terray, 1975a: 121).

In the slave-supplying States, capture took on decisive importance and war replaced raids as the indispensable means of supplying human commodities. War became all the more necessary to the captors of slaves in that demand from the Atlantic slave trade was less for women and adolescents than for adult men, who were more difficult to capture in raids and ambushes. In order to capture men in sufficient numbers, it was not enough to lie in wait in the fields or at the wells. The men were armed and they protected the women at work. In order to be captured they first had to be disarmed; there was thus a resistance to be broken. This implied more radical and more generalized attacks, aimed at the population as a whole. In order to reach the men, the very heart of the social system had to be attacked. These tougher offensives

necessitated additional numbers and thus greater mobilization of the aggressor's means of attack.

When the demand for male slaves fell with the ending of
the Atlantic slave trade, the slavers did not revert to raids as
the main means of capturing women. On the contrary: the
rising demand for female slaves on the African market provoked by the circumstances created by the slave trade and the
establishment of States whose reason for being was still capture led to an increase in warfare. The falling returns, mostly
in captives, from war had to be compensated for by a rise in
their frequency and intensity.

Distance, like resistance on the part of the population,
favoured warfare rather than raids. We have seen how the
flight of populations and the subjection of those who stayed
within the orbit of the kingdoms combined to force the
armies to cover greater and greater distances in response to
the departure, disappearance or transformation into subjects
of the social material. Furthermore, as military States multiplied, they came into competition: rivals had to be fought
and forces of equivalent strength had to be mobilized against
them. For these States, war became 'the great task of the
kings' (Tardits, 1980a: 191, with respect to Bamoum). Echo-
ing the Jawara of Kingi, who devoted themselves to these
wars of capture, the warriors of Dahomey declared: 'Our
fathers did not cultivate with hoes but with guns. The kings
of Dahomey cultivate only war' (Le Hérissé, 1911). 'Ashanti
is a nation of warriors', corroborated King Osei Bonsu, for
whom men 'are made on the battlefield' (Terray, 1982a: 388).

Just as war involved society as a whole, so recruitment, in
order to satisfy the demand for men, was extended to the
civil population and no longer only to specialized warriors.
The army was composed of combatants who were numerous
but irregular, so that it needed a staff, a supply corps and an
ideology which could act as a stimulant in place of booty,
which was reduced by division among greater numbers of
men. Thus a military hierarchy was set up with control of an
organization and of arms, manipulating values which were
presented as essential to the existence of society. The existence of this hierarchy challenged political relations between
the army and the civil authority, between the dominant class

and the people, and, finally, between the slaves, who were the product of these wars, and the court.

Since wars of capture were both military and slaving, as well as being the principal apparatus of reproduction of the State and the dominant class, they brought class conflict into the heart of free-born society, between the people and the aristocracy and between rival houses within the aristocracy; while the slaves, by exploiting these divisions introduced by their existence as a class, tended to remove the sovereign from the power of the nobles and subordinate him to their own.

Thus in order to overcome the resistance of the raided populations and the competing States – and also to resolve the problem of distance – the army had to be swelled and the principal forces of the State had to be involved in warfare. Indeed, the armies of the slave-hunting States took on considerable dimensions. I have already referred to those of the medieval empires which supplied the slave trade in the Maghreb (Part I, Chapter 1). Comparable figures are reported for the States which supplied the Atlantic slave trade. At the beginning of the nineteenth century, Robertson (1819) credited the Ashanti army with 40,000 men (A670) and Bowdich (1819: 317) with more than 200,000: 'All the males capable of bearing arms are obliged to equip themselves and to join the army when there is a national war'.[10] It was indeed a matter of general mobilization. The king of Benin could assemble an army of 20,000 in a single day (Dapper, A616, in Walckenaer, 1842, 11: 59–61): 'With a little more time he can put 100,000 men into the field' (ibid.). In Dahomey, Snelgrave (1734: 77) found that the army was divided into 'regular troops numbering some 3,000 men' and a multitude of at least 10,000 men who followed, bearing 'baggage, provisions and heads [of their dead enemies]'.

According to Elwert (1973: 37), 'each [Dahomeyan] village had to deliver a precise number of young men' for war, for one month or several months in succession. These recruits had to bring their own basic subsistence. In principle they were given arms and ammunition, but since the loss of a gun was punished by death, they also brought their own arms if they could. The kingdom of Juida (Whyda) could 'without much expense, field an army of 200,000 men' (A577, in Walckenaer, 1842, 10: 353–9), although it seems they were rather badly commanded.

While the size of the armies was to influence the outcome of military actions, their social composition caused far-reaching problems. Extended recruitment incorporated into the army peasants without any military experience. As a result there was a need for an organization which could bring these troops into the field either to carry out auxiliary functions or even to fight. This organization necessitated discipline and training. This explains Snelgrave's reference to the division of the Dahomeyan army into two parts: a corps of regular soldiers on one hand and a militia recruited from the people on the other. In the same way, among the Wolof, 'each *lamane* [vassal of the king]', according to Geoffroy de Villeneuve (1814),

> has in his service a certain number of soldiers whom he provides with arms and horses. Several of them stay close to him and are then fed at the master's expense; the rest stay in the villages and are obliged to march as soon as they are required. The faithfulness of these soldiers often make the *lamanes* into so many little tyrants who oppress the people.

These remarks sum up the main characteristics and effects of this twofold recruitment, which will be further discussed below.

In the Ashanti army, according to Bowdich (1819: 298), a merciless discipline was exercised by the staff on the battlefield. The army leaders, with their elite troops, followed closely on the recruited fighters, 'forcing them, sword in hand, to march and immolating all those who tried to flee'. The 'elites' of the Ashanti army were made up of soldier-slaves, captured as children and trained for the work (Reindorf, 1895: 132). Similar discipline seems to have reigned in the Benin army, where, according to Dapper (in Walckenaer, 1842, 12: 59–61), no one dared to leave his post for fear of death. The organization of the Dahomey army, as described by Snelgrave (1719: 77s.) made provision, in the companies – each of which had its own flag and its own officers – for the training by each soldier in the royal army of a young boy, maintained at the expense of the public, so that he could be prepared for war at an early age. A similar division can be found in Samori's army: according to Binger (1892, I: 100–04) this army included permanent soldiers (the *sofa*); their officers (the *keletigi*), who were responsible for recruiting, in each region, 'anyone who is able and owns a gun'; and among them the *kurusitigi* ('wearers of trousers'), adult, married warriors and temporary soldiers.

In aristocratic societies the military staff was usually composed of nobles or professional warriors who had won a place in the dominant class, or of local chiefs whose role was to raise a militia and sometimes to accompany it into the field. But as the army developed, the permanent core was increasingly composed of chiefs recruited among captives taken in war, themselves supervised by more senior slaves. Samori's *sofa* were young slaves who had been entrusted since their capture to the army's regular warriors (whose own origins were similar). Reindorf (1895: 119) said that the recruits in the king of Asante's army were 'either captives in a recent war or his own subjects . . . bought as slaves'. The latter stayed in their villages, but the others had to live in their captain's home town; he himself lived in the capital. The Bamoum royal palace guard was composed of several hundred captives from a neighbouring tribe (Tardits, 1980).

Among the Nupe of the Sudan, the infantry, armed with guns, and the cavalry were made up of slaves and mercenaries. The slaves who served in the cavalry were the sons of titled slaves, and each noble house established this sort of corps for itself (Nadel, 1942: 109). The king used these slaves like a police force to maintain order in the markets and in the street (ibid.: 91, 99). Loyer (1660–1715, in Roussier, 1935) notes that the slaves of Issinie formed the larger part of the army and that each general owned 500 to 600 armed slaves. Among the Yoruba, the only permanent army was composed of slaves who were maintained by their chiefs (Johnson, in Forde, 1951: 23–4). The Bamoum case is particularly interesting and well documented (Tardits, 1980). In the early part of its existence, according to Tardits (perhaps in the seventeenth and eighteenth centuries), the kingdom waged expansionary wars in which the whole of the population took part. Lands were conquered, but at the expense of the local populations. Population density dropped to the extent that in the second phase, under King Mbuambua (182?–4?) wars were no longer fought to conquer lands but to capture men. From this time on, the demand for labour-power was continuous and the dynamics of slave reproduction took over in the same way as in the kingdoms which supplied the slave trade. However, unlike the latter, Bamoum slave society supplied itself, and itself alone, with slaves, with no intermediaries.[11] Tardits (ibid.) finds a transformation of the society as a result of slavery. The number of palace servants rose considerably (ibid.); in the same way, the captives kept in the palace as guards or used on expeditions began to number in the hundreds. But during this reign the tribute paid by the populations also increased: 'In the time of Nsara [Mbuambua's predecessor], little, very little, was given, but when Mbuambua became king and had vanquished several tribes, one gave a lot' (ibid.: 779). Slavery introduced an additional burden for the people and at the same time was used as a repressive means to force the people to carry this burden.

This phenomenon is visible in many other cases also. The slaves attached to the palace and to the different fractions of the dominant class were generally used by this class as instruments for the domination and oppression of free-born popular classes:

> The Asante army also maintained the peace and order of the Asante State against threats from within. The state acted directly when it confronted social unrest among its lower order. The slaves in the Asante army were an ideal 'foreign legion' for suppressing social disorder. (N. Klein, unpublished, 67)

Elwert (1973: 40s.) reports that the Dahomey army was used to ensure the payment of the tribute, in goods and also in people.

In Sonxai, the phenomenon is clearly evoked by the author of a contemporary chronicle: 'The population which, under the reign of the Kharedjite Sonni Ali, was entirely called to arms, henceforth divided into two categories: the army and the people' (*Tarikh es-Sudan*, 1964 ed: 118). Olivier de Sardan sees this transformation as an important stage in the history of Sonxai (1975: 127). This separation of free-born society into two classes as a result of slavery and the existence of slaves was not complete in all cases, but it represents a tendency which is all the more interesting in that it throws light on the nature of the State, of power and of class relations in societies devoted to the capture of slaves.

Preferential recruitment of slaves in the regular army can be explained by factors whose underlying cause is always the social nature of the slave, his extraneousness, his state of stranger in the city. This state originates, it must be remembered, in the slave mode of production which prevents the slave from reproducing himself within the social system.

Capture through war became less rewarding for those who practised it, and in particular for peasant recruits, as it became more distant and more brutal, and met greater resistance. The booty could be relatively well shared out among those who took part in a raid, but less so among all the fighters in a war. The takings did not increase in proportion to the growth of the armies. It does not seem, from an examination of forms of distribution practised within the armies, that the majority of the foot-soldiers had much chance of getting rich. Distribution benefited the king in the first place, then the officers, the aristocrats and the regular troops. According to Dapper, the king of Benin admitted only his general to the sharing-out of the booty. Samori reserved all the young men and half the captives for himself, giving the other half to the chiefs and to the warriors who were responsible for the takings (Binger, 1892, I: 100s.). In most other cases, the king kept all the slaves and distributed them as he wished. The possibility of rewards certainly did still sometimes exist, but other forms of encouragement had to be found to induce men to go into battle.

Thus ideology was brought into play to compensate for the reduction or absence of material rewards and to overcome the fear of being wounded or killed, which was more likely in war than during raids. In the clan societies of the savannah – for instance, in Segu – the praise-singers were the agents of this ideological pressure (Bazin, 1982: 345): 'The heroic ethic is constantly manipulated by the professional storytellers in the service of the court, in order to encourage the warriors to exchange their miserable lives for a glorious destiny.' Glory was bartered for death, fame for existence. Shame or disgrace, courage in the face of death, motivated the troops as much as the fear of capture, which was presented as social death and an indelible stain.[12]

Among the Bamana or the Soninke, during the long nights before combat, the fighters, filled with the heroic songs of the praise-singers and the encouragement of the women, promised to accomplish astonishing feats of bravery or to perish (1965 Mission). The Arab nomads brought the most beautiful women in the tribe into the battlefield when fighting declared war (not on raids) to encourage or boo their men, depending on the outcome of the fighting (Daumas, 1858: 324s.). This exploitation of ideology was linked to the mobilization of the population as a whole for purposes of war, as opposed to raids.

But in the most important and least homogeneous States, when mobilization reached the most rural and least affected strata, this often rather crude ideology was complemented by the most brutal forms of discipline, like those used in the Ashanti army referred to above: a staff of soldier-slaves of alien origin forced the peasant recruits forward, whipping or massacring them if they retreated. Non-native troops were usually assigned to these staffs rather than citizens who would be more likely to fraternize with the foot-soldiers.

Through war, the authorities increased their pressure on the people – not only by drawing them into combat but also on the economic level. In most cases the slave-guards and the servile armed corps were fed by their masters. These troops were armed by their masters, and sometimes provided with horses (in contrast to the militia, whose members had to bring their own arms). During the campaign, the soldier-slaves were given rations while the recruits were expected to bring their own subsistence.

The consumption of the armies maintained by the nobles, and particularly by the king, was added to that of the aristocratic and merchant classes which developed with war and the slave trade. Demand for subsistence goods increased. At the same time, growing urbanization made the cities dependent on peasant agricultural production. The hazards of war, which sometimes spread throughout the kingdom, further diminished the productive capacity of agriculture. The tributes which burdened the peasantry, even though it was freeborn, tended to rise and increasingly had to be extracted by force. The examples of Bamoum, Nupe, Dahomey, Ashanti or Kayor show that it was the armed corps composed of slaves which was responsible for repression 'in the street and in the marketplaces'. Thus, whether within the nation or within the army, slaves could be used effectively against the people in a repressive corps: particularly since, being aliens and not citizens, they had neither kinship roots nor affinities which might have tempered their activities.

Thus the soldier-slave opened the way to the restructuring of free-born society by providing the slaving aristocracies with the means of restricting and repressing the free peasantry. The class relation between master and slave was transformed into an ancillary, military and administrative relation: it carried exploitation into the heart of free-born society and made it the medium of class relations.[13]

However, we shall see that the exploitation of free-born peasants did not necessarily replace that of slaves – though this was conceivable – and that the two generally coexisted. Slave exploitation was rarely the sole mode of production.

Before discussing the nature of class relations in aristocratic slavery, however, it is necessary to describe the mode of reproduction internal to these military corps. Not only the recruitment, maintenance and arming of these slave corps, but also their renewal, were controlled by the court. The men who belonged to these corps could be given female partners only by the king. The king maintained his right to the

progeny or the first-born of these women; the boys were expected to join the corps in their turn and the girls to be their
partners. This form of renewal was used in the court of the
Mossi *naaba*, for example, and was assimilated to *pogsyure*
marriage.[14] (Delobsom, 1933: 164; Izard, 1975: 291).

Some of these corps of armed retainers – in the kingdom of
Senegambia, for example (Sin Salum, Walu, Jolof) – were
not necessarily composed of slaves but of children given to
the sovereign by their parents. It seems that the king applied
the same rules of reproduction to them. Thus the king-
master ensured the loyalty of his armed retainers by granting
them the privilege of one or more partners. He was dependent on men who depended on him in every respect. He had
given birth to these men for arms and he gave birth to them
again every day, by sparing them from death (Izard, 1975).
Like a father, he fed them, he gave them a mate, and
although the slave, unlike the son, could not claim paternity
for his progeny, the master took over as a replacement for the
ancestor, as absolute forebear and father. With respect to the
ceddo (armed retainers) of the *damel* of Kayor (present-day
Senegal), V. Monteil writes: 'They were the only section of
the population on which the king [the *damel*] could absolutely
depend' (1967: 269).

In fact, these slaves were originally 'reborn' in the host
society only as orphans and could therefore give birth only to
other orphans.

As we have seen, the non-paternity of the slave results from
his *economic* use. At this level, it was a practical means of exploitation which enabled the cost of reproduction of the producer to be avoided. Since this placed the slave outside social
relations, he *ipso facto* acquired the quality of non-kin which
made him suitable for political and non-productive employment. Once he was used for these tasks, his economic position was transformed. Instead of maintaining the master, the
slave was maintained by him. Thus the cost of his genesic reproduction was no longer a question of profit but of opportunity. The slave's chance of living with a woman, of recon-
stituting a cell around himself which had the appearance of a
family and of being formally assimilated to free men, was a
(reversible) privilege which distinguished such a slave from

others and tied him even more strongly to his master. But since he was still a slave and incapable of making this cell function as an organism which could help him build up a family and a patrimony, since his very state meant that he was dispossessed of his genesic or material product, he had no rights over his progeny, even if they lived with him (which was not always the case), even if he fed them (with what the master gave him). The armed slave was still socially sterile. For their part, the progeny of these slave men and women could inherit nothing from their genitors. The children were dispossessed of their parents, as of their own children – no links were created between generations.

Birth did not contribute to the emancipation of the armed retainer in the way that it had social effects on the free man. This was true both of his own birth, since it took place outside the space of the free-born, and of that of his possible progeny; he never acquired the authority over the progeny which would have reduced his dependence on the master on whom he himself depended. In the armed corps which were subjected to this slave mode of reproduction, birth was confiscated from each slave for the benefit of the corps to which he belonged. This sort of reproduction was designed not to allow families to come into their own but to reconstitute a permanent social corps whose members would have no relations between them other than those chosen by their sovereign-master. Such a mode of reproduction could present a danger to the king if the distribution of women was not strictly controlled; as a result *de facto* families were constituted which might acquire power based on their military functions. In order to avoid this risk, if the chief was not the sovereign himself, he was generally not chosen from among the members of the corps. He usually belonged to another category of servants or was recruited from those with executive functions.

The division which the use of soldier-slaves introduced within the free-born class, between aristocrats and peasants, touched the very heart of the aristocracy itself.

In the kingdom of Segu, Biton, the first sovereign and,

initially, *primum inter pares*, established a guard of soldier-slaves [*sofa*]. It seems to have numbered 3,000 men. Ngolo, who was put in command of the guard, used it to usurp power and during his reign its numbers rose to 12,000 (C. Monteil, 1924: 50, 70). When he seized power in 1750, Ngolo rejected the status of his predecessors: he refused to swear by the idols, since 'this is due only from slaves'. The reign of the *ton-jon*, the companions, had ended and that of the kings [*mansa*] had begun.

War had enabled direct recruitment by the sovereign of numerous young captives placed under the command of chiefs, also captive in origin but owing allegiance only to their master (Tautain, 1884: 349). Unlike the 'companions', these new recruits were not privileged to become the peers of their abductors. Their condition of slavery meant that from then on they were subordinated to their master and not to an association. The *ton-jon*, anxious to preserve their status, did not extend it to these new recruits, so that a distinct and competing social and military corps was formed. Latent conflict can be detected between the *ton-jon* and the *sofa*. C. Monteil reports that the latter were used by the king to make the former see reason. The *ton-jon* would have been able to resist better if they had been able to constitute themselves into a permanent army. But during the great confrontation between King Dakoro, one of Biton's sons, and his *ton-jon*, in which the *ton-jon* were defeated, Dakoro forced them and their men to continue to cultivate the land (C. Monteil, 1924: 55, 302). In this way the king tried to avoid the establishment of a military aristocracy hostile to him, free of the obligation of agricultural labour and all the more dangerous in that its members could turn to raiding as an autonomous means of subsistence.

C. Monteil (1924) notes the consequences of this use of military slaves in the neighbouring Bamana kingdom of Kaarta: 'The corps of the *sofa* is . . . particularly powerful and the *fama* can easily use it to counter attempts at insubordination on the part of the *ton-dyon* chiefs'; initially his companions-in-arms and his peers.

The servile armed corps was not invariably a royal prerogative. The military chiefs could also use their captives as soldier-slaves for purposes both of war and of repression. As instruments for the assertion of power by the military aristocracy as a dominant class, against not only the slaves but also the population as a whole, these troops were also engaged in internal struggles among the kingdom's powerful men or between them and the king. They were the arm of a class power which divided the society of free men, both between aristocrats and peasants and between military houses.

3

The Divine Court

The power of a king was never established without allies and
compromises; and those who had contributed to its creation
expected to wield some power themselves. When royalty – as
was often the case – was the result of conquest, of domination over an alien group, an alliance was generally formed between the occupiers and one or more families who were
locally acknowledged to be masters of the soil.[1] Furthermore,
the conqueror granted privileges, lands and prerogatives to
his companions. He sometimes accepted other families into
the collectivity. It was agreed that important decisions should
be taken in concert. At a given moment in their history, a
council was established around the sovereign in all African
royalties. It was made up in the first place of the representatives of the great noble families and sometimes of those who
had lived in the area before conquest, or had come later and
been accepted. In Walo, the advisers of the *brak* [king] were
the delegates of the three great matriclans of the kingdom. In
Kayor and in Baol, as in many other dynastic societies, the
king was elected from among aspirants belonging to the eli-
gible family or families, by eminent men in other noble families. He could also be dethroned by them (cf. Gamble, 1957:
56). In Sin and in Salum, the *bur* had to be of aristocratic origin but was chosen by those of high rank at the court. Similar
procedures can be found in Oyo, in Dahomey and in the

neighbouring kingdoms, as well as in southern African States such as Kongo and Monomotapa. However, according to Bowdich, in Ashanti the Royal Council intervened more in foreign than in domestic affairs, while in many cases officials of high rank who were not of the aristocracy but were slaves or eunuchs took part in the decisions of the Council. Within these Councils, the king, the aristocrats and the court officers were, in fact, to fight over power.

1 THE KING SURROUNDED

Royal absolutism was both the product and the reaction of a king faced with the intrusive power of the notables. This was particularly threatening when the Royal Council had the power to order the death of the king or those close to him, as was the case in a number of kingdoms such as Oyo, Mono-motapa and Kongo.

In Oyo, according to Morton-Williams (1967), the notables in the aristocracy exercised power attributed to them by the constitution. Power seems to have been fairly well balanced between the great families, which doubtless competed at various moments in their history. In principle, the king had to govern with the aid of a council made up of six representatives from these families; they could condemn the sovereign to commit suicide if they considered him incapable of continuing to reign.[2] This raises the question of who really held power. Who is the more powerful – those who can decide on the king's death, or the king himself, who is subject to this decision? Surely nothing reveals the weakness of an individual more clearly than his arbitrary condemnation to death? When the Oyo notables condemned the king to commit suicide, was power in the hands of the king? In fact, in many kingdoms, with the growing absolutism of the Council of Nobles, the king could be condemned to death on all sorts of pretexts, most of them quite outside his sphere of competence. He could certainly be condemned because the kingdom had suffered a military defeat for which he could, directly or indirectly, be held responsible;[3] but the king was more often condemned because of a prolonged drought, because he was ill, or even – as in Monomotapa – because he had lost an incisor. These pretexts were so numerous and so futile that the king was exposed to the most arbitrary decision of the Council.

The Council of Nobles could reduce the king to this level of impotence through various means, which were the same almost everywhere. The most important was the right granted to the Council to intervene at the critical moment in the succession. Its power was built and extended around this prerogative and this crucial moment.

The more difficult a succession was, the more necessary it became to appeal to arbitration by the Council of Nobles. The more frequently successions took place, the more often the Council could intervene.[4] It was in the interests of the aristocratic families which were rivals to the royal lineage, and did not directly wield power, to multiply and complicate these successions. The king's multigyny was another way to weaken the royal house. The homage which the noble families claimed to pay the king in offering him their daughters in marriage, the encouragement of royal polygyny with free or slave wives, confused the criteria for succession and made it more difficult to discriminate in terms of dynastic heredity. The king's paternity was diluted, and with it hereditary appointment. The criterion of elderhood among numerous children born soon after each other or at the same time was complicated by criteria relating to the rank of the wife, the status of the mother, the sister, and so on. Any choice could be contested. Under the pretext of ensuring that the pretender chosen by the king had the qualities necessary for government, the Council of Nobles could give preference to one candidate chosen from too many and, with the help of the diviner, attribute to him the marks of power and plot in advance with him to make him into their instrument, triggering off the succession by various conspiracies.

Divisions between the members of the council during these intrigues might perhaps restore some of the king's power to intervene, even if the weapons at his disposal were no more powerful than those of his rivals. For the more numerous the 'heirs' were, the more bitter and bloody the struggles. Whether an heir had been chosen by the Council or the king, he attracted the hatred of his brothers and his position was immediately weakened. The royal family was torn apart instead of being united each time there was a succession. The king found only enemies among his kin, ready to make alliances with his rivals in the other families. In order to stave off these struggles, custom sometimes provided for the assassination of all the applicants except the one chosen by the king. But although he had been chosen and although the issue seemed clear-cut, the king's position was no stronger, since these family murders, which were the very negation of kinship, tended further to isolate the sovereign from his own milieu. The dynasty no longer existed except in name, the royal family was dissolved and the king was left *alone* to face those who ruled over the succession.

The weakness of the dynasty could be exploited by all those with power who were likely to oppose the king, such as the *cabecere*[5] Francisco de Souza in Dahomey, who plotted a *coup d'état* against King Adandozan (1818). 'As for finding an Agossouvi [sovereign] who would agree to replace Adandozan, Francisco's only problem was that there were too many to choose from. There were many princes and each dreamed of reigning before his death' (Sy, 1965: 211). The successor chosen by the Council always seems to have been the one chosen by the king, but this is because the king anticipated the Council's refusals. Sy (ibid.: 205) relates how Agonilo eliminated from the succession one of his sons whom he knew would be turned down by the Council, using the pretext that his toes overlapped (from Dunglas).

It was at this point that the divinization of the king completed his isolation from temporal matters by locking him into an illusory omnipotence.[6] K. Hopkins (1978, ch. 5) provides some interesting reflections on the divinization of the Roman emperors. In his opinion, divinization ensured that power lasted beyond the person of the emperor, reconciled the moral and temporal orders, provided a 'catholic'[7] vocation for the empire through its universality, and consolidated the nation in its diversity. These explanations seem to me correct with respect to all monarchies founded on divine right. But divinization was also, as Hopkins additionally – but less emphatically – points out, a weapon to be used

against the king's authority. It increased his isolation by the
extreme formalization of all contacts with his subjects, even
the most eminent, with foreign ambassadors and with all
those who, in spite of their position, were less than a god. He
could see only those who watched over his divinity and
locked him within it so as to replace him in the exercise of
temporal power. Divinization relegated the king to the use of
ritual power with no effect on reality. In particular, he was
subject to the decisions of an immediate entourage which
acquired rights of life and death over him, if at an opportune
moment it was discovered that his earthly image did not conform to that attributed to God.

The rituals which were inflicted on the divine king de-
socialized him by reversing kinship relations: he had to eliminate, exile or kill his rival brothers. In Oyo the king killed
his mother, who was replaced by a fictitious mother recruited by the court from its midst. The king sometimes had
to marry his sister, which deprived him of relations of affinity. In Monomotapa some of these rituals were contemptible,
like the one which obliged the king to copulate with a female
crocodile during his enthronement, his divinity supposedly
protecting him (perhaps) from this de-humanization. Finally,
the ritual killing of the king, as well as his wives and those
close to him, represented the ultimate subordination of his
divinity to the true power, that of his entourage which took
the decision.

The protocol imposed on him, designed to increase his
spiritual majesty, revealed his temporal powerlessness and
his dependence. He could not leave the palace; sometimes he
could not even be seen; he had to address the people through
a spokesman (it is true that this is common in Africa, but here
it was added to other restrictions). When he was authorized
to appear in public, he was weighed down by so much sump-
tuous finery and regalia that he could not move or make a
gesture without help. When he was authorized to assert his
'omnipotence', it was in the most ridiculous way: the king of
Uganda could throw a javelin over the wall of his palace and
kill at random. The act of omnipotence was robbed of all intention and thus of political significance, and if it helped to
impress the people, it had no more than symbolic content.

The divinization of the 'father-king' was the logical development of the power of an aristocratic and dynastic class. It diluted the royal family, but on the other hand it strengthened the political ideology of kinship by allowing this ideology to sanction class relations and at the same time to neutralize them through fictitious filiation: it justified domination of all the children of God by the king and by those who dominated him. The king could be used as an emblem for the social and political ambitions of the aristocratic class as a whole, and for its desire for conquest. The aristocratic class could spread this ideology without danger to itself, since the divine omnipotence of a mortal could be matched only by his temporal impotence.

When the 'logic' of religion is applied to its god (that is, when the irrational is applied to itself) God becomes the creation of his own creatures. In order to preserve his supernatural powers the king accepted the dictates of diviners, priests and councillors who set to work to freeze him in the timeless immobility of the pure in spirit or to free him under any pretext from his fleshly form. The fate of gods, which are the inventions of man, is to be kept in existence only if they have been tamed and have become the obedient instruments of their priests.

The origin of divine kingship has been sought in religion or in the superstitions of the people. According to Frazer, it was individuals gifted with power over nature who were chosen, at the beginning of man's history, as magician-kings and witch doctors; later they were ambiguously identified both with nature and with their people, whereupon they became divine kings.

This argument merely reformulates the quibblings of the priest-ideologues in these populations; it is an irrational reconstruction of history. The facts generally point not to the coming of a dynasty of witch doctors but to a process of sanctification of the king as kingship lasted and was weakened through its contradictions. While the first sovereigns usually took power through war, through their personal authority, their exploits or their capacity to resolve certain crises facing the population, while these early kings shaped the power they wielded, it was their successors who, sooner or later, became trapped in the nets and rules of the supernatural. The king did not impose his divinity on his entourage: it was his entourage who decked him out with divinity. It was a manifestation not of the king's absolutism, but of his absolute weakness. The sanctification of the king took place when royalty had already been diminished by quarrels over succession, when the royal family was in the process of being dissolved, and when the dynasty had been compromised. The isolation of the sovereign at each succession made him receptive to the suggestion that he was unique, while his growing dependence on those who had isolated him and the effective loss of his temporal power induced him to transcend his worldy impotence by the omnipotence of the solitary god. In order to elevate him from the state of king to that of god, it was necessary only to take to their extreme the virtues which legitimated his functions, using the ideological resources available in history and culture.

From then on, the characteristics of divine kingship could no longer be explained with reference to kingship alone but in terms of the transformations and logical contradictions imposed on ideology during the process. In anthroponomic societies, the sanctification of the king seems to have developed in two ways. The first was based on patriarchal notions borrowed from the ideology of kinship in domestic societies; the second on a resurgence of sacerdotal functions entrusted in certain lineage societies to 'sacred' persons.

'The king', wrote Aristotle (*Politics*, I: 1259), 'is in the same relation to his subjects as the head of a family to his children.' This analogy is frequent in royal systems and leads in fact to practices which are the reverse of the father–children relations found in domestic societies, as we shall see in the part of this book which deals with the war economy.

At the political level, this led to the justification of divinization. As he transcended the function of father, the king's ancestrality was extended beyond that of all the other fathers and doyens in the kingdom. If he was to be the father of their children, his ancestors had also to be the fathers of their ancestors. The king's genealogy tended to be traced further and further back in time. As the number of his subjects increased, so his ancestors went further and further back. At the limit, the ancestor reached eternity and became a god, the king became his 'son' incarnate and the whole of humanity became the king's children. The claim that royal power was universal was the corollary of the king's eternity. These were the two logical dimensions of imperial absolutism.

On the other hand, the divine king calls to mind the sacerdotal persons, weighed down by restrictions, whom one finds in certain domestic societies. These persons were taken in hand by the community; their function was to concentrate bad luck in their own persons.[8] In order to be close to supernatural forces, they had to respect several constraints: they were confined to their court, they could neither eat nor sleep in public, they could not marry or have sexual relations. Their company was considered dangerous, except for certain individuals like children before the age of puberty or women after the menopause. The kingdom's ideologues found it convenient to transform these functions into divine posturings and to inflict them on kings who were already partly reduced to statues and unable to refuse this other image of kingship, in spite of the fact that it was incongruous for them to be their own priests.[9]

Divinization was the road to this priesthood. To be god meant to be close to God, to submit oneself to rules of behaviour which were different from those of ordinary people. It meant accepting rituals, restrictions and prohibitions. In this ideological framework, the king had to learn to be divine and thus to submit himself to those who, having put him in this position, claimed to be able to teach him. To be divine was to accept the responsibility for supernatural manifestations which only a supernatural being could control: rain, calamities, the results of battles. The king's fate was bound up with the nation's destiny.

In the process of weakening divine power, the role of

divination, as an effective means of influencing – or even controlling – power, must be emphasized.

The diviner[10] was the constant companion of the royal councils. It was he who consecrated the heir to the throne by discovering in him the marks of royalty. He decided whether or not the king had the charisma which could transcend fate and guarantee his legitimacy.

As regards ordinary people, the diviner could certainly turn to the interpretation of signs provided by chance according to a conventional code. At this level of society the oracles operated within the field of probabilities. But at the level of politics, at the very heart of the intrigues which created and destroyed power, divination acquired such importance that at critical moments it could only reflect decisions which had already been taken or successful schemings in order to stamp them with the irrefutable marks of fate. For the court diviner's clairvoyance depended only on himself and on those with whom he had contact. His divinations were, therefore, merely opportunistic.

Through divination, the king's capacity to decide in the last resort was separated from his capacity to govern. If the king himself had been the diviner, his power would have been considerable; but, deprived of the capacity to decide, or forced to submit his most important decisions to the ratification of the diviner, he was powerless.[11] Thus divination, whose commands the king was obliged to obey, blinded him to his own divine nature and deafened him to messages from the supernatural, which he could hear only through the intermediary of the priest. In this way divination helped to dispossess the sovereign not only of his royal attributes but also of the gifts which his divinity should have granted him.

 These divine kings – isolated, immobilized, deafened and sooner or later comdemned – were the masks and sacrifices of the real power, which was wielded in the shadows of their artificial brilliance.

Is it so easy, even for a king, to accept death – particularly by execution?

It is said that one of the kings of Monomotapa, who in

earlier times might have agreed, refused to kill himself because he had lost a tooth, as his Council ordered, and continued to rule for a long time. Times had changed. This king had managed to free himself from oppression.[12] If he refused to die for such a futile reason, in spite of the example of his forebears, how can one believe that others accepted without demur?[13]

Moreover, the king usually does not die alone. His wives were very often condemned with him, as well as his closest and most faithful servants: none of those who might be capable of accumulating knowledge which was essentially royal could be spared, and the new king could not be left with a court experienced in government. Although all these victims allegedly accepted their fate for the joy of serving their beloved master even in the next world, it must have been disagreeable for them.

Thus the king, his servants and his wives, his slaves and his eunuchs, were bound together in their terrible fate. Bound and thus allied. For the palace slaves, protecting the king against death was also self-protection. Their loyalty to the sovereign became the security for their own lives and for his. The court slave was encouraged to block the aristocratic absolutism of the councils of nobles. For this purpose, the ancillary functions of the palace slave officers were transformed into decision-making powers. A new form of government was to be established, composed, recruited and perpetuated according to rules imposed by the state of the slave.[14]

2 HENCHMEN

Court slavery seems to have existed in all slave-owning aristocratic societies.[15] Sometimes its extent was stupefying: we know that the 700 eunuchs who belonged to the *askia* of Sonxai were constantly at his side, ready to hold out 'the sleeve of their clothes for him to spit into' (*TEF*: 208). But not all slaves had such futile and prestige-related functions. The *askia* also used eunuchs as leaders in war (*TEF*: 129). We shall see later that in Dahomey, women slaves, sometimes in their thousands, were absorbed by 'the capacious bellies of the various royal palaces' (Skertchly, 1874); they filled almost every conceivable function, from the most humble household tasks to war, spying, administration, procreation and pleasure. Men were also employed in the palaces in positions of trust and command, including the highest (Manning, 1975: 90). The *damel* (king) of Kayor employed slaves as leaders in war, governors of the provinces, tax collectors, and so on. These slaves gave orders to free men and themselves had the use of goods, slaves, cattle and lands. They were titled and inalienable in practice, and occupied the posts of true dignitaries of the kingdom (Arch, OM: K18: 10). 'They made and unmade kings' (V. Monteil, 1967: 269). Samori had placed one of these slaves, 'who were called "*dougoukounasigi*", at the side of each village chief: the slave gave orders to the village chief and in fact represented the Almany' (Binger, 1893: 33–4). Nadel remarks on the wide spectrum of their functions at the Nupe court, where they ranged from slaves employed in the most material tasks to the eunuchs of the harem, the bodyguards, the police, the provincial delegates, the messengers, the tax collectors, and so on. These slaves also had titles granted by the king.[16] But once they had been appointed, writes Nadel (1942: 106–7), they were civil servants of the kingdom rather than the king himself. This last remark contradicts the observations of most other authors. It does not seem that in other areas the slaves acquired, merely through their appointment to a position of responsibility, such a degree of civic conscience.[17]

In fact, Fisher and Fisher note that 'slave officials of all kinds were recurrent features of African government aiming at centralization and often at despotism' (1970: 137). The appointment of court slaves was often the sovereign's prerogative. Political functions, badly carried out by foolish princes, fell into the hands of zealous servants. Dunbar (1977: 171) points out that in Damagaram at the end of the nineteenth century posts held by members of the royal lineage were passed to slaves, such as that of commander in chief of the armies or chief receiver of revenue. The same evolution took place among the Kom of what was formerly British Cameroon, a slaving State and a provider of slaves, where

Chilver and Kaberry (1967: 148) find a growing distinction between the Council of the country's notables, governed according to the rules of kinship, and the Council of the king, recruited among 'common people' but not hereditary. Becker and Martin (1975: 294–5) point to the dominant influence which the 'captive chiefs' and the *tyedo* (armed retainers) had acquired in the political life of Kayor and Baol, as well as to the diminished role of the *laman*, representatives of the rural families.

Wilks (1967: 209) similarly finds among the Ashanti

> the rise of a controlled bureaucracy, the eclipse of the older traditional authorities, the growth of elaborate organizations of household troops (and palace eunuchs . . .). The increasingly authoritarian character of Ashanti kingship was mirrored in the increasingly absolutist nature of the Ashanti State.

This bureaucracy, which supplanted the power of the Amantoo chiefs, *primus inter pares* with the king (Wilks, 1967: 209), was made up of individuals of servile origin. Wilks seems reluctant to admit this, although Rattray (1923: 43–4), to whom he refers, as well as other authors, mention the employment of slaves at court and also in the army. (See also Terray, 1976: 312).

Randles reports a similar evolution in the seventeenth century in the ancient kingdom of Kongo (1968: 62):

> The personal authority of the king increased in the capital while that of the State Council and the ruling caste tended to decline. In 1632, the king's entourage consisted of slaves, since he could no longer trust either the nobles or those who were his councillors in name only.

Slaves also seem to have had an increasingly important position among the former royal servants of King Mogho Naaba (Mossi), at the expense of the noble lineages (Izard, 1975: 283). It was they who surrounded him, while 'the agnatic blood relatives of the king were systematically kept at a distance' (ibid.: 292). Apart from the apparently neutral

functions which made the household officers into an anceocracy,[18] they were also army leaders and responsible for repression (Skinner, 1964).

In Benin, the nobles who in principle chose the king's successor lost their power to individuals nominated by the king
with non-hereditary titles, the Eghaebho (Bradbury, 1967:
16): 'At Maradi most royal title-holders were systematically
divorced from administrative responsibility, jural and economic power and economic resources. They were dependent
on the largesse of senior officials [who were slaves or
eunuchs], on gifts . . .' (Smith, 1967: 108). 'All princes were
under the eunuch Galadimas' jurisdiction, their behaviour
being reviewed critically to select the most suitable successor'
(ibid.).

A similar development may be observed in the kingdom of
Porto-Novo, where power fell into the hands of a tyrannical
slave (Akindele and Aguessy, 1953: 45), while in Oyo the
powerful Council of Notables was weakened when the most
important among them, the commander of the army, was replaced by a eunuch, the Otun Efa (Morton Williams, 1967:
41).

Thus, in all these examples – and others can be found –
slave henchmen were close enough to the king to form a barrier against the representatives of the noble families.

3 EUNUCHS

Eunuchs were almost invariably in a crucial position among
court slaves. They were present wherever court slavery
existed. It is true that eunuchs were sometimes prestige
objects (as at the court of the *askia*) which some sovereigns
forbade their subjects to own; they were preferred as guards
for the *harem*: but this is not the main reason why this category of slaves was castrated.[19] Women in the harems could
have been much more securely guarded by other women
than by castrated men, whose desire and capacity to fornicate
were not, it seems, removed by the operation.[20] In fact there
were two forms of emasculation: one, 'against the belly'
(Deschamps, 1971: 19), which removed the entire genital

organs; and another which was limited to the removal of the testicles. Only the first made coitus impossible. However, emasculation was generally performed by the second method to prevent mortality, which was already high and costly, affecting 75 to 90 per cent of the young victims.[21] This mortality raised the value of the survivors, who were worth four to ten times as much as an ordinary slave of the same age (Cuoq, 1975: 68; Abitbol, 1979: 217).[22]

The high number of eunuchs (in spite of the cost and the importance given to their 'conditioning')[23] shows that demand exceeded the needs of the harems alone. In practice their employment was much more political in nature.

Wittvogel (in Hopkins, 1978: 188, n.42) and Coser (1964) found that in China the rise of the eunuchs under the Tang and Ming dynasties coincided with attacks by the emperors on the hereditary power of the nobles. Dunbar finds a similar phenomenon in Damagaram in Africa, where the employment of eunuchs dates from between 1822 and 1846, under the reign of Ibrahim, when they were used more and more often at court: 'at the end of the century five of the top officials at the court were eunuchs' (1977: 163). During this period, 'critical changes occurred in the organization of the military and bureaucratic structure of the kingdom', at the expense of the aristocrats (Dunbar, 1977: 172). It is indeed the particularity of the eunuch not to be able to pass on anything – not life, nor goods, nor titles, nor functions. By replacing an aristocrat with a eunuch in government, the sovereign could retain his control over the prerogatives and goods he entrusted to him. He retained control over his own succession. He satisfied himself that no lineage was likely to seize titles and spared himself the problem of taking back from an heir the prerogatives attributed to his own person.[24] The other advantage was the possibility of disposing at any time of an individual who was still a slave and over whom the master thus still had rights of life and death.[25]

But for all this, the eunuch was no different from the slave, who was also deprived of descendants. Why were court slaves, who had been deliberately chosen because of their social inability to be parents, replaced by eunuchs?

The eunuchs with whom the sovereign surrounded himself in order to keep his political rivals at bay were invested with functions which were all the more important in that they were used as a barrier against persons of higher rank.

Although at first the shift of power towards slaves took place to the detriment of the rival noble houses, it later worked to the disadvantage of the members of the royal lineage itself. As the functions entrusted to slaves brought them close to power, and as the slaves replaced kin who might have aspired to power, the condition of the king's court members necessarily became more and more incongruent with kinship. While the court slaves were instruments of attack or protection against rival families, the eunuchs seem to have been those among the slaves who could counter threats from closer at hand, from the members of the reigning family itself. Thus the presence of eunuchs at court seems to suggest that the sovereign was protecting himself not only against nobles in rival houses but also against his own kin. Their presence seems to be an indication of the sovereign's isolation within his own house and of his distrust of his own 'brothers'.[26]

Eunuchs were a better means of keeping the members of the royal family at bay than ordinary slaves. It is true that their use was generalized and that they were also used to keep at bay nobles in rival families. It was not always possible, nor was it necessary, to distinguish between threats from the aristocracy and those from the dynasty. But the emergence of the eunuch and his functions in the dynastic system were probably based more on his role as anti-prince than as anti-noble. In this way the eunuch pushed to its limit that aspect of slavery which is the opposite of kinship and revealed its dialectic. Through his mutilation the eunuch incorporated the social state of the slave, who was denied kin only by law. But once the eunuch was sterile in body, it was no longer necessary for his state to be that of a slave, or even for him once to have been a slave. His physical constitution exempted him from this state. This is why in Rome there were numbers of enfranchised imperial eunuchs, while in imperial China poor free-born families castrated their children in the hope that they would carve out careers at court. Though slaves labouring the land were also forced into the total sterility demanded by profits from slavery, non-productive slaves like armed retainers or court slaves (henchmen) could form couples. Nevertheless, this prerogative, which resulted from their separation from economic activity, made them into a threat if they came close to the political activities of the court, since it could provide them with a means of building lineages with administrative responsibilities and of taking over power through a network of matrimonial alliances.

Through castration, therefore, the court slave was reduced to his essence. The eunuch was the slave *par excellence*, the slave whose physical state locked him into his legal state, whatever his juridical fate might be; and who, in particular, unlike the court slave, was unable to build a hereditary aristocracy or a dynasty which could usurp power.

4 ALL-PURPOSE COURTESANS

Since women can do anything, from cooking to fighting wars and even to having children, they can be very extensively and very subtly exploited. Within a dynastic system racked by malignant forms of kinship, filiation and succession, they could be exploited as women and active agents or as slaves and neutral agents of kinship, according to the desires of the sovereign. The widespread use of slave courtesans in all sorts of roles is illustrated by the pre-colonial kingdom of Dahomey.

Dahomey was first and foremost a warrior State, where the dominant class which emerged was military and aristocratic, backed up by a powerful army. This class organized itself around an economy and an authority based on class slavery, which ensured both its military power and its ability to dominate the Dahomeyan people as well as the peoples among whom it captured. The instruments of this internal and external domination were the army, the palace and the plantations. Supervision and labour were essentially carried out by slaves in all three institutions, but it was in the palace that women played a major role.

The palace, site of power, was filled with contradictions which developed and were resolved according to the model described above. Since at this stage of the development of the aristocracy power emerged from domestic society, and since this power was applied to and dominated the domestic communities, it tended to borrow the trappings of kinship to enforce its ideological domination: the king was the 'father' of his subjects, the people owed tribute to the king just as cadets owed labour to their elders, the country was ruled by one family among other families, and so forth.

But in practice the exercise of power and class domination could not conform to the rules of domestic society in the strict sense. The preservation of power within a single aristocratic lineage reduced social kinship to biological kinship: collateral succession opened the way to bloody quarrels and royal multigamy diluted elderhood and filiation through arbitrary choices. In contrast to domestic societies, membership of an aristocratic or royal family was a source of rivalry, not solidarity, between kin. Brothers or sons, even more than wives, became potential or real enemies. In order to protect himself from their pretensions to succession, the king had to keep them at a distance and thus govern without them or even in opposition to them. Since he rejected family collegiality, he was forced to surround himself with councillors who were dynastically neutral and whose status prevented them from laying claim to the throne or to an inheritance.

In a system of virilineal filiation, the slaves (especially the eunuchs among them) *but also the women* had the advantage of *dynastic neutrality* and provided the safeguards the sovereign sought.[27] However, in surrounding himself with anti-kin, the king exposed himself to another danger. The servants of the king who were useful for his protection gradually formed a barrier which isolated him from his family, his class and the people. Masked by a king who was more and more paralysed by the hieratic rituals imposed on him by his entourage, the anceocratic college filtered information before it reached him, selected the individuals he could meet and reduced the sovereign to a symbolic and representative role. Power

shifted towards them. The king could only sporadically recover part of his power by using his royal image or the instruments of matrimonial control left to him (cf. above).
This anceocracy, often servile in origin and – at the Dahomey
court, for example – female, could not recruit according to
the rules of kinship without itself being placed in the same
vulnerable position from which it profited. It therefore recruited through co-optation of other socially neutral individuals – that is, of other slaves and other women. In this context women slaves were doubly excluded from dynastic
pretensions. This twofold incapacity gave them a twofold
advantage which explains the apparent power of the women
at the Dahomey royal court. Some were the counterparts of
male civil servants in various districts of the kingdom. From
inside the palace they controlled the administration of the
country (Bay, 1983). But the women who filled these administrative functions were not the representatives of other
women; they did not owe their position to their emancipation as members of a dominated sex. Even if they seemed
emancipated as slaves, they were still alienated as women.

Thus the demand for slaves in general, and for women
slaves in particular, was high at these courts. E. B. Bay
shows that the women in the 'harems', who are often
described as being designed for the king's pleasure, also – and
perhaps primarily – had a political function. It seems that at
the Dahomey court there were few activities to which
women were not assigned. Their tasks included household
work, cooking, pottery, sewing, spying and even war. It is
true that many were also the king's concubines, and they
were indisputably used as procreators as well as for pleasure.[28] But the purpose of this was less to provide descendants for the sovereign than to generate a 'social species' from
which the queen 'mothers' of the sovereign as well as his
wives could be recruited, and around which a fictitious kinship was reconstructed conforming only to rules which could
easily be controlled, such as co-optation rather than birth (cf.
Chapter 7 above).

The employment of women as a matrimonial instrument
of social control must be added to their use as agents of administrative and political power at court. This was one of the

methods used by the court to ensure the loyalty of the social
corps in the service of authority (armed retainers and henchmen) which had been entrusted with executive powers that
could be used against this authority. The harems and con-
vents where such high numbers of young women – many of
them captives – were held constituted reserves from which
the court drew wives who could be assigned to the men in its
service, whose status denied them access to free women. In
this way women and their progeny were provided for the
royal military guard, as we have seen above, in terms of a
system which was self-perpetuating. For instance, it was
agreed that the first-born of all the children of a union would
be returned to the sovereign: if the child was a boy he would
be educated for membership of the guard and thus ensure its
reproduction; if the child was a girl she would be given 'to
one of the members of the guard under the same conditions
(see also Keim, 1983: 14).[29]

Alongside this institutional form of control over the reproduction of a social group, the sovereign – or the court –
could give captive women as a reward or remuneration to
those in favour. Glélé, for example, 'had women distributed
to the people of Agouli who had built the palace of Jegbe'
(Glélé, 1974: 161).

If the use of women at court was peculiar to the Dahomeyan system, the mode of devolution of wives and their
progeny was comparable to the one which prevailed in domestic societies under the aegis of the doyen of the community.
It was indeed as 'wives' that women slaves were exploited
here. Unlike in merchant society, as we shall see, a policy of
reproduction was carried out at the level of the court in
which the female nature of the captive was preserved but
alienated. In every other respect, it was as slaves rather than
as women that they surrounded and protected the king; and
as warriors that they became de-feminized into Amazons.

5 'THE KING'S FLY IS KING'

The slave was the ideal servant, the near-perfect minister,
because the slave was the child of man [*viris*] alone. In

Bamoum images described by Tardits (Seminar, 1975, un-published) the palatine slave was compared to the king's ex-crement, as if the king had given birth to him without re-course to a woman. The king appropriated him directly, without the intervention of wives or affines. The man – par-ticularly the warrior – who captured the alien gave birth to the slave: in this way he acquired the procreative power of a woman, with the difference that the slave produced by him belonged to him alone. The slave, dependent on his master alone, was therefore expected to be loyal to him alone.

Thus the responsibilities entrusted by the sovereign to the slave were accompanied by a specific relation: the trust the king placed in his slave and the loyalty of the slave to his master. The state of the slave favoured this relationship: 'The master found in his captive one in whom he could place the greatest trust, the trust which one places in persons who owe one everything' (Piault, 1975: 348). An obedient *dimajo* (slave), according to a Fula dictum, 'is more useful than a dis-obedient brother' (Labouret, 1955). Such was the extent of this trust that in a Soninke noble family a slave was entrusted with the functions of doyen until the heir reached maturity (Meillassoux, 1975a: 239). It was also a slave who took over between one reign and another in the kingdom of Jara (Jaw-ara, 1976–7: 27).

A Soninke legend describes how Wakane Sako, one of the Wagadu notables (sixth to seventh century), owned a valo-rous slave who was his companion in arms. He was said to kill 99 enemies each time he moved forwards and 99 each time he moved backwards. Maxane's praise-singer is said to have exclaimed: 'Maxane of Kingi, Maxane of Jajiga, Max-ane Sako, child of Maxane the generous, the slave and his master must not accomplish the same feats!' So, the legend concludes, Wakane made his slave into a 'porridge of blood'.[30] In this way the class of masters protected itself against any threat which might be posed by their slaves, not only because of the slaves' defects but also because of their virtues. 'Since he comes from nowhere, the slave can be sent back there at any time' (Terray, 1982a). In Jara of Kingi, the slave who had taken over between reigns was executed when the prince was old enough to reign, 'since, once one has wielded power, one gives it up only with death' (M. Jawara, 1976: 27).

These examples of the absolute authority of the masters over even their favourite slaves reveal their fear that the slaves might usurp their functions and thus their class power. In effect, the service of the master implied relieving him of all effort, undertaking on his behalf all the tasks necessary for his existence and, soon, also the functions for which he was responsible. Through a natural progression this meant replacing him in more and more functions as the service came closer to perfection. It meant gradually identifying oneself with one's master and, if he was king, reigning in his stead. At the Bamoum court, Tardits notes the invasion of power by the slaves:

> The strength of the servants raised the question of whether they would remain an instrument in the service of the power or whether the authority which they wielded through their intervention would result in a new shift of power into their hands. (1980a: 191)

The evolution of the kingdom of Oyo, which provided an example of a king surrounded by a council of nobles, is characteristic of this process. The absolutism of the king, originally conquered or reconquered over the nobility, was once again reduced to the benefit of henchmen slaves who were transformed from the king's weapons against his peers and his kin into his mentors and protectors.

Thus, late in the history of Oyo, the grand eunuch controlled the palace, assisted by other eunuchs and by court slaves chosen by the first among them. Visitors could have access to the king only through the intermediary of the second eunuch. The latter *impersonated* the king in his religious duties, while the first eunuch dealt out justice *in his name*. The third eunuch received the notables of the Grand council *in the king's place* when the king was indisposed, and could also *impersonate him*, dressed in the royal finery, at public ceremonies. It was he who chose the titled slaves responsible for administrative tasks. Among them, the second slave received visitors to the palace. At the same time, each of the palace officers, including the king, was given an adoptive 'mother', whose social origins are not mentioned by Morton Williams (but who was probably of servile origin). The king's 'mother' was present during all visits to the sovereign. She had higher rank than the nobles of the Council. The kinship link between the king and his 'mother' was actively and strictly institutional, since it was created by the *execution of the king's true mother* at his enthronement. Thus a relation of nomination replaced a kinship relation.

At first, these slaves and eunuchs who were nominated by the king or even by the Council of Nobles probably only exploited their ancillary functions, their positions as intendants or as intimate servants of the king in order to keep nobles and kin at a distance from him. Through their closeness to the king they became his spokesmen and, in the same way, his only source of news from the outside world.

Thus in Oyo the king seems to have been surrounded by these officers without birth, by these women who watched him all the time and these eunuchs who replaced him and even incarnated him on the most important occasions. But the king no longer even had the choice of these officers.

To protect himself against threats from a class of hereditary nobles, the dynast had surrounded himself with another corps, whose members were nominated and, in principle, totally dependent on his choice. But once it had been established, the administrative functions performed by this *de facto* government, which existed alongside the outdistanced and formalized government of the aristocrats, enabled it to make its own rules. Dynastic and kinship relations ceased to function as relations of reproduction for those who wielded power. The trust put by the king in his nominated servants gave them the prerogative of nominating other servants in their turn. Once those who had been nominated could in turn nominate, this new governing corps, through a logical progression, ceased to be selective and became *co-optive*. This process is illustrated by a Mossi legend about the origins of power: the prime minister had a handsome young man, whom he had met by chance, nominated in his own place by the Mogho Naaba. The young man met another and had him nominated second minister. The process of co-option was presented as inherent to the origins of the kingdom! (Delobsom, 1933: 63, n.1).

The court slave and the eunuch created a new model of government underlying the old, a new political system in which functions were now neither hereditary or lifelong. This bureaucratic system, founded on relations and hierarchies which were not those of kinship or birth, was imposed even on its creator. As the king was locked within this bureaucracy he tended to become the last of his kind. As the only member of a dynasty within a co-optive system, he was subject to the latter's laws in his own turn. He was a dynast in name only, since the succession soon escaped his control. It was the eunuchs, in Oyo, who watched over the behaviour of the princes and chose the most worthy among them. It was they who finally co-opted the hereditary king! Any dynast is reduced to impotence once he can no longer refer to filiation or active right to paternity in order to choose his own successor, on his own. In government by the eunuchs, the multigamous king, the paragon of kinship and a father a hundred times over, was excluded in his turn from heredity and castrated by the castrated. Isolated by his servile entourage, the king could thus be directed, maintained or relegated to a divine role as the mask of legitimacy and the hereditary backing of a court run by shadowy masters.

The political problem was no longer posed at the level of kingship, which had become bloodless and weak, but at the level of this corps which was servile in origin: could it constitute a *political* class which could replace the aristocracy? There are some rare examples of the usurpation of power by slaves in the history of some African kingdoms. It was said that in Melli in the thirteenth century Sakura was a slave who had seized supreme power for the period of his reign. A similar case is reported in detail in Bamoum history (Tardits, 1980a: ch. 3), where the reign of a *panka* (chief of the servile guard) lasted twenty years before the return of the legitimate lineage. In Porto-Novo, the *lari*, a slave nominated by the king, wielded real power under the nominal reign of Demessi (Akindele, 1953: 55–6).

These seizures of power were shortlived. At most they lasted as long as the usurper survived, for the slaves always adopted monarchic and aristocratic forms of power during their reigns. They inserted themselves into an already existing system without modifying its organic structures, so that their domination came to an end as soon as the question of its renewal arose. Hopkins correctly notes, with regard to the eunuchs at the court of the Roman emperors, that, unlike a clergy, 'they had no corporate existence by which they could transmit inherited wealth' (1978: 190). This is true also of the slaves, to the extent that their state continued to deprive them of legitimate descendants. However, in their case this obstacle was not physically insurmountable, as it was for the eunuchs.

Thus, in order to exist politically with the mode of recruitment which was theirs, the slaves lacked an essential dimension: that of being able, like the Christian or Brahman clergies, to be granted or to assume the right to corporate existence, with rights of ownership and of transmission of goods and prerogatives among themselves: renewal by co-option could then become an organic mode of social and political reproduction and the basis of collegiate power. In the absence of this, the mode of recruitment and renewal on which the political power of the slaves was based (co-option) was only a delegated form of royal power (nomination) dependent on the existence of a central authority, even if this authority was itself nominated.

Once the usurper personalized his reign he could govern only by perpetuating the monarchy, either by hiding behind a puppet monarch or by declaring himself king. In the latter case the usurper, if he was to take usurpation of power to its logical conclusion, had to re-create a dynasty in order to have an heir. This was impossible for the eunuch, but not for the court slave. But in so doing the new sovereign merely substituted one dynastic system for another, without changing the forms of power. The specificity of government by slaves, as it functioned under the monarchy (through co-option), disappeared with the usurpation of supreme power by the slave. This was not a case of a bureaucratic class replacing an aristocracy but only of a courtier creating for his own benefit a dynasty and a court which were similar to those he had supplanted, without changing their basic structures.

If 'the king's fly is king', the court slave, invested with supreme powers because of his closeness to the throne, was no more than a king. The first aristocrats of servile origin, the authors of *coups d'état* against their masters, owed their nobility only to the usurpation of titles which corresponded to functions they already performed. It was their descendants who were to become aristocrats by birth.[31]

Although it also grew out of a corps of slaves, this court nobility of servile origin differs from that of the warrior barons who emerged from brigandage and plunder, like the *ton-jon* of Segu. The latter were the actors in a revolt; the former were merely the artisans of a palace revolution. The warrior barons were the product of a confrontation with the aristocratic class; the court slaves were the product of this class. The warrior barons created and built their power by force; the court slaves diverted power which already existed.[32]

However, in neither case did these slaves manage to lead their congeners towards freedom. Slavery persisted under the reign of the slaves. This was an evolution, not a revolution: it raises the question of class relations in slaving societies based on a war economy.

B

The War Economy

In military slaving societies, slavery emerged not from the war economy but from capture.

Military specialization and the emergence of an administration and a permanent army with an increasing need for men and arms created a social and political gap within society between rural populations producing subsistence goods on the one hand and specialist corps secreted by the aristocracy, detached from the land and thus dependent on the rural population for their provisions, on the other. The supply of food to the palace, the barracks and the non-agricultural population of the royal quarters was a difficult problem to resolve in an economy where productivity was low. It involved internal relations of production which affected the population as a whole and defined its components. The resolution of the problem triggered off class divisions within free-born society, between aristocrats and peasants, which were added to and articulated with the divisions between masters and slaves.

A few historical examples show how this problem arose, which social fractions were involved and which relationships were built between them. They show that in these societies slavery was never the only relation of production, nor was it the main source of production. These examples illustrate how the dominant class could be located at the pole of two

class relations. They also show how the process of trans-
forming social relations can be traced back (though it did not
reach the same point in all cases) along a path parallel to that
of the political transformations described above.

1

Cases

In the practice of war, as soon as campaigns last several days, the military authorities are faced with a problem of supplies; to resolve it the relation between soldiers and agricultural production must be defined. Is the soldier to produce his own rations or is he to consume the surplus-product of other producers? In the latter case, how is the society to be organized in order to effect this transfer?

1 THE PEASANT–SOLDIERS

In the kingdom of Segu, each man was in principle both a peasant and a soldier: 'When war broke out, those who had to go to war, went. When the war was over, everyone returned to the fields. This is why the kingdom of Segu is powerful' (Jara royal tradition, in Sauvageot, 1965). Even the troops who depended directly on the king produced their means of subsistence in the framework of village organization (Bazin, 1975: 176s.; Roberts, 1984).

In the savannah, the division of the year into two distinct seasons of nearly equal length, with only one being devoted to agricultural work, meant that men could be kept on the land during the rainy season and sent to war during the dry season. The choice of this military season certainly had strategic advantages: the armies could move more easily over dry land, new harvests could be plundered, herds which had come down from the Saharan pastures could be raided, and so on. Moreover, since the army was not mobilized during the agricultural season, the peasant–soldiers could produce their own food for the year and thus provide their own means of subsistence for the campaign. In order to compensate for military losses which might disorganize production, the authorities were concerned to reconstitute pseudo-lineages from their captives[1] (Bazin, 1975: 178). On their side, the *ton-jon* and the *sofa* could employ their booty of men and women captives to produce their own subsistence, although these ruffians were more likely to drink away the proceeds of their abductions.

Thus captives in Segu were destined for several uses. Some were sold by the court in order to procure horses, arms, equipment, prestige goods and also food. The *maraka* community which had settled in the merchant towns and exploited slaves for cultivation and in the production of craft goods was one possible outlet. Some proportion of the slaves belonging to the king formed a sort of military corps, cultivating for themselves or employing slaves for this purpose. Still others seem to have been used exclusively for agriculture, waterway transport or crafts, sometimes supervised by artisans of caste.

This form of organization, in which soldiers and cultivators were mixed, was not completely advantageous; it encouraged combatants to desert the battlefield to return to their fields as soon as the rains came, even if the military operation had not been concluded. After three months besieging Kirango, when winter came, the soldiers of Segu muttered: 'Our fields will produce nothing; we would do better to return to them' (C. Monteil, 1924: 53). It also limited the involvement of Segu's allies: 'My men can well stay during the dry season, the king of Dina explained to Biton, who had come to ask for his support, but they will have to come back in winter to cultivate' (ibid.: 41).

The subordination of war to the agricultural cycle impeded the formation of a permanent army and the constitution of a corps of professional soldiers, which would have been the logical result of the mercantilism linked to wars of capture. Indeed, in Segu tendencies towards military professionalism appeared. Dakoro, Biton's son and successor, was compelled at one point brutally to order the *ton-jon* and their men to go back to their fields, triggering off a crisis which led to his assassination (C. Monteil, 1924: 55, 302). Exempting the *ton-jon* from cultivation meant renouncing the doctrine of self-sufficient militias on which the organization of the kingdom had been founded; it meant allowing a permanent army to be built up, dependent on the production of a class of exploited peasants, and thus establishing relations of production parallel to those of slavery and allowing class relations to develop among free Bamana.

These developments did in fact take place in Segu – through exchange with the *maraka* communities, who took over part of this exploitation, probably delayed them – but it was in other States that their consequences were most striking.

2 SUBSISTENCE SLAVERY

Permanent war led to a permanent warrior hierarchy and the emergence of a military class which was detached from all productive activity. This specialization was accompanied by an ideology which reinforced it. The dangers faced by the warrior encouraged an exaggeration of martial virtues to the exclusion of all others, and a contempt for all peaceful activity. The aristocratic class generally does not cultivate the land and has a poor opinion of those who are involved in such lowly activity. 'The Tuaregs are too proud', wrote Daumas (1857: 143) 'to cultivate the land like slaves.' Saliou Balde reports similar attitudes on the part of the Fula of Fuuta Jallo (1975).[2]

Thus the nobility detached itself as the first social and institutional form of the permanent and non-productive army. But its existence as a *social class* presupposes the simultaneous establishment of relations of production through which part of the social product is allocated to it and which contribute to its renewal. Evidently, it was war which provided the means.

Geoffroy de Villeneuve (1814), who visited Senegambia at the beginning of the nineteenth century, sums up in a few lines a situation which seems to have been common to military aristocracies: 'All the great men and the rich, especially in the conquered territories, have a large number of slaves . . . [who] cultivate the land, look after the cattle and are responsible for all servile labour.' The dominant class among the Nupe, which owned the land, Nadel reports (1942: 252), did not work on it. It employed slaves, pawns and clients for this work. N. Klein (unpublished: 59) notes that 'officialdom and even the "middling orders" in Kumasi depended largely on slaves to produce their food'. In Bamoum country, the aristocratic families supplied themselves from their rural estates which were cultivated by slaves and servile families (Tardits, 1980a, ch. 8); the same was true of the dominant class among the Mawri (Latour, E. de, 1981: 262). The aristocracy – which, because of its functions, was a permanent army – constituted itself into a social and political class through the establishment of relations of production based on capture. The king, as we have seen, confronted this aristocracy with his own armed slaves, another form of permanent army but one which depended on him and was gradually detached from all productive activity. The consumption of this military corps was added to that of the aristocratic class. Furthermore, the development of the court as an instrument of government and the management of war and the State, as well as the political bastion of a growing bureaucratic corps, the increase in the number of the king's wives, the multiplicity of artisans responsible for military equipment and for prestige goods – all contributed to a growth in consumption which necessitated continuous supplies.

The Bamoum court provides a relatively clear example of urban development and the role of slavery. At the beginning of the century this court numbered 15,000 out of a total population of 70,000 (Tardits, 1980a: 922); thus more than 20 per cent of the population can be said not to have produced their own means of subsistence. In fact the court was fed by thirty royal *domaines* maintained by subjugated labourers and free-born families. If one adds 7,000 aristocrats belonging to 700 lineages who were fed by the slaves on their own lands,

there were some 23,000 people to be fed by a total peasant
population (of all ages) of 47,000. This last figure, represent-
ing almost exactly two-thirds of the population, is also the
figure given elsewhere by Tardits (1980a: 524) as the number
of 'Slaves' in the kingdom.

In fact, the royal and seigneurial *domaines* which supplied
the dominant class of the Bamoum were cultivated both by
slaves of various ethnic origins, deliberately mixed together,
and by settlers. The slaves could be sold, they were at the
mercy of their master; some were granted allotments and
attached to the land which could be sold or ceded with them.

The slaves cultivated a strip of land which supplied their
food, even during the time they worked on the masters'
lands. Men, women and children worked on the masters'
lands under the supervision and at the demand of an intendant of servile origin, to complete the tasks necessary for
cultivation. Among these tasks, weeding, clearing and har-
vesting, both on the individual strips and on the masters'
lands, were assigned to women, as well as the heavy, slow
work of transporting the product weekly from the land to the
masters' residences in the capital (the return journey sometimes took the whole week). It therefore seems that the
women's share of agricultural work in this non-commercial
food production was considerable, though we do not know
how many women were involved relative to men.

Only a limited number of slaves were 'married' (Tardits,
1980a: 467) – or rather, 'settled' – and the agricultural population was maintained 'by the regular campaigns which the
Bamoum constantly waged against their neighbours until the
arrival of the Europeans' (ibid.).

Slavery, to the extent that we have defined it as reproducing itself through capture, seems thus to have dominated relations of production at court and among the aristocracy. But
it was not exclusive, since an indeterminate proportion of
agricultural labourers were allotment or settled slaves, whose
social status was inferior but who were permitted to live in a
couple and to have progeny. It does not seem that any kind of
'patriarchal slavery' developed among ordinary people.

3 THE TRIBUTE OF THE 'TRIBES' OF THE *ASKIA*

The chronicles report that *Askia* Mohamed (1493–1528) (the first of the Sonxai dynasty to bear this title) inherited from the predecessors he had supplanted – the kings of Melli and the Shi dynasty – no fewer than twenty-four 'tribes' subjected to different forms of exploitation. Among three of them, the men were not allowed to marry until the king had given '40,000 cowries to the bride's parents to ensure that they and their children would still belong to him' (*TEF*: 107–8). In other words, by going through the motions of paying bridewealth for the bride, the king reserved her progeny for himself and dispossessed the husband of his paternal rights. By making use in this way of the custom of bridewealth in domestic society, the king reactivated the juridical state of non-paternity of all the members of these 'tribes', in each generation. Without buying them but by endowing the women, he became the legal father of all their children. He might in turn endow their children, and thus formally fulfil the functions of a 'patriarch'. But, to the extent that he also reserved the right to sell some of these children in order to buy horses (as was often the case), he in fact behaved like a slaver. These individuals were juridically alienable; thus their state was still that of 'slaves'. Yet the system of exploitation was not strictly 'slave', since the king had to pay a certain sum when he settled the slave and reproduction was organized to take place genetically, not through acquisition. In juridical terms these individuals were maintained in a state of slavery, alienable and without rights over their progeny; while their mode of economic reproduction situated them in economic conditions similar to serfdom.

In spite of this situation, these three 'tribes' were subjected to changing forms of exploitation which illustrate changing conditions. During the rule of the kingdom of Melli, each household had to cultivate 40 cubits of land for the king. Under the Shi, 'people were recruited in groups of 100 persons', men and women, to work together, to the sound of the flutes, in the 200-cubit fields, and the product was shared between the king and his soldiers. Finally, under *Askia*

Mohamed, a progressive tax in kind, up to 10 measures of flour, was imposed on the population. A similar progressive but limited tax was applied to the dried fish produced by the Zendj, a tribe of fishermen, who had also to supply pirogues and crews if required. With one exception, only the king could employ and sell the members of these three 'tribes'. Alongside them, the 'Arbi' provided 'servants, confidants, aids and messengers' for the prince (p. 111). Their daughters were employed in the service of the royal wives; the young men provided the king's escort, both in war and peace. They were not obliged to pay dues in kind, but according to the *Tarikh* they did also have to cultivate for the king. Finally, five 'tribes' of smiths had to pay the king fixed dues of 100 spears and 100 arrows per family per year (p. 112).

A system of slavery in the true sense was added to this form of exploitation , which seems to have affected only part of the servile population, during the reign of *Askia* Daouda (1549–83). It seems that in this period (*TEF*: 179s.) the court was supplied by royal rice plantations, each cultivated by 20 to 200 slaves under the direction of *fanfa* ('bosses'), themselves of servile origin. We know that one of these plantations employed 200 slaves supervised by four *fanfa*, who were themselves dependent on a fifth. 'The product which the *askia* extracted from this production was one thousand *sounou* of rice: it was a fixed product which could neither be increased nor reduced' (*TEF*: 179).[3] The *sounou* (*TEF*: 188, n.1) was a measure of volume. Bearing in mind that the minimum capacity of a *mudde*[4] was probably one litre (or one kilogram), each slave must have provided the king with

$$\frac{240 \times 1,000}{200}$$

or 1,200 kilograms of rice per season. This is high, given what we know about the productivity of agriculture under the hoe. Now, the principal *fanfa* on this plantation was 'saturated with riches' and in one year was able to supply the king, at his request, with 1,000 additional *sounou* left over 'from the previous year's harvest', plus some 230 others which he gave as an additional present to the king (ibid.: 187). To this surplus-product must be added the subsistence production which the slaves produced for themselves. Once again, although these figures may not be exact, such high productivity shows at least that the totality of the slaves' sur-plus-product must have been confiscated and that, therefore, they could not have had enough to feed a family. Thus these producers must have been reproduced through capture or purchase, in conformity with the strictest mode of slave ex-ploitation.

In certain years it seems that the total production on the plantations was 4,000 *sounou* (ibid.: 179), or about 960 tonnes. If this quantity represented the whole of the surplus-product, taking into account the slaves' consumption, one can esti-mate that at the rate of productivity above it represented the production of some 800 slaves and the annual consumption of 4,700 free-born persons. Assuming that the *fanfa* kept an equal quantity for themselves – probably a maximal assump-tion – this number must be doubled to give a total of 1,600 labourers subjected to this slave mode of production.

The royal plantations seem to have been widely dispersed, since the *Tarikh* does not suggest that the sovereign moved his court periodically, as was the case in other kingdoms: it is not clear how these far-flung plantations were used.

These descriptions suggest that the Sonxai State contained several forms of exploitation of agricultural labour simulta-neously.

The first was royal slavery as described above, involving labourers organized under the supervision of guards and re-plenished by inflows of new captives. The figures – whose value is merely indicative – suggest that this mode of exploi-tation was limited, since 800 or even 1,600 slaves is a small number needing barely more than 80 to 160 replacement slaves a year. In fact, slavery and the exploitation of lands by supervised teams seem to have been reserved for the court. This restriction can be explained by the pre-eminent right of the sovereign to all captives taken in war: the king must thus have had at his disposal captives whom he could use on his own plantatons, while waiting to sell or redistribute them. Probably for this reason, their numbers varied. The author of the *Tarikh* writes that '*in some years*' the product of these royal lands was 4,000 *sounou*. This can be taken to mean a maxi-mum, resulting either from a favourable climate or from a higher number of slaves on the land because of trends in war or trade. The variability of these numbers also explains how the principal *fanfa* on a plantation – whose dues were fixed – could extract such considerable quantities of rice. Finally, it explains the high returns referred to above, as being the result of a higher number of slaves.

In any case, royal slavery, random and limited, could not have been sufficient to supply the needs of the court. Other forms of exploitation were in operation. The main one was based on dues and affected some of the 'tribes' mentioned earlier: duties in labour, dues in services and in products. The populations subjected to these dues were grouped into 'villages', which seems to mean that they were constituted into para-domestic cells, reproducing genetically but without legal rights over their progeny. Part of this population originated from the deportations of whole villages captured during distant campaigns, some of which kept their original place-name (*TEF*: 214). This was thus a population of slaves, in statutory terms (they had no rights over their progeny and they were legally alienable); but their economic exploitation was similar to serfdom (they set up households and owed only a fixed part of their labour or their product). Under *Askia* Mohamed, this exploitation was transformed. Dues were no longer fixed but became progressive, with an upper limit, which implies a change in the status of the producers. The exploitation of these populations, unlike those on the royal slave plantations, was not undertaken by the king alone. He presented whole 'villages' to notables and particularly to holy marabouts, including both the land and the labour force, for their subsistence and well-being (*TEF*: 30, 137–8). Thus to the royal agricultural slaves must be added those – of whose numbers and mode of exploitation we know nothing – exploited by the aristocrats, the marabouts and other notables of the kingdom, on their own lands. These gifts of villages have sometimes been seen as a Sonxai feudalism.[5] But the *askia* did not grant fiefs; he granted lands whose benefits were uncertain and on which worked populations who were bound to the land – subject, perhaps, to conditions similar to serfdom, but dependent on the king.[6]

We know nothing about the numbers of these servile

populations as a proportion of the total population, or about their composition. It is very probable that a peasant free-born population lived alongside them, but contemporary documents are silent on this subject.

4 PLANTATIONS AND TAXES

The example of Dahomey provides some – incomplete – information on the coexistence of slavery with a free peasantry. In Dahomey, as in most military monarchies, the king (or the palace) received all captives, in terms of a pre-eminent right to all the beings and goods in the kingdom. Snelgrave (1734: 10) reports that the soldiers were given, in the name of the king, five cowries for each slave captured;[7] this was a ridiculously low sum which enabled the confiscation of captives from the rank and file under the guise of payment. Thus the king had the sole use of this booty; part of it was sold and part was used to renew the numbers of soldiers and labourers, some being distributed among the nobles, the most eminent of the warriors, the king's officers or his representatives. The others were immolated.

Commentators have given little attention to the organization of subsistence production. We know that fairly late, at the turn of the century, the king owned plantations which were worked by *captives in the process of being exported* (Le Hérissé, 1911: 53). During the time of Béhanzin, 'dumped in their thousands around the Abomey plateau, they cleared the forests and replaced them with palm trees and particularly with food crops. Thus they fed the population of the palace and the permanent warriors, that is, a population of 20,000 persons' (Le Hérissé, 1911: 90). 'Most of the [king's] slaves were entrusted to the Sogan'[8] and 'dumped in the fields under cultivation' (ibid.). Le Hérissé adds that in his time 'the ruins of six of these encampments' could still be seen.

Thus capture was the sole mode of renewal of the labourers on these royal plantations. The fact that they were employed for only part of their active life and worked in the fields under the direction of royal agents clearly demonstrates a mode of production typical of slavery. Furthermore, these slaves were distinguished from other servile individuals who were given a strip of land and seem to have been employed mostly by the aristocrats. They were also different from the *glési* (labourers who had been servile from birth), who were inalienable in principle but were assigned by the king to the cultivation of lands designed to feed certain of his courtiers (Le Hérissé, 1911: 57). The existence of the aristocracy depended on the distribution of captives by the king. Yet, again according to Le Hérissé (ibid.: 52), 'the gift of a captive was a favour granted to few', mainly princes and servants of the court. They could not be sold without royal permission. The king had sole rights of life and death over all captives in the kingdom and remained their *de facto* owner. The rest of the people do not seem to have had access to captives. We know that captives taken in war were confiscated in exchange for minimal payments, and that the people – except for a few brave warriors whose good fortune gave them entry to the privileged class – did not benefit from royal gifts. It seems that internal trade in slaves did exist in Dahomey, but it appears to have developed late and probably only the rich in the kingdom could afford to buy slaves because of their price.[9] Until the emergence of trade in palm oil, the peasants had few opportunities of producing commodities for sale. The system of royal dues and distribution, combined with the self-sustenance economy, did not favour the development of a market.

The peasant class, which received few or no slaves, was nevertheless subjected to various taxes, dues, fines and duties over and above its burdensome participation in warfare.

Le Hérissé refers to 'sleep money' [*argent du sommeil*]: a poll tax of 4,000 cowries per head, based on an annual census; a mortmain lump sum of 20,000 cowries paid on the death of the head of the family; and, in particular, dues in kind, estimated according to the production of each village, paid in sorghum, maize, spices and later in palm oil. Revenue from these dues (to which Le Hérissé adds the tolls which more particularly affected traders) represented, according to various estimates, one and a half million French francs at the time, out of a total revenue of two and a half million francs.

Dues in labour were paid through an institution, the

dompe, in the form of collective labour (which traditionally took place at village level). Through a process of distortion the *dompe* became a system of forced labour owed to the king by each of the villages in turn. The king pretended to be a member of one of these *dompe* himself and went through the pretence of obeying its rules. Each village also had to supply a required number of young men for the annual wars (Elwert, 1973). They had to bring their own basic needs for the length of the campaign. In principle these recruits were armed by the court, but they preferred to bring their own arms, since the loss of a gun was punishable by death (ibid., from Skertchly). Finally, some categories of artisans had to provide the court with certain products in determinate quantities: the smiths, for example, had to supply bullets for guns, the weavers had to supply lengths of cloth and the wood-workers wooden articles.

Thus a free population and a population of artisans, both subject to extractions – whose nature will be discussed below – coexisted in Dahomey with slaves who were subject to specific exploitation by the aristocracy.

5 SUBCONTRACTING OF WAR

When the inhabitants of a region were brought into submission after repeated plundering, they were not immediately incorporated into the State. They did not immediately become subjects, particularly if the subjects were not exploited. The aim of the capturing State was not conquest, since this would have deprived it of hunting-grounds. Mass selling of an entire subjugated population would have made its reconstitution impossible (while if the population was left behind its defences, it could reconstitute itself). In general, submission was resolved by tribute. The conquered peoples had to hand over goods, including slaves, to the victors. In this way a *modus vivendi* could be established under which the populations agreed peacefully to supply an annual contingent of slaves rather than to be victim to the violence of periodic and repeated invasions. This was the case of the 'tribes of the Sonxai' (cf. B, ch. 1, 2 above), who were obliged to deliver part of their human substance to the *askia*. These peoples were seen as destined to be slaves.

The last of the peoples to come into the orbit of the slaving aristocracies were – logically enough – those who had to pay a tribute in slaves (Bradbury, 1967: 10). Men and women who had previously been raided were voluntarily handed over to the conquerors. This arrangement did not lift the state of war between the two populations, since failure to pay tribute immediately provoked armed reprisals. Some of these tributary populations, rather than delivering their own members, became hunters in their turn and handed over as tribute the captives they had taken. This was true of the Vute of Cameroon, who are the subject of a particularly interesting study (Siran, 1980).

Raided by the armies of the *lamido* of Tibati (in the north of present-day Cameroon), who supplied the Atlantic slave trade at the end of the nineteenth century, the Vute of the Adamawa plateau were brought under submission by their powerful neighbour, after long resistance. However, part of the population escaped to the south. This population rallied to two legendary hunters and warriors and reconstituted itself into a military society. In order to avoid confrontations with the *lamido*'s cavalry, these Vute agreed to pay tributes in slaves and, in order not to have to hand over their own members, began to go in for capture. This society of expatriate cultivators, which had no military tradition, transformed itself into a warrior principality, inventing its own arms, techniques and strategies. Young warriors and hunters brutally confronted their elders. Kinship was replaced by other relationships built around prey, in hunts or in war, through the distribution of game, slaves and women. A military State was established which captured many more slaves than the *lamido* required. The whole of the population, including the women, took part in war. Nevertheless, it was noted at the time of the German conquest that only the notables owned enough captives to free themselves from labour. The distribution effected by the prince seems to have reduced democracy among warriors and replaced it with the power of an aristocracy. The sovereign handed over the tribute in adult captives to the *lamido*, sold the excess to the merchants of Kano,[10] and kept the women and the adolescents, whom he distributed as he chose. Among the latter, he recruited young men for his personal guard, whom he equipped and provided with wives. He chose his confidants from this entourage.

In the case of the Vute, the demand for slaves originated from their powerful neighbour, but the military and dynastic structures which developed as a result of wars of capture were similar to those found elsewhere, in Segu or among the Mawri, during the early phases of the constitution of warrior societies (Piault, 1975, 1982). Wars of capture tended to re-create the same types of social and political relations. Relations of filiation and elderhood, proper to domestic society, were at first replaced by relationships based on co-option, where members were recruited on the basis of their qualities (military valour); later the military class which had been constituted in this way was penetrated by dynastic practices which led it towards hereditary aristocracy.

The Vute system emerged in response to the demand for slaves, and had no other reason for existing. Its dependence on the slave trade and on the *lamido* was absolute: 'As soon as it was no longer possible to wage war, this sort of political system necessarily collapsed', writes J.-L. Siran (1980: 52). Various indications suggest that in this society, now a warrior society, agricultural activity had almost disappeared and relations of production were unimportant relative to the relations which resulted from warfare. It seems that, as in Segu, an indeterminate but doubtless significant proportion of needs was supplied by pillage or by trade in booty. Vute society at this state was no more than a war machine; class relations between warriors and peasants had not developed to the point where a mode of production could be established between them which could be perpetuated independently of its insertion into the sphere of world slavery. They were the cutting edge of world slavery within the slave-supplying regions. At the other extreme were the slave-buying populations, within which the slaves found their final employment and their masters. The disappearance of one end of this chain led to that of the other, and vice versa.

But not completely due to African market. (handwritten marginal note)

2

Analyses

In all the examples presented above, war had a centralizing effect. Even when raiding persisted, and in spite of the resistance of the aristocratic houses or the anarchy of the troops in the field, 'the great work of war' led to the concentration of the military – and thus the political – organization of the State.

It is true that royalty itself – when it takes on the trappings of patriarchal ideology – tends to function through dues and redistribution, which put the palace at the top of a huge hierarchized system of circulation. But only war can create, maintain or accentuate this concentration, by linking power to sovereign monopolies.

Thanks to war, the 'king' managed and distributed the booty, including the captives who were the essential ingredient of the war economy. They were the primary and sometimes the only resource which could be sold by the slaving State in order to import arms which could ensure its military superiority over the peoples it raided – particularly horses and guns. Converted into slaves, the captives contributed to the war economy through the exploitation to which they were subjected on the spot, the product of which – agricultural or craft – was exchanged for imported goods. They were indispensable to the perpetuation of the conditions of the warfare of which they themselves were the product, and to the workings of the slaving warrior State; they were assigned primarily to the State and to those who identified with it – the chief, the king, the notables. Few captives reached the people.

1 ECONOMIC ASPECTS OF WARS OF CAPTURE

On the basis of the cases described above, several sociomilitary systems can be distinguished with different relations between the authorities, the people and the slaves.

The raid did not exclude any member of society. It was undertaken either under the direction of a temporary chief, or by egalitarian bands. Capture was a source of riches for all those who went in for it. It did not establish differences between social classes, since permanent hierarchical relations were not built up around it.

Once a political society was constituted through the enlargement of the band – as we have seen in the early history of Segu – the right to capture tended to be extended to all those who penetrated that society and took part in its military activities. And once the numbers of those involved rose sufficiently to make true warfare possible, the prerogatives of the raid could, for a while, be extended to war, though they were modified. The population as a whole took part in the collective enterprise of capture and benefited from it. Expeditions were undertaken by militias rather than armies, and at this stage power was based on the capacity to direct these military operations. There was no organized exploitation of the free-born by the leaders. The whole of the free-born class benefited, in differing degrees, from the captives taken in war, selling them or exploiting them as subsistence slaves. The type of social formation which was established in this way can be assimilated either to what Engels called a *military suite* or to the Greek *laos* described by Benveniste (1969: 89s.).

But the soldier did not keep the whole of his booty from war, as had been the case in raids; he gave part of it to the chief, or he was given a part of the common booty. Even in Segu, where the *ton-jon* received their booty in flesh and blood, they did not keep it (see above). Accumulation of captives did not take place among the Bambara warriors, since it was held that 'to capture slaves makes one great, but to own them corrupts' (Bazin, 1975: 153). In contrast, 'there was intense accumulation at the level of the State' (ibid.).

Similarly, among the Mawri the distribution of the booty was very unequal and 'the servile labour force was used by only a very small fraction of society' (Latour, E. de, 1981: 269, 266). 'The captives were mainly in the hands of the aristocrats. . . . The peasants, in contrast, seldom managed to keep their captives: they sold them for sorghum' (ibid.: 280). It seems, furthermore, that among the aristocrats there was a concentration of slaves around the court (ibid.: 263).

Bosman, a Dutch trader in Benin in about 1700, noticed that 'the king maintains a prodigious number of slaves'; this can be explained by the fact that 'all war captives belong to the *onige* [chief]', as did vagabonds and even anyone who had the bad luck to fall into the latrines! (Bradbury, 1957: 71–2.) In the military monarchies which concern us here, unlike in merchant societies, slavery functioned primarily for the benefit of the court and the members of the dominant class. In Bamoum country, a third of society lived from servile labour (Tardits, 1980a: 524). Thornton (1979: 81–4) calculates that in the seventeenth to eighteenth centuries, 15 to 20 per cent of the total population of the kingdom of Kongo was fed by slaves. In contrast, employment of slaves among the rural communities seems to have been negligible, if not non-existent.

There are several reasons for this difference. In the first place, the export of large numbers of slaves left a limited number of captives, who were reserved first for the court, the aristocracy, the military chiefs and the king's protégés. Secondly, the weakness of internal merchant exchange, which might otherwise have competed with the circuits based on dues and redistribution which functioned in the kingdom (and on which the monarchic and aristocratic structure was built)[1] made it difficult to acquire slaves through purchase. In any case, it would doubtless have been humiliating for the aristocrats to provide themselves with slaves in the same way as merchants. Finally, and perhaps most importantly, the development of agricultural slavery among the productive peasantry was not really in the economic interests of the dominant class.

The labour of slaves employed by peasants tended purely and simply to replace the labour of their masters, without increasing total production.[2] The employment of slaves was counterbalanced by the additional mouths to feed from a roughly equivalent volume of production, since the productivity of slave labour was not much greater than that of free peasants. Thus taxes to the State would have been levied on a lower surplus-product. If these slaves had been employed by the peasant communities on the production of commodities for export or for sale on the domestic market, they would have enabled these communities to escape the constraints of the distributive economy and encouraged their insertion into the merchant circuits which competed with it. Access to slaves would have been a means to the economic and thus political emancipation of the people, which the authorities blocked by a series of convergent measures all linked to the distributive economy. It was only at the beginning of the twentieth century, with the emergence of trade in palm oil, that a popularization of slavery began – as, for example, in Dahomey.

2 WHY WERE THERE SACRIFICES?

Among the institutions which limited the employment of slaves by the people was what is called the prestige economy or the economy of ostentation. The effect of this mode of accumulation, apparently pointless, was not only to reserve a larger relative share of wealth for the privileged; it also neutralized wealth and prevented access to it by the dominated classes. Some of these riches became luxuries or prestige goods only when accumulated; the same goods would have been necessities in smaller quantities in the hands of the less privileged. This was particularly true of pubescent slaves held in the palace for the king's pleasure and kept idle and *de facto* sterile. The neutralization of their productive and reproductive potential through their accumulation at court deprived the peasantry of them and ensured that this peasantry remained locked within its domestic structures (Meillas-soux, 1968).

I believe that the 'sacrifices of slaves' can be explained in the same terms. Once the demand of the merchants and the economic and military needs of the dominant class had been satisfied, in the absence of a domestic market – as was generally the case in the redistributive economy – on which slaves or their products could be sold, excess captives became useless mouths to feed. Rather than distribute them to the lower classes, the aristocratic classes usually preferred to eliminate them under the cover of 'sacrifices'.

It is true that practical reasons are given for these killings: they were said to be a means of getting rid of ageing and un-productive slaves. Snelgrave (1734: 46) also suggests that it was feared that old slaves 'who had become wise with age and long experience' might be likely to plot against their masters. Individuals who were considered unsaleable and beyond redemption were also killed.[3] It is true that many of these victims were men, considered to be more dangerous and less useful economically, but women were also killed, and not only old women. In Dahomey, the pretexts for these murders were numerous and often futile. Herskovits (1978, II: 229) estimates that 200 men and women 'messengers' were dispatched to the ancestors each year to pass on to them some sort of information or to ask questions about the digging of a well, the timing of a marriage, the arrival of an alien or the creation of a new dance. But it was especially for annual 'customs' and during royal funerals that men and women were massacred in large numbers. In any case, a choice was made between the assassination of these slaves and their dis-tribution among the people. Whatever the pretexts for or aims of these killings, the 'sacrifices' of slaves blocked the spread of slavery among the free peasantry and deprived the latter of a way of getting rich and thus of political emancipa-tion from the authorities.[4]

3 SEPARATE ECONOMIES

The distribution of slaves between aristocrats and peasants did not only mirror the different conditions of the nobility and the people; more importantly, it defined two distinct economic sectors, one slave-owning and the other domestic, each functioning according to distinct relations of production. In the first, the class relation between productive slaves and aristocrats operated to the benefit of a dominant minority which, in the examples above, does not seem to have exceeded a third of the free population.

The second sector, where domestic relations of production were preserved, remained the infrastructural basis of peasant reproduction.

Both these sectors could function autonomously. Apart from the exploitation of slaves (while it lasted) and the sale of them, the aristocratic sector benefited from other resources: the material booty and tributes paid by the conquered. The sale of captives led to an export and import trade from which the court profited: in slaving States of this type this trade was often entrusted to official representatives appointed by the king and closely dependent on his favour (Polanyi, 1965). The trade in which alien merchants were involved was subject to royal taxation or to obligations in gifts. When the productive and merchant sector of the economy was left to autonomous communities – as it was in Segu – these communities were periodically 'reaped' to the benefit of a bankrupt sovereign.

Finally, around the court and the aristocracy a social corps emerged which contributed to the direct and indirect exercise of power by the dominant class; the *clients*.[5] Thanks to the agricultural goods produced by the labour of slaves or the free peasantry, the court and the aristocracy could maintain in their sphere of influence craftsmen or individuals who provided services, whose products or labour were entirely reserved for their own use. Since they were inserted into a relation of clientelism, the production and circulation of these specialized products were kept outside the commodity circuits. In this way specialization of labour which might have encouraged the development of a market economy was drawn into the sphere of redistribution, and the class of merchants was excluded from an entire realm of transfers and circulation of products. The relation of clientelism is not essentially a relation of exploitation, but it could be a channel for relations of extortion. Nevertheless, this was not the essential function of clientelism. More importantly, it gave the court control over goods which were indispensable to activities which it reserved for itself, such as war; or over economically strategic goods, such as agricultural implements.

During periods when capture and the slave trade prospered, the aristocratic economic sector, fed by slavery, trade and clientelism, could function and perpetuate itself independently, without recourse to exploitation of the peasantry. As for the domestic economy, we know that it existed before the aristocracy and that the disappearance of the aristocracy would only give it back the autonomy which was inherent to its operation.

Could these two sectors nevertheless be linked in an organic relation? Did specific relations of production develop between the slave-owning aristocracy and the free-born peasantry? Did the economics of capture – in which the whole of the social system, represented by the dominant class, was engaged – depend on such a relation?

4 EXTORTION IN THE NAME OF THE FATHER

The relation between the two sectors, slave-owning and domestic, manifested itself socially and politically as a relation between two social fractions; the aristocracy – including the king and his court – and the free-born peasantry. The former was locked into a class relation with *productive* slaves, but the nature of its relations with the peasantry varied according to the degree of economic autonomy of each sector with respect to the other.

The links between aristocracy and peasantry were ideologically represented as links of 'kinship'. The aristocratic class was assimilated to a category of seniors, the king to a father or an ancestor, and his subjects to an obedient progeny.

These relations of seniority justified the apparently domestic system of circulation based on dues and redistribution of which the doyen–king was the centre.[6]

In order to evaluate the grounds for this ideological assimilation, the nature of domestic relations of production must be reassessed in the light of this confrontation. In the self-sustenance domestic economy, at the level of the communities, the labour-time and the share of the product which had to be returned to the labourer were not defined in any contract. As regards essential goods – that is, food – the entire product of the active labourers belonged to the community under the responsibility of the doyen. This product was reinjected into the community, to all its members, *productive and unproductive*, through the mechanisms of reserves and communal cooking. *Thus the relation of production was established between all the productive members and all the unproductive members.* If there had been a class relation in this mode of production, it would organically have been between these two categories. But this relation did not lead to the exploitation of productive members of the community by unproductive members, since the food consumed by the latter was used to produce future producers whose product would belong in its entirety to the community; nor were they exploited by post-productive individuals, since these in turn received from their cadets, through this investment, what they themselves had produced in their time, for their elders.

In this relation of production, the doyen was responsible for the management of the community, by virtue of his precedence in the agricultural cycle – or, in other words, in his capacity as *the elder of the productive members*.[7] However, he generally retained this precedence even when he reached post-productive age in order to manage the political and matrimonial affairs of the community. Thus his position of authority did not necessarily coincide with the post-productive phase of his life. An individual could be doyen of the community before or after he became unable to work. So if the doyen, once he reached old age, consumed the product of his cadets, this was not by virtue of his rank or his functions, but because his reduced physical capacities placed him in the class of the unproductive. In contrast, there would have been exploitation (or extortion) to the benefit of the doyen or the elders in general, if the possibility of consuming without producing had been linked to rank, independently of participation in production: if, for example, the elder, while still of productive age, had used the argument of elderhood to exempt himself from labour.

Now, the ideological transposition of the king and the doyen (or father) is based precisely on this confusion between unproductiveness and idleness, idleness and elderhood, elderhood and management, management and appropriation of the product. In aristocratic society, the doyen was no longer designated by his precedence in the agricultural cycle: he was the individual whose birth placed him in the class within which 'seniors' were recruited, irrespective of age or true precedence. It was on this basis that the king claimed the management of the collective product and even the right to dispose of it freely.

The domestic and purely functional relation between productive and unproductive individuals was transformed into a hierarchized relation between one social fraction whose functions were exclusively political and another which was assigned to productive tasks. It is interesting to note that when domestic ideology was transposed in this way into a hierarchical society, appearances were generally preserved. Thus the sovereign very often undertook ritual 'labour' on the land. Through this gesture (which is usually seen only as abstract symbolism linked to fertility) the king unequivocally placed himself in the class of agricultural producers. Thus the king of Dahomey belonged to a *dompe* (association of individuals of the same age engaged in collective agricultural labour) and took up a hoe for a few moments: whatever his age, he chose to present himself as the *elder of the productive members*, so as to demonstrate that dues were owed to him on this basis.

Nevertheless, the relations based on dues and distribution which resulted from this ideological assimilation were not necessarily a channel for exploitation; they could be a channel for extortion.[8] In effect, the redistributive circuit sometimes functioned occasionally and sometimes regularly, depending on the case.[9]

In its occasional form – among the Mawri, for example (Latour, E. de, 233s.) – the quantity of dues owed by the peasantry was neither fixed nor measured. Gifts were given to the authorities *on the occasion* of certain celebrations, enthronements, funerals, feasts, first crops, only some of which were regular. Contributions could also be required *on the occasion* of war. Conversely, the authorities redistributed the booty among the population *on the occasion* of a victory, food *on the occasion* of a scarcity and gifts *on the occasion* of certain exploits or achievements by their subjects.

While the redistributive circuit functioned in this *occasional* way in both directions rather than regularly, while it was not accompanied either by periodicity or by accounting, the relation between the aristocratic and domestic sectors was not organic: it could even function without either of the two parties profiting from it. *Since each sector was economically autonomous, the economic attitude of the authorities or the dominant class towards the peasantry was dictated by conjunctural political considerations.* Indeed, several commentators find that there was a concern to moderate extractions from the peasantry.

Thus dues and counter-dues took on the appearance of 'fair' reciprocity between the authorities and the peasantry: the peasants donated to the king or lord according to their abilities and received from them according to their needs. Clearly, all sorts of pressures could be applied by those in power in order to benefit from this system, but this does not invariably seem to have been the purpose of these extractions. Indeed, the surplus-product appropriated from the peasantry could be merely an occasional complement to the aristocratic sector's own resources: booty from war, the products of the exploitation of slaves, taxation of the merchants, confiscations, fines, tributes paid by the conquered, and so on. While the aristocracy was master of these resources, it is conceivable that the two sectors functioned independently of each other, or that exchange between them was equal. In other words, there was no necessary economic relation between the two sectors, nor was there a systematic organization of exploitation, although the situation did present opportunities for extortion. I shall call this social formation – which was made up of two economic sectors, one aristocratic and slave-owning, the other peasant and domestic – *warrior despotism.*

5 MILITARY TYRANNY

The beginnings of exploitation appeared when the slaves cap-tured by the peasant recruits were not only confiscated from them but also used against them as military supervisors and as the repressive corps of the State. Then the peasant recruits were locked into a relation of dependence on the aristocracy, whose agents were the slaves whom the peasants had helped to capture. Exploitation took place to the extent that the military activities of the people came, in this way, to maintain the relation of domination and exploitation to which it was subjected. Through supervision by the soldier-slaves, the peasant militias tended to be reduced to an unpaid military labour force, where each recruit brought his own basic needs and sometimes also his weapons and his means of subsistence. This was true of the Ashanti troops, for example: they were fed either from the land or from the flour which each soldier had to bring with him.[10] Binger's descriptions of Samori's supply lines also suggest that for the most part the soldiers were supplied from their own resources or left to fend for themselves.

The military exploitation of the peasants meant that the material and human cost of capture was not borne only by the aristocratic class (though it appropriated all the captives) but also by the peasantry: their free contribution benefited both the aristocratic class which sold slaves and those who bought them.[11]

However, the military exploitation of the peasants could be neither stable nor organic, since they were exploited not as cultivators and producers but on the basis of an activity – war – which was foreign to their condition and to which any social group could be assigned. In fact, this military relation between aristocracy and peasants tended to disappear as its effects became positive: captives from war were transformed into soldiers and replaced the armed peasants who had captured them. Soldier-slaves took the place of conscripts. There was no reproduction of the relations of production.

The cases described above thus correspond to three models of social organization, based on capture and the employment of slaves:

a. a warrior society emanating from bands and raids, involving the entire population in wars of capture and the sale and/or exploitation of the captives; which I have called, following Engels, *the military suite* and which is comparable to what Benveniste (1969: 89s.) calls the *laos* (Greek);

b. a social formation consisting of two economic sectors, one aristocratic and slave-owning and the other domestic, between which there were only inorganic and occasional relations of extortion (*warrior despotism*);

c. a slave-owning aristocratic State, backed up by a corps of armed slaves, militarily exploiting peasants who were forced to participate physically in the capture of slaves but did not themselves benefit from slavery (*military tyranny*).

If we examine the nature of the relations which were built up within the slave-owning military society, we notice that three social components were involved: the military or aristocratic class, the free-born peasant population, and the slaves. Relations between them were different in each of the three cases. In the military suite, the people and its chiefs – sometimes also the court – all benefited from capture, albeit to different extents, either by selling captives as commodities or by exploiting them as slaves. There were no relations of exploitation between the free-born. In warrior despotism, slavery benefited only the aristocracy; in addition, it imposed occasional extortions on the people. Finally, in military tyranny, the aristocracy organized some of the slaves into a repressive corps in order to force the free-born peasant population to undertake the labour of war.

Slavery benefited the free-born population as a whole only in the first case. The free-born peasantry was excluded from slavery in the second case, and in the third it was subjected to a form of military exploitation.

Unlike the raid, wars of capture thus tended to create class relations within the free-born population, by encouraging the accumulation by the warriors of captives who were used for the repression and supervision of the peasants. In this way the military class was placed at the pole of a *double class relation*: it was master with respect to the slaves and lord with respect to the peasants. On the basis of the respective employment of each in terms of this class relation, different political systems were elaborated.[12]

Thus slavery could be the foundation for different political forms. It could benefit part of the free-born population only, or it could contribute to the creation within the free-born population of forms of exploitation which could coexist with those of slavery and even replace them. Thus is opened up the way to serfdom.

6 FROM MILITARY TYRANNY TO SERFDOM

As capture became more distant and more costly and sources of renewal of slaves on the land dried up, the burden of agricultural exploitation fell more and more heavily on to the free-born peasantry. In order to intensify its exploitation, the aristocrats and their soldier-slaves diverted their military activity from wars of capture towards internal repression, while the servile corps of the court constituted the administrative instruments of aristocratic domination over the peasant class. The condition of free-born peasants and that of agricultural slaves became confused into similar relations with the aristocracy. In fact, in these conditions, it was no longer necessary for the aristocracy to keep the agricultural slaves in a different state from that of the peasants. On the contrary: it became necessary to grant allotments to agricultural slaves and to let them form couples so as to encourage their reproduction. The improved condition of the slaves tended to approach the deteriorating status of a peasantry weakened by growing and constant exploitation.

At this stage the economy was no longer composed of two economic *sectors*, as it had been in warrior despotism, but of two social *classes*. The relation of exploitation was between the aristocracy and a productive population composed of free-born cultivators and allotment slaves, mixed into a new peasant class. Since from then on supplies to the aristocracy and its social corps depended *entirely* on this class, a strict form of extraction had to be established to ensure a *regular* surplus-product and to enable the *constant* transfers necessary to the maintenance of the dominant class and its means of domination. This was serfdom: the 'corvée' and the tax became the principal forms of an extraction which was no longer occasional but periodic.

a. Corvées

In most aristocratic States royal buildings, military works and, usually, all works which took a long time were built through the requisitioning of serf and free-born village populations rather than through the mobilization of slaves. These corvées were undertaken by the villages in turn, for a few days each year. As in the case of the peasant militias, this raised the question of supplies, since those working on the corvée had to be fed during the period of their work. When the corvée was brief, as it usually was, the peasant agriculturalists could feed themselves from their own harvests. They could more easily provide a costless labour force than the slaves, who had to be maintained in large numbers, permanently, on the basis of long-lasting requisitions of food and the difficult organization of supply lines. This is why these works were undertaken outside the agricultural season and why the villages nearest the court were usually requisitioned.

b. Taxes

Even more than corvées, which always necessitated a form of coercion, it was through the institution of taxation that economic relations between the peasantry and the aristocracy were *organically* established. By diverting greater numbers of servile individuals from production to repressive or admi-

nistrative functions, the aristocracy made the transfer of subsistence goods more and more indispensable to the maintenance of this growing unproductive corps, while the corps
itself became more and more necessary for the enforcement
of ever more burdensome requisitioning.

Unlike the occasional extractions imposed on the people
through the system of dues or the tributes inflicted on alien
populations brought under submission, taxes were a regular
contribution, quantitatively measured and socially determined on the basis of an assessment. In aristocratic societies,
the assessment first distinguished those strata of the population who owed taxes from those who were exempt from
them. The distinction was made on the basis of ideology, not
of wealth: dependants – that is, the peasantry – had to pay;
the aristocrats and the court were exempted.[13] The assessment rarely took place on the basis of resources, since at the
level of the people the tax was a poll tax. Each household or
each adult in a household owed the same lump sum, and the
doyen of the community was responsible for its payment.
(With Islam the more sophisticated system of the tithe was
sometimes introduced, proportional to the volume of production.)

The complexity and administrative clumsiness of the tax-
collecting apparatuses, even the simplest, in societies without
writing and without numbers, must not be underestimated.[14]
Taxation necessitated censuses, collections, stocking and so
on, and hence a large qualified staff, able to use the various
methods of accounting available. It was backed up by a relatively complicated administration which took a long time to
establish, and it seems likely that the final result of all this
effort was to the advantage of the court.[15]

For various reasons taxation was more effective than the
system of dues in creating profit for the court. With taxation
the peasantry's contributions were no longer occasional but
obligatory and regular, while royal redistribution in favour
of the peasantry was still circumstantial and arbitrary. By setting off relatively constant resources against variable dis-
bursements, the authorities could ensure a positive balance.
Furthermore, the social identification of resources through
their definition in assessments guaranteed their transfer from

one class to the other.

Apart from these material advantages, taxation enabled the State to act as a regulator of the social system. In this respect the objects which composed the State must be separated into those destined for prestige or for the State apparatus and those which entered the productive cycle. The most important of the latter, apart from human beings, were subsistence goods. Obligatory taxes in subsistence goods, made possible through the mastery of the administrative and repressive apparatuses, not only ensured the flow of provisions to the non-productive population but also allowed the State to exercise decisive control over the economic and social re-production of the peasant population. Through taxes on sub-sistence goods relations of production could be established which led to the transformation and disappearance of slavery.

Doubtless, this qualitative transformation was merely potential, and it is envisaged here only as the hypothetical product of internal developments. In reality, many of the predatory States disappeared before reaching this stage, because they had used up all the human material on which they fed. But with taxation on subsistence goods the elements of evolution towards generalized serfdom were present.

Some authors consider that serfdom existed in the Sonxai empire (Tymowski, 1974b), for example. The *askia* gave whole villages, lands and men, to his faithful or to the holy marabouts. The very fact that this was possible presupposes that the cultivators concerned were forced to stay on these lands, irrespective of their owner. Furthermore, these peasants were 'villagers', which must be taken to mean that they reproduced themselves within a family.

Serfdom is still the condition of the inhabitants of numerous hamlets in Africa, who are obliged to pay fixed dues and services to their masters but who nevertheless live in families, sometimes under the authority of one of their own kind (Dorman, 1973). They are sometimes dependent on aristocrats and sometimes on merchants. But this mode of exploitation must not be confused with feudalism, since serfdom, in various forms, can exist independently of vassalage or of dubbing (Duby, 1973).

c. Reserves

Because of the cyclical nature of agricultural production in the short term and its uncertain nature in the long term, the existence of *reserves* (of grain or seed) was indispensable to the production and reproduction both of individuals and of the productive cycle. In the domestic economy, each community had its own reserves to finish off the agricultural year and, depending on storage techniques, to survive catastrophes for as long as possible. But the efficiency of a system of reserves improves when the area of production is extended to cover regions which are not likely to be affected by the same climatic fluctuations or the same calamities at the same time. While the domestic communities could compensate for variations in production *over time* through the stocks in their granaries, each covered too restricted an area to be able to compensate for them in space.[16] The kingdoms, because of their size, were better able to achieve this balance over space. Since they could use taxation as an administrative means of extraction, they could concentrate agricultural products in one place, stock them and redistribute them, thus counterbalancing geographical variations. Thus the central administration was well placed to organize the regulation of the food supply.[17]

Once the royal reserves were used for such regulation, they tended to be constituted through taxes at the expense of domestic reserves. Compensation for production on a spatial scale replaced that performed by the granaries on a time scale. The functions of elders in this respect were taken over by the central power. After each poor harvest, the domestic communities thus became dependent on the court for food during periods of dearth and sometimes for seed during longer famines. This relation became organic once the reproduction of the peasantry was dependent on the existence of these reserves, themselves dependent on peasant production.

Political control over food reserves and seed – and thus over human energy – was not necessarily (and never in practice) exercised over the entire food production. It needed only to affect the fraction necessary for reproduction during the least productive periods, in order to be effective. This control could also be exercised on a scale smaller than that of a kingdom, since at one time or another the serf was always, after a bad season, unable to pay his *fixed* dues, while the lord, thanks to the fixed nature of the dues, accumulated the surplus-product of good harvests.

In addition, this wealth of food enabled the aristocrats and the court to maintain the craftsmen-clients mentioned above within their sphere of influence and to ensure for themselves the exclusive control of their products. When these were agricultural implements, the mastery of the dominant class over agriculture was even more effective and self-perpetuating. In the case of arms for use by the army-police, the peasants, by providing food for these craftsmen, were, once again, contributing to their own subordination.

It is thus conceivable that under serfdom, subsistence goods - although apparently consumer and not producer goods, since they entered into the energy cycle of the production of labour-power - represented the principal material content of the relation of exploitation between the aristocracy and the peasantry, and thus the basis of an authentic mode of production.

Once again, at the level of class relations, slavery was the agent of its own disappearance. Once slaves had only administrative or military functions and once their maintenance was indirectly ensured by the labour of the people and directly by the dominant class, they no longer constituted a class but a *social corps* secreted by the aristocracy to undertake on its behalf certain tasks which were necessary to the establishment and assertion of its power. The length of the productive life of these agents – unlike that of agricultural slaves – was no longer of interest. Their fidelity was more important than profits which could be made from them. Their material lot improved relative to that of the people, and their loyalty was better guaranteed by heredity than it had been by capture. The state of the slave became blurred as his new function shaped him into a different agent needing different qualities. When at the same time, as we have seen, the 'labour' of these henchmen successfully reduced the peasantry to servitude, there were no longer any juridical obstacles to prevent agricultural slaves from becoming peasants. And if, as one might imagine, this evolution took place at the same time as capture became less profitable, there were sound economic reasons why, as was the case in numerous historical examples, slavery should be transformed into serfdom.

Nevertheless, this evolution of aristocratic slavery was only one of the ways in which slavery as an institution was transformed. The development of slavery within the merchant framework differs from that described above: through the incorporation of his labour into commodities, the profit-slave himself became a commodity and was permanently barred from a political destiny.

Think about this in context of U.S. — does it apply?

Part III
GOLD:
Merchant Slavery

Merchant Slavery

The aristocratic economy provided slaves and retained those who were necessary for its own use. It supplied the market but did not function through the market. In contrast, the merchant economy developed entirely around the market. The merchants bought captives from the aristocrats, conditioned them (made them into merchandise), transported them and exported them to distant lands from which demand had been transmitted through the merchants. In doing so they contributed to the spread of slavery, opening up markets along their routes wherever local production could be exchanged for their merchandise and, in particular, for their captives. In this way they reorientated and diffused slaving exchange, by making it accessible not only to aristocrats but also to ordinary people, as long as they had the means to acquire slaves. These markets multiplied between the Middle Ages and the nineteenth century in Africa. In Part I we have given an indication of the routes and slave markets which existed in the nineteenth century. Their location in this zone of Africa points to the regions where the slaving economy developed. The slave trade, produced by demand which originally came from far away (the Maghreb and the Atlantic), in turn created a supply of slaves destined for African societies situated close to the zones of capture.

Far from suggesting a problematic genesis of slavery on

the basis of kinship systems in African societies (Miers and Kopytoff, 1977: 26) and the spread of trade on the basis of this internal differentiation, the facts seem to show that slavery in peasant societies emerged in response to inducements from the merchants, the closeness of these societies to the markets, and their integration into an expanding area of exchange. The thesis according to which the slave emerged from the midst of domestic society excludes *a priori* his exchange or the exchange of his product, and thus does not explain the slave trade in which these societies were involved. The market on which slaves were sold was also the site of purchase of the products of their labour. Slavery could not therefore be perpetuated or developed outside this commercial context. Trade in slaves within Africa emerged as the combined result of war and trade between plundered regions and those which, situated within the markets' sphere of influence, bought and exploited slaves, thus feeding a continental economy where slaves and their products were exchanged side by side.

interrelation of aristocratic
+ merchant slavery.

1

The Land of the Merchants

In the ancient kingdom of Sin (present-day Senegal), towards the fourteenth century, the acquisition of wealth by an ordinary man was seen by the court as subversive. The *bur* (sovereign) sent his *ceddo* (armed retainers) to raid the upstart, or paid him a visit lasting several days, emptying his reserves and departing laden with gifts (from Mbodj, 1978: 53).

This is one of many illustrations of the conflicts mentioned above between two classes which were economically complementary and politically competing: the warrior aristocracy which supplied captives and the merchant class which sold and sometimes employed them. The productive and merchant economy created within the kingdom the political threat of the acquisition of wealth without birth, and when this threat became too serious the aristocracy could not allow the establishment of a class within its sphere of influence which was not its client but its rival.

As we have seen, the merchant in these kingdoms was usually an 'alien', almost always kept at a distance from power because of his outsider status. Those who had been settled for a long time and converted into the king's subjects were kept at the edge of society or 'reaped' when they became too rich; sometimes they were introduced to the titles and obligations of nobility which justified wealth under the aristocratic regime but also made it dependent on channels of favour and status. Relations of protection or clientelism were extended by the aristocracy to the social corps and classes which threatened its superiority, in order to lock them into relations based on dues or on hierarchies which conformed to aristocratic norms. Terray (1975a: 405) explains how this worked in the Abron kingdom:

> Wealth could be acquired autonomously only within relatively narrow limits, and wealth amassed within these limits did not automatically lead to social influence and political power. A man who had built up something of a fortune could hope to retain and increase it and to use it for his social and political ambitions only if he put it at the disposal of the established power. There were two ways in which he could do this: he could directly contribute to the king's treasury and that of the provincial chiefs, whose expenses were heavy and who were often in difficulty; or he could recruit and equip at his own expense a company of warriors which in times of war he placed in the service of the sovereign. The king or the provincial chief rewarded him by appointing him *safohen* and entrusting him with the supervision of a certain number of villages: he then exercised judicial power over these villages in the first instance and thus collected part of the fines; he participated in the collection of dues and took his share of them: the recognized mechanisms of distribution and concentration of wealth then worked to his advantage. In short, wealth could lead to power only to the extent that its owner could use it to insert himself into the existing political hierarchy, and only this insertion could enable a man to acquire more wealth without running the constant risk of its plunder and of his own collapse.

This integration into status society was possible when, as was the case in coastal societies, local merchants were confined within the narrow boundaries of the kingdom and further subjected to royal annoyance.

The merchants of the savannah, who circulated throughout West Africa, had more freedom with respect to the princes and could impose their own rules to a greater extent (Wilks, 1971).

1 MERCHANT IDEOLOGIES

The emergence of a merchant power, wielded by a merchant (or 'bourgeois') social class, was faced with difficulties in areas dominated or plundered by military and predatory societies. Wherever war was the dominant activity, the aristocracies also dominated and imposed their own criteria of access to power and wealth: birth or exploits. Sometimes commercial agricultural production was hampered by the restrictions which the sovereign could impose on access to land on the basis of allegiance.

However, history shows that in the interstices of these aristocratic areas, spaces were formed which were managed by the merchant class and subjected to its rules – the market-towns and their dependencies – and that links were established between these spaces to form a business network which backed up a sort of reticulated merchant 'State', with neither territory nor central government (cf. Meillassoux, ed., 1971d). Among themselves the merchants maintained mercantile relations which necessitated ethics, means of payment and arbitration. The preservation of patrimony, which at this stage was much the same as merchant capital, was backed up by a re-interpretation of kinship relations in a form which was neither that of domestic agricultural society nor that of the aristocratic family.

Men of science, juriconsuls, moralists emerged within merchant society to elaborate, express and interpret the new law and the ideologies which backed up these transformations, to judge contentious cases relating both to persons and to goods, and to place morality under the supervision of an omnipresent god. The common interest of the traders in the maintenance of moral and cultural conditions favourable to their business, and their desire to keep business at a distance from greedy princes or States which dispensed justice, led them to accept the immanent and inhibiting policy of Islam. The merchant slaving class applied to slavery rules which were its own, codified by its own religion.

The commandments of the Koran concerning slavery are not very numerous, but they refer directly or indirectly to 'production', exploitation, and reproduction of the slave. None of these rules, although they have been the object of doctrinal interpretations, has, to my knowledge, precipitated schisms.[1]

The Koran unambiguously identifies potential slaves with respect to religion – *Surah* XLVII: 4–5: 'So when you meet those who are unbelievers, strike them on the neck until you have them at your mercy! Then tighten the bonds' (transl. R. Blachère, 1980: 538).

Marc Bloch has shown how Christianity displaced the notion of 'alien' from its geographical context in order to make it into a notion of faith (1947: 165). Islam was used in the same way to identify the *kafir*, the unbeliever, as an alien suitable for enslavement. It did not, in principle, authorize the enslavement of believers, but notions of schism or heresy could opportunely be used to lift this restriction. There are numerous examples of this.

As regards exploitation, the remuneration granted by the Koran to slaves was the wealth (more precious than that which had been taken from them) which God would set aside for them in the next life if he saw the uprightness of their nature and the good in their hearts (VIII: 7). On the other hand, if they were not obedient, Allah gave their master the right to dispose of them as he wished (ibid. 72: 71). With respect to their capacity for reproduction, the Koran is very strict (XXIV: 32): 'Marry those of your slaves, men and women, who are honest. . . . If they are hardworking, Allah will make them sufficient to themselves through his favour.' When it was granted, the manumission of slaves freed the master from all responsibilities towards them but did not free the slave of all obligations. The rule which prevailed in the merchant class with respect to slaves was linked less to the exercise of absolute power over a being who was seen as inferior – as was the case for the aristocracy – than to their exploitation. The productive function of the slave and his or her value as merchandise subjected him to arbitrary decisions up to a certain point. In that they formed a social class which was constitutive of society and on which production and profit were based, and because of their dispersal among numerous owners, slaves were ruled by the public interest and not exclusively by the private interest of each of their masters. In practice, Islam (and the Islamic State) took on this civil responsibility by imposing rules which could reduce and avoid the spread of conflicts resulting from relations of exploitation. It imposed its own arbitration on the parties concerned, particularly as regards punishment, seeing to it that this did not aggravate tension. Islam treated slavery as a class relation and tried to resolve conflicts as class conflicts.

Human sacrifice was ruled out. The execution of a slave by his master was permitted, but could be only rare and circumstantial. Islam recommended that the slave should be correctly fed and that his labour should be moderate. If these rules were not applied, the authorities were allowed to sell the slave who had been badly treated, in spite of his master. Islam advocated a form of ideological integration which gave the slave the chance of belonging to the community by becoming a Muslim. It advocated manumission both as a hope which could be held out to pacify slaves and as a means of making old slaves look after themselves. These rules organized the alienation of slaves and their more effective subjugation. 'The master must inculcate into the slave the principles of religion (through punishment if necessary) . . . so that he becomes incapable of doing wrong to a Muslim' (in Daumas, 1857). Reward for his labour and his good behaviour was postponed for the future, in the paradise which was presented to him, if he deserved it, as his true enfranchisement. Thus if Islam withdrew from each individual master the absolute and arbitrary power to punish or kill slaves, it offered the *class of masters* the ideological and juridical means of efficient social domination. Through the moderating arbitration of Islam, the slave escaped the absolutism of the master and was partially re-civilized (Samb, 1980: Sanneh, 1976a).

As C. Aubin-Sugy (1975, II: 510s.) shows with acuity, Islam introduced the social conditions which were necessary for the development of an individualistic profit economy. Islam sanctioned property through the cruel punishment of thieves. Theft, which in domestic society was merely a lack of respect for authority, became an attack on property. Property was extended to the land, which until then had been inappropriable and inalienable (ibid.).

Islam imposed the division of inheritance: applied to the land, this gradually dissolved the domestic community and favoured the emergence of landless peasants.[2] But by then real wealth lay in the ownership of goods, gold and money (Rodinson, 1966) more than in the patrimony of land. C. Aubin-Sugy again emphasizes that if Islam preserved caste discrimination, it criticized the praise-singers[3] who encouraged the aristocrats to spend all their wealth to acquire renown, while Islamic puritanism tried to direct them towards saving. In '. . . Timbuktoo, the imam Mohammed Baghayogo (may God be satisfied with him) tried to preserve harmony among the inhabitants, by preventing the development of the people's tendency to ruin themselves or to plunder each other and to squander the goods of orphans' (*TEF*: 227). Religion was no longer founded on the clan ancestor, as C. Aubin-Sugy once again notes, but on a common god. Supernatural life no longer depended on the quality of elder or doyen of the community destined to become an ancestor, but on piety and individual virtue. Social classes asserted themselves. The 'infidelity' which identified pagans as slaves enabled servile labour to replace the collective labour which was part of the social infrastructure of the domestic community. Furthermore, the prohibition of fermented drinks dissolved community social relations linked to their consumption, to the benefit of an individualized commodity – cola (Aubin-Sugy, ibid.).

Accumulation became possible, the acquisition of wealth brought access to Islamic education and accentuated social differences. 'The slaves freed Jaxanke children of school-going age from long spells of agricultural labour', notes L. Sanneh (1976a: 60, n.57); he also points out that the merchant Islamic community of Senegambia preserved its cohesion and its strength 'largely as a result of the additional work supplied by slaves' (ibid.). Pilgrimages to the rich Arab countries sanctified those who undertook them – and made them into profitable commercial expeditions (Aubin-Sugy, ibid.). It must be added that this was offset by the development of a class of poor. Alms, which were the pride of Islam, were the – modest – price of the acquisition of wealth by its most adept members through the dispossession of a growing fraction of the domestic peasantry by the believers. Holy war against paganism and infidelity displaced thousands of individuals and expropriated them totally. Others were reduced to poverty in depopulated villages, their granaries burned or pillaged and their lands plundered or threatened, deprived of their women who had been abducted by the raiders. Old slaves, charitably emancipated once their strength gave out, were reduced to begging.[4] The division of the land impoverished the weakest among the relatives. Islam provoked and assumed poverty.

Islam was also a code (a set of gestures and passwords) which enabled believers, particularly those whose business obliged them to travel, to recognize each other through prayer and spare each other from capture. The *salaam* conquered space and brought peace, to the benefit of believers, businessmen and the pious. It underpinned huge networks which stretched all over the world, opening up the way to the circulation of captives over the great distance on which, as we have seen, their exploitation depended. On the other hand, it deprived infidels who did not own this passport of the privilege of trading over distances or in Islamic countries without serious risk of capture.[5] *outsiders*

There were, it is true, Islamic families devoted entirely to religion, to the teaching of Islam or to healing. H. J. Fisher is correct in reminding us of this. But this specialization was not the rule, and these families were often shown to be a branch of a larger clan which included other fractions involved in trade. Could proselytizing alone have imposed Islam on pagan populations which already had their own beliefs, teachers, thaumaturges and healers? In Sahelo-Sudanese Africa, for example, some of these functions were performed by smiths: the healing of madness and other illnesses, the taking of oaths, burial . . . these functions were taken over from them by the marabouts. As late as the nineteenth century, Samori's councillors included pagan thaumaturges, smiths and marabouts, all on an equal footing. In contrast, the numerous merchants whose services he used were all Isla-

mized. The concentration of Muslim clerks in the big towns
– which depended on trade for their existence – and their circulation over large areas followed the movements of the merchant caravans; their routes joined up with the networks
established by the traders which guaranteed the safety of all
Muslims, bazaar merchants or *wali*.[6]

Islam did certainly appear to be superior to paganism,
thanks to writing, to books and to a solid body of beliefs and
ethics. Cosmopolitan Islam, in particular, provided the be-
liever with a faith which opened up to him a social space out
of all proportion to the narrowness of the village. But was
this 'moral' superiority not a means for the conspicuous
acquisition of wealth by Muslims, by virtue of this same
space? A new faith could take hold over individuals from a
peasant and pagan milieu only if economic and social conditions changed. Where trade – or, more precisely, production for exchange – did not penetrate, Islam was resisted:
from the outset the peasant communities fought against the
destructive effects of trade, which were immediately visible.
The transformation which created an environment favourable to Islam must be sought in the new social relations
which sprung up from the market and the exploitation of
labour. The pagan converted to Islam when he found himself
compelled, out of fear or self-interest, to have dealings with
this new society which imposed its rules on him, often by
force: when he emigrated to towns where the cultural values
of his village milieu gave him no foothold in the wider
society into which he penetrated; he became Muslim when, a
slaver in his turn, he found it necessary to resolve relations of
production from behind the shelter of an ethic, and to justify
them. The princes were often the first to convert when Islam
consecrated their wars of capture as *jihad* and thus allowed
them to enter the religious realm of the great trade in slaves,
as suppliers. The same applied to their subjects when they
entered the realm of the market.

2 MERCHANT TOWNS

In a West Africa strong in commercial capacity and ideology, a merchant realm esablished itself in the interstices of the kingdoms. It inserted its urbanism in quarters adjoining the capitals or in towns separate from them, with their shops, their caravanserais, their mosques and all the 'beautiful buildings and very elegant houses' described by El-Bekri.

This was a reticular realm, barely visible within the moving masses of the empires, but it nevertheless had to provide itself with some form of protection. In Agadez:

> each merchant owns a large number of slaves to form his escort on the road from Cano to Borno, where the way is infested with an infinity of tribes who travel all over the desert. These people, who resemble the poorest of the Zingeri, constantly attack the merchants and kill them. The latter therefore take with them well-armed slaves. Then these robbers can do nothing. When he reaches his destination, he [the merchant] uses these slaves for different tasks so that they earn their living and keeps ten or twelve for his personal use and to guard the merchandise. (Jean Léon l'Africain, 1550/1956: 473–4)

In Timbuktu, the merchants established their own units of defence, the *jonbugu*, composed of armed slaves. Some families were said to have owned 700 young armed retainers in the period when the Arma aristocracy, although weakened, still reigned over the city in the nineteenth century (1893).[7] The power of the kingdoms was often inadequate for the protection of the merchant caravans. It was even a threat to them when the zones to be crossed were ravaged by war between princes, forcing the merchants to encroach on the military function of the aristocracy by organizing their own defence.

However, no free-born merchant city was beyond the reach of the aristocratic States. The subordination of the merchant communities to the power of these States was never total, but it was always present. Sometimes the merchants

occupied only a part of the town and had no political existence; sometimes they governed fortified and armed towns
which had negotiated relations with the kingdoms. In other
cases, the merchant community – powerful, organized, size-
able – maintained a sort of (sometimes painful) symbiosis
with the local aristocratic power. *Merchant society* emerged,
nevertheless, as soon as the balance of power was reversed
and strength based on arms yielded to the 'power of things' –
that is, of commodities; as soon as conjunctural factors made
trade the infrastructure of wealth and power. Léon l'Africain
notes (pp. 463–4) that after the merchants deserted Walata the
lord of the town became 'poor and powerless'. He also reports (p. 467) that the son of the great Sonxai sovereign *Askia*
Mohamed Abu Bakr Iskia (1493–1528) gave two of his
daughters in marriage to two merchant brothers because of
their wealth: a remarkably demeaning act for a noble!

The merchants were travellers: 'they circulate constantly,
prospecting in all the neighbouring lands', notes Léon l'Africain (1956: 479). In their wake a way of life and a series of
establishments developed which favoured travel. These men,
deprived of households, needed places to sleep, to eat and
sometimes to amuse themselves. The manufacture of and
trade in prepared food emerged in response to the passage
and the needs of the merchants. These activities required a
relatively large – and generally female – labour force, because
of the existing techniques of cooking. Léon l'Africain refers
to slaves without veils who sold 'all the things one can eat' in
Timbuktu (p. 467). Binger found in Tenetu, a village of 800
inhabitants, some 100 passing merchants and as many captives, all of whom needed food. Everything – or almost
everything – was sold in these towns, even water and wood
for heating (Caillié, 1830, II: 312). Buildings had to be
planned and maintained to lodge the caravaneers and their
escorts. In the same way, commercial services – courtiers, re-
tailers, lenders, dealers in cattle and in slaves – emerged.
    Transport necessitated a labour force which was mobile,
and preferably alienable, like the merchandise it carried. In
the towns where the merchants stopped, money circulated

which was sufficiently fungible and divisible to make current transactions possible. Coffers were needed to hold it, solid houses were needed to protect the merchandise without armed guards, and thus an architecture developed which differed from that of the peasants or the aristocrats. 'In Borno, the king left to hunt slaves and the merchants waited for him, at his expense, sometimes until the following year' (Léon l'Africain: 480). In Timbuktu they stayed six to eight months, according to Caillié (II: 309). In order to help them pass the long weeks or months of waiting which good business required, places of entertainment and a new artistic culture developed. El-Bekri describes the young girls 'of handsome countenance' of Aoudaghost, 'with white skins, light and slender in body', who had 'firm breasts, small waists, the lower part of the back well rounded and wide shoulders' (1965: 348–52); or those of Tamekka, 'of such perfect beauty that those of other lands cannot compare with them'. These 'tourist' notices came from information provided by the merchants to other merchants. In the fourteenth century, Ibn Battuta took offence at the excessively complaisant attitudes of the women of Walata (1968, IV: 388s.). In the nineteenth century, Félix Dubois (1897: 310s.) reports how the 'high life' of Timbuktu was, still, described to him: 'Business often leaves time for leisure. One has to wait for certain articles to arrive or for the price of others to rise or fall.' Dinners with friends, dinners offered by the ladies of Timbuktu (who were also known for their beauty and their talents as hostesses), dancing and music, presents given to women who were the mistresses of passing merchants, often ate up a large part of profits.[8]

Jenne and Timbuktu were the twin trading towns through which exchange took place between the savannah and the Sahara, in the continental West African trade: Jenne was the northern port of the Sudan and Timbuktu the southern port of the desert. The Niger, flowing between the two cities, almost exactly from north to south, was the waterway which carried this trade. Jenne drained off food products (cereals, market garden produce),[9] textiles and craft clothing as well as slaves and gold from the lands of the Sudan; Timbuktu sent back salt, horses, guns, luxury goods (cloth from Europe, amber, coral), books, paper, tobacco, and so on, from the desert and the Maghreb. One of these towns was Sudanese, the other 'Moroccan'.

a. Jenne

Of all the merchant towns in this Sahelo-Sudanese region, Jenne certainly came closest to franchise. The town's origins were cosmopolitan. Merchants from various areas, called _Maraka_ – or, locally, *Nono* and *Jennenke*[10] – who had probably been settled in the surrounding area since the second century of the Hegira, won the goodwill of the inhabitants, fisher populations which occupied the lower Niger delta. Together, at an unknown date, they founded the town known as Jenne on land surrounded by water when the river was high.[11] These new urbanized populations were peaceful and concerned mostly with merchant wealth and religion, as is shown by the fact that in the sixth century of the Hegira the town numbered 4,200 *ulema* (*TES*: 23). Jenne's role as a commercial metropolis dates from this period, with the sultan Konboro's conversion to Islam. The mercantile concerns and cosmopolitan nature of the inhabitants are, almost naively, expressed in the favours which were asked of Allah on this occasion:

> Konboro . . . charged Dienné to pray God to grant three things: first, that he who, chased from his land by poverty and misery, comes to live in this town, may find in return, thanks to God, abundance and wealth, so that he may forget his former fatherland; second, that the town may be peopled by a number of foreigners which is higher than that of its nationals; third, that God may deprive those who come to trade their merchandise here of patience, so that, tired of staying here, they sell their goods at rock-bottom prices, which will benefit the inhabitants. After these three prayers, the first chapter of the Koran was read, and these prayers were granted, as all can see *de visu* today. As soon as he had been converted to Islam, the sultan demolished his palace and replaced it with a temple de-

voted to the worship of Almighty God; this is today's great mosque. He built another palace to install his court and this palace is beside the mosque, on the east side. The territory of Dienné is fertile and populous; numerous markets are held here each day of the week. It is said to contain 7,077 villages which are very close to each other. (*TES*: 24)

According to another version reported to me in the field, one of these prayers asked that all the traders of Jenne be granted *baraka* (grace) so that they could make profits from their trade.

The town was governed by these Islamized and peaceful populations. From the sixteenth century, according to C. Monteil (1932/1971), the highest authority was entrusted by the elders of the main families to one of their number, the *were*, who gradually came to be chosen always from the same clan. This college of electors constituted the Council of Jenne, in which the representatives of the Arab and Berber traders with interests in the town also participated. The task of this government was to ensure the best possible conditions for trade, to ensure the security of the markets and to finance the pursuit or punishment of plunderers. The *Jennewere* also administered the surrounding villages which were dependent on the town and collected dues from them, which it used to safeguard the land's independence. This, therefore, was a mode of government which differed from that of the aristocrats. The *Tarikh el-Fettach* relates that the town, at one time, was the prerogative of the wife of a sovereign of 'Mali',[12] but the *Tarikh es-Sudan* specifies that the town had never suffered a military defeat until Sonni Ali (sovereign of Sonxai) brought it under his authority in 1468 and reigned over it. It is said that he besieged the town 'for seven years, seven months and seven days' and that, having won this difficult victory, he left a sort of consul but preserved the existing political structures.

b. Timbuktu

At the same time Sonni Ali took over Timbuktu, where he applied the same type of indirect administration, as did all the successive Sonxai sovereigns.

Until the latter were supplanted by the Arma, invaders from Morocco (1591) who were to install the government of the Pashas over the whole of the Sonxai and over its towns, Timbuktu was also governed by juriconsuls whose power was only judiciary. 'At this time, the town of Timbuktu had no magistrate other than the magistrate responsible for justice: it had no chief or, rather, the chief was the qadi,[13] who was the chief of the town and alone had the right to pardon and to punish' (*TEF*: 315). The inhabitants carried 'neither spear nor sabre, nor knife, nor anything but sticks' (*TEF*: 315):

> At this time Timbuktu had no equal among the towns of the land of the Blacks, from the province of Mali to the outer limits of the Maghreb region, as regards the solidity of its institutions, its political liberty, the purity of its moral standards, the security of persons and of goods, the mercy and compassion shown to the poor and to foreigners, the courtesy shown to students and men of science and the help given to the latter (ibid.: 313).

On the other hand, the merchant class does not seem to have been concerned with the military protection of the town. Timbuktu was not fortified. Its notables preferred to use negotiation or corruption to settle differences rather than resort to hazardous armed solutions.[14] These entrepreneurs knew that their productive activities, the commercial organization they controlled and the economic institutions they dominated, were necessary to the general acquisition of wealth, and the princes knew it too. The wealth of the merchants did not consist of accumulated treasures which could be seized, once and for all. It was built on a constant process of production of consumer goods and on the uninterrupted flow of exchanges which attracted merchandise from other, distant, lands to the houses of the great and the wealthy.[15] They knew that the warrior classes had no choice but to 'protect' them; they could sometimes tax them or extract them, but they could never destroy them without depriving themselves of the benefits of this wealth.

In this merchant society, attacks on goods were seen as an affront. When the Moroccan conqueror Jouder had some houses and shops which belonged to rich merchants knocked down, in order to fortify the town, 'no greater or more cruel trial had ever been forced on the people of Timbuktu, nor any more bitter than this' (*TEF*: 280). The Arma mobilized the inhabitants' slaves and even forced free men to undertake these works, but the worst example of 'violence and excesses' reported by the author of the *Tarikh es-Sudan* was the 'tearing down of the doors of the houses and the knocking down of the trees in the town' (*TES*: 282). While it was true that the trees sheltered the ponds and were doubtless even then 'a gay green belt around the city, sheltering its streets and its squares under fresh domes of greenery' (Félix Dubois, 1897: 291), the disappearance of the doors of houses, the only protection for the citizens of this open town, exposed their goods to the covetousness of the plunderers.

All relations between Timbuktu and its neighbours, whether violent or peaceful, centred around these goods. The Tuareg from the north came to pillage houses and warehouses; the sovereigns tried to impose their taxation on trade. The merchants' vulnerability to plunder by the former more or less obliged them to accept the protection of the latter. The administration of the 'protectors' was judged in terms of their capacity to ensure abundance and prosperity and to safeguard the conditions necessary to the working of the market and the transit of goods (Abitbol, 1979: 93, 96, 104).

However, one of the purposes of the Moroccan presence in the bend of the Niger was the provision of slaves for the Sultan:

Apart from gold, the sultan's caravans brought back ivory, wood for dyeing, horses and, of course, slaves, to Morocco.

The latter are mentioned in all the sources, but estimates

of their numbers are rare. However, all the indications are that their numbers were particularly high. This is why, in the early period of the conquest, the selling price of a slave in Timbuktoo itself was between 200 and 400 cowries, or about a tenth of a *mithqal*, while the current price was six *mithqal* at the beginning of the sixteenth century and ten *mithqal* in the middle of the century.

In 1594 the caravan of prisoners of Sankoré numbered 1,200 slaves. Five years later, Djouder brought back to Marrakesh 'a considerable number' of eunuchs and slaves of both sexes, including the daughters of the *askia* Ishaq II himself.

The following year, *Amin* al-Hasan al-Zubayr prepared to send another contingent of 900 captives to Morocco. The slave trade did not spare any of the populations of the Niger bend, not even the Muslims – Sonxai or not. Its dimensions were such that, it seems, it provoked upheavals and qualms of conscience within Moroccan society. (Abitbol, 1979: 80)

In these conditions, the preservation of the merchant apparatus which was necessary to these supplies imposed moderation on the occupiers as regards taxation and their interference in the management of the city's affairs. The pasha imposed few regular taxes on the basis of a fixed assessment. He exercised only limited prerogatives – usually penal rather than civil, and usually with respect to the Arma and to aliens (Abitbol: 121). When one day the pashas' armed retainers imagined they could claim their master's aristocratic privilege in order to rob and seize the merchants' goods, they came up against violent resistance from the merchants. These peaceful merchants, suddenly enraged, massacred the insolent, and the pashas did not dare to intervene.

If the pashas' exactions were, nevertheless, frequent, they were gradually won over by the prospect of gain. In their turn they made use of their prerogatives to exploit the land through a new category of servile individuals, the *harratin* (Abitbol, 1977: 156), to acquire herds and slaves of both sexes, to accumulate wealth and even to participate more closely in trade by lodging passing merchants (ibid.: 157).

Finally, the usual division of trade in slaves was established between the Moroccan warriors, who plundered the surrounding lands, and the merchants in the cities (Abitbol: 70).

Apart from commerce, Timbuktu had a craft industry which supplied part of the merchandise for exchange, particularly textiles. Twenty-six houses, each with some fifty apprentices, were involved in the production of clothing. Spinning, dyeing, weaving, the sewing of loincloths and of cotton and woollen garments seem to have been important activities. In contrast, fishing and the cultivation of cereals, although they produced the means of subsistence, apparently did not produce enough to constitute reserves against droughts and other calamities (Cissoko, 1968), and certainly not enough for export.

We do not have much information about urban slaves. Caillié, who visited the two towns, noted that in Timbuktu (II: 310) 'they seem less unhappy than in other areas. . . . They are well clothed, well fed and rarely punished; they are obliged to practise religious ceremonies . . . but for all that they are still seen as merchandise.' 'Most of the traders are rich and have many slaves', he continues, without giving any further information. They drew water, and the women cooked and engaged in petty trade in the streets. The masons also seem to have been slaves (ibid.: 320, 321, 324).[16] In Jenne, Caillié noticed that certain slaves were well dressed and did not work much (II: 204): 'these are trusted domestic servants . . . they keep house, count cowries, carry the merchandise on to the boats'. It is possible that in these towns slaves assigned to ancillary or craft tasks benefited, through their proximity to their masters, from better conditions than slaves who were 'responsible for cultivation' (ibid., II: 205). The rural slaves – probably far more numerous – who supplied the means of subsistence of the citizens and a large part of the merchandise were in the hands of the Maraka.

3 THE MARAKA

Most of the products for export to the north, particularly food products and cotton, came from the hinterland of

Timbuktu, in the Sahelo-Sudanese region. The chronicles cite the names of contemporary towns, which were merchant towns like Timbuktu but were also agricultural and probably more closely involved in production than Timbuktu. They were Islamized towns, situated within the sphere of influence of the kingdom of Melli, of Segu or of other sovereigns and also enjoying prerogatives; their religious status protected them from the intrusion of military power and sometimes even from its administration. Referring to the judiciary form of government in Timbuktu, the *Tarikh el-Fettach* notes:

> the same was true, during the time of the domination of the kings of Melli, of Diaba, a town of jurisconsuls situated within the territory of Melli: the king of Melli never entered it and no one except the qadi had authority there. Whoever entered the town was protected from royal violence and annoyance, and even if he had killed one of the king's children, the latter would not have been able to claim the price of blood. It was called the town of God.
>
> The same was also true of the town called Koundiouro, situated in the Kaniaga province; this was the town of the qadi of this region and of the country's *ulemas*. No soldier could enter and no civil servant who might oppress those he administered could live there. However, the king of Kaniaga visited the *ulemas* and the qadi of this town each year during the month of Ramadan, following an ancient custom in the region, bringing alms and presents which he distributed among them.

These were generally the so-called '*maraka*' towns: some of them still exist today and have preserved their trading, slaving and Islamic character.[17] They were located within the sphere of the African contintental market. These towns – Sansani (or Sansanding), Marakala, Marakaduguba, the seven-sided town of Marakaduguworoula, Nyamina, and so on – were located on the margin of the Sudan or on the edge of the Niger, generally at the point where the camel took over from the donkey as means of transport. They sheltered the *maraka* class, which was represented here by Muslim families devoted to slave-owning merchant production.

Their activities and their religion had allowed them to establish a *modus vivendi* with the military class of Segu. In return for certain privileges (exemption from conscription, extraterritoriality) they were obliged to supply dues which were either material (the provision of products) or spiritual (prayers and talismans), particularly on the occasion of celebrations or war by the Segu monarch (Bazin, 1972). We have some information on the practice of slavery in these industrial towns: 'Maraka slavery', writes R. Roberts, who studied Sansani in the field, 'clearly reveals an organization directed towards the market' (1978: 320). 'The production of grain and that of cotton cloth were the two pillars of economic life in the Maraka commercial centres' (ibid.: 314, 317).[18] R. Caillié (II: 242) also mentions that

> The land of Banan (Banandugu) (some fifty kilometres down the river from Mopti) is independent of that of Sego-Ahmadou; . . . its inhabitants are all Mahometans, they have many slaves whom they use for cultivation. They also engage in trade, construct pirogues and voyage to Jenne or Temboctou. . . . They . . . manufacture cotton cloth which they sell to their neighbours . . . and also cloth from the wool of their sheep: they make of it an article for trade.

No precise information is given on the mode of agricultural exploitation. It varied according to opportunity. In Sansani, captives often spent the rainy season working in the fields of their Maraka owners before being sold (Roberts, 1978: 317) (the same happened, as we have seen, on the plantations of the king of Dahomey). Others lived in hamlets separated from the town. They worked under the supervision of an intendant, himself a slave, or of one of the master's sons; both had the right to inflict corporal punishment. The most effective punishment was said to be the denial of food, which suggests that the labourers did not control their own food production. In fact the entire food production was stored in the masters' granaries, which were filled by slave labour. Their rations were drawn from these stocks (ibid.). Here again, the system of redistribution and of control over reserves was the organic instrument of the exploitation of labour.

Some of these subjugated individuals seem to have lived in households, cultivating a strip of land, but only during their free time – that is, after cultivating the master's fields during the day and sometimes also those of the intendant or the master's eldest son. According to prevailing custom in the Maraka population, the slave's working day during the agricultural season lasted from sunrise until 3 or 4 p.m. for the master, and could be extended until 6 p.m. for the wife or son of the master or for the intendant. He had only one free day in a seven-day week, and then only if he was not expected to perform other tasks for the master or for members of his family. In any case, he was not granted either enough land or enough time to produce his own means of subsistence. Unmarried slaves were attached to 'households' and ate with them (Roberts, 1978: 317).

As a result of the growing commercialization of grain during the colonial conquest, according to the accounts of several administrators (ibid.), the slaves' food rations were very meagre, from 350 to 420 grams of sorghum per day per head, while a minimum ration of 1 kilogram is thought to have been necessary for hard labour.

It seems that in other cases labour was not collectively performed on a single plantation. Each slave cultivated a field and had to hand over a given fixed quantity of production each year. In other words, agricultural exploitation took place through the extraction either of a rent in labour or of a rent in products, each of which contributed to the realization of profit. The implications of these different forms will be discussed below.

Textiles were the other pillar of Maraka slave exploitation. Maraka women took advantage of the general increase in wealth brought about by trade to obtain slaves of both sexes from their rich husbands or from their own families, or were allowed to use part of the labour-time of the family slaves. There is no doubt that slavery brought considerable benefits to women of noble or merchant condition, particularly since most of the slaves were women who could replace them in their work. If, with the coming of Islam, free-born women led more cloistered lives, they were also freed from domestic and agricultural labour. Most of them took up textile production, assigning slaves to this work. Women slaves cultivated the cotton, carded and spun it. They also cultivated indigo, prepared it and dyed the cloth. Weaving was exclusively reserved for servile men, who also sewed the lengths of cotton. These textiles were destined for the market and particularly for export. The Maraka women handed over these lengths of cotton and cloth to relatives or to merchants of their acquaintance, to be sold on distant markets and exchanged for jewels or other goods which became these women's property.

The slaves involved in these tasks, particularly perhaps the women, also had to perform household tasks, so that they could scarcely work for their own benefit. According to Roberts, these slaves were 'doubly exploited', since they had to spend the usual five or six days working for the wife's family and the rest of their time working for their mistress. They had no free time to cultivate a strip of land. In contrast, allotment slaves could engage in certain craft activities apart from their agricultural subsistence labour – sometimes paid, sometimes on their own account. Plaiting mats, for instance, or manufacturing potash and soap, enabled them to market goods which swelled the merchants' trade and profit. The men were sometimes given bonuses for their weaving which increased their pittance.

The most exploited were the slaves of slaves, whom Roberts also found in Sansani. Once a slave reached a certain age, if he had accumulated sufficient savings, he could buy another slave to help him or replace him in some or all of his dues to the master. Moreover, the slave's slave had to supply his slave-master's means of subsistence as well as his own. 'Thus the *jonmajon* (Bamana, slave's slave) was doubly exploited and doubly dependent' (Roberts, 1978: 316). He was fed by his slave-master, who controlled the whole of his production. He was usually not 'married'. In this way the slave was responsible for his own economic (not genesic) reproduction, at his own expense, at a time when he was in the process of becoming unproductive. Through this mechanism his earnings – which, as we have seen, never really belonged to him – were returned to his master. The slave benefited from his savings only to the extent that part of the surplus-product of his *jonmajon* was left over after the satisfaction of the master's needs and of those of the *jonmajon* himself. As a result the exploitation of these sub-slaves was all the more intense. It contributed to a rise in the general rate of exploitation of labour. It must also be noted that, as in this case, an exploited individual could exploit another without, for all that, freeing himself of his class condition.

State does not change, regardless of condition.

2

The Spread of Slavery within the Peasantry

1 THE INTENSIFICATION OF WARS OF CAPTURE

a. El Haj Umar

We do not know in what proportions slaves were employed by the Maraka at the time of Segu (seventeenth to nineteenth century). The first estimate dates from 1863: according to Mage (1868: 276), the Kuma (one of the two great Sansani families) owned several thousand slaves. In 1887, an inhabitant of Sansani told a French officer that 'each family owns 1,000 to 2,000 slaves' (Roberts, 1978: 290). The figures given in the colonial census of 1904 vary in the order of one to twelve, depending on whether they were provided by the masters (who tried to minimize their wealth) or the slaves (ibid.: 291). But in any case these figures indicate that the numbers were large.[1]

These numerous slaves were the product of more and more intense wars of capture, waged from the mid-nineteenth century in the entire Sahelo-Sudanese region, by El Haj Umar, Samori, Tieba and others who emulated them; they resulted in the spread of slavery. A military aristocracy claiming inspiration from Islam replaced the pagan princes of

Segu when, the Atlantic slave trade having dried up, the growing demand for slaves, particularly women, on the African continental market had to be satisfied. Could these increasingly brutal wars, which had become less profitable since the main outlet for male captives had disappeared, be more easily sanctified when waged by Islamized warriors? In any case, the very progress of Islam, since it increased the number of Muslim princes and subjects, would have severely reduced potential captives if the faith of some had not been asserted as superior to that of others, so that the latter were transformed into infidels, suitable for capture.[2] As a result of the new momentum which the slave market acquired in this way, new Maraka cities developed, while slavery spread among peasant milieus in the areas which were spared from plunder.

El Haj Umar, the founder of Tijanism, started his holy war of capture [*jihad*][3] as early as 1852 in Tambura. He did not undertake raids but true wars, involving several thousand men with imported firearms and sophisticated methods of warfare. In 1855 he invaded Kingi and took Nioro, putting one of his sons, Agibu, in power. In 1856 he sacked the Baxana area on the edge of the Sahel; in 1859–60 he attacked the territory of the kingdom of Segu and took its capital in 1861, installing another of his sons, Amadu. The following year he seized Hamdalay, capital of Masina, a Muslim but rival State (Mahibou and Triaud, 1983).

The spiritual significance of the wars waged by El Haj Umar and his sons seems meagre compared to the material benefits they brought, through the destruction of hundreds of villages and the death or enslavement of thousands of men, women and children. Mage, a French officer who had come to negotiate a treaty with Amadu (son of El Haj Umar) and was held by him in Segu from 1863 to 1866, relates some of these campaigns, in which he took part with his men, as a heroic French soldier, pretending to see these wars of abduction as 'the War' (Mage, 1868: 432–8).

Togu was a big Bamana village some 60 kilometres from Segu, which refused to accept the domination of Amadu. On 7 April 1865, Amadu attacked the village with 10,000 men. The inhabitants defended themselves courageously:

*The taking of Toghou by Amadu (Mage, 1868: 432–8), 31
January 1865*

Towards four o'clock the Bambaras had all, or nearly all,
succumbed; in the village occasional gunshots were fired.
Since a few of the enemy[4] were still hiding in the huts, [the
army] did not dare to enter because of the darkness and
waited for them to escape. Ahmadou came from the left,
then from behind the village, on the hill where the day
before the Bambaras had still been encamped . . . Firing on
the undergrowth started almost at once. The Bambaras
who were there had tried to flee to the East, but they had
encountered the Peuhls, who had forced them back to the
village. They stopped firing only towards nightfall, and
the *tabala*[5] was constantly sounded . . .

1 February 1865.
Dawn had hardly broken when the whole army went into
the bush to finish them off: the Bambara were found there,
defenceless, and were horribly butchered. A band of
twenty-seven, perhaps hoping for mercy from the conquerors, laid down their arms and came out of the undergrowth crying: Pardon! [*Toubira!*] They were immediately
taken to Ahmadou, between two tight ranks of Sofas. All
of them were delivered to the executioner . . . In the evening, wanting to see how many had died, I passed by the
field of execution; they had been taken there, all closely
surrounded by the crowd and held simply by human arms;
in the centre of the circle stood the executioner, who had
started to cut off their heads, randomly, in no particular
order, as soon as they were within reach of his arm. Some
heads had not even been detached from their trunk!
  It is impossible to describe the spectacle of Toghou. In
the houses and the streets bodies were lying in all sorts of
positions. In the hideout which had been so long defended,
each hut had been transformed into a horrible charnel-
house. The roofs which had been set alight from the top
had burned hundreds of unfortunate people, whose death
agony had been revealed only by their muffled cries. In
some of the huts people had hanged themselves in despair;

at one of the gates of the town more than five hundred
bodies were lying on top of each other; this was the gate
which had been attacked by the Talibes.[6] Later I went into
the bush: one could say that the whole village and its surroundings was no more than a field of dead, and the following day, when the half-burned bodies had been removed from the burning rubble of the village and taken on
to the plain, the horrible smell they gave off infected the
air over a great distance. It would certainly be less than the
truth to say that two thousand five hundred Bambara had
perished there, and later, when the Peuhls returned on
horseback, their still bloody spears bore witness to the
blows they had given to the fugitives . . .

This village was prodigiously rich and could resist a
long siege. There were powder and sorghum in immense
quantities, not counting all the other nutritive substances
such as beans, rice, etc.

During the whole of the first night, the army had eaten
chickens, goats and sheep in the village, and when one re-
members that an army of more than ten thousand men had
lived on this, it is not surprising that the next day I could
not find a single chicken. However, everyone was chew-
ing gourous.[7] Many had filled their sacks with cowries and
the booty was such that it could not be carried . . .

The departure from the village was difficult. Each man
loaded himself with baggage; some had sent for donkeys
to carry the booty, and it was truly strange to see the warriors of the previous day transformed into merchants of
old scrap. Everything was useful to them; some carried big
calabashes, others sacks of sorghum, native candelabra
from the area . . . others took away a door, guns, spears,
axes or the tools of smiths or weavers. Some had cotton,
others tobacco or balls of indigo; and then there was the
line – or rather the lines – of captives. I did not know how
many they were until Segu, where they were distributed.
About three thousand five hundred women or children
were there, bound by the neck, heavily laden, beaten by
the Sofas while they walked. Some of the women, too old,
fell under the weight of their burden and, refusing to walk
further, were assassinated. A shot in the kidney and it was

over: I was forced to see this and I had to stay calm and not cut off the head of the miserable individual who had committed this crime. Our *laptots* [native boatmen in the French colonial army] and even some of the Talibes were shocked by this; but they were the exception and the masses passed by with a gesture of disdain, finding only the epitaph: Keffir.[8] And let it be known, those who committed these atrocities were themselves Keffirs, Bambaras, slaves from father to son, former slaves of the Massassis of Kaarta or of the Courbaris of Segu, whose savagery and cruelty had been doubled by a dash of Islamism as it is preached in Africa.

In Kenenku, where Mage once again took part in the taking of the village, he associated himself with the results: 'We took many prisoners, and we took nearly all the women. The prisoners were summarily interrogated and immediately executed by the light of the campfires' (1868: 472). These captures and executions were routine. The aim was to seize a certain type of merchandise – women, particularly, and able-bodied children – and to get rid of those who could not be sold – adult men and old people of both sexes. The job was apparently done with professional competence and detachment.

b. Samori

While El Haj Umar turned to the east, towards Fuuta Jallo, another 'great conqueror', Samori Ture, distinguished himself among the plunderers who operated on a fairly small scale in the region. Unlike Captain Peroz, who favoured alliance with Samori, Galliéni (1885: 519–59), who fought a war against him, does not present him in such a favourable light:

For about two years[9] the Sankaran has been devastated by Samory . . . Many of the inhabitants of the Sankaran, like those of Ouassolou, have been taken away into slavery: the market at Kankan is the usual selling place for these unfortunate people . . .

It is said of him[10] that he turned *Malinke* so as to show
that he had ceased to be a merchant and had become a warrior.[11] His suite is made up of young people who are well
armed, mounted on excellent horses and used to success.
At the end of each winter[12] he places himself at the head of
this troop, descends on the neighbouring lands and reaps
an abundant harvest of captives and cattle. In this way he
has successively ruined Baleya, Dioumo, Belimena,
Amana and the land of Kankan. He even exacts tribute
from this famous market. His former village, Dougourou,
once fairly poor, is now gorged with booty.

These long devastating excursions were not accomplished by Samory alone. The chief of Dinguiray, Agui-
bou, would perhaps not have allowed such fruitful raids to
take place at two or three days' march from his fortress
without taking part himself. Thus Toucouleurs and
Malinke have acted in concert against the Bambaras. But
. . . the well-armed and belligerent bands of Samory are a
danger to the Ahmadou's brother . . . and Dinguiray
would be in a difficult situation were it not for the intervention of a new chief of plunderers, called Mor-Birahim,
who has already fought with Samory . . . Today he lives in
Molokoro and attracts many of those who were formerly
faithful to Samory and are hostile to the Muslim religion . . .

The Morebeledougou can be crossed without too
much fear by the Dioulas, who have recently been able
to make numerous and very remunerative purchases of
captives there, which the war delivered to them at low
prices.

Batedougou lies on the banks of the Milo and its principal village is the famous market of Kankan, which René
Caillié has already visited and described . . . Captives flow
in from Ouassoulou, from Sankaran and from the lands
ravaged by Samory . . . Kankan, located behind the
English colony of Sierra Leone, is said to be frequently
visited by traders for the English merchants, and many of
its inhabitants travel to the ports of call on the British
rivers . . . Amana and Baleya are neighbouring and have
suffered more or less the same fate . . . Samory has sowed

ruin everywhere and dispersed the inhabitants. Baleya has suffered particularly harshly: it is said that nothing is left ... The Dioula continue to cross this desolate land, but they have difficulty finding places to stay.

The rivers of Djoliba and Dioumo are situated near the confluence of the Milo and the Tinkisso rivers with the Niger ... Samory came to bring ruin to this land also, but he respected important sites like Tiguibiri and Damoussa, which are in a good position for trade ... Kenieradougou comes after Dioumo on the right bank of the Niger ... The population contains mostly Malinkes from Manding. Its main occupation is war. During each dry season, the young warriors go to Ouassoulou and the other neighbouring countries to raid for captives, who are then crowded into the *tatas* [see note 6, page 352] of Keniera.

As I have said, this market is one of the most important from the point of view of the slave trade: it is as well known for this trade as Dialikrou for transactions in gold. The Dioulas whom we questioned told us that in Keniera there was always a large supply of slaves to be sold. In times of war, the number is still higher. Also, the price of human flesh is lower here than anywhere else, and in times of abundance one can buy up to two captives for one bar of salt (about 15 kg). Samory, having destroyed Baleya, Amana and Dioumo, came to strike at Kenieradougou ...

The Keleyadougou, located to the north-east of the former, belongs to Malinkes, who are fighters and cultivators. Once the harvest is over, they arm themselves and go out for gain, one of the young men of the area told us ...

The Tiakadougou contains numerous and populous Bambara villages; there are a few Malinkes on its western edge. The main town is Tenetou, which is an important market visited by caravans travelling from Segu to Boure and to Keniera ... Ahmadou's columns have already started to attack it from the north, carrying off the population of several villages into slavery. These incursions are renewed and will continue to be renewed each year, and little by little the Tiakadougou will be sucked into the States of the Toucouleur sultan, who seems to want to reach the Ouassoulou the classic land for captives.

The Banandougou, a large territory situated to the north of the former, has already been partly subordinated to the Toucouleurs, who go to supply themselves with captives there during the dry season. It is known that raids are the only means of existence for the Talibes of Ahmadou. The fortress of Tadiana keeps the conquered villages under submission; without the Toucouleur garrison there they would revolt every winter, like the inhabitants of Bele-dougou. The Bambaras of Banandougou are beginning to realize what fate awaits them, and their resistance is weakened as a result. While we were at Nango, the first column of Talibes covered the land in all directions, burned three villages and gave in before a fourth which had enough energy to resist the attackers. But the column had hardly returned to Segu before a new troop, composed of Sofas, set off for Banandougou in its turn: the terrified village took flight, abandoning some hundred captives.

Nothing can equal the horror of the scenes of carnage and desolation caused by these ceaseless wars in regions which are known for their unusual fertility and their wealth of metal products. The villages are burned down, old people of both sexes are put to death, while the young people are dragged off into captivity and then shared out among the conquerors.

In 1827 Caillié passed through the same region; he noted that in Sankaran 'the independent chiefs often wage war against each other to procure slaves whom they sell at very high prices' (p. 416). The slaves were used in the neighbouring Bure to exploit the gold mines of the sovereign of the Jalonke and of private owners. In the Baleya also, bands abducted captives. In Kankan, the slaves lived in hamlets and were used for cultivation: 'a Mandingo who owns a dozen slaves can live at ease without working' (p. 415). But he does not mention the sale of captives in the Islamized town of Kankan, the region's main market. Honey, cloth, wax, cotton, animals and gold were sold there, brought by neighbouring populations including the Toron, pagan agriculturalists who resisted the Muslims and lived in independent villages. Slaves were bought, he was told, in Kissi (to the west, in present-day Guinea): '. . . The current price is one barrel of powder weighing twenty-five pounds, a poor gun worth five gourds[13] and two measures of pink silk' (p. 415). The bridewealth of women consisted of two or three slaves. In contrast, the people of Amana lived peacefully, although their villages were surrounded by 'a double wall of earth 10 or 12 feet high'. Further to the east, the Wasulu, which was to become one of Samori's main warrens, seemed to Caillié to be prosperous and well populated. The inhabitants were peaceful cultivators and pastoralists, living in spread-out hamlets where the only protection was the palisades erected for the cattle. They were weavers and smiths but they did not engage much in trade and 'do not travel, since their idolatry would expose them to the most horrible enslavement' (p. 447). Nevertheless, they welcomed Muslims with kindness.[14]

Thus although the villages to the west of Kankan had already been affected by slaving raids and forced to protect themselves behind fortifications, circulation does not seem to have been seriously affected. To the east the populations were self-sufficient and pagan and lived without protection. All these lands were to be brought under submission by Samori, and their inhabitants were to swell the African slave market to such an extent that prices fell sharply.

Under Samori the region was divided geographically in functional terms: the peripheral areas, pagan, whose lineage populations lived in hamlets which were dispersed and therefore vulnerable, were the zones for capture; the Islamized towns and the markets were spared, along with their inhabitants, as channels for the sale of human merchandise; a political zone under the authority of Samori, who established himself at Bisandugu in Wasulu, developed with the *pax samoria* whose economic and political orderliness was admired by Peroz (1896: 359s.); finally, beyond the zones of plunder, towards the north, lay a hinterland irrigated by the slave trade, whose inhabitants bought labourers cheaply for use in the production of goods and merchandise.[15]

In the villages of the Sahel, as in the Wagadu or the Gajaga, joining Samori's troops was seen as a sure way of acquiring wealth by bringing back captives who could be added to those bought on the southern markets as far as Sikasso, where captives from Beledugu were sold (1966 Mission). Furthermore, engagement in the French colonial troops, which fought on the same ground, had similar advantages. 'Irregulars', as the African volunteers who joined in the fighting were called, were not paid and the French officers, in accordance with a well-established military tradition, turned a blind eye to the behaviour of these troops during campaigns. El Haj Umar, Samori and the French colonial army made a considerable contribution to the supply of the Sudanese slave markets during the second half of the nineteenth century. As a result of these campaigns slaves became cheaper and were no longer the privilege of Islamized merchant Maraka families. Slavery spread within peasant populations, more and more of whom entered the circuits of merchant slave production.

2 SLAVERY AMONG THE PEASANTS OF THE SAHEL

According to a legend which seems to date back several centuries, the mother of Dinga, founder of Wagadu, was a slave, Faduwani Bafonje: 'Faduwani Bafonje had one hundred and one heads on a single neck and one hundred and one eyes. At each daybreak, she put one hundred and one jars on her head and went to draw water from the well at Tiri'.[16] This is the portrait of the ideal slave, of the *tumbare* engaged in her characteristic functions, but it is also the portrait of a formidable woman and the mythical ancestor of one of the oldest Soninke clans! According to this text, certain 'slaves' were thus intimately connected with noble families. The legend also describes how a sort of cousinly relation was established between the hero Maren Jagu Dukure and a young slave girl, Henten Kuruba, who had been substituted for him to protect him from the hatred of a tyrant. In spite of having been saved by her, Maren Jagu was forced by an oath to cut the young girl's throat; she was resuscitated by her own magic powers. When he came to power, having killed the tyrant, he put her at his side on the mat which symbolized both the throne and the conjugal bed, to the great displeasure of his elders. Yet it

is from Henten Kuruba's family that the 'slaves' of the
Dukure are descended, even today. Thus servitude was not
new among these populations; however, how can one date
each of these descriptions from the often anachronistic
accounts passed on by the praise-singers, and how can one
characterizse them? How can one detect the social fantasies
which they underpin? The same legend also refers to a more
modern form of slavery. It says that to be a slave means, first
and foremost, to cultivate another's land; that 'the slave is a
stallion' and not the father of a family; that the child belongs
to the mother's master; that the lineages of the enfranchised
bear the name of a female ancestor. The legend tells of hamlets exclusively populated by slaves. One learns that the free-
born protected each other from enslavement by a pact and
that through another pact they pledged to return escaped
slaves (and wives) to each other.

We know a little more about more recent slavery as it developed among these populations, probably in the nineteenth
century, as a result of contact with the Moors, whose commercial activities had opened up the region to exchange.
Close relationships had existed for some time between the
transhumant pastoralists of the southern Sahara and the agri-
culturalist populations of the Sahel (see Meillassoux, 1971d).
Each year, the latter were hosts to the pastoralists during the
months of the dry season. They let them use their wells or
ponds to water their cattle; the cattle grazed on the hay left in
the sorghum fields after the harvest and simultaneously
manured the soil. The Sahelian peasants paid in sorghum for
the transport of the harvest by the Moors' oxen or exchanged
it for milk and other dairy products; they exchanged raw cotton cloth for bars of salt. Because of this relationship, the
Moors did not plunder the Sahelians. They attacked the
Bamana populations (whose name had become synonymous
with slave) further to the south and sold the captives whom
they did not keep for themselves to these Sahelian populations.

These exchanges between sedentary cultivators and nomad
pastoralists were primordial: they lasted until the wars of El
Haj Umar and they explain the presence of agricultural villages on the edge of the desert. An early form of slave peasant

economy had developed around this trade, but we have no precise information about the numbers involved, the condition of the slaves or their price. However, since it had already been inserted into the circuit of exchange, however limited, and since it produced goods for trade and benefited from a surplus-product, this economy was structurally capable of taking advantage of the new circumstances created by the wars of capture waged by El Haj Umar, Samori and others of their ilk.

There were two ways of benefiting from these wars: by taking part or by buying the booty.

After El Haj Umar's passage through the region and the surrender of the villages, several local heroes went to join the fight and brought back captives. However, most of the slaves were bought: some from passing merchants who brought El Haj Umar's takings, from Sokolo to the east, but most from the markets on the banks of the Niger which were supplied by Samori and Tieba. Armed caravans which included the principal slave-traders were periodically organized by the Islamized families. The villagers, who did not enjoy the safe-conduct which applied to Muslims, gave them goods to exchange, with instructions about the type of slave they wanted in return; they also sent trusted slaves (whose capture would be less important) to see to the transaction. At the time of El Haj Umar, these caravans reached Banamba, Nyamina, Segu, Banambile. They did not cross the Niger. During Samori's wars the better-armed caravans went further, to the regions of Sikasso and Wasulu.

Exchange took place in kind, and the terms of the exchange were expressed in respective quantities of merchandise. The local money, the cowrie, was accepted as such only within the frontiers of the kingdom of Segu (where it was also used to pay taxes), particularly in the towns. The main export articles were raw cotton cloth and sorghum. They were bartered, before departure or during the journey, for goods which could be exchanged for slaves on the markets to the south. Bars of salt were obtained from the Moors and exchanged for so-called 'Guinean' cloth of European origin, guns, amber and coral with the Futanke, who crossed the land from the coast. The merchandise was converted into cowries in Muruja. A considerable trade in horses developed at the same time as Samori's wars (Roberts, 1984: 310) and whole convoys of the animals, bought from the Moors (who had in turn procured them from the Arabs), were taken to the regions occupied by Samori.

On the way the horses carried on their backs the goods whose counterpart was carried by the slaves, on their heads, on the return journey. According to certain enthusiastic informants, the value of these horses was fabulous: they were said to be exchanged for ten, fifteen or even twenty captives. Others said they were exchanged for two to five captives, Roberts found two to ten captives per horse (ibid.). In fact, the slave was not a standard measure, since the price of slaves varied according to sex, age, social and geographic origin and personal characteristics. Since the same applied to horses, such large differences are understandable. These transactions continued and increased during the campaigns of the French colonial troops, with the contribution by 'irregulars' of their human booty. At the time of the French occupation, when censuses of slaves were taken, they represented 30 to 50 per cent of the total population of several Sahelian towns.

Most of these numbers were reached during the years before French occupation. The case is quoted of the planter who owned between 100 and 300 slaves in 1908, when he was forced to free them, while in 1901, when he had been 'poor', he had owned only two.

The distribution of slaves between the families was unequal (Meillassoux, 1979a: 248). Islamized families were among those who owned the most slaves and exploited them in similar fashion to the Maraka.

In this peasant society, the slaves were not immediately made profitable to the same degree as in the merchant Maraka class. Many owners assigned them to the production of the family's subsistence rather than to the manufacture of goods. At first slaves were a luxury, relieving their masters of part of their labour and cultivating at their side; then, as their numbers increased, in their stead. Young people of good family left agricultural work. Dressed in beautiful clothes and in trousers cut wide between the legs, they became idle, spending their time chatting in the village square,

impertinently making fun of their elders or organizing themselves into bands to hold the caravans to ransom. Some,
stimulated by the exploits of Samori or Tieba, dragged off
their companions and some of their slaves to fight strange
jihads against the nearest Islamized towns.

During the wars or the mutual raiding of the *kafo*[17] and
their neighbours, the slaves were mobilized to carry food and
water and sometimes to fight, armed with single-barrelled
guns (double-barrelled guns were reserved for the free-born)
or with picks to knock down the walls of besieged villages. It
was imperative for a slave to bring back his master's body if
he was killed. Certain slave 'families' were installed at the entrance to a town – which was not fortified – so as to take the
first shock in case of attack.

Here again free-born women drew great benefit from
slavery. Their *gada*, or court girl, took over cooking and all
domestic tasks; the *tumbare*, women of all work, undertook
the heavy duties such as carrying water and wood, pounding
and cleaning. . . . At the end of the century, free-born
women did not work in the fields. They had family slaves for
the cultivation of vegetable gardens, cotton and indigo. Like
the Maraka women, some benefited from the product of a
private field cultivated by their slave or slaves. They made
the women card and spin and the men weave the lengths of
cotton which they sold for their own profit.

In this way social differences were established within the
peasant milieu between families which followed the same
lines of exploitation of slaves as the Maraka and others whose
participation in merchant slave production was limited to the
renewal of a troop of slaves for their own use.

3

Forms of Exploitation

Although the peasants were concerned with profits later and to a lesser extent than the Maraka, they were nevertheless compelled, in order to replace their slaves, to make them produce commodities for sale on the market. As a result, different forms of exploitation can be found in both populations, none of them being reserved exclusively for the peasants or the Maraka.

1 TOTALITARIAN EXPLOITATION

In the simplest, most characteristic and most widespread form of slave exploitation before colonization, the slaves supplied, on demand, the whole of their labour-time to their masters, the only limit being that of exhaustion. In Gajaga, they were called 'slaves who rose early'; in Kingi, *koccinto* (bound). *A priori* these were polyvalent labourers of both sexes (more often women than men, in Africa) who were totally available and ready to perform any task assigned to them. According to the season or to market conditions and the needs of their masters, the labour of these *drudge-slaves* was primarily applied to agriculture during the rainy season, to household tasks, to the production of goods for sale, and so on. Sex did not affect the task to the same extent as among

free-born persons. Sexual specializations were mainly the result of customary forms of skill transmission between
women or between men. The women helped or replaced
their mistresses in the labour of cooking. In the dry season,
men and women resurfaced habitations and undertook craft
work to meet domestic needs or those of the market. In the
least qualified tasks – such as the drawing and transport of
water, the collection and cutting of wood – men and women
were used depending on opportunity, independently of any
notion of 'dispensation' linked to sex.

These slaves were fed from household production, to
which they were the first to contribute: sometimes from a
common plate, sometimes from leftovers. For a time they
had to go naked or be beaten. With the coming of Islam it became customary to give them a few old clothes. They were
lodged in huts which usually had no furniture. They had no
recognized right to progeny and in practice they rarely gave
birth. No institution provided for the reproduction of these
slaves by procreation. However, births could take place as a
result of the promiscuity in which they lived. But in the
absence of a host institution, the children born in these circumstances were either fed from the common plate of the
master's household, once they had been weaned, or handed
over to settled women. This reproduction was incidental and
was often seen as hampering the women's labour.

In contrast to the unlimited labour-time provided by the
slaves, their earnings were limited to their measured individual needs. These earnings were not proportional to time
worked, to production, or to family responsibilities. The
only measure used in this mode of exploitation was the uniform measure of food. Rations could be reduced in times of
dearth or famine, the slaves being among the first to suffer
hunger and to die. But as a rule, for fear of losing his slaves,
the master was careful to provide what was necessary for the
reconstitution of their strength and their daily maintenance
even when they were not working. Since drudge-slaves had
no time of their own, the labour necessary to the satisfaction
of their needs was confused with the surplus-labour undertaken for the benefit of the master. But unlike wage-labour,
where the same confusion is found, remuneration was paid in

kind, in food in the form of meals, and not in money: it was not proportional to the time worked by the slave, nor to the volume or value of his or her production. Once bought by the master, the slave had to be maintained permanently. His or her earnings in food could not drop below a physiologically necessary minimum, otherwise the owner himself would suffer. On the other hand, it could be limited at all times to this minimum. Thus the surplus-product does not appear, here, as a distinct physical entity, and surplus-labour does not appear as the result of a measured length of time (as it does in the forms described below). The benefits the owner drew from this type of slave were not, strictly speaking, either surplus-labour or surplus-value, but what I call an *excess* which confuses the two and could be at the disposal of the master in the form both of labour-energy which he could apply to any task, whether remunerative or not, and of the non-consumed product of the slave. Depending on whether this mode of exploitation functioned in the framework of self-sustenance or in relation to the market, the excess product could be kept or used as profit.

This form of exploitation is thus characteristic of slavery. It must not be confused either with wage-labour or with the forms of exploitation described below, which generated *rent* (in labour or in kind) but were common to serfdom.

When totalitarian exploitation functioned within the framework of the self-sustenance economy, where labour was primarily applied to food cropping and was thus limited to a part of the year, the only way to increase the surplus-product of the drudge-slave was to reduce his or her rations or increase the intensity of his or her labour. But with merchant slavery an increase in the length of time worked became possible, since *outside the agricultural season* slaves could be used to produce goods for the market; furthermore, this production could be intensified either by punishment or by material incentives. Thus some of these slaves, if they were skilled, could be assigned to profitable artisanal tasks which sometimes contributed to improvements in their condition. This totalitarian exploitation was certainly the form which affected the greatest number of slaves, although after colonization its importance was greatly reduced. Drudge-slaves were considered the most vile and were the most despised. Because of their condition (and, thus, of the fact that they were single) they have left neither memories nor traditions, so that they are barely perceptible retrospectively, unlike settled or even allotment slaves.

2 RENT SLAVERY

As the slave trade dried up, the slaves' condition changed. The number of drudge-slaves, whose renewal depended on the market, fell, while the number of those who were allowed to cultivate the land in order to produce a *rent* in labour or in products, rather than an *excess*, rose. In certain regions, such as Kingi (M. Diawara, oral communication), it seems that this new form of exploitation was generalized after the colonial conquest. We know from Klein (1983) and Roberts (1984) that in some regions French colonization attempted to negotiate the status of the slaves with their masters, and that apparently traditional forms of serfdom emerged as a result.

Thus the importance of rent slavery in the Sahelo-Sudanese region must not be overestimated. Before conquest, only a fraction of allotment or settled slaves worked in material conditions which were linked to some form of emancipation, whose social forms were described in the first part of this work.

a. Rent in labour

Some of the slaves whose condition I have described as being that of 'allotment' slaves (Part I, Chapter 5, Section 2) thus had a *measured* amount of time at their disposal to grow their own food on a strip of land. Here the slave's time was divided between the labour necessary for the production of all or part of his or her means of subsistence and surplus-labour which he or she provided, free, to the master. In the Sahelo-Sudanese region, the time available to the slave varied from one slave-owning population to another. It could be

from one to three days in a seven-day week, plus evenings
from about 4 p.m. after the completion of work on the
master's fields and on fields belonging to those of his dependants who had a right to this labour. The slave was fed by the
master when he or she worked for him – that is, during the
agricultural season, usually at the midday meal. The slave
provided his or her own food in the evening, on holidays
and, during the dry season, on days when he or she did not
work. These slaves lived either in yards adjoining those of
the master or in hamlets reserved for them, under the
authority of one of them who had been appointed by the
master. Most of those who were appointed were themselves
slaves who had been bought, since only people of the same
'species' could live in these hamlets. They could form a
couple, if they so desired, only with the permission of their
respective masters, and each 'partner' continued to work for
his or her master if they did not both belong to the same
family.

Since he renounced part of the rent in labour, the master no
longer had, as in the previous case, to keep the slave alive all
year round, irrespective of the labour he or she performed.
Because the slaves were given – limited – access to the agricultural means of production, their basic needs were considered to be met by their private labour and they were supposed to be able to feed themselves during periods when they
were not employed by their master. Only part of the labour-
energy used up had to be compensated for. This fraction
could, therefore, be varied in terms of the labour which was
effectively supplied. Here the slave's earnings tended to
become proportional to his or her labour-time. However, it
was preferable not to allow the slaves too much time to work
for their own benefit, and in particular not to allow them to
build up reserves which would enable them to become independent of their masters for their food needs and reduce
their incentives to work for these masters. In any case, their
condition as slaves meant that they did not own their granaries, if they had any; these belonged by right to their
masters. As we have seen elsewhere, when the master's
authority was no longer exercised on the person of the slave,
a principle was established in terms of which the master,

through his management of reserves, intervened during bad years as the only way of ensuring the reproduction of the agricultural cycle.

This form of exploitation, which I have called *allotment*, did not necessarily imply life in a household in the same way as in the case of the *settled* slave. However, it is possible that the different lengths of time granted to these slaves by the different populations which employed them were linked to a policy of reproduction through procreation. Among the Soninke, for example, who were more fully integrated into the merchant circuits and among whom the great majority of slaves were renewed through purchase, settled slaves had only one day a week, plus their evenings, free. Among neighbouring populations who were more attached to domestic traditions and among whom the insertion of slaves conformed to a greater extent to this perspective, they had two to three days free. During their free time they could do craft work, some of which was remunerated by the master and some of which was for their own profit. This additional length of time allowed settled slaves who lived in couples to use a larger part of their surplus–product to feed a progeny and perhaps also to accumulate savings which might allow them to be settled through redemption.

b. Rent in kind

A small minority of slaves were freed from dues in labour and allowed to cultivate land which had been allocated to them in return for dues *in kind* (in this case, sorghum), which were fixed by convention and independent of the result of the harvest. Settlement and redemption of this sort (Part I, Chapter 6, Section 3) were generally granted to settled slaves who were expected to take charge of minors born of their union or entrusted to them. When these children reached productive age, identical dues were demanded to redeem their labour. This was the case when a boy reached the age of 'wearing trousers' or when a girl was married. In the latter case the master demanded dues in kind from the father, who had to claim them from his daughter's husband. Children on whose behalf these dues were not paid worked on the master's lands. These dues were comparatively high, and those affected said that they had difficulty meeting their obligations. In Gumbu, for example, 150 *mude* (2·4 kilograms per *mude*) were demanded per active individual per year. Among other populations in the region the dues were only 80, 90 or 100 *mude*. As a very approximate estimate, if annual dues were 150 *mude* per productive adult, over twenty years – the average active life of a couple – allowing for seed requirements and bad years, the total volume of dues must have exceeded the surplus-product (Part III, Chapter 5). Thus it seems unlikely that the slave household, even without children, could have built up reserves. If the annual dues were 90 *mude*, a couple would scarcely have had enough to feed more than one child up to productive age. In both cases, reproduction did not take place and reserves were totally used up.[1]

When the master's family called on relatives and neighbours to undertake collective work, settled slaves had to send as many of their adult members as possible, as they did for village works in the public interest. In principle they could use the rest of their time, particularly in the dry season, to satisfy their other needs. Two types of remunerative activity were open to them. Skilled men could hire out their services to their master, or even to others, as weavers. Spun materials were supplied by the contractor, who remunerated the weaver on a variable basis.[2] The women were paid for spinning in equivalent weights of raw cotton. Slaves could also manufacture ropes or mats from materials which they procured through their labour and keep the entire proceeds of their sale. Here again, however, this revenue was never entirely theirs, since the old slave whose strength was declining had, if he wanted to free himself permanently from dues, to present his master either with a donkey or with a slave (sometimes two) bought from these savings. Thus the old slave who had become unsaleable managed to sell himself to the only buyer who was likely to consider him of value and want to buy him: himself. When the slave was manumitted free of charge, the sum advanced was not reimbursed but the slave did not become a burden to his master in his old age.

Through settlement and redemption, the slave was

supposed to meet his own needs with respect to the *reconstitution* of his labour–energy, his *maintenance* during periods when he was not employed, and his *economic reproduction*.

Thus the master extracted from the settled slave:

1. a fixed *rent in food*, which in the long term was barely lower than the total agricultural surplus-product;

2. a *rent in labour* converted into profit realized by the sale of commodities produced outside the cultivating season;

3. the possible reconstitution of the *initial investment* in the purchase of the slave, when the slave redeemed his dues.

As regards *reproduction by natural increase*, settlement of slaves appeared to be the most favourable social framework. However, we know that at the economic level the volume of dues required prevented settlement from being fully realized. This situation doubtless stimulated the slave to do craft work for his or her master during the dry season. Once he had bought back his dues in labour, the settled slave had to be remunerated. (He was usually remunerated in food, and then only in excess of his reconstitutive and maintenance needs which were covered by his agricultural labour.) It was this paid labour which brought him the additional, if not the total, revenue necessary to bring up children. It must be noted, once again, that the labour of these children, when they reached productive age, belonged to the master of the genitrix, even if she and her partner had been settled and redeemed. Thus the labour of the slave in bringing up a replacement to productive age profited the master, who received either the total surplus-labour, if this replacement was not redeemed, or the agricultural surplus-product, if he was settled in his turn.

In merchant slavery, every slave was directly or indirectly defined in terms of the market. He came from the market, he produced for it, sometimes he took part in trade, and above all, he or the members of his household could in principle be sent back to the market at any time.

In spite of the variety of conditions which we have described among slaves, their state, although always marked by alienability, irrevocably situated them in relation to the market. And the historical evolution of this state, as the study of merchant slave reproduction shows (Chapters 5 and 6), also depended on the evolution of the market. If the market narrowed, the slaves were sent into serfdom; if it was extended to cover all their products – and in particular the means of subsistence – it opened up the way to wage-labour.

4

The Internal Market for Slaves

Trade was the condition for the existence and development of what we have, as a result, called merchant slavery. It was the agent of slave reproduction: it was through trade that captives came into the hands of the slave-owners, and through trade that the products of slaves were sold. But this slaving trade had certain specific characteristics in the regions studied. Exchange took place mainly in kind. Exchange, in the Sahelian regions and elsewhere, was expressed in terms of products which were not always convertible one to another. Part of the goods produced by caste (and court) artisans continued to circulate according to the principles of clientelism, through dues rather than merchant exchange. The use of fiduciary money (such as cowries) was limited and circumscribed. It did not intervene in certain exchanges, such as the purchase of heavy goods – specifically slaves, horses or arms – which were exchanged for other goods. This fiduciary money circulated within the towns, sometimes within the frontiers of a State, but because of its bulk it rarely circulated between one market and another. In some cases, such as in Segu, it was a means of paying taxes, but it did not intervene between different sites of production as means of arbitration which could bring about the realignment of costs through the movement of capital. No other commodity filled this function, which would have placed slavery in a competitive system closer to capitalism. Even gold was far from being generally convertible. It circulated mostly, along with other export commodities, in distant exchanges, sometimes as a sort of interzonal currency. In short, these limitations were the sign of a trade which was mostly turned towards the outside, but did not create a true internal market.

These circumstances can doubtless be explained by the still weak implantation of the merchant economy in societies which were still dominated by the domestic economy, where certain important production goods were not to be commercialized. This was particularly true of the land. In this respect slave society as we have examined it was the heir of domestic society within which the land, like air and water, was a life-giving gift of nature; at first private appropriation of the land did not exist, nor did rent from it. Slave-owners took advantage of this to obtain land free of charge in order to settle their slaves, either within their own community or by negotiation with local populations.

If we limit ourselves to the cases we have examined, it is clear that whatever their form of exploitation, the slaves as a whole grew their own food. Their masters did not systematically buy food to feed them. There was, it is true, a market for food, and grain was exported to arid zones, but there was no internal market for subsistence goods destined for slaves. Even the urban merchants generally owned hamlets of slaves who fed them and their servants. Slaves were overwhelmingly self-sufficient, either individually or within the framework of the slave cell to which they belonged.[1] But the self-sufficiency of slaves, which might have been the result of historical circumstance, also had its own logic which was self-perpetuating and thus also perpetuated the nature of trade as we have seen it.

For the slave-owner, the purchase of a slave was the determining factor. The initial investment in the acquisition of a flow of labour, incorporated in a living being and not realized in use-value, forced the purchaser to maintain the bearer of this value until it had been fully realized – that is, to take responsibility for the slave constantly and completely during the whole of his active life, irrespective of his actual profitability and irrespective of the circumstances. While the capitalist can obtain the wage-earner's labour-power by paying only the cost of its reconstitution, the slave-owner also had to pay for the slave's upkeep, at all times. The fact that the slave was initially purchased meant that he had to consume in order to provide surplus-labour; the food necessary for his surplus-labour could not be dissociated from the food he absorbed to keep himself alive, as is possible under wage-labour. In order to obtain even part of the first – labour – the slave-owner had to provide for the second – life – in its entirety.

I do not consider it illuminating to compare the slave to 'capital' and his energy to 'labour-power'. If the slave were 'capital', he would have to combine in himself, in contradictory fashion, both constant capital, which does not modify value, and variable capital, which does (*Capital* I: 209). In capitalist terms, in order to extract profit from the variable part of 'slave capital', the constant part – which had, however, already been paid for by the owner – would have had to be remunerated. In order to avoid these contradictory ambiguities, I shall call the slave a labour-potential, which must be given compensation in food if labour-energy is to be extracted.

Because the slave's body contained both labour-potential and labour-energy, compensation in food had to be constant and could never fall below the slave's maintenance needs throughout his active life. Self-subsistence was the form of production which was best suited to this requirement, since it did not dissociate producer from consumer. Through this simple fact it ensured that a constant proportion was maintained between food production, the number of slaves and the length of their active lives.[2]

If, within the food-producing sector, the slave's consumption was always proportional to his agricultural labour, this was not the case in the merchant sector during slumps, when commodities could not be sold. The slave, in these circumstances, was fed but did not produce profits.

In the capitalist system this situation would be resolved by the dismissal of the workers. In slave-owning society, where this solution was not available, were supernumerary slaves to be sold? Two situations could arise. One, in the circumstances described above, is hypothetical. If the slaves were fed through the purchase of food because they did not themselves produce any, when their commodities could not be sold they would, in the absence of income, be threatened with famine and the slave-owner's enterprise with ruin. If on the other hand – as was in fact the case – the slaves were self-sufficient in food, their double employment in food production and in the merchant economy limited the usefulness of selling them as a solution. A reduction in merchant production through the resale of slaves because of market circumstances would also have meant a reduction in food production which also depended on other, possibly contrasting, circumstances (climatic, for example). In their capacity as agricultural producers of food, the slaves preserved their use-value as long as their total subsistence production did not exceed internal needs, storage capacities and sales. Thus when sales of commodities were low, only slaves who exclusively produced these commodities (assuming that such specialization of labour existed) should have been sold – that is, the very slaves who would not have found a buyer in such circumstances.

During the discussion of the social state of the slave earlier in this work, we noted that certain authors use the argument of the restrictions which in practice were observed when slaves were resold in order to assimilate their condition to that of kin. I argued against this interpretation on the grounds that the state of the slave was preserved as long as the market for slaves – and thus the possibility, even hypothetical, of selling them – continued to exist. But if, at this level, limitations (in practice, not in principle) on the sale of slaves improved their condition without changing their state, on the economic level, on the other hand, these restrictions are a sign of the absence of a 'labour market' in the strict sense within the slave-owning economy.

In fact, the internal market for slaves was usually limited to the (non-circumstantial) resale of defective or marginalized individuals or to the liquidation of patrimony. Except in the – negative – case of ruin, the resale of slaves by their masters was more often a sanction than a transaction.

The resale on the market of a slave by his or her owner did not have the same effects at the sale of a captive by a trader. With the captive, the merchant introduced a new, additional value into slave-owning society: in selling his slave, the owner merely transferred the value of the slave within society. Thus these exchanges are not the same, even if they took place in the same terms and the same forms. Exchanges of slaves between slave-owners did not affect the total volume of production. In fact, the slave market within slave-owning society did not play the role of regulator of the circulation of agents of labour, or of their productive energy. It was not a 'market for labour-power'. The economic conditions of the formation of rent in food through self-subsistence, which was at the origin of merchant profits, withheld the slaves from circulation. The relative weakness of the internal market was both an effect and a cause of this.

Since the whole of the slave population and their masters were fed from the production of the slave class, and since the peasant populations still depended on the domestic economy, the vast mass of subsistence goods was outside the reach of internal trade. The absence of a true internal market for food was reflected in its means of production: the land, essentially free of charge, was not transformed into a commodity; slaves, as we have seen, were exchanged rarely and with difficulty between slave-owning producers.

The implements and materials for food production were generally limited to those which the slaves could produce themselves. They were rarely bought on the market, for several reasons: because the funds available were mostly used for the purchase of the slaves themselves; because higher returns from food crops were less directly profitable than those from merchant production and priority was given to investment in the latter; because food production was always proportional or more than proportional to the number of slaves involved as a result of self-sufficiency, and there was therefore no need to increase the productivity of food production; because the incorporation of a fixed material capital in food production would, as a result of the need to repay this investment, have drawn it towards the commercialization of food products and of land, and thus towards the disappearance of rent and the end of slavery. The initial purchase of the slave and the tying-up of available funds in this investment, the permanent maintenance of this labour-potential which could be realized only with obsolescence, were factors which led to the self-sufficency of slaves, the limited commercialization of all what is related to food production, and the low productivity of labour in this sector.

The slave, early form of economic property. – Two factors combined in this context to make the slave into an object of ownership: his quality as a commodity and the purchase of his total capacity for labour before his lifelong use. In order to be bought on the market and perhaps resold, the slave had to be alienable. In order for the master to benefit from the product of the slave in proportion to the disbursement necessary for his acquisition, the master had to be sure that he could keep the slave as long as he was useful. Thus in practice the three legal rights characteristic of property were applied to the slave: the right to use him on the part of his buyer [*usus*]; the right to benefit from his labour, his products and his services, with no limit in time [*fructus*]; the right over his person, including the right to sell him or to put him to death [*abusus*]. In spite of circumstances which in fact limited these practices, these rights were conceived of as unrestricted.

With respect to domestic society – and any other self-sustenance society – the slave represented the first historical form of property applied to a means of production. In this historical process, ownership of slaves preceded that of land. The slave market developed before the market for land. Under slavery the relation to the land could continue to be based mostly on patrimonality, whether in terms of kinship or of royalty.

Now, we have seen that once introduced as an expensive instrument of production, the slave, far from communicating his commodity nature to the land or to his products, tended rather to preserve the patrimonial nature of the land as long as it remained the instrument of food production and as long as the self-sufficiency of slaves remained a condition for slavery. In this way patrimoniality of the land was a guarantee of ownership of the slave. Inversely, at the strictly juridical level, the ownership of the slave helped to delay the generalization of the ownership of land. Since the slave was himself an object of property, he could not be an owner: whatever he possessed was the possession of his master. Without his master's permission he could not have access to any good, and particularly not to land. Thus it was not necessary to make land an object of property in order to protect it juridically from unwarranted appropriation by the slave. Ownership of the slave was sufficient.[3] Ownership of land could protect it only against citizens with full rights. The state of slaves reserved land for the dominant class, within which patrimonial relations prevailed. Thus everything contributed to make the slave into an object of property before land. Although the slave was still associated with a patrimony – like land in merchant peasant societies or industrial capital for the hereditary bourgeoisie – he was the first of the means of production to enter the sphere of property.

This observation may help to clear up the confusion which is often made between the capitalist social system, built exclusively on the ownership of the *material* means of production, and the systems which preceded it. In *domestic society* no means of production, whether material or human, was appropriated. Under *slavery*, it was human beings who came into the orbit of the market and became objects of ownership. With *serfdom*, it was rather subsistence goods: as for the serf, he once again formed part of patrimony, linked to the land, and both constituted a complete and indissociable means of production which could be transmitted, given, inherited in the form of *domaines*, prerogatives – or even fiefs when this organic patrimony was used to back up a military and political hierarchy. But these lands, once deprived of their serf labour force, were not the object of any merchant transaction. It was not until the bourgeoisie gnawed away at this feudal tie, through trade in subsistence goods, that land also entered the market as a commodity, dissociated from those who produced on it, and that in turn it drew in its wake all the other means of production.

When the *ownership* of the *material* means of production is

conceived of retrospectively as the base of all modes of production, they are all retroactively assimilated to capitalism;
capitalism is held – as it is by liberal economists – to be the
universal and everlasting model of economic organization. It
seems to me more in line with Marx's perspective to look for
historical differences between social systems, rather than
analogies.[4]

[handwritten notes]

Patterson,
1979

"On Slavery & Slave
formations,"

inquel for slavery

as a form of

capitalism.

5

To Buy or to Breed?

Three possibilities were available for the replacement of a slave when he was no longer capable of fulfilling his function: capture of another slave; eco-demographic reproduction through procreation and the bringing to maturity of a replacement slave; merchant reproduction through the purchase of another slave on the market.[1]

Reproduction through the capture of another slave took place in the case of military societies, which have been described above: we shall not return to this.

In societies which did not capture slaves themselves, the choice was between allowing a servile class to be born and bred in their midst and the purchase of captives.

1 BREED THEM?

The reproduction of any population does not take place only through births. It is necessary for a new generation of producers, at least equal in number to those they replace (in the case of simple reproduction) to be *brought to maturity* (that is, to a culturally defined productive age). Thus minimum female fertility must be further corrected by this new generation's survival rate up to the age of economic maturity, and thus by the quantity of subsistence goods available to bring it to this age. This form of reproduction therefore presupposes: (a) a sufficient number of women to ensure a birth rate which is at least high enough for survivors of productive age to replace the active population, given mortality before productive age; (b) the capacity of the active members to feed the new generation from birth to economic maturity, given losses of subsistence goods due to mortality among pre-productive individuals, on the one hand, and shortfalls in production due to mortality among productive individuals before retirement age, on the other.

In the case of a subjugated population which had to pay dues from its food production, the disposable surplus-product after extractions had at least to equal that necessary to feed the new generation. Dues paid to the class of masters could not be allowed to eat into the needs of this generation by the extraction of the total surplus-product, as was possible under slavery; otherwise the reproduction of the servile class would be compromised. Agricultural rent was then correspondingly reduced. Thus the number of individuals reaching economic maturity in a serf population was limited both by the *productivity* of labour in food production and by the level of deductions. The same is true of the annual demographic output of children reaching maturity each year; this was regulated not only by the length of time it took to reach maturity but also by the average interval between births, which in turn depended on the means of subsistence left to the serfs after extractions by their masters.

In order to illustrate my method, some numerical examples of rates of eco-demographic reproduction, based on quantitative estimates of food production and consumption, are given. These estimates may be questionable in themselves, but their purpose is to provide measurements which can be compared with the rates of merchant reproduction of slaves discussed below. The numerical results are less important than the argument developed in this chapter to explain how these results are reached.

I shall call the number of children who can be brought to maturity by the productive generation each year, during the length of an active life, the *rate of eco-demographic reproduction*. The calculations refer to a *couple* of productive adults and are based on the fertility of a pubescent woman and the productivity of the couple. This is not a 'household' but an *abstract* couple, in which at any moment, within the economic cell, the average production of an active man and an active woman are added together; and which is renewed in each generation to ensure the constant material and moral upkeep of progeny, since in practice the active life of the 'parents' generally comes to an end before the maturity of the last-born. In fact, in domestic communities with adelphic succession, this constant upkeep was undertaken by the fraternity and later perhaps by the elders in the following fraternity, in the generation of the children of 'brothers' or 'uncles'.

As regards production and consumption, I have used the following figures of annual cereal production and consumption:

Production of the couple:	1,530 kg
Consumption of the couple:	480 kg
Average consumption of a non-productive individual:	180 kg

I make the following assumptions: that one year in three is a bad year; that 15 per cent of production is put aside for seed; that children who die before reaching the age of fifteen absorb 10 per cent of the total consumption of pre-productive individuals. I do not take into account adult mortality before 'retirement' age, nor food consumed by post-productive individuals. I assume that economic reproduction starts at fifteen and that the length of the couple's active life is twenty years.

1. *For a free-born domestic community* (which pays no dues) the rate of reproduction is calculated as follows:

Annual surplus-product of the couple:
1,530 − 480 =   1,050 kg

Annual surplus-product after provision for seed (15%):

$1,050 - 157.5 =$ 892.5 kg

Surplus-product over 20 years, taking into account bad years (a reduction of one-third):
$\frac{2}{3} \times (892.5 \times 20)$ 11,900 kg

Deduction of the consumption of deceased pre-productive individuals
(10%):   1,190 kg

Balance of surplus-product (rounded off)   10,710 kg

Consumption of a child up to 15 years of age
(less two years before weaning):   2,340 kg

Number of children fed to the age of 15
   during these 20 years:
$10,710/2,340 =$ 4·57

Average interval between births of surviving children:
20 years/4·57   4·37
                      (Approximately 4 years, 4 months)

Annual rate of eco-demographic reproduction per couple:
4·57/20   0·228

Annual rate per individual (given sex ratio of 1:1):   0·114

I have not counted reserves, since they are assumed to be absorbed in bad years.

2. *Reproduction of slave couples paying dues:*

(a) *Annual dues of 90 'mude':* (216 kg)

   Volume of dues over 20 years:
   $216 \times 20 \times 2$ 8,640 kg

Balance of surplus-product after payment of dues:
11,900 − 8,640 =   3,260 kg

Number of children fed by the couple over 20 years:
3,260/2,340 =   1·39

Annual rate of eco-demographic reproduction per couple:
1·39/20 =   0·07

Individual rate: 0·035

Average interval between births:
20/1·39 =   14·4
(approximately 14 years, 4 months)

(b) *Annual dues of 150 'mude' per active person over 20 years:*

That is, 150 × 2 × 20 =   6,000 $mude^2$

Conversion into kilograms at 2·4 kg per *mude* = 14,400 kg

If production over twenty years is the same as that of a free-born couple, the dues exceed the surplus-product. They must be covered either by the reduced consumption of the couple or by remuneration for craft work performed during the dry season.

Textile production necessary to meet the needs of a replacement, given annual dues of 150 *mude* (360 kg):

Food shortfall over 20 years:
14,400 − 11,900 =   2,500 kg

Food needs of a replacement, given mortality before 15 years:
180 × 13 = 2,340 kg
+ 10% =   2,574 kg

Total needs:
2,500 + 2,574 kg =   5,074 kg

Remuneration per *tama*[3] (Gumbu example):
4·5 *mude* = 10·8 kg

Number of *tama* to be woven over 20 years:
5,074/10·8 = 470

or 23·5 per year, in order to breed (taking no account of mortality) a single replacement over the whole of an active life.

2 BUY THEM?

a. Robber's value

The primary superiority of slave reproduction was based on capture, though capture was not costless and in merchant slavery the slave was not without a price. The initial theft of human beings and their transformation into commodities through trade were at the base of structure of production which, in order to reproduce themselves, acquired characteristics which were specific to merchant slavery as we have observed it.

We have already noted that some authors see capture as an act of 'production' but that this perspective eliminates the true producers of slaves, the communities where they were conceived, fed, bred and then captured. Now, as we have seen in analysing the domestic community, the sale of children brought no benefits from those who had given birth to and bred them, since, because of the principle of *identical exchange*,[4] the only equivalent of a dependant was another dependant. This transfer could therefore take place only through abduction. Abduction brought two phenomena into play simultaneously. One value was substituted for another, and in this way the nature of exchange was transformed. While the purchase of a slave from his or her community of origin – if it had been possible – would have preserved the slave's 'labour-value'[5] (to which the cost of commercialization would have been added), abduction eliminated it and replaced it with the indeterminate costs of kidnapping, harbouring, sale, and so on. Once stolen, the captive did not arrive on the market bearing his or her original 'labour-value'; while the captive's use-value remained intact, it was no longer the basis of exchange-value. Another market value prevailed, corresponding to the costs and efforts involved in capture, transport and marketing of the captives, and so forth. We shall examine the implications of this substitution below. But this was not all. At the same time as the slave's value was transformed, its content changed. The demand, in this process of capture and marketing, was not for the ingredients necessary to the physical reproduction of the slave (means of subsistence and pubescent women) but for the material means necessary for war or the slave trade, whose value had no organic or logical relation to the labour-value incorporated in the slave. Yet capture was the basis of the captive's market value, which determined the volume and nature of the commodities necessary to the reconstitution of the slave trade. Thus, the commodities exchanged for slaves might be inert goods, without regenerative capacity. Not only was the slave not exchanged at his or her 'labour-value', but the products necessary for the slave's acquisition were not necessarily those which contributed to his or her physical reconstitution. A double rupture was therefore provoked by the single fact of the purchase of a captive: on one hand, the social substance, the basis of the slave's use-value, was not compensated for; on the other, the living captive could be acquired in exchange for an inert product which had no regenerative capacity.

In the merchant economy the captive was transformed into an inorganic being, in the image of the commodities which created him or her.

b. The market of metamorphoses

In merchant slavery, as long as slaves produced their own food, profits from the sale of the commodities they produced were net profits. They were equal to the difference between revenue from these sales and the purchase price (assumed to be constant) of the slaves: the necessary labour did not need to be remunerated except through the slave's own food production.

Once the number of slaves was high enough for their surplus-product in food to cover their own needs and those of their masters (including reserves), any excess could be used to feed slaves who could be exempted from agricultural tasks and assigned exclusively to the production of commodities. The labour-time necessary for the subsistence and upkeep of the slaves as a whole was reduced – to an even greater extent if the number of slaves belonging to a single owner increased relative to the number of masters whom the slaves had to feed. In the absence of an internal market for subsistence goods, the only outlet for the rent in food was the feeding of a higher number of slaves specialized in the manufacture of commodities. When slaves were used in this way, on the self-sustaining large farms, food production generated a constantly growing demand for them.

However, in merchant slavery demand could in principle be satisfied only through the purchase of slaves on the market, and thus through the production of commodities. The number of slaves who could be bought thus depended on the prices of these commodities relative to the price of slaves. In order to establish the merchant rate of reproduction and to compare it with that of eco-demographic reproduction, the notion of *amortization* must be introduced, as the ratio of revenue from the sale of the slave's products to his or her purchase price, which is assumed to be constant.

But on the slaving market, the nature of the slave's products was also relevant.

In this slave-owning merchant economy, the foodstuffs produced by the slaves themselves could not be used to purchase slaves. Indeed, exchange of this sort would have restricted their capacity for economic reproduction to the volume of the food surplus-product. Returns from slaves bought with this balance of food surplus-product could not be higher than those from eco-demographic reproduction. The owner could not procure more slaves with this surplus-product than those whom he could have bred himself on the basis of it. Trade in slaves against foodstuffs, if it had existed, would in fact have presupposed the purchase of slaves from professional breeders whose profit would have depended on their ability to procure foodstuffs at lower prices than those produced by their customers' slaves, which eliminates this hypothesis. In fact, no lasting slave-breeding enterprises seem to have existed.[6]

In contrast, agricultural products other than food, since they had no regenerative role with respect to slaves, were by definition inert. They could profitably be exchanged for slaves if their production did not hamper food cultivation and if it was an addition to the necessary surplus-product. This seems to have taken place in the East African plantations described by Cooper (1977), to which we shall return.

In the final analysis, the commodities which could best be produced and exchanged for slaves were non-agricultural goods which could be produced all year round and which, through the process of the slave trade, could be transformed into living beings on the market. This transformation had two consequences which favoured the merchant slave mode of reproduction with respect to eco-demographic reproduction.

The reproduction of slaves through the sale of inert commodities on the market made all the producers of these commodities, irrespective of their sex, age or social condition, reproducers of slaves. Men, old people, women before puberty and free-born individuals could all give birth to slaves, through their economic activity.

In the second place, since it was possible to buy slaves with commodities which were inert and thus manufactured outside the food-growing season, the labour-time of all these producers assigned to merchant reproduction could last over the whole year.[7]

Merchant slave reproduction, because of its three advantages – the transformation of inert products into human beings, the extension of reproductive labour-time over the whole year, and the transformation of all producers of both sexes and all ages into reproducers of slaves – had a higher capacity than eco-demographic reproduction, which depended on the number of pubescent women and the productivity of labour in food production alone, during a limited part of the year.

3 RENT IN FOOD AND MERCHANT PROFIT

Within the slave-owning cell, the slave took part in two sectors of activity: the agricultural food-producing economy from which he drew his means of subsistence and his maintenance; and the economy of production of inert goods through which he was reproduced. The reproduction of the first sector depended on the second, and production in the second depended on the first. But despite the close links between the two sectors, no material exchange took place between them. Only forms of labour passed from one to the other, without any regenerative compensation. The merchant sector delivered to the food-producing sector labour-potential in the form of captives who were both commodities and regenerative goods. In his capacity as slave, the captive, activated by his own labour-energy applied to the production of subsistence goods, produced the surplus-labour used in the sector of merchant production. The inert commodities, manufactured on the basis of this surplus-labour and sold on the market, led, through a distant and destructive alchemy, to the emergence of the captive, bearer of living labour.

Each of these two sectors operated according to its own constraints. Food production was limited in time during the year; merchant production knew no season. The first was subordinated to natural events; the second to prices. Food products could stay outside the market; commodities owed their existence to the market. The absorption of foodstuffs depended on conditions of production more than on demand, in contrast to that of commodities. The first had to be stored; the second had to be sold at once. Each had its own means of production and, in particular, its own productivity. Finally, while slaves and subsistence goods contained their own regenerative value, this was not true of commodities. Not only did these two sectors of activity have their own laws; they also had distinct types of revenue. From one, a *surplus-product in food* emerged, equal to the total production of subsistence goods by the slave less the slave's consumption during the whole of his or her active life $(\alpha B - \beta B)$, from which *rent in food* was extracted. In the other, *profit* was extracted, equal to the difference between the selling price of the commodities produced by the slave during his or her active life and the purchase price of the slave on the market $(mB - H)$.[8]

It is necessary here to point out the difference between peasant slavery and merchant slavery in the strict sense. In each case both sectors, food-producing and merchant, had to function in order to feed and replace slaves, but while for the peasant slave-owner profit was subordinated to the production of a rent in food, the reverse was true of the merchant slave-owner. The purpose of peasant slavery was to substitute the labour of the slave for that of the master, particularly in the production of subsistence goods. Since the extraction of a rent in food was the main goal, the conditions for the acquisition and reproduction of slaves were different from those in merchant slavery, which was aimed at the creation and accumulation of profits.

As long as rent in food was the purpose of slavery and profit was secondary, the slave's purchase price could equal the total revenue from the commodities produced by the slave during his or her active life and sold on the market. The slave's surplus-product in food remained intact, but he or she brought no merchant profit. The slave could even be bought at a price which was higher than profits if the master also contributed to agricultural or commodity production. Thus, paradoxically, the peasant communities which procured slaves only for their own use were able to pay high prices for these slaves, in spite of low profit rates, equal or even lower than one:

$$\frac{mB}{H} \leqslant 1.$$

However, these communities were a mediocre outlet for the market, since while they could, in these conditions, pay high prices for slaves, they bought them at long intervals and sold few commodities.

It was not these peasant communities which 'made up the market', but the slave 'farms' which extracted their profit from the multiplicity and frequency of their operations on

the market. It was these merchant slave-owners – sooner or
later joined by part of the peasantry – who formed the components of the slaving market and on whom our reasoning
must be based. For them, rent in food, while it was certainly
essential, was nevertheless a seasonal by-product of the
slave's production of commodities. The profit extracted
from this production was their principal objective.[9]

4 COMPETITION

On the internal market, since the living reproduction of the
slaves was not compensated for and since their upkeep was
ensured by their own labour alone, the commodities they
produced could be sold, like the slaves themselves, at a market value stripped of all regenerative value. The market value
of the totality of the slave's products were objectively lower
than their social value, the value which determined the price
necessary for the reconstitution of all the social conditions of
reproduction for the human means of production employed.

For an equal productivity of labour, slavery must therefore
have had decisive advantages over the other modes of production which competed with it historically, if they produced for the market. Could the domestic community or
serfdom endure, with respect to the market and in the context of a merchant slave economy? How can the fact that they
did coexist with slavery be explained?

Once it had been introduced into the commercial circuit,
the domestic community could also, by applying its surplus-
labour outside the agricultural season to the production of inert goods, put on the market commodities which were similar to those produced by slaving enterprises. To begin with,
the domestic community had a relative advantage over merchant slavery. If, on the one hand, the food surplus-product
was totally consumed for domestic reproduction, and if, on
the other, the number of slaves in the slaving sector was such
that the whole of the surplus food product was consumed by
the masters, given equal productivity, the return from labour
in the domestic community was the same as that in the slaving cell. However, in the latter, part of the slaves' surplus-

labour had to be used for their replacement, while the whole of the domestic surplus-labour could be used to produce net profits. This was the price paid by the slave-owners for being freed from working on the land themselves. In this situation, the domestic economy was still competitive on the market.

However, as soon as the number of slaves exceeded that necessary to feed the class of masters, a surplus-product of food emerged, which could be reconverted into labour. We have seen that it was necessary only to withdraw some of the slaves from food production, in proportion to the food surplus-product used to feed them, and to assign them to full-time commodity production. From this moment, after deduction of the necessities for the replacement of these slaves, the average labour-time incorporated in each unit of merchandise was lower than that in the domestic community.

The domestic community could nevertheless continue to put commodities on the market, even at market prices determined by the new conditions of slave-owning production, since it supplied itself, totally, with necessities produced during a labour-time which was not reduced by the production of commodities, and since no commercial requirements were imposed on its reproduction. Whatever it acquired on the market appeared as a net benefit, irrespective of its volume. An increase in commodity production could take place in the long term with the rise in the community's numbers. But, since it was linked to the rate of eco-demographic reproduction, this increase was always proportional to the relation between the number of productive and unproductive individuals; this relation, for any given productivity, always varied within the same limits, unlike the acquisition of slaves at the rate of merchant reproduction, which in theory was not limited by pre-productive consumers of food.

Thus, with the growth of the market economy, the slave-owners gained an increasing advantage over the domestic economy. As the number of slaves rose relative to the slave-owning population, so the cost of their product fell, and with it the domestic community's revenue from its production of commodities.

What applies here to the domestic economy applies *a for-*

tiori to serfdom, since under serfdom the surplus-product had to cover both the reproduction of the serfs and that of the masters. At the same level of productivity, since the net surplus-product was lower, it was less likely that it could be redistributed to allow the freeing of serfs from food production, and the demographic increase of the serf class was also less likely.

Finally, competition between slaving cells was merchant in character. It was proportional to the food surplus-product redistributed among the slaves in each enterprise – that is, according to the numbers of productive slaves and idle masters. The bigger farms produced more efficiently, though their profits from each additional slave tended to decrease.

If commodities were sold proportionately to the average labour-time spent by all the slaves, in both the food-producing and the merchant sectors, the small slaving cells made smaller profits, so that some probably tended to be eliminated with each fall in commodity prices.

However, falling prices did not threaten the existence either of serfdom or of the community as long as the food-producing and merchant sectors continued to be separate – that is, as long as commercialization did not spread either to subsistence goods or to their means of production. In particular, as long as the land did not become a commodity, the domestic community and serfdom could not be destroyed by the laws of the slaving economy; they could only be eliminated from the market. But the interpenetration of the subsistence economy and the merchant economy did not threaten only these competing modes of production; it threatened slavery itself.

5 COMPARATIVE RATES OF REPRODUCTION

It is true, however, that the reproduction of slaves through the market gave slavery an overwhelming advantage.

Since the amortization of the slave took place entirely within the merchant sector, merchant reproduction depended only on the productivity of labour applied to the production of commodities. This is why this mode of production had its own specific rhythm, and why it was possible to increase the production of slaves up to the limits of slave exploitation and the exhaustion of raided populations.

For profit to be at a maximum, the period of amortization had to be as short as possible relative to the average length of a slave's active life. If, given an average price of slaves on the market, the period of amortization was equal to the average length of the slaves' active lives – as we have seen with respect to subsistence slavery – the only revenue during this period would be the agricultural rent extracted from the slave; there would be no merchant profit. Hence the amortization period necessary for the extraction of profit was shorter than that needed for the extraction of rent in food alone. If slavery was to be preferred to serfdom, this period of amortization also had to be shorter than the period necessary for eco-demographic reproduction; that is, shorter than the average interval between the arrival at maturity of children born into serfdom. The scanty data at our disposal suggest that this was in fact the case.

In former French West Africa, some observers and colonial administrators tried to compute the amortization period of a slave. Towards 1818 the explorer Mollien crossed the village of Pacour in Bourba Iolof, which belonged to a single master who had populated it with his slaves; he writes that their 'labour increased his wealth and gave him the means to double [their] number each year' (1967: 89–90). In 1846, Raffenel (p. 385) calculated that 'in one year a hard-working man can extract [from the gold mines of Bambouk] the value of 4 to 5 captives', which gives an amortization period of two to three months.[10] Deherme, who in 1904 was put in charge of collating the reports on slavery of the colonial administrators in French West Africa, calculated that a slave was amortized, at a rate of 200 remunerative working days a year, in three years (Dakar Archives, K25: 220-M224). The administrator of Podor considered that a slave produced his own value in five to six years. According to my own calculations, a slave in Gumbu repaid his own price, through labour in textiles alone, in about four years.[11] For Pollet and Winter (1971: 239) amortization took three years.

F. Cooper's study (1977: 72s.) provides numerical data on

slavery on the east coast of Africa, where the Omani owners cultivated mainly agricultural products for export: cloves, copra, cereals. The amortization period of slaves varied considerably according to circumstances. In 1839, when clove cultivation was started in Zanzibar, a slave was amortized in 73 to 122 days. In 1870, because of poor market conditions, the price of cloves fell and it seems that profits reached zero. But in 1873, the slave who produced cereals for export – and therefore worked for only part of the year – paid for himself in only one year. Now, according to Cooper's data, the maintenance cost of a slave – estimated in Omani dollars – was $2 to $3 at the time, while the slave who paid for himself in one year cost $40 on the market. In this specific case, $1 invested in the purchase of a slave was doubled in one year (and reached $60 in the sixth year), while the same dollar used for the purchase of a serf would have brought no returns for thirteen years, the time necessary for him to reach maturity.

It must be added that the breeding cost of slaves quoted by Cooper is only a monetary estimate and does not reflect the social conditions of production. In fact, 'each slave grew his own food on a plot provided him', writes Cooper, and 'plantation slaves were capable of meeting much of the essential subsistence needs of the plantation' (1977: 64). It does not in fact seem that there was a market (for manioc) aimed at the feeding of slaves, on which breeding costs could have been established.

On the basis of these limited empirical data, a comparison may be attempted between the respective rates of merchant[12] and eco–demographic[13] reproduction.

The figures above give a rate of merchant reproduction which varies from 0·16 to 5. On the plantations studied by Cooper, the rate would have been between 2·99 and 5·0. It was zero in 1870. Now, according to our calculations, the rate of eco–demographic reproduction of a couple which was free-born and therefore paid no dues was 0·228, or 0·114 per person. That of settled slaves who had to pay dues varied from 0 to 0·035 per individual,[14] and was thus always lower than the merchant rate.

These figures illustrate the reasoning above. It is logical that merchant reproduction was faster and higher than eco-demographic reproduction. Surplus-labour time was longer in merchant slavery, since it was based on the labour of producers of both sexes and all ages, and since all sorts of commodities were exchanged for human beings on a market which was supplied by capture and not through demographic growth.

For the businessman involved in slavery the need for labourers was always urgent, all the more so in that the price of their products on the market was high. The availability of the labourer appeared to the slaver as an immediate criterion, much more so than the relative costs of the bought slave and the bred 'slave' (which in any case could be estimated only in magnitudes which were not comparable). The planter bought slaves according to the relation on the market between the price of the slave and the current (and hence expected) price of the commodities he could produce. To the extent that land was still available and in the absence of investment which could have raised productivity, profits rose only with a rise in the number of slaves. 'Strength is slaves', one of Cooper's informants summed up (1977: 87). Quantity and immediate availability were imperatives which could be satisfied only through the slave market, not by the slow coming to maturity of a generation of servile individuals, expensive to breed from a large, cumbersome and dangerous population. 'If you wait for children, you will not get rich' (Harms, 1978: 237).

Nevertheless, the idea of a slave population which reproduced itself and represented wealth was fairly widespread among slavers. In fact, as our argument shows, this idea, often impregnated with the master's desire to be the 'patriarch' of a society rather than the owner of a slave stock, was based on a false perception of reality. Any comparison of the economic advantages of eco-demographic and merchant reproduction is intrinsically fallacious. It abstracts from the effects of war and trade on slaving exchange and from the transformations they wrought in the nature and value of goods. The idea that a bought slave could be equivalent to a bred 'slave' implicitly assumes that identical economic laws governed self-sustenance and merchant slave production. But the 'values' of bought and bred 'slaves' cannot be compared because they belonged to sealed economic spheres which could be joined only through an act of violence. Capture was necessary to displace the slave from one system to the other. Through capture he was transformed into an object stripped of social substance and bound to a value in terms of commodities which locked him within the logical imperatives of the slave-owning economy, and thus into a specific and immutable state. The slave's imprisonment in a social class which could not be compared with that of the masters expressed the incommensurability between the commodity value which was inflicted on him and his social value.

6 EXTRA-UTERINE REPRODUCTION

All the above shows that merchant slave reproduction had to free itself of demographic constraints in order to strip the slave of his or her social substance.

The fact that slaves were reproduced through the manufacture and exchange of commodities rather than through the fertility of women had consequences for the fate of female slaves in merchant slave society.

While eco-demographic reproduction was closely tied to the number of pubescent and fertile women, merchant reproduction generally depended on women only within the conventional and cultural – and thus changing and sometimes irrelevant – limits of the sexual distribution of tasks.

Thus the participation of women in the slave economy was to depend on their productive rather than their reproductive capacities, and therefore on their price relative to that of men.[15] While in societies where women were still in demand because of their conventional domestic or craft specializations they were more expensive than men, this was not the case in plantation economies, for example, where these qualifications were not useful and the choice of the sex of slaves assigned to labour depended only on their respective purchase prices. The examples below seem to suggest that the de-feminization of women slaves increased, in merchant slavery, as merchant production intensified.

In the trading towns of Upper Zaïre, where in the nineteenth century a merchant class operating on distant markets was concentrated, new economic and social situations emerged, with effects on the sex ratio of slaves (Harms, 1983). The merchants' travels created a demand for prepared food, either for those who were on expeditions or for passing traders. The commercialization of cooked food brought in its wake that of ingredients and cooking utensils, and thus the development of market-gardening and of pottery, among other activities. Thus the share of female labour was still large, particularly in the preparation of food, which increased the number of domestic tasks and led to the emergence of trade by free-born women or sometimes by female slaves who employed other female slaves. In particular, urbaniza-tion created a growing differentiation between an urban population – which did not produce its own means of sub-sistence and depended to an ever greater extent on the market to supply its needs – and a rural sector which supplied it with food. It was women who were employed in agriculture, whether in the cultivation of manioc or of market-gardens, since both were traditionally female tasks. In the towns of Upper Zaïre, slaves were more often women than men. Still, Harms reports that the price did not vary according to sex: 'Don't buy men, don't buy women, just buy people' (Harms, 1983: 99).

If *a priori* no preference was shown for either sex, this was because slaves were needed as *asexual agents of labour* and because the procreative capacity of the women did not affect their value. If they were, nevertheless, more numerous, it was because the sexual distribution of tasks still determined the choice of sex. But the equivalence of prices shows that it was possible here to replace women with men. In Mombasa, Strobel (1983) shows that men participated to a greater extent in the production of commodities: of foodstuffs (through agriculture); of meat and ivory (through hunting); of slaves (through raids). It was perhaps in this way that men slaves gradually acquired a value comparable to that of women: through a modification of activities and the sexual distribu-tion of tasks.

The information provided by Cooper (1977) concerning the eastern coast of Africa also reflects this transformation.

The data show an average sex ratio of 52 men to 50 women. Towns contained more men than women, while women were more numerous in certain rural areas. However, since the proportion of urban to rural slaves was 1 to 10 or to 15 (p. 182, n. 130) it could not have been the only reason for this balance. Cooper also shows that 52 per cent of adult slaves and 61 per cent of children bought between 1874 and 1888 were male. This should lead to the deduction that the number of men on the plantations in certain rural areas was increasing to such an extent that it could offset the higher number of women in other regions where a count was taken. Unfortunately there is not enough information to test this hypothesis. In any case, this change in the sex ratio of slaves expressed either a new type of employment for men or the substitution of men for women in certain ancillary or rural activities. It is conceivable that the plantation system accentuated the social division of labour and came to dominate the sexual division. As soon as the specialization of tasks no longer imposes the choice of one sex at the expense of another – given the fact that supplies of men were less costly because of their lower price on the African market – male slavery tended to predominate. Its nature resembled that of slavery in the West Indies and the United States, for economic reasons which were probably comparable and conformed to the laws of slave reproduction in what seems to have been their universal application.[16]

Caught between women slaves stripped of their sex and distant mothers stripped of their children, the slave class was born only of a womb of iron and gold. Being thus born of matter, the slave could not be born into life: the slave was used up like 'black ore'.[17]

6

The Disintegration of Slavery

At the level of the slave-owning economy as a whole, including both the populations which were dispossessed of their children and those which had the use of them, slavery led to a general fall in food production. In slave-owning society the entire class of masters and part of that of slaves did not produce their own means of subsistence; in plundered societies the relative number of active individuals dropped. Thus slavery did not create what one might call a 'surplus' or a 'superfluity', although it did allow *accumulation* through a transfer of the social product from the plundered populations towards the plundering populations, and, within the latter, from the slaves towards the masters.

This accumulation without a surplus could only result in the decrease of the pillaged populations. Stripped of their demographic growth, albeit only once, because of the reduction in the numbers of pubescent women and the active population as a whole, they could reconstitute themselves only at a slower rate than that of the slave-owning societies which preyed on them. In the long term, independently of the resistance of these peoples or of distances from the sources of captives, the flow of supplies to the slave markets could only dry up.[1]

As for the African societies on which we have focused, the relative brevity of the period of the spread of merchant

314

slavery and its interruption by colonization make the decisive transformations which resulted from these factors difficult to detect. However, the process of abolition initiated with French colonization in the Sudan provides some interesting lessons.[2] R. Roberts (1984) has pointed to some of its most characteristic aspects.

After the French army had contributed, as we have seen, to slaving capture in order to pay its African mercenaries, the colonial administration was most reluctant to apply instructions from the metropolis regarding the struggle against the slave trade and slavery. An argument which was often put forward was the risk of such measures for local trade. The pivotal position of slavery in exchange had not escaped the notice of those who were trying to justify colonial conquest by demonstrating the economic viability of the colonies and hoped to use established flows of exchange as a means for the penetration of French products on to the African market. The colonial administration was also tormented by another worry. Mobilization for war and forced labour, urbanization which had been accelerated by colonization, raised the problem of the provisioning of the troops, the labour camps and the towns. Abolition threatened to interfere with agricultural food production in societies where this was assigned to slaves. Once the slaves had been freed, how would they have access to seed, held by the masters, in order to start another agricultural cycle? How could the masters cultivate without a slave labour force?

In fact, in the Sudan, cereals (sorghum) for the capital (Bamako) were supplied by the Maraka. R. Roberts (1984) points out and analyses the effects of the colonial conquest on this economy. On the one hand, war against Samori and Bademba had dried up the supply of slaves to the market. On the other, the demand for cereals was rising for the reasons given above. The only solution was the increase in the labour-time worked by the slaves and the reduction of their rations. In Marakaduguworowula, an important Maraka sorghum-producing centre, slaves fled in their masses, complaining to the administration that they worked too hard and did not eat enough. This intensification of exploitation, in a colonial context which allegedly advocated its abolition, provoked successive and massive exoduses of slaves seeking the protection of the administration. It is estimated that 20,000 left Marakaduguworowula before 1905–6. Later the exodus reached other regions of the western Sudan, involving tens of thousands of indivduals (Roberts, 1984: 470).

Most of them were said to be first-generation slaves. In fact, I think it would be correct to say that they were drudge-slaves, who were the most numerous and the most exploited. But it seems, from the statements of some of the escapees reported by Roberts, that they also included allotment slaves and perhaps settled slaves, who had been subjected to an intensification of their exploitation: perhaps women had been made to work in spite of their redemption, or their progeny had been confiscated by their masters. It may be that slaves grouped into hamlets, separated from their masters, also tried to seize independence on this occasion. However, as a whole the allotment slaves, and particularly the settled slaves, remained numerous in the masters' villages, and it seems that there were more women than men. This is why abolition did not, as one might have expected, lead to the regrouping or consolidation of free-born houses around their doyens, but, on the contrary, to their fragmentation (Pollet and Winter, 1971). The older members, in their capacity as guardians of the patrimony, kept the remaining slaves who paid dues in order to meet their own needs, while the cadets were invited to reconstitute autonomous cells and to pay their taxes to the French on their own account.

Although large numbers of escaped drudge–slaves or those who had been enfranchised by the French administration returned to their region of origin, it is unlikely that many returned to their villages, since the shame of having been captured would have made reintegration difficult. However, some resettled where their villages had been before destruction by their captors. The French administration drew some ex-slaves into its army or into the Liberty villages [*villages de Liberté*] which were used as reserves of labour. The immediate result of abolition was the drying-up of the slave trade and the liberation of some of the slaves. Those who stayed where they were, and were objectively already in relations of serfdom, preserved similar but slightly improved relationships with their masters. The change in their state was mainly the result of the suppression of the slave trade: they were no longer alienable, since the slave market had practically disappeared. Sales and purchases of persons were still found long after abolition, but it was no longer a question of a slave trade or a market which dominated transfers of the labour force. In fact Roberts shows how the beginnings of a capitalist economy were established around the emergence of wage-labour. The policy of the administration, which wished to reconstitute a labour market, was combined with that of the traders, both European and African, who wished to encourage the sale of cereals: 'The availability of food imports permitted full-time commercial agriculture, rubber gathering or mining', as Roberts perceptively notes (1984: 455) on the basis of the administration's commercial reports between 1905 and 1908. A market for food and the disappearance of slave-sufficiency were indeed the preconditions for the establishment of wage-labour. But while the Maraka slave-owning plantations helped to supply this market, the spread of wage-labour which it fed contributed to the disintegration of these plantations.

M. Klein (n.d. and 1983) shows, with respect to the Fulbe of Masina, that the colonial administration also had a plan for the resettlement of slaves and the improvement of their relations with their masters which advocated sharecropping. This mode of exploitation, where dues were proportional to the harvest, contrasted with serfdom, where dues were fixed. The change provoked endless conflicts which were never resolved. Klein notes that in the long term this attempt came to nothing, but that it nevertheless helped the slaves to acquire certain rights on the land they cultivated.

The drying-up of the slave trade and the generalization of trade did certainly lead to the abolition of slavery but not to the immediate disappearance of servitude, alienation or the prejudices linked to it. With the colonial abolition of slavery in French West Africa, thousands of men (though fewer women) thus left their masters. But while the opprobrium of capture still weighed heavily on them in their villages, where could they go? Many of these men found themselves in the 'Liberty villages' created by the colonial administration, where they were soon transformed into cheap labour. Many others joined the army to conquer Africa in the name of the Republic. In Mali, during emancipation, important administrative and sometimes governmental positions were filled by the descendants of slaves in the towns, who were closer to colonial culture and whose knowledge of things Western was often better than that of the aristocrats who had stayed in their remote provinces and despised the colonizers. In Bamako, after independence – which in this respect represented a brief social revolution – the status of this or that individual was no longer mentioned: the government had it struck off the administrative registers. However, no one was in ignorance of it. The praise-singers, pretending to mistake their clients' patronym, sang to their new patrons the praises and genealogies of their former masters.

But still! Once a slave, always a slave. Even today, whatever their social rank, public opinion still attributes to them all sorts of stereotypical defects: greed, dishonesty, lack of moral values, obscenity, and so on. As soon as one of them gives in to the temptation of corruption – like most of his colleagues of high birth – he immediately becomes the living proof of the indelible nature of the servile stain. Prejudices are still so strong that some despise all Black Americans because they are all seen as the descendants of slaves. One does not give one's daughter in marriage to a person said to be of slave descent, whatever his social or political position. Some of the new generation fight these prejudices, but mixed marriages are still rare. In hostels for immigrant workers in Europe, conflicts arise when some try to escape the permanent service of others. Not so long ago, when migrant workers of servile origin went back to their villages, they had symbolically to hand over all their earnings and all their purchases to their former owners, who chose their presents. Among the nomads, the condition of servants has hardly changed today and a clandestine trade in slaves still exists.

It is to be hoped that these unpleasant situations are residual in nature. Slavery as an economic phenomenon of exploitation is destined to disappear. But in the countryside it is still a real problem for those who, legally enfranchised, still depend on their former masters for access to the land. Even today, if the behaviour of these ex-slaves is not considered to conform to their former status, they cannot stay in their villages. In order to disalienate themselves and to be reintegrated as full persons, they have to emigrate to a place where their status is not known. But their patronym, their accent, their habits or the news transmitted by praise-singers and gossips almost always denounce them to the numerous persons who scrutinize the liver[3] and kidneys of their congeners and are delighted to find there the stain which so conveniently shows that they themselves are superior beings.

In other contexts, depending on the historical period, the exhaustion of supplies of slaves seems to have led to serfdom or to wage-labour, depending on whether rent or profit was preserved.

In societies where the emergence of a market for land was blocked by patrimonial ownership and the self-sufficiency of the labourers was generalized, the drying-up of supplies of slaves tended to lead to the drying-up of the market as a whole. Deprived of its pivot, trade could only involve a reduced volume of exchange. Transactions became less and less numerous and limited to luxury goods. The market's lack of fluidity did not favour either exchanges of articles for current use, like subsistence goods, or the generalized use of money. Since the conditions for self-sufficiency were maintained, the economy fell back on to the preservation of rents in food. If there was no progress in subsistence agriculture, the surplus-product, now based only on eco-demographic reproduction, dropped, and with it dropped the capacity for surplus-labour. Since the volume of the food surplus was low, it tended to be stocked rather than sold; since surplus-labour had been reduced, fewer commodities were produced. Finally, since labour was reproduced within the serf community, the lord was not compelled, as the slave-master had been, to produce for the market in order to renew his human herd.

In turn, serfdom, which resulted from the patrimonial ownership of the land, its use by a sealed food-producing sector, the low level of surplus-labour and the sluggishness of exchange, further weakened the internal market. In contrast, it seems that it contributed to the maintenance of long-distance trade, less through its demand than through its indirect social effects. In order to procure from the market the arms and prestige goods which were indispensable to his domination, the lord had to supply it with the product of the surplus-labour of his serfs. In order to increase this surplus-labour, he had to keep fewer peasants on the land than the domestic economy had supported. As a result, peasants were expropriated and migrated to the towns.

In the urban centres to which the dispossessed peasants came, food, supplied to the market only sparingly by the lords' *domaines*, was scarce. On lands bought from the nobles with the promise of eternity, the clergy re-established subsistence agriculture which enabled it to exercise a charitable exploitation over lay brothers and sisters and *idiota*. But the bourgeois in the towns, if they were to employ this expropriated labour force, had to have at their disposal the means of subsistence necessary for its upkeep as well as for their own. They had to bypass the huge areas of serfdom and go beyond them to reach distant regions which produced foodstuffs. Long-distance trade in grain replaced trade in slaves and began to build the foundations of what much later was to become a market for labour-power.

The transformations of modern colonial-type slavery are different, because they are affected by the economic context of world capitalism in which they have taken place. The establishment of a wage-earning labour force in competition with slavery took place entirely through the operations of the market.

It was with the use of slaves for the cultivation of cash crops that the way was opened for wage-labour. The commercialization of the products of the land led to that of the land itself. The value of agricultural commodities was communicated to the land; returns to it were evaluated in terms of commodities; it acquired a value and even a price which was in turn communicated to all its products, including subsistence goods. Even when the social structures of production put a brake on the effective commercialization of the land, it had a latent value which tended to be extended to all its products, without exception. The internal commercialization of foodstuffs reached a critical point when, land having become transferable, the market for it contributed to social inequalities in access to the soil or to the specialization of certain land-owners in cash-cropping. With the commercialization of the slaves' food, other problems arose from the arrival on the internal market of a mass of foodstuffs which had previously been consumed in the context of self-sustenance. This necessitated the marketing of equivalent commodities or the overvaluation of those already on the market. It encouraged the rise of a money which could reduce these differences, and thus of a political authority which ruled over it. In these circumstances the slave-owners, forced to buy food for their slaves, found themselves in the situation described earlier of having to make constant and fixed – and now costly – payments to slaves whose production of commodities was sold in market conditions which varied. At this point the logic of profit led from the purchase of subsistence goods for slaves to their remuneration in money; and further, from fixed remuneration to remuneration which varied according to work done or results achieved.

This form of remuneration bought only labour-power, delivered independently of the labourer's basic needs; it was not based on any evaluation of the minimum needs for the upkeep of an individual, whether or not he worked; there was no quantified concern with his reproduction. This is wage-labour. Its establishment corresponded to the opening of a labour market where 'free' labourers competed with slaves; these labourers might be more expensive per hour worked, but in the long term they cost less. These wage-earners necessitated no investment of capital or disbursement before employment, and they were employed only as long as the purchase of their labour-power was profitable.

Although the advantages of wage-labour were overwhelming, the resistance of the slave-owners can be explained. It was linked to their material interests and to the business and social relationships they maintained with the apparatus of the slave trade. It was linked to their investment in a slave stock which lost its merchant value with the emergence of the market for labour-power. The capital invested in the slaves could not be recovered, and this put the slave-owners at a disadvantage with respect to their capitalist competitors, who could invest in the means of production and in improvements in the productivity of their wage-earners. If the slave-owners managed to buy machines for their slaves to work on in spite of this handicap, the amortization of these machines forced them to amortize their slaves at the same pace, even at the risk of exhausting their strength. Just as investments in fixed capital complicated slavery, so they were simplified by capitalism.

Rather than the conversion of slave-owners to capitalism, the substitution of one exploiting class for another can be observed – in the United States, for example. In the world context of an industrial, money economy, abolition became the stakes in a war between two competing exploiting classes, rather than a class struggle between masters and slaves.

Did slavery in fact give rise to class struggles? There are no obvious examples of this in Africa. Slave rebellions were rare. *Captives*, held in barracks waiting to be taken away, did certainly rebel; slaves tried to flee; usurpers of servile origin seized power. But there were no organized revolts aimed at taking over control from the masters. In this respect we have already referred to the hierarchization of the slave class, its univocal link with the master and its inability to find grounds for collective organization where the stakes were higher than those granted at the master's pleasure. De-personalization, the ideology with which these women and adolescents were impregnated upon their enslavement, the pain and terror inspired by cruel punishments, the collective action by the class of masters which contrasted with the disorganization of the slaves. . . . The harsher exploitation is, the more it deprives the exploited of knowledge and free time, and the more limited are the possibilities of consciousness. Revolution is not inversely proportional to repression, as revolutionary romanticism would have it. Beyond a certain point human beings are crushed under the need to survive. The most cynical of the exploiters are aware of this and deliberately worsen the material conditions of those they exploit, not because it benefits them – since the costs are sometimes higher than the gains – but as a means of locking the exploited into absolute materiality. Freedom is won little by little through the exploitation of the interstices created by contradictions in every social system which force the exploiters to give in so that they themselves can survive. Each social conquest is not sheer victory: it can also be an adjustment necessary to the perpetuation of the mode of exploitation. The settlement of slaves, which was an improvement with respect to drudge-slavery, was not the fruit of struggle. It was useful to the masters, while it also introduced further divisions among the slaves. The working class, more than any other, has been capable of positive struggle, but it could be a dangerous illusion to believe that an action need only be massive and organized in order to succeed completely without, partly, serving the interests of the masters.

Conclusions

The few cases of slavery described in this work evidently do not exhaust the matter, and still less the search for a theoretical conceptualization. But in order to pursue this search through the study of classical cases like those of Antiquity, the Muslim East or the Americas, analysts must first agree on a characterization which renders them comparable.

In this work I have suggested that slavery can be identified in terms of its 'mode of reproduction'. Yet I have been criticized for having, in a previous work, placed this notion – which does not exist in the writings of Marx! – 'on the same level' as that of the 'mode of production', which in fact would contain it.

I have stated elsewhere (1981) that I do not consider the 'mode of production' to be an operational concept. Even in the works of Marx it is a convenient notion used temporarily until such time as the question is clarified, to describe differing and not always very clearly identified forms of economic organization, with no conceptual content being applied to them in a uniform fashion. It is in any case by no means certain that one can give this notion a homogeneous content in terms of which all possible modes of production can be discovered by a logical process of transformation.[1] On the basis of present research into slavery, I shall confine myself for the time being to the following considerations.

324

In the historical framework of its productive forces, a society is not based on production alone, but also on the reproduction of the conditions of production. Without, as we shall see, putting them 'on the same level', I consider the organization of the relations of production as the 'mode of production' and the organization of the relations of reproduction as the 'mode of reproduction'. From this point of view the juridical, political, ideological and cultural 'superstructures' seem to me to be instruments of the mode of reproduction. A *society* is made up of the organic organization of its modes of production and reproduction, whose specificity characterizes the *social system* which underpins it: the domestic community, slavery, serfdom, capitalism, and so on. Since the historical notion of the 'mode of production' in Marx's work refers to the economic infrastructure (I,1: 82n.), it can be applied only as a synecdoche – as Marx himself sometimes applied it – to the totality of the 'social system'.

At each moment of its history each society inherits *productive forces* which are made up of accumulated intellectual knowledge and material assets, as well as the political, social and ideological capacity to put them to work, for its own guidance and also *relative* to other societies. At any moment these productive forces determine the limits and the nature of the society's relations with all that is external to it, both the natural environment and 'alien' societies – that is, those with which its relation is based on force and not on institutions. In this general framework of determination essential and restrictive relations of production are established, which are indispensable to the material upkeep of the members of the society and the system of production. Within the same framework of determination, social rules governing the relations of reproduction aimed at the constant reconstitution of the relations of production and the human beings which are inserted into them are elaborated. But, unlike the relations of production, they are not directly subordinated to material constraints.

For, although the social conditions of production are located within a framework which is determined historically by the level of the productive forces, social organization must be made to conform to them through appropriate action. The

notion of determination applied to the social sciences does
not imply automatism. History offers a framework for determination in the sense that the relations of production it makes
possible are limited in form and content; but only through
organized action by members of society, to create institutions; which establish and constantly renew the relations of
production, can these relations be implemented. These institutions, such as kinship or wars of capture, for instance,
are institutions of reproduction. Like all institutions, they are
found at the apex of power relations: their existence implies a
political choice which is liable to affect the productive forces
or the way they are put into operation, and thus to shift the
point at which they become determinant. Through this intervention – which can take place only at the political level,
since it is not directly determined by the material conditions
of production – society escapes absolute materialist determinism. It is in this respect that society enjoys a degree of freedom. However, the constraints of material production are
still determinant, although they are subordinated to the
effects of the modes of reproduction which they generate. In
other words, it is through the putting into operation of a
mode of reproduction which organizes the mode of production in terms of the historical and material imperatives which
weigh on it that the relations of production 'freely' conform
to the determinism of the productive forces.

In domestic societies, for example, the productive forces
operate within the limits of self-sustenance as it applies to a
population in which the relations of reproduction are
governed by kinship. Kinship, which organizes the social
framework of procreation (marriage) and the devolution of
progeny (filiation), constantly generates relations of production in conformity with the historical conditions in which
they have to operate in order to be efficient and to maintain
the material conditions for the perpetuation of the society.
When historical conditions change, and thus relations of production must also change, relations of reproduction have to
be adjusted accordingly. This adjustment can initially take
place through a 'subversive' fraction of the population,
before spreading to and imposing itself on the social set as a
whole; the social authorities can conform to this adjustment

or oppose it, provoking a crisis, and so forth. The same mode of production can apparently fit different modes of reproduction. The main feature of the domestic relation of production, built around food cultivation (lifelong relations, relations of anteriority and the intergenerational distribution of the product) can adapt to patrilineal or avuncular filiation. Slave reproduction can originate in war or in raids, which as we have seen had different political implications, while still underpinning similar relations of production.

Under the capitalist regime, the modes of reproduction imposed on the working class distinguish an integrated, relatively stabilized proletariat from one which is migrant and temporary: the first is backed up by institutions of social security and the other by the administrative and police apparatus which organizes shifts of populations between the domestic and the wage economy.

In domestic society, the relations of production and the relations of reproduction are not confused but are, however, congruent, since they apply jointly to the whole of the population. This is not the case for slave-owning society, where the mode of production is not directly determined by the productive forces alone, but is also determined *relative to those of other societies* whose demographic increase it can constantly and regularly plunder. Slave exploitation is organically founded on an alien mode of production, the domestic mode of production, which 'produces' the men and women whom the slave mode of reproduction transforms into slaves. As a result, the domestic mode of production (which is not founded on any other) and the slave mode of production are not homogeneous: they do not fit, term for term, into a single category, 'mode of production', which in this context cannot, therefore, be seen as a concept in the true sense but only as a notion.

Since slave society is a class society, the dominant class also has to operate the institutions which reproduce society at large; those which ensure the reproduction of the dominated classes alongside those which perpetuate the relations of domination and exploitation. In aristocratic society, the houses which make up the dominant class together wage slaving wars, which are the means of reproduction of the slave class and thus also of slave-owning society as a whole. For this purpose they build up military and political alliances which contribute to social reproduction.

Through the plunder of other societies by the slave-owning society, aliens fall into the hands of gentles. This relation is at the base of the primary class relationship established within this society between masters and slaves. Distinct relations of reproduction are constituted within each class and a more general relation of production is constituted between them.

The aristocracy, more concerned to organize itself around war and power than around agricultural food production, sometimes reproduces itself in co-optive forms – like the band – but more often through a model of dynastic kinship backed up by the ideological and segregative notion of consanguinity.

The merchant class's relations of reproduction centre around the transmission and reconstitution of patrimony, while it provides itself with an ethic which sanctions the market, the instrument for the reproduction of the slave class.

For the slave class, the institutions of war and of the market, set up by the dominant classes, are the framework which governs its reproduction and which, in this historical context, evacuates kinship.

Dynastic or patrimonial kinship on the one hand, capture and purchase on the other: these forms of social reproduction were mutually exclusive and thus sanctioned the class relation through an 'agamy' which prevented the emergence between these classes of relations capable of generating kinship. Only relations of production existed, operating between dominant and dominated classes.

Finally, when individuals of lower classes were incorporated into relations of reproduction which were not centred on kinship - like wars of capture – they were constituted not as a class but as a *social corps* with its own specific mode of reproduction and its own specific relation to the dominant class.

To take only the mode of production into account in the examination of a social system is to analyse it as if it always reproduced itself in an identical form. It implies restricting the analysis to a model of simple or equilibrium reproduction, of a functionalist type. But since societies in history do not exactly repeat themselves, the mode of reproduction opens up the model to the contradictions which transform it dialectically, in conformity with the principles of historical materialism.

Research undertaken from this perspective opens out several paths, which unavoidably lead to the transdisciplinary approach inherent in historical materialism.

In order to distinguish the mode of reproduction of slavery from that of serfdom it was essential, in examining serfdom, to take into account both the demographic conditions of the emergence of new generations and the economic conditions of their growth up to productive age. A generalization of this 'eco-demographic' approach is likely to lead to the discovery of laws of population particular to different social systems (and thus also to the specification of their content). Such a study of population laws presupposes an anthropological examination of the social divisions between the sexes. This refers back to the notion of 'woman' which results from the social recognition of the woman's reproductive function and the cultural positions she occupies in this capacity. The study of slavery, a system in which all sorts of manipulations are possible, shows how what appears as 'human nature' intervenes as an explanatory principle only once it is culturally defined. This *social* definition of the woman in turn orders the rules of kinship, since it is through her that the relations of kinship are established, although she may not be at their apex. The case of mixed births in unions between masters and slaves shows how kinship relations which supposedly rule an entire 'tribe' are in fact subordinated to the principles which regulate class relations. The problematic of the so-called 'complex societies' of structural anthropology, most of which are class societies, cannot, in terms of this view, be founded within a purely structural logic which imposes itself on the social system as a whole.

Although for theorists of kinship slavery is all the more

instructive in that it is antinomic to kinship, it has not as such held the attention either of the structuralists or of the functionalists, except to be situated in the universal scheme of a kinship which is implicitly consanguine – that is, essentially aristocratic! The fact of procreation cannot, in any society, be considered a 'natural' starting point for the elementary social relation of motherhood, and still less of fatherhood. These relationships can be created only through active material exchanges between adults and children. Between slaves, these parental relationships depended on the masters' goodwill. They existed only slightly, and precariously, in the context of the functioning of the institutions which, as far as the slaves were concerned, replaced kinship: capture or sale.

Nor is birth the pivotal point of social reproduction. It was given less significance in anthroponomic societies than the successive stages of entry into productive and reproductive life. In fact the reproduction of a society is not completed with the birth of a new generation, but only with its coming to economic maturity. However high the fertility of the women, the proportion of children who reached maturity depended, in the final analysis, on the active individuals' labour productivity in food production. Demographic potential was subordinated to productive capacity.

What is more, we had to define what 'production' meant in this context. In order to do so we had to single out the goods which enter into the maintenance of life, which we called 'regenerative goods'. Marx placed the productivity of the sector producing the 'necessities of life' at the origin of capitalist surplus-value. Indeed, the productivity of this sector determines the value of the products bought by the labouring classes and thus, in the final analysis, their wage and their reproduction. However, although Marx distinguishes analytically between the two great sectors of capitalist production, that of consumption goods and that of producer goods, he confuses regenerative goods with all consumption goods. Yet his own reasoning leads to the sharpening of the distinction between them and to the singling out of the regenerative sector and its specific laws. The slave-owning economy cannot be explained without such an analysis. And even today, because of the strategic position in the world capitalist economy of the food-producing sector, States – even those which advocate free trade – intervene to subject it to economic laws which are different from those prevailing in other sectors of production, with an important impact on what is called 'the population explosion' (Meillassoux, 1983).

Even more importantly, this distinction, which highlights the incommensurability of the social value of human beings and their labour-power (Itoh, 1985), makes it impossible to see them as 'human resources', as reificatory economics would have it.

In the transdisciplinary approach schematically set out above, ethnology, economics and demography are not juxtaposed as they are in a multidisciplinary approach; rather, they tend to fade away as disciplines to be reconstituted in a general perspective imposed by the problematic of social reproduction. They do not serve only to contribute information or facts, nor to 'clarify' the so-called 'different facets' of a single phenomenon: each supplies relevant information which is linked and ordered in an articulated argument.

In the 'liberal' view of the economy, slavery represents one of the first, if not the first, form of the 'liberation' of labour: these women and men, torn from their native communities where they could work only within the framework of the indissoluble and restricting ties of kinship, were transformed into a labour force supplied to all those who had the means to appropriate it for themselves. In this way a huge shift of labour-power took place, along with its concentration and its reorganization according to different norms of production. But can slavery, for all that, be considered as objective economic progress in the sense of a historical advance of the productive forces? Was this destructive mode of exploitation the springboard for an accumulation which enabled a step towards the improvement of the means of production? Engels, in response to the moral but scarcely scientific judgements applied to slavery, underlined its merits. Nevertheless, the result is uncertain.

We have already noted that in global terms slavery led to a drop in food production and thus in population; that the immobilization of potential capital in a slave restricted the growth of labour productivity. Slavery provoked transfers of the surplus-product but also its reduction. Slavery was a means not of exploitation but of overexploitation. To its credit can be attributed the fact that it created and stimulated large-scale trade, the specialization of tasks and the diversification of production, and thus the rise of a merchant class which could rival the military class, while still depending on it. However, the potential capacity for accumulation of merchant capital through this class was realized in a context which, while it put labour on the market, made it too easy to replace and did not grant labour-power market value. The increase in production took place in a manner which was destructive rather than progressive, through the intensification of wars of capture and the accumulation of numbers of slaves: there was no incentive to increase the labour *productivity* of the exploited. Merchant capital had less potential than military wealth, which was the real agent of economic growth. The coexistence and combination of aristocratic and merchant societies and of their respective slaveries favoured an economy stretched between subsistence and luxury, in which 'productive' investments were mostly limited to the instruments of war.

Serfdom, with fewer means of accumulation because it limited the number of labourers available at any moment, and although it was accompanied by a decrease in trade, probably led to greater advances in labour productivity: the swing plough, draught animals and the use of natural energy emerged with it.

The surge of philosophical or political thought in ancient Greece or Rome is partly attributed to the leisure time slavery made available to the ruling classes. But did this thought, for all that, help them to see more clearly the real conditions of their existence? Marx remarked that the unequal value of men had blinded Aristotle to the respective value of their labour. Cicero, who advocated torture and the death penalty as means of bringing slaves into submission, held the crudest prejudices against these 'aliens', identical to those which inspire the worst racism today, which made him incapable of recognizing any civilization other than that which owned slaves.

In Pompeii, in a fresco illustrating domestic and craft tasks, the artist replaced the ugly slaves who usually performed them with sweet and smiling cherubs. The Pompeiians lived in a myth in which everything seemed to them to have come from heaven as a natural and deserved reward for their obtuse refinement. Like all exploitation, slavery leads to the alienation not only of the exploited but also of the exploiters. It leads to a negation of the humanity of men and women, to contempt for them and to hatred. It is an inducement to racism, to arbitrariness, to cruelty and to purifying murder, which are the characteristic weapons of the bitterest class struggles. If by any chance slavery did contribute to some sort of material progress, the intellectual guides which it has bequeathed to us are philosophers and politicians whose consciousness was the product of this blindness and these prejudices. Is it not perhaps because their alienation has communicated itself even to us, borne by the unquestioned and uninterrupted culture of the exploiters, that it is still imperceptible to us and that it still presents as humanist societies which were built on the plunder of man?

Glossary

Words *in italics* in the definitions refer to other words in the glossary.
(This glossary was compiled in close collaboration with Jean-Luc Jamard, CNRS.)

Abbreviations:
\# as distinct from
conv. converse: terms which refer back to a word used conversely, e.g. elder/cadet, father/son
ant. antonym
syn. synonym
cf. see
neol. neologism

acquisition (of slaves): capture or purchase

adelphy (neol.): set of individuals whose *filiation* refers to the same *doyen*; *adelphic* (succession): succession from *doyen* to *senior* in an *adelphy* and from elder to cadet in a *fraternity*.
\# lineage

adoption: placing of an individual in a new relation or context of *kinship*.

affiliation: conventional social tie which binds an individual who is not *kin* to an *elder* or a *doyen* who sanctions his or her membership of the *community*.
\# joining
cf. filiation

affine: a community may distinguish two categories of affines: the kin of women married to *gentle*-men of the *community* and the kin of the husbands of *gentle*-women of the community.

affinity (narrow sense): the relationship between a husband or wife and the *kin* of his or her spouse (from Littré); (wider sense): relations between two or more individuals based on the fact that at least two members of their respective *communities* are linked by marriage.
alliance

agamy (neol.): matrimonial exclusion.

alienation (1) apprehension and assumption by an individual, as part of his or her social personality, of the constraints imposed by the *exploitation* of which he or she is the object or the agent; (2) alienation of a good: absolute disposal of a good (in the case of slaves, through sale or immolation).

alliance: joint, complementary or reciprocal undertaking sanctioned by an act (oath, pact, treaty, etc.) outside of *kinship* or *affiliation*.

allotment: minimum measure of land necessary for the subsistence of a man and his family.

amalgam: mixture, by marriage, of distinct populations.

anceocracy (neol.): power of servants (male or female).

anteriority: concept of seniority and the elders.

anthroponomic (neol.): describes a social system in which the administration of men rather than of things is dominant; through the manipulation of the means of human reproduction (women and the means of subsistence) rather than of the material means of production.

aristocracy: social *class* established by armed force; co-optive in origin but tending towards a dynastic organization.
cf. brigandage, band

avuncular: *filiation* between the *doyen* of an *adelphy* and the progeny of the *sororities*.
de facto syn. matrilineal

band: group constituted for the purpose of and during a specific activity – hunting, collection, pillage or abduction – where this activity is the principal link between its members.

breeding: set of operations designed to bring an individual to *maturity*.

brigandage: act of plunder or abduction carried out by a *band* within its own society.

raid, foray

capitalistic: society dominated by merchant capital, in which profit is subordinated to gains from trade.
capitalist

captive: a person who has been captured but not yet acquired by a master. The captive is a commodity; the slave a means of production. The captive consumes; the slave produces.
slave (who is under the authority of a master)

captor: a person who seizes other human beings to make them his *captives* (cf. Rinchon, 1929, in Gaston-Martin, 1948).

civilization: process through which an individual has access to social rights guaranteed by arbitration between him or her and the parties on whom he or she is dependent.

client: person who receives goods or services, working for a *patron* who sees to his maintenance, without any relation of material equivalence between their respective duties.
obligor
conv. patron

collective means of production: those which are the result of the collective labour of several production cells but are used by each of them for the satisfaction of their own particular needs.

community: set of *gentles* in a *house*.

concept: operational* instrument of analytical or synthetic thought, which creates distinctions.
notion

condition (of the slave): social situation defined by the slave's place in the relations of production or reproduction in the society in which he or she is employed.
state

congeners: those who were born and have grown up together as fellow-members of a community.
cf. franchise

contradiction: abstract description of a process inherent in a situation undergoing radical change.
(Thus different from 'conflict', 'opposition', 'opposite', etc. – meanings which the word has abusively been given in Maoist and Stalinist

---

* operational: capable of creating other concepts.

thought.)

co-option, co-optation: mode of recruitment of a group by its members where predefined individual qualities are the criteria for selection.

culture: the sum of intellectual production and knowledge in a social milieu, potentially transformable into an ideological force.

deme or *gamodeme*: 'matrimonial circle within which at least 90 per cent of marriages take place' (from Bounak, 1964, quoted by Gomila, 1976: 18). cf. matrimonial set

divination: arbitrary and conventional (therefore often esoteric) correlation between fate and the physical ordering or the appearance of certain objects.

doyen: the elder of the *seniors*.

drudge-slave: slave whose entire labour-time is supplied without restriction to his or her master, who in return provides the slave with the basic necessities of life.

dues: fraction of *surplus-product* or *surplus-labour* due from a dependant to the individual who has authority over him or her.
tax
cf. rent, surplus-product, surplus-labour

dynasty: organization which brings together kin of the *aristocratic* class with rights of access to power.

dynastic kinship: hereditary mode of transfer of power and titles which tends towards monogamy and direct father–son filiation.

eco-demographic reproduction: takes into account both female fertility and the *productivity* of regenerative labour in a given society.

eldership: anteriority within a *generation*.
(Introduces the notions of *elder* and *cadet*.)
seniority

enfranchisement: operation through which a slave is wholly *redeemed* and becomes the equal of a *free-born* individual through the total obliteration of his or her previous *state*.
manumission

enslavement: the *state* of the slave.

excess: the *surplus-product* and *surplus-labour* of the *drudge-slave*.

exploitation: relation between *social classes* in which one class collects all or part of the *surplus-labour* or *surplus-product* of the other and this transfer

ensures the reproduction of the relations of exploitation.
extortion

extended reproduction:
(1) demographic: when each individual supports more than one individual of the next generation to the age of maturity;
(2) economic: reproduction of the means of production, either in increased quantities or with greater social returns.

extortion: the arbitrary and occasional, but inorganic, withdrawal of an indeterminate part of the social product by those in power.
exploitation

extra-economic: a flawed vision of history (Marx: *Grundrisse*, pp. 488–9).

father: man to whom are attributed the children of a woman recognized as his wife or those entrusted to him by adoption.

feud: state of deadly warfare between families designed to avenge insults or crimes.

filiation: membership of a *kinship* group shown by dependence on the person who has the authority of *doyen*.
cf. affiliation

formal (domination): exercised over a producer who owns his own individual instruments of labour but not the social means of production (including the land).

franchise: status of the *gentle* as long as he or she is linked to his or her *congeners* by *kinship* or *affinity*.
freedom

fraternity: masculine collaterals of the same *generation*.
adelphy

free-born: free of all *servitude* through membership of a *social class* or through *enfranchisement*.

generation: individuals of both sexes belonging to the same *sorority* or the same *fraternity*.

gentle: individual who, born and brought up in a *free-born* social milieu, is acknowledged to be free of all *servitude*.
syn. free-born

henchman: subjugated person whose functions depend on trust.

homogeneous (society): where the *social components* have homologous structures (for example, domestic society is composed of *communities* whose social structures are based on the same organizational principles).

ant. heterogeneous

horde: unstable reproductive group constituted for productive activities with immediate returns; new members enter the group by *joining*.
cf. band

house:
(1) in domestic society, a group made up of individuals of various origins producing and consuming under the authority of a *doyen*;
(2) in *aristocratic* society, the set of relations with the same political *patrimony*.
cf. community, stock

hypergamy: marriage of a woman of inferior condition with a man from a superior *social class* or *order*.
ant. hypogamy

ideology: rationalization or naturalization of social prescriptions or representations which establishes their restrictive or indisputable nature.

inert (product): which is not used for the physical regeneration of the human being.
ant. regenerative

joining: act through which an individual of productive age voluntarily joins a production group organized for immediate returns (whose product is not deferred) or a *band*.
\# affiliation
cf. band, horde

kin: set of *congeners* linked by lifelong relations of production or reproduction and hierarchized according to *eldership*.

kinship: juridico–ideological representation of relations of production and reproduction in domestic communities; refers to relations of reproduction only with respect to *free-born social classes* within other *anthroponomic* societies and to all classes within capitalist society.

labour-energy: describes labour-power as a use-good, not a commodity.

labour-potential: slave's ability to supply *labour-energy* at any moment in his or her active life.
\# capital

manumission: condition of the slave *redeemed* of his or her obligation to work.
\# enfranchisement

marriage: institution through which the children born or to be born to a woman are recognized as being *affiliated* to her husband's *community* (in patrilineal society) or to that of her *elder* (*avuncular* filiation).

matrimonial set: set of communities which reproduce demographically and socially among themselves.
cf. deme, gamodeme

maturity: age at which an individual is considered capable of economic production and/or social reproduction.

model: coherent abstraction from a historical *social system* reduced to the essential features of its reproduction (the model is dialectic if contradictions likely to lead to its transformation are thrown up by its own internal logic).

multigyny or multigamy: polygymy where the number of wives is such that primogeniture loses its relevance as a means of designating a successor and is replaced by a selective mode of succession.

necessary (labour-time, product, etc.): the part of labour-energy, labour-power, or the product used for the reconstitution of this energy and the maintenance of the producer's life.
cf. surplus-product, surplus

neighbour: alien living 'within reach' with whom relations subject to conciliation are maintained.

notion: descriptive or categoric generalization.
(for example: 'junior' is a notion, 'eldership' a concept).
concept

obligor: a person who, in exchange for services received, places himself under the influence and freely at the disposal of his protector or his guarantor.
client

order: institutional and juridical notion of *social classes* and *social corps.*

organic: describes an essential relation inherent to a social system of which it is thus constitutive.

patrimony: set of goods, in principle inalienable, in the possession of an organized collectivity, transferred unilaterally within it (by gift or inheritance) independently of exchange.
property

patron: cf. client

primary (material or good): which is used in the production of another good.

productivity: relation between the production and consumption of an active worker.

return

property: used in the Roman sense of *usus, fructus, abusus*.

protector: conv. of *obligor*.

puberty: the period of her life during which a woman is able to procreate, not the beginning of the reproductive cycle.

raid: plunder or capture by a *band*.
war
syn. foray, incursion

redemption: release from all or part of the dues in labour or products owed by a slave to his or her master for the purpose of *manumission* or *enfranchisement*.

regenerative: product or material which contributes to the reconstitution of *labour-energy* and the maintenance of the producer's life.
ant. inert

relations of production: *organic* relations between active members of a *society* through which the production and the distribution of the social product are organized.

relations of reproduction: organized relations between the members of a *society* which order its demographic and institutional perpetuation.

rent (in labour or in products): that part of the *surplus-labour* or *surplus-product* of the slave or serf which is appropriated by the master or lord.

reproduction, simple (see also *extended reproduction*):
(1) demographic: when each active individual can provide for a single replacement up to maturity;
(2) economic: reproduction of the means of production with the same economic capacity.

self-sustenance: characterizes an economy capable of producing the basic necessities of life and the means of production using materials and know-how directly within reach.
autarchy

seniority: when referring to two or more *generations*, describes membership of an individual to a previous generation.
conv. junior
cf. doyen
eldership

serfdom: *exploitative social system* based on the extraction by an *aristocratic class* of a *rent* in labour or in products from the *surplus-labour* or *surplus-product* of a *class* of serfs who produce the necessities for the reconstitution of their own *labour-energy*, their maintenance and their reproduction on a minimum of land granted for this purpose by the dominant class.

\# slavery

servitude: exclusive dependence on a master or lord independently of all *kinship* ties.

slavery: social system based on the *exploitation* of a class of producers or persons performing services, renewed mainly through *acquisition* (used also, by extension, to mean *enslavement*).   *capture or purchase*

snatch: seizure of an isolated person, far from his or her home base, to take him or her *captive*.

social class: *social component* placed in *organic* relations of *exploitation* with respect to another.

cf. social corps

social component: social cell whose specificity in a *society* is determined by its relation to other (homologous or converse) social components (e.g. clan, domestic community. social class, order, enterprise, etc.).

social corps: group generated by a *social class* in order to perform certain functions which are essential to its survival and of which it cannot itself take complete charge. For example: soldier–slaves for the military aristocracy; the police, the army, company executives for the bourgeoisie; the trade–union bureaucracy for the working class; state bureaucracies, etc.

\# class

social means of production: those which are produced within the social division of labour and used for the production of social good.

\# collective means of production

social system: abstract model of the organic and institutional organization of modes of production and reproduction in a certain type of *society* and of their juridical, political and *ideological* expression (see Conclusions).

society: historical and local form of a *social system*.

cf. social system

soldier-slave (or servant): servant or slave armed in the service of his master.

sorority: female collaterals of the same *generation*.

sovereign: presumed holder of supreme political power.

sovereign monopoly: exclusive control by those in power of the production and circulation of a good.

state: social and juridical situation of an individual deprived of *status*: status is defined by a set of prerogatives, state by a set of privations.

State: governmental and administrative apparatus of sovereignty which is at stake in the struggle between social classes or fractions of the dominant class.

status: set of *de jure* and *de facto* prerogatives enjoyed by an individual through membership of a *class* or an *order*.
state

stock: set of *gentle kin*.
cf. house, community

subject: free-born individual who is dependent on a sovereign.

subjection: process through which an individual is placed under the political authority of a *sovereign*.

surplus-labour: labour-time available over and above *necessary* labour-time.

surplus-product: part of the product available over and above the *necessary* product.

symplectic (society) (neol.): one whose *heterogeneous social components* are not amalgamated but are held together by various compulsive *alliances* which can carry out some functions of a centralizing power.
cf. homogeneous

tax: periodic levy based on an assessment of the income and the goods of defined social categories.
tribute

tribute: *extortion* from conquered populations or those without civil rights.

vicinal: to do with neighbours (e.g. vicinal war: war between neighbours).

war: organized and planned recourse to violence by a society or a social class against another.
raid, foray

yield: quantity produced by a production cell or by each unit of the physical means of production during a given period.
productivity

Notes

INTRODUCTION

1   In primitive Roman law, the slave is explicity an object and not a person (Monier, 1947: 211).

2   This is also Finley's thesis (1981): he considers that the demand for slaves precedes supply.

3   This is the name usually given to a fragment of the *Grundrisse*, in Marx (1964).

4   Marx, ibid.

5   It is precisely this position which I have criticized in Miers and Kopytoff's work (1977).

6   'But man is individualized only through the process of history.' The same is true of apparently individualized relations such as that which binds the slave to his or her master (Marx, 1964).

7   The same reasoning can be found in the work of contemporary authors such as Leslie White (1969: 128): 'Slavery did not exist during the hundreds of thousands of years before Neolithic times because culture had not developed sufficiently to make it possible for a producer to be more than self-supporting.' Strictly speaking, this assertion implies the extinction of the human race before its emergence.

8   The exchange of commodities at their approximate value and not at their 'price of production' takes place, as in slavery, 'so long as the means of production involved in each branch can be transferred from one sphere to another only with difficulty . . .' (*Capital* III, 1; ch. X: 177).

9   Meillassoux, ed., *L'esclavage en Afrique pré-coloniale*, Paris, Maspero, 1975.

INTRODUCTORY CHAPTER

1   Saliu Balde correctly translates the term *Beyguure*, which describes the extended family among the Fula of Fuuta Jallo, as *'croît'* (growth). The link between the productive and reproductive cycles is also demonstrated by the assimilation of progeny to their nourishment, as Jaulin notes among the Sara (1971: 242) or P. Weil (1970) among the Mande, where 'by association [the women] symbolically treat the production of food and that of children as one and the same'.

2   From this perspective, in a virilocal system the girl is a gentle in her community of origin but an alien as a wife in her husband's community.

3   *The individual surplus-product* of an active adult, *over his or her lifetime*, is equivalent to the difference between the adult's food production from farming and his or her consumption during his or her active life; or:

$$\beta B - \alpha B$$

The social distribution of the individual surplus-product is made up of:

$$\beta B = x_2 + \alpha B + \frac{1}{x_2} \Sigma \alpha C$$

The concept of *surplus-product* has nothing in common with the term *surplus*, which is used generally, without specifying to what period (a year or the length of an active life) it refers, whether or not it includes the quantities necessary for demographic reproduction and at what rate, if seeds and stocks are to be deducted and if so, for how many years, etc.

β   annual production of an active individual

α   annual consumption of an individual

A   length of the pre-productive period for young people (in years)

B   length of a producer's active life (in years)

C   length of the post-productive period (in years)

x_1 number of (pre-productive) children fed by a producer during his or her active life

x_2 number of descendants who share the care of their elders (post-productive individuals) and of the disabled (Meillassoux, 1981).

4   In Aboh, the term *osu* describes a person who gives his labour free of charge. 'He could not be obtained from within the patrilineages of "free" Aboh', as Nwachukwu-Ogedengbe correctly notes (1977: 140).

5   Meillassoux (1979e).

6   Paul Bohannan (1963: 180) is among the first, if not the first, to have pointed out this essential feature of slavery: *'anti-kinship'*. P. Riesman provides a very interesting elaboration of the relation between procreation and the status of individuals and comes to the same conclusions using a different method. In particular, Riesman finds that the root of

the Peul word *rimaïbe*, which applies to slaves, means 'he who has not given birth', as opposed to *Rimbe* (the gentle), which apparently comes from *rim*, 'to give birth'. Gaden (according to Labouret, 1955) finds in the word *rim-ay-be* (the plural of *dim-â-dyo*) the root *dim*: 'to be pure of all stains', which does not contradict Riesman's findings, since according to Ba and Daget (1962: note p.66) *rim* comes from *rimde*, 'to breed'; *rimdude*, 'to be pure, to be born'. Thus the *rimaybe* are not born; the *rimbe* are pure, noble (and born).

7   According to the administration's report on captivity in the Kissi (Guinea) (Dakar Archives, K14-1894), 'captives are only exported, never imported', since 'they do not know what to do with them . . . being sufficiently numerous in each family to meet their own needs'. Whatever the value of this explanation, it expresses the reluctance of this type of domestic society to employ subjugated persons.

8   P.-P. Rey uses the word 'slave' to describe those who have been captured, yet they only become slaves once they have been sold to a master. I think that the word 'captive' is more appropriate here.

Part I The Womb:
The Dialectic of Slavery

1: THE HISTORICAL DIMENSION OF SLAVERY IN WEST AFRICA

1 This chapter is a reworked version of an article published in *Anthropologie et Sociétés* (Quebec), 1978,2,1: 117–48.

2 Capture of slaves was doubtless practised under the dynasties of the pharaohs, from 2000BC, when the troops were made up of Nubians. Between 1500 and 1450BC, 'military expeditions on the Upper Nile were frequent', aimed at the provision of recruits and of 'servants' (Vercoutter, 1976). Sesostris III (12th dynasty) wrote: 'The Nubian . . . I have captured his women, taken away his subjects . . .' (ibid.: 83). It seems that the Koushites and the Meroites, to the south of Egypt, constituted themselves into military slave-supplying States, on the Egyptian model, between 800 and 300BC.

3 Some archaeologists (Thilmans *et al.*, 1980) suggest that the megalithic civilization of Senegambia – dated between 594 and 790 – disappeared as a result of attacks by slave-hunters installed south of the Sahara. Basing his argument on archaeological discoveries by Munson (1972) in the Tishitt region, A. Bathily (1975: 43) considers that slavery in the area dates back three or four centuries before our era.

4 Which seems to suggest that capture was a reason in itself and not the by-product of wars waged for other purposes (on this point, see Part II, A, Chapter 2 below).

5 *Sudan*: Black.

6 A generic name given by Maghrebin authors to the so-called savage populations of tropical Africa, among whom slaves were captured.

7 In this and the following quotations, the emphasis is added.

8 Or Edrissi.

9 These figures may not be accurate, but they indicate considerable numbers.

10 The name Barbara was given by Arab authors to several populations which were very distant from each other. Here it refers to the Sudanese. The Amima might have been the inhabitants of the ancient land of Mema or Mima, which is generally located in the semi-desert region to the west of Lake Debo.

11 Founder and chief of the Almoravid brotherhood.

12 Or an area of 1,800 kilometres.

13 Sovereigns of Sonxai (which straddled what are now Mali and Niger).

14 Belonging to the caste of the *mabo*.

15 Goody (1971) considers that cavalry (and guns) gave the princes a decisive advantage over the peasants. I have discussed this point of view in *Africa*, XLI, 4, October 1971: 331–3. The horses seem sometimes to have suffered during expeditions to hot regions like Gurma (*TES*: 426). On this point, see also C. Aubin-Sugy, 1975, ch.IX; McCall, 1967; Daumas, 1858; Law, 1975.

16 In a more recent period, Telem habitations and the *tata* of the Bamana or the Malinke are examples of this (Meillassoux, 1966).

17 C. Aubin-Sugy (1975, ch.IX) suggests that the use of slaves in the cavalry contributed to a more disciplined organization of the army.

18 'In the twinkling of an eye, the troops of the *askia* were routed'. This is how the battle between the 30,000 soldiers and horsemen of the *askia* and the 1,000 Moroccan invaders is summed up.

19 On the relative effectiveness of firearms, see the special issues of the *Journal of African History*, vol. XII, nos 2 and 4, 1971.

20 M. Izard (Seminar on War in Africa, 1978) dates this withdrawal very much later – towards the end of the seventeenth century.

21 See in Brunschvig, 'Abd', *Encyclopédie de l'Islam*, pp. 27 and 32, the permanent justification provided by Islam for the capture of slaves, under the cover of holy war. This justification betrays the slave-owning character of the civilization which developed at this time, and prefigures its incessant demand for slaves.

22 The overwhelming importance of the capture and sale of slaves is clearly established by O'Fahey (1973) with respect to the Dar-Fur of the eighteenth and nineteenth centuries. Abitbol (1979) also highlights the importance of slaves and of salt in trans-Saharan trade between the sixteenth and nineteenth centuries, and Devisse (1970:118, 127) notes the low tonnages of gold exported and the drying-up of gold supplies from Ifriqiya (Africa) from the second quarter of the twelfth century.

23 In the same way, the conquest of the Taghaza salt pans by the sultan of Morocco led, later, to the drying-up of production.

24 This exhaustion is disputable, since the Bure and Bambuk gold deposits were still being exploited in the contemporary period. In 1937, the deposits of French West Africa produced three and a half tons, on the basis of artisanal methods (Hopkins, A.G., 1973: 46). (See also A. Bathily, 1975: 56–7.)

25 In the more recent period, traces of the exodus of numerous populations as a result of raids can be found in the oral tradition of so-called palaeonegritic peoples. (See, for example, Pontie, 1973.)

26 Terray (1982) found a similar process among the Akan.

27 Similarly, in the eighteenth century, the people of Dahomey could not be sold by their sovereign. The fall of the kingdoms was often the result of the breaking of this rule, as the history of States like Wolof and Oyo shows.

28 Here a distinction must be made between the information provided in the original manuscript and that in the later *TEF* manuscript (Levitzion, 1971), which mirrors a change in the conception of subjugation – *contra* J.-P. Olivier de Sardan (1975).

29 '700 eunuchs surrounded the king, ready to offer their sleeves for him to spit into' (*TEF*: 208). The daughters of the royal soldiers were at the sovereign's disposal, for his pleasure.

30 The same process can be observed in Adamawa in the nineteenth century (Burnham, 1980: 51s.).

31 In El-Bekri (eleventh century) numerous references can already be found to merchants, markets, routes, currencies, and so on, which show that trade was well established in this region, even if in the *Tarikhs* it is obscured by the military history of the empires.

32 According to Niaré tradition, the first merchant families settled in Bamako towards 1640 (Meillassoux, 1963 – *contra* Marty, 1920–21: 65).

33 See the Islamization process of Mali, before 1300, in Triaud, 1981.

34 The history of Africa provides examples of this: the crumbling of the Kongo kingdom (Balandier, 1965; Ekholm, 1972); the disintegration of the principalities of the Senegal valley (Barry, 1972); the collapse of the kingdoms of Senegambia (Klein, 1972). I have discussed elsewhere the capacity of the merchants in the savannah to escape the control of the States (Meillassoux, 1971a). See also Terray (1974) on the relations between power and trade, and Bathily, 1985.

35 Yet the two terms are not interchangeable. If the Bamana, Bozo, Senufo, Minyanka populations referred to the Soninke as Maraka, this is because the word was applied in pagan milieus to Islamized families and peoples, and in peasant milieus to merchant or warrior and conquering families and populations. 'Maraka' was also the name of a population in Upper Volta which seems to have had nothing in common with the Soninke populations. See also Roberts (1978) on the

Maraka of Sansani.

36 Mauny (1961: 379) considers that this trade involved two million people each century. Malowist (1966) considers this to be an over-estimate.

37 J. Vansina has shown the importance which must be attached to silences in tradition.

38 This should be read as 'Maraka'. C. Monteil also made the mistake of seeing the two terms as synonyms.

39 See also Bazin (1972) and Roberts (1978, 1984).

40 The accuracy of these dates, which is questionable, is less important than the event reported here – that is, the strengthening of the mer-chants and their towns, at the expense of the military aristocracies and their empires.

41 Cf. Part II, A, Chapters 1, 2 below.

42 For an analysis of the condition of the subjects in the kingdom of Segu, see J. Bazin, 1972, 1975, 1979, 1982; Dumestre, 1975 and below, Part II, Chapter 2, 2.

43 *Talibe*: disciple.

44 See the pretexts used by El Haj Umar to justify his holy war against the sovereign of Masina (Mahibou and Triaud, 1983).

45 *Dolo*: sorghum beer, prohibited by Islam.

46 The reasons for these preferences are discussed in the body of the work.

47 Made up of parts and corps which are distinct but closely interwoven.

48 The phenomena described here have their counterparts in other regions. M. Klein (1971) notes the role, in the same period, of the Yoruba civil wars, the commercial wars in Sierra Leone and slave raids in the Fulani emirates of Zaria, Adamawa, Kontogara and Senegambia, as sources of supply for the growing demand of slave-producers.

49 Senegal Archives, series K.

50 This reconversion is particularly well illustrated by B. Barry (1972), Part III, Chapter 1.

2: Extraneousness

1 Exoticism: describes that which is not native to a country (Littré).

2 In Europe, the aristocrats and traders used slaves, particularly female slaves, as domestic servants. There were 3,000 such slaves in Bordeaux in the eighteenth century and 20,000 in London in 1764, the objects of continuous trading.

3 C. Aubin-Sugy (1975) describes these populations as 'non-economic' or 'non-commercial': in other words, outside the State's circuits of production.

4 The reader is referred here to the accounts by Niger peasants inter-

viewed by J.-P. Olivier de Sardan (1976) of their magical and practical methods of defence against pillaging incursions. J. Goody (1971: 57–72) describes the prohibitions which, among the peasants of central Gonja, still apply to horses, which were the instruments of their enslavement.

5 F. Héritier provides details of the organization of one of these domestic societies, the Samo, and their reactions to pillage by the Mossi (1975).

6 *Tata*: high, wide fortification (some 3 metres high and sometimes as wide) made of adobe, with towers at the angles. See plans in Meillassoux, 1966a.

7 Part II, 1, 2 below.

8 G. Elwert (1973), in his analysis of the 'mode of production based on the abduction of men', takes this approach.

9 This identification of slaves with animals is fairly generalized. According to Herodotus, 'the Guaramantes hunt Egyptian troglodytes . . . who are fleet-footed. They feed on lizards and all sorts of reptiles. Their language cannot be compared to any other, but only to the cry of the bat' (in Deschamps, 1971: 11–12). In the same work the author points out that in Great Britain domestic slaves in the eighteenth century were treated like favourite animals to which collars were attached. Farias (1980: 128) notes that *zang*, the stereotype used to describe slaves, has the connotation '*enslavable barbarian*'. In Soninke country it was said that 'slaves are like cattle'; in that, as for the Sonxai, slaves were part of the patrimony in the same way as cattle. (1965 research trip and J.-P. Olivier de Sardan, 1973. See also Cicero in Deschamps, 1975: 58.)

10 It is true that the relation of otherness can be modified over time. Sometimes a tribute in slaves was imposed on populations near the pillaging society, in terms of an agreement which presupposed communication of some sort. But the individuals delivered by these tributary societies were chosen from the group of marginals who were least likely to be socially identified or were captured in neighbouring populations (cf. below).

11 Theoretically Islam and the Muslim State did not grant rights to pagans. *De jure*, relations between pagans and Muslims could be based only on force. In fact pagans were part of the 'war territories' [*dar el harb*] and could therefore be submitted to enslavement (from Lansina Kaba, forthcoming).

12 Engels's argument sees the State only as the product of relations between classes which belong to a single social formation; but the slave State could also be seen as the product of a relation of extortion involving *distinct societies* – that is, as a relation both between *natio* (in the original sense of those of the same birth) and between classes. It is only later that internal class struggles reinforce and remodel the State

according to the forms of exploitation which are established between masters and slaves on the one hand and within the free-born classes on the other, as I shall try to show below (Part II).

13 According to Le Brasseur (1778) in Becker and Martin (1975: 289), the Moors left Brack and Damel (sovereigns of States in Senegambia) only those inhabitants 'who were necessary to supply their annual pillage'.

3: STERILITY

1 E. Terray (1975a) claims, in contrast to Hindess and Hirst (but without providing a demonstration any more than they do), that generative reproduction was more economical than capture.

2 'When they were able to sell their prisoners, the kings fattened them up, looked after them and gave them little work; now that they do not know what to do with them, they slit their throats by the thousand so as not to have to feed them, or they abandon them near their huts, chained, with no clothes and not a single grain of maize, *waiting for their time to come*' ('Daumas, 1857: 19–20. See also below, Part III, Chapter 2).

3 This must be taken to mean slaves who had children with other slaves and not the concubines of the masters.

4 The white slavers of Cuba had recourse to the same medicine (Barnet, 1967).

5 Snelgrave (1734) tells how he often saved babies who would have been 'thrown to the wolves' by the dealers, so as to be able to sell the mother more easily.

6 As Brunschvig also notes in the *Encylopédie de l'Islam* (art. 'Abd', p.27): in Muslim regions, the import of women slaves and their marriage with free men meant that their progeny was born free: 'Slavery could hardly have survived without the constantly renewed supply of peripheral or external elements either taken directly in war or imported commercially under the pretext of the holy war from foreign territories.'

4: PROFITS AND ACCUMULATION

1 See below, Section 5 and Part II, B, Chapter 2 and Part III, Chapter 5 for an examination of the conditions of acquisition.

2 He or she incorporates αK (where K is the slave's age at the time of capture and his or her annual subsistence consumption). αK is maximized if the slave is captured at the beginning of his or her productive period (when $K = A$, where A is the length of the pre-productive period).

3 Thus the profit realized from each slave is $\alpha K + (\beta B - \alpha B)$. If the captive is integrated before productive age A, $\alpha(A - K)$ must be deducted from the surplus-product over a lifetime – that is, the amount which

the slave would have consumed without producing. If the captive is integrated after productive age (K>A), his or her lifelong surplus-product will be $\beta B - \alpha(K - A)$ instead of $\beta B - \alpha B$. (At this point I have not taken into account the cost of acquisition; this will be covered in Part III, Chapter 5.)

4 'If your master does not give you someone in marriage, you do not marry', confided a slave to J.-P. Olivier de Sardan (1976: 166). The same applied to Greek slaves: 'The slave *puer* has no legal access to women, he thus is not the master of his biological reproduction. Just as he has no parents, the slave, properly speaking, has no children' (Maurin, 1975). Among (Fulani) slaves studied by Riesman (1974: 88) 'marriage does not confer rights to paternity'.

5 This is one of the reasons why I do not subscribe to Terray's reasoning (1982b). He sees this rationing as a means of procuring a differential rent through an assumed (but unsubstantiated) exploitation of 'cadets' in 'lineage' societies.

6 Engels thought that slavery necessitated higher productivity than that which existed in the communities (1884 [1954]: 55). The reasoning above shows that this was true rather of serfdom; slavery, because of its mode of reproduction, could adapt to the same productivity as the domestic community.

7 This is the definition of the 'manse' (Littré), or 'hide' of land (a unit of land area used in the Domesday Book).

8 B. Jewsiewicki has pointed out to me that during the transition from serfdom to the market economy – for example in Poland or in Russia in the nineteenth century – when the land became a commodity the serfs were *sold* along with it (oral communication).

9 K. Hopkins (1978: 21, 34) found an average life expectancy of twenty-five years for Roman slaves and fifty for freemen; this implies that given a slave's active lifespan of ten to thirteen years, the slave population would have had to be renewed four to six times to ensure the subsistence of a generation of freemen.

10 See also Terray, 1982b; Meillassoux, 1967: 128.

11 Terray (1982b) notes that among the Asante 'the productivity of labour is constant. The system can grow only through extension.'

5: UNBORN AND REPRIEVED FROM DEATH

1 They were not covered by laws governing citizens (see below, section 4).

2 Benveniste (1969, I: 356–7) finds a distinction in European languages between 'captured' and 'captive', but does not explore its implications. Augé and Bazin (1975) make the same distinction. Rey (1975), on the other hand, assimilates capture to slavery. For professional slave-

dealers, the term 'captive' had a precise meaning: it referred to a captured individual who was already or was to be the object of transactions, but was not yet in the hands of his or her owner-employer (master), when he or she would become a *slave*. There could be no slave without a master, and the dealer was not a master.

3 This authority was recognized only to the extent that it referred back to the primary authority of the elder.

4 A slave explained to Olivier de Sardan (1982: 94): 'Any race can be reduced to slavery; all that is necessary is to be cut off from one's community.' Finley (1969: 260) emphasizes the importance of the slave's alien origin and the transmission of this alien state to his or her 'descendance':

> What sets the slave apart from all other forms of involuntary labor is that, in the strictest sense, he is an outsider. He is brought into a new society violently and traumatically; he is cut off from all traditional human ties of kin and nation and even his own religion; he is prevented, in so far as that is possible, from creating new ties, even to his masters, and in consequence his descendants are as much outsiders, as unrooted as he was.

Finley does not, however, explain how, in the situation he describes, the slave could have 'descendants'.

5 Dakar Archives, K14: Kissi, 1894.

6 This was true at least until the time of El Haj Umar, who only occasionally recognized this custom.

7 Brunschvig, 'Abd', *Encyclopédie de l'Islam*, p.34; Hunwick, 1970. In the *Tarick*, '*zanj*' refers to all social categories subjected to the power of the sovereign, but not specifically to slaves. According to Labouret (1955), *zenj* is an Arab term used by the literate in Timbuktu to refer to the Soninke. This claim is doubtful. Many of these literate persons were themselves of Soninke origin; it seems unlikely that they would have used a derogatory term to describe themselves.

8 Such as *hurr* (in Arabic), which became *horon*, *horo* in Maninka languages, meaning free-born individuals as opposed to slaves.

9 *Jon* is the name of a Dogon people who were for a long time raided by their neighbours. *Contra*: according to C. Monteil (1915: 344s.), '"*dyon*" comes from the same root as the word "*sin*", to vanquish, and really means "the vanquished"'.

10 Massa Makan Diabaté, oral communication.

11 Even in our modern law, the loss of certain social attributes is assimilated to *civil death*.

12 Benveniste (1969, I: 327) also notes that in Indo-European languages

this distinction is made between members of the class of 'well-born' individuals and members of the class of 'those who are not "born"'.

13 In India, the extreme hierarchization between Varna had driven the lowest order, the Sudra, outside 'real' birth. At first only the aristocracy and the clergy were considered to be *dvija*, 'twice-born'; it was second (institutional) birth which opened the way to social relations. The Vayshiya fraction of the people were granted this privilege later, as a result of their economic activities and their wealth. In the eyes of the lawmakers only the Sudra were denied the social ties which came from second birth and through which the person was constituted.

14 Apart from a difference in vocabulary, C. Monteil (1915: 344) makes the same point regarding slavery among the Xasonke: 'The primary origin of slavery is captivity. Capture removes all personality from the individual. He finds himself cut off from his milieu and not accepted into the new society. It is this absence of state [I have used the word 'status' – C.M.] which really characterizes the situation of captives.'

15 On the link between the shaving of the head and birth, see Baduel and Meillassoux, 1975.

16 C. Monteil finds this practice among the Xasonke of the savannah (1915: 344–55; 1966). The *Tarikh el-Fettach* (p.179) recounts the case of a very rich slave called Missakoulallah: 'he who is the cause of all is God' (in Sonxai).

17 The Soninke distinguished 'reclining goods' (or dead livestock) from 'standing goods' (or living livestock) such as slaves and cattle.

18 See Chapter 7 below.

19 For example, dowry seen as a 'compensation' for the labour-power lost by the fiancée's family, or as a 'purchase price'.

20 Such as J. Fage (1980) in an article which in other respects is extremely well documented; and J. Goody (1980), several of whose other arguments are nevertheless in line with my analysis.

21 See below, Chapter 7.

22 Noting in 1892 that women slaves were more expensive than men in the Bonduku region, Lang wrote: 'A woman is more useful than a man and does more work. In fact whether or not they are slaves, the women do almost all the work' (quoted by Terray, 1982b: 390). See also Strobel (1983), who notes the importance of feminine labour in the physical reproduction of society.

23 In caravans of captives, the men were shackled but 'the women's hands were left free, not out of respect for their weakness[!] but so that they could bear huge loads of rice and grain, which they were obliged to carry on their heads, as well as the children who could not walk or ride horses behind their abductors' (from Gray and Dorchard, 1816–1821, in Walckenaer, 1842, 7: 146–7).

24 See below, Part II, A, Chapter 3, Section 4.

25 For Saint Thomas, master–slave relations came under private law; they were not governed by public law (in Lengellé, *Encyclopaedia Universalis*, 'Esclavage'). See also Rattray (1929 [1969]: 42): 'If you have no master, a beast will catch you . . . ' (ibid., 3, n.1: 129).

26 Maurin (1975: 226) points out that the torture of slaves in ancient Rome shows that 'violence was the only means of communication between city and alien, city and slave'.

27 This custom was doubtless inspired by Malekite Islamic law ('Abd', *Encyclopédie de l'Islam*, p.30) in terms of which the victim of damage caused by a slave was granted the author of the damages in compensation.

28 Functions which were hereditary or elective but not delegated.

6: PROMOTION OF SLAVES

1 In this way the master could recover the slave's savings. According to the reports on slavery by the French colonial administrators at the turn of the century, in the Bafulabe district (Arch. K4), in Kaedi (K18) in present-day Mali and in Bakel (ibid.) (Senegal), the basic redemption was estimated as the value of two slaves or 60 guineas for each member of the enslaved family. In Baol (present-day Senegal), the slave redeemed himself by leaving his children to the master and giving him, in addition, a granary of sorghum each year or the equivalent in money (K18).

The manumission of Xasonke slaves is well described by C. Monteil (1915, 4: 347–50); of Soninke slaves by E. and G. Pollet, 1971; Meillassoux, 1975a.

2 Manumitted slave.

3 *Kome*: slave; *xoore*: big.

4 They were probably no more numerous when, before emancipation imposed by colonization, a total count of at least twice as many slaves was made in Gumbu.

5 In French medieval law, manumitted individuals who paid taxes to the king – that is, who were no longer under the sole and strict authority of the master – were enfranchised.

6 This implies that *public* ceremonies supposedly aimed at enfranchisement could not in fact fulfil this purpose, since they did not cleanse the benefactor of the stain of slavery but on the contrary confirmed it in the eyes of all.

7 In a later work (1984) the author adopts a more nuanced position.

8 The arbitrary aspect is an essential element in the notion of slavery, notes Marc Bloch as regards medieval slavery (1939/1968: 357).

9 The master's intervention in unions between slaves is mentioned in

most of the administrative reports on slavery: in particular, Dakar Archives, K18-21, K18-2, K18-10: 'The absence of family is the cause of the captive's abjectness' (Capt. Gallana, K18-11, etc.). Islam imposed several conditions on slave unions: 'The master is not obliged to allow the marriage of a slave who asks to be married. He or his heirs can annul a marriage contracted against his will . . . the married Negro [slave] must maintain his wife, otherwise he is separated from her . . . ' (in Daumas, 1857: 330). The same was still true recently: 'If the slave does not work for the master, he does not have the right to take a wife . . . the union can be approved only by the master', explained a Soninke to M. Samuel (1977, unpublished).

10 See above, Chapter 5.

11 See also Lovejoy (1981) on slaves in Sokoto.

12 As we have seen, this was the case among the Zerma Sonxai as regards the *cire bannya* and also as regards the slaves of slaves: 'even if the captives have been with the *horso* for a long time, even if they have been there 20,000 years' (Olivier de Sardan, 1976: 172).

13 In Gidimaxa, the slave's condition, however far back his enslavement reaches, depended on the master's arbitrary decisions: 'Even if the slave is rich, he is rich because the master wishes it to be so. The day that the master needs his wealth, he takes it' (Mody Camara, oral comm.). This dependence on the master reached its height with Islam: 'The marabout gave the slaves to understand that access to paradise depended on their master's consent' (ibid.).

14 This is what enabled the King of Segu to proclaim that all his subjects (and he himself) were *jon* (Bazin, 1975).

15 This permanent nature was confirmed clearly by Bossuet in the seventeenth century: 'To condemn this state . . . would be to condemn the Holy Spirit who orders slaves, through the words of Saint Paul, to remain in their state and who does not in any way oblige their masters to enfranchise them' (quoted by Lengellé, in 'Esclavage', *Encyclopaedia Universalis*).

16 Throughout Soninke and Bamana country, it was always a few *jon* and *woloso* who performed obscene dances at feasts. For the Sonxai, cf. Olivier de Sardan (1984: 36).

17 When, after a long and serious discussion in Gumbu with a *woroso* (settled slave) family about the difficult lot which had once been theirs and the cruelty to which they had been subjected, I asked the oldest of my informants if I could take a photograph of them, they immediately started to make faces in front of the camera. I asked the reason for this surprising exhibition on the part of men who had seemed so composed and even venerable, and they replied that as *woloso* they felt obliged in the circumstances to act the fool.

18 In Gidimaxa, not even manumitted slaves had the right to build a *biire* (a sort of veranda) in front of their hut, as the free-born did. The *biire* was the place where the free man or woman received their relatives (Saint-Père, 1925: 36).

19 In Dia (Masina, Mali) we listened to an old slave who had been captured as a child explain why, when emancipation was imposed by the colonizers, he had refused to leave his masters, whom he considered to be his protectors and whose good deeds he praised.

7: HALF-BREED SLAVES

1 In other respects Peroz was very well disposed to Samori, praising his intelligence, his organizational capacities and his good taste, and inviting the French government to make him into an ally.

2 These measures were also part of the 'Code noir' in the French West Indies.

3 See also C. Monteil, 1915: 338.

4 This 'enfranchisement' was circumstantial and thus fictitious (cf. above, Chapter 6, Section 5).

5 Research trip, 1966, EK3. See also A. Bathily, 1985: 336s.

Part II: Iron Aristocratic Slavery

A Slavery and Power

1: THE COMING OF THE BRIGANDS

1 Brigandage, raids [*razzias*] and war are three distinct activities which will be dealt with separately in this part of the book.

2 Present-day Mali.

3 On the Sudanese hero, see Dumestre, 1979: Amselle *et al.*, 1979; Meillassoux *et al.*, 1967; Meillassoux, 1978a.

4 There is some doubt, which I share, as to the exact period to which some of these remarks refer. In the thirteenth century, however, the Maninke were probably among those peoples called Lam-Lam which were a source of slaves for the Saharan slave trade.

5 Other traditions point out that the Mande numbered thirty 'houses', twelve of which were *jasa* or military houses (including that of Sunjata) and four clans of clients of caste (Diabaté, 1970: 40, 55; Niane, 1960: 138).

6 *Niya*: to be in front; *moko*: individual. He who goes in front, the first, the chief.

7 It does not seem that Kamissoko's account can be interpreted as telling of the 'abolition of slavery' in Mande, as Y.-S. Cisse's translation might suggest. The context of the account shows that Sunjata was famous for having put a stop to the capture and trade of Maninka by other Maninka, but not to the enslavement of alien captives, as numerous references to the existence of slaves among the Maninka after Sunjata's victory demonstrate (Kamissoko, 1975, III: 201; Niane, 1960: 140, 437, etc.).

8 Benveniste (1969, II: 14) suggests the following meaning for *Rex*: he who delimits 'the interior from the exterior . . . national territory from

alien territory'. As regards the concept of 'society', he shows that it was known by the name of 'kingdom': 'the limits of society coincide with a certain power which is the power of the king' (ibid.: 9).

9 On the geographical situation of Melli, see Hunwick, 1973; Meillassoux, 1972f, g.

10 This tradition is also found among the Soninke-Kusa, in the legend of Maren Jagu, for example (Meillassoux, 1967); a hero whose destiny was also to eliminate tyranny but who came up against the resistance of his congeners as soon as he tried to impose his power over them. See also the attempts by the Bamana of Wasolon to prevent domination by a person predestined for 'power' (Amselle *et al.*, 1979).

11 *Suba*: one of the names by which Sunjata was known: thaumaturge.

12 These royal characteristics are attributed to him in a later praise-song.

13 *Miskin* (Arabic: small) was a term adopted in several Mande languages to designate people of common birth, free-born but not noble.

14 Marx (in Engels, 1884/1954: 100) describes this type of organization as 'military democracy'. The term 'democracy' is doubtless excessive in that these bands had no popular support. It was only among their own members that relative equality existed. For Benveniste (1969, II: 89): 'The *personal* relationship between a group of men and their chief was expressed in ancient Greece by *laos*. *Poimen* was the chief of this "virile and warlike community".'

15 Even in the nineteenth century, according to Vallière (in Galliéni, 1885: 320), the inhabitants of Wasolon (part of present-day Mali) captured each other and abducted their close relatives in order to sell them: 'When the villages had finished the harvest, the young men grouped together in armed bands and attacked their neighbours so as to "earn a bit" while the chiefs sold their own subjects.' Galliéni adds that 'the armed bands . . . scoured the countryside, living outside the control of the chiefs, even sometimes fighting against them' (1885: 598). A similar situation is reported in Minianka country to the south-east of Segu (D. Jonckers, 1981: 150).

16 C. Monteil uses the word *tribe* in the sense in which I use *clan* and the word *clan* to mean *association*.

17 It was also through the murder of the old men that Chaka, the Zulu (Nguni) sovereign, replaced domestic patriarchal society with a military society.

18 Cf. similar practices among the Asante (N. Klein, unpublished: 121).

19 *De facto* brigandage was used as a means of repression by the Segu State against rebel villages which, through their insubordination, put themselves 'outside': these villages were sacked.

20 According to Roberts (1978: 34) the practice of brigandage (*tegere* or *jadoya*) was seen in Segu as a serious crime against the State. Le Hérissé

(1911: 292) similarly reports how in Dahomey the people of King Aïsan who hid along the roads to stop women and children, whom they sold as slaves, were punished. 'This fact was an outrage which directly touched the king of Abomey, who sent his warriors to kill Aïsan.'

21 See also Dumestre (1979, Intr.) for an interpretation of this process.

22 Fields under cultivation.

23 'Without the camel . . . the Sudan would be unknown. We would have no slaves . . . with them [camels] the desert has no space' (in Daumas, 1857: 161).

24 According to E. Terray, on the contrary, the raid could have taken place only under the protection of a strong military State which could provide a refuge for the plunderers (1982a: 390). I think that this is true only when the raid affected immediately neighbouring populations, which was in effect the case of the strong States. In any case, the raid could not have been at the origin of these States, as Terray suggests (pp.385–6), if they had to be in existence already so as to provide bases for withdrawal.

2: THE GREAT TASK OF THE KINGS

1 I use the term ethological determinism to describe attempts to find the prefiguration of human behaviour in the behaviour of animals. Ethology is a scientific discipline when used with scientific rigour, but it sinks into ideology when, as is too often the case, it proceeds by analogy.

2 There were a number of theories on war in the Middle Ages in Europe, which, though competing, were all founded on human 'passions'. In the works of two authors, Jean de Lagnano and Honoré Bouvet (fourteenth century), 'war appears to be a phenomenon which is all the more natural in that it has a cosmological character', since the stars were thought to influence earthly bodies and the passions, sources of conflict, to have their origin in the movements of the stars. Several authors do not seem to have progressed since this period.

3 But according to Kouroubari (1959: 547), in order to induce his brothers to go to war, Samori told them: 'Beyond the Niger, there are slaves, chargers, sorghum in quantity. Let us go there!'

4 This opinion is shared by Arhin (n.d.): 24.

5 Former State south of the present-day Republic of Niger.

6 Small kingdom centred around the town of Aboh and situated at the entrance to the Niger delta (Nigeria).

7 Cf. Bathily, 1985: 409.

8 Elwert (1973: 29) founds his analysis of the Dahomeyan mode of production on the periodicity of wars.

9 M. Jawara, 1976–7 and oral communication, KC1.

10 In the same way as for the medieval armies, these figures provide an order of magnitude rather than accurate statistics. (For a discussion of the numbers in the Ashanti army, see Terray, 1976: 318s.).

11 Although Tardits minimizes its importance, the Bamoum State captured in order to export slaves. Slavery also intervened in trade, through the export of food, which came mostly from the slaving zones, and craft goods, part of which were manufactured by individuals in a servile condition.

12 According to Snelgrave, the Dahomeyans' main fear was of being eaten by their enemies.

13 This shift in the function of 'captives' is observed by M. Piault (1975) in his study of the Kabi and Mawri regions.

14 This, however, was very different from *pogsyure* marriage as it took place among free-born families. Here, a daughter born of the marriage between a woman surrendered by one family to another should marry into her mother's family. The reciprocity which was practised here was deformed, in the case of the soldier-slaves, to the sole benefit of the king. He remained the sole owner of the children of his women slaves, as in any system of slavery.

3: THE DIVINE COURT

1 Fuglestad (1977: 102) finds an exception to this practice in the Agasuvi conquerors of Abomey.

2 See also Rattray, 1929/1969: 16; R. Law, 1971, 1977a.

3 This was also the case among the Burgondes (Benveniste, 1969, II: 27).

4 Vansina (1975: 148) reports that the rule among the Kuba of Kongo was that the king had to be the oldest biologically and genealogically. As a result, reigns were short and devoid of power.

5 Grand officer of the court responsible for commercial transactions.

6 For a discussion of the notion of divinization, see Tardits, 1980b. See also CEJC, 1979, for an ideological interpretation of this phenomenon.

7 This term, which I use here in its etymological sense, is not that of Hopkins; however, I believe it sums up his thinking, which is extremely rich.

8 Girard (1969), who studied this personage in Casamance, calls him 'rex-sacer' and sees him as the 'scapegoat' of the collectivity. Yet he was not a king, nor was he, strictly speaking, responsible for the community's errors; nor was he immolated. He was merely a sort of 'magnet for fate'.

9 The usual logical separation of the god from his priest cannot be used here in opposition to this twofold function. Irrationality has always been an integral part of religion. It is used, in the modern scholastics of contemporary religions, as the mysterious dimension which 'proves'

the unfathomability of the revelation.

10 In Mossi, the diviners, whose opinion was decisive in many matters, were 'assimilated to captives' (Izard, 1975: 293). This remark is interesting because few authors describe the social status of these persons.

11 When the sovereign wielded *de facto* power, he surrounded himself not with a single diviner but with several. Samori or the kings of Segu, for example, consulted several competing diviners using different forms of divining, as well as marabout, which enabled them to choose the predictions which conformed most closely to their plans.

12 In 1774 the king of Oyo refused to kill himself at the command of the Council of Nobles and sanctioned the resulting revolt by the massacre of the prime minister and all his men (Dalzel, 1793, in Law, 1971: 37–8).

13 The only known reaction (which is held to be true) of a god incarnate when faced with death is the 'agony' (anguish) of Jesus Christ on the Mount of Olives: 'Father, let this cup pass from me'.

14 Max Weber describes this tendency towards centralism assumed by court slaves as 'sultanism'.

15 Ibid.

16 See the numerous cases discussed by Fisher and Fisher (1970: 137–43) with respect to the Muslim States of Africa, to which we shall return.

17 This behaviour, similar in every respect to that which is expected from the British *civil servant*, seems unlikely in a civilization where allegiances were personal.

18 Neologism: power of servants.

19 For their use in African Muslim States, see Fisher and Fisher (1970: 143–8).

20 Hopkins (1978: 194) quotes Cyril of Alexandria's warning against women's licentiousness with eunuchs. In contrast, it was young eunuchs who were responsible for the bodily care of the *askia* Bani, sovereign of Sonxai (*TEF*: 240).

21 Nachtingal (in Fisher and Fisher, 1970: 146) gives mortality of 70 per cent; Deherme (1908: 373) gives 80 per cent; Mercadier (1971: 41) and Dakar Archives (K25: 201) refer to three to four children out of five. In Rome, under Justinian, 87 young boys out of 90 who had been operated on are said to have died (K. Hopkins, 1978: 190 n.50).

22 It is to be noted, however, that these prices did not compensate for losses.

23 Castration took place in certain specialized centres. It was forbidden by Islam, and the Muslim courts procured eunuchs from Christians or Jews or from certain pagan tribes. The Mossi surgeons had a reputation for particular skill in these operations, and were said to incur fewer losses than others (Bovill, 1968: 246). Mossi, Damagaram (Dunbar,

1977: 163), certain centres in Sudan (in Cuoq, 1975: 65), the Tuaregs (Daumas, Mercadier, 1971: 27, 33, 41) were producers and exporters of eunuchs. 'The "*setasy*", the ten-year-old eunuch, who measured six spans from the lobe of his ear to his ankle, was the standard of value' in Chad, Kanem, Wadai, Darfur (Dakar Archives, K25: 201).

24 We know that in principle titles were originally not hereditary under the feudal system. Nevertheless, custom tended to pass the title on to the heir; in this way lineage heredity was applied to the transmission of functions which were external to the lineage.

25 K. Hopkins (1978: 190) points out that in Rome the eunuchs, grand servants of the palace, were sacrificed to popular rage as scapegoats by the Roman emperors.

26 In the absence of eunuchs, a similar distrust led other (Christian) sovereigns to entrust these functions to priests who had taken a vow of chastity.

27 Lorenzo Anamia (1573) relates that in Bornou the king was served by 'eunuchs and by young women who are made sterile by certain potions' (in Lange, 1972: 347). In this way neutrality with respect to kinship (and to the dynasty) was physically inflicted on women also. I do not know of other cases of female 'eunuchs'.

28 Captives destined to be concubines were the object of specialized trade in the Middle East. These women were captured very young, educated, trained and conditioned to their role by merchants of repute who followed them throughout their career (cf. Kouloub, 1958).

29 This institution, which existed in many societies, also had the effect of weakening the matrimonial capacities of the noble families – in the Mossi kingdom, for example (Izard, 1975).

30 Jiri Silla, unpublished: translation Mamadu Sumare.

31 Engels had noticed this phenomenon in medieval Europe: 'Among the Francs, slaves who had been enfranchised by the king played an important role first at court and then in the State: a large part of the new nobility came from among them' (1884/1954: 134).

32 The Mameluks from Egypt were a rare case of slaves in power retaining for themselves a slave reproduction system.

B The War Economy

1: CASES

1 See above, Part II, A, Ch. 1, Section 2.

2 This attitude has always been characteristic of warrior aristocracies: '. . . the very vocation of the noble forbade him any direct economic activity. He was devoted, body and soul, to his true function: that of warrior' (Marc Bloch, 1939/1968: 403). 'A prince can have no other object, no other thought, nor take anything else to heart, other than the fact of war and the organization of military disciplines' (Machiavelli, 1571/1938: 92). For Aristotle, men of State had to know the art of war, 'so as to become the masters of those who deserve to be reduced to slavery' (*Politics*, quoted in Finley, 1973: 156–7). Military activities and contempt for the people always go hand in hand.

3 The *Tarikh* emphasizes that these dues were fixed once and for all and were required from the principal *fanfa*: though he could keep any excess, he was responsible for deficits.

4 Today the *mudde* varies according to region and sometimes according to family. It can exceed two litres, but the *Tarikh* commentators set its capacity as approximately one litre.

5 See, however, the detailed work of Tymowski (1974a, b).

6 M. Amady Dieng (1974: 15) correctly notes that 'the mere existence of a military or religious aristocracy is not sufficient to characterize a mode of production as feudal'.

7 Fifty cowries in the nineteenth century, according to Le Hérissé (1911).

8 Intendants.

9 Le Hérissé gives prices from 160 to 300F and estimates that the king gave the soldiers a sum in cowries equivalent to 5F, plus a cloth;

according to the same estimates, the annual poll tax was 20F.

10 'Trade was so intense that there was a permanent colony of 500 Hausa merchants in Ngila [the capital]' (Siran, 1980).

2: ANALYSES

1 The limiting of the internal market and the preservation of the distributive economy seem to have been the concerns of the Dahomeyan court, which reserved all sorts of objects for itself (Burton, 1864, I: 119–20; Herskovits, 1978, I: 107–8). This was the case for a large part of utilitarian craft production, such as hoes, which were then redistributed. In Ardra 'the king is given the first sight and the choice of all the merchandise' (Voyage of Elbée in 1680, in Walcknaer, 1842, 10: 426).

2 In Abron, 'the wealthy captive bought other captives. He could then escape the duties in labour which his master expected of him' (Terray, 1975a: 414).

3 The slaves who were sacrificed at the death of the Abron chiefs were 'bad', 'recently bought', or too old (Terray, 1975a: 410).

4 Among theories which try to explain these bloody sacrifices, that of Ryan (1975) suggests that sacrifices had a 'publicity' effect which was thought to attract 'adherents' to those who practised them. But the author's laborious mathematical demonstration is not convincing.

5 The client was a person who received products or services, working at the request of a 'patron' who in turn ensured his maintenance; relations of equivalence were not established between them.

6 The king of Oyo's relations with the chiefs of conquered lands or villages were assimilated to the father–son relationship and mediated by 'little fathers', slave agents delegated by the third eunuch (Morton-Williams, 1967: 64).

7 For a more complete demonstration, see Meillassoux, 1981.

8 *Exploitation* implies organic relations of production between two classes, through which one collects all or part of the surplus-product of the other, where this transfer is indispensable to the reproduction of the relations of production. *Extortion* is the inorganic and occasional extraction, by physical or moral force, of an indeterminate fraction of the product of an individual or a group of individuals. (See also P.-P. Rey, n.d.: 151.)

9 This distinction between occasional duties and regular taxation is also made by R. Thapar (1980: 658) with respect to the emergence of the State in India. Terray (1983: 118) notes that in the Abron kingdom the shift from one to the other took place during what Wilks has called 'the Kwadwoan revolution'.

10 From Bowdich, in Walckenaer, 12: 151–6 and Monrade, ibid.: 399–402.

11 An analogous situation appeared in the Atlantic slave trade. On the slave-ships the exploitation of sailors recruited at low prices and often, like the slaves, losing their lives in the transport of the 'ebony wood', helped to reduce the price of slaves on the market.

12 In contrast to what seems to have happened in Rome, for example, the cases which are examined here rather show that slaves were assigned to military tasks more often than to agriculture.

13 With respect to the nobles, the king preferred to use extortion, thus demonstrating that the relations between those of the same rank were, in principle, reciprocal.

14 Cf. Goody (ed.) 1968: Intr.

15 Terray, 1983: 118.

16 When it took place in space and not only in time, this compensation could be effected even in the case of food which did not last well from one year to another, such as tubers.

17 It is true that it was not impossible for the domestic communities to organize among themselves for this purpose. We know, for instance, that during famines villages or hamlets which were short of food were helped by relatives living in areas which had been less seriously affected. There are also cases of collective granaries independent of political centralization (J.-M. Vincent, AFA Communication, 1981). Thus while the centralization of stocks favoured the centralization of political power, it was evidently not the 'cause', as naive materialism might suggest; any more than the centralization of power necessarily led to that of reserves.

Part III

Gold

1: The Land of the Merchants

1 The recommendations of Ahmed Baba, juriconsul in Timbuktu in the sixteenth century, are in accordance with this (Zeys, 1900).

2 The Soninke-Kusa of Wagadu still specify that their espousal of Islam was accompanied by a rejection of this prescription (Mission, 1965).

3 'One does not see a single praise-singer among the Dioula . . . ', Binger remarked in Kong (I: 338).

4 'Some of them, enfranchised by their masters because they were too old or no longer able to work, so that it had become useless to feed them, wandered in the crowd, blind or crippled by rheumatism, their joints swollen by yaws or with hideous wounds which they showed without shame. They were naked or nearly naked. A layer of earth from their retreat stuck to their bodies, which were emaciated and drained of colour . . . These people asked for alms. They were pushed aside by the foot or with a stick.' (Account of a Timimoun slave to Mercadier, 1971, 147.)

5 Park, 1799: 215; Caillié, 1830, II: 4. Sometimes the pagan kings behaved in similar fashion towards the Muslims, like the king of Dahomey (Le Hérissé, 1911: 303).

6 Holy men of Islam.

7 The robbers attacked the Mandingo caravans, noted Caillié (1830, I: 425), 'but never the caravans of the Saracolets, because they knew that the latter carried guns'.

8 Long-distance trade encouraged the development of culture and arts designed for the leisure of this wealthy class of travelling merchants, as can also be observed, to a greater extent, in the societies of ancient

369

Greece, of India or of Japan during their great trading periods.

9 For the Aïr and Azawak regions, Lovejoy and Baier (1975: 555) calculate that the nomad population, estimated at 50,000, had to receive
7,500 tonnes of sorghum per year to feed itself. The desert was a market for cereal production without which the nomads could not have
survived.

10 The three words were equivalent in Ja and in Jenne. They were used to
describe 'foreign' and Islamized merchants and sometimes warrior or
old families. They did not apply to a tribe and still less to a race, as
Delafosse has claimed (1912). The term was probably analogous to the
older term 'Wangara', which C. Monteil correctly defines as 'being
used locally to describe indigenous Islamized people and traders' (1932:
52).

11 See Spini and Meillassoux (1984) and particularly Gallais (1967).

12 There was probably, as Hunwick suggests (1973), a political formation
called 'Melli' in the sixteenth century between the Mandingo country
and the interior of the Niger delta. It cannot be identified a priori either
with the Mali of Sunjata or with the Melli which Ibn Battuta visited in
the fourteenth century (Meillassoux, 1972b).

13 Judge.

14   If the flotillas which came to Cabra had been stopped on the
    way by the Touariks, the inhabitants of Temboctou would have
    suffered the most appalling scarcities. In order to avoid this mis-
    fortune, they make sure that their shops are always amply sup-
    plied with all sorts of food. I found those of Sidi-Abdallahi full
    of large bags of rice, a grain which keeps much longer than
    sorghum.
        This consideration stops the flotillas which come down the
    river to Cabra from fighting with the Touariks, in spite of all
    they suffer as a result of their demands. I was told that if anyone
    dared to strike one of these savages, they would immediately
    make war on Temboctou and they would intercept all com-
    munications with its port; in which case it would not receive
    help from anywhere. (Caillié, II: 313)

According to Caillié's descriptions, the safety of the pirogues on the
Niger does not seem to have been threatened from Jenne to Sa (on the
Bara Issa, a branch of the Niger, some 32 kilometres south of Nia-
funke). The boatmen were neither armed nor protected by armed men;
there were no guards during the night (II: 253). After Sa, the pirogues
which continued their voyage as far as Timbuktu travelled together to
protect themselves from the 'Sourgous' or Tuareg.

15 Cf. the hypothesis of R. Roberts (1980a) on the multiplier effect of
'interzonal' trade in West Africa.

16　It is probable that Caillié did not have at his disposal all the information
necessary to distinguish between different sorts of servile individuals.
In fact the Timbuktu masons were more likely to have been Bozo
fishermen, just like the bargemen, whom Caillié also considered to be
slaves (ibid.: 275). In fact this was a native pagan population employed
to perform certain services. The king of Masina, according to Ba and
Daget (1962), classified them as 'slaves', but we do not know exactly
what this term means here.

17　According to its present inhabitants, the town of Marakaduguba on the
Niger also had these ancient privileges (Mission, 1966).

18　According to J. Bazin (1975: 155), the Maraka of Sansani made the
slaves produce grain only for their own subsistence and not for trade.

2: The Spread of Slavery within the Peasantry

1　These figures are of the same order as those given by Hogendorn (1977)
and Lovejoy (1978) for the caliphate of Sokoto, another major centre of
production in West Africa, in the nineteenth century. The Sokoto caliphate was an aristocratic society within which a merchant economy developed and where some of the plantations were devoted to the supply
of the dominant class and others to the supply of the market. The
former were owned by nobles who employed slaves in their thousands, the latter by merchants who owned 100 to 500 slaves. Hogendorn (1977) gives the example of two villages in the caliphate inhabited
by allotment slaves who cultivated the food plantations of the former
or the cotton and tobacco plantations of the latter: 'Apart from their
strips of land, they cultivate the masters' lands at certain times of the
day and the year, in brigades of 25 persons of both sexes under the
supervision of a guard of servile origin.'

　　Lovejoy (1978) indicates that in the northern part of the caliphate at
the end of the nineteenth century, some 50,000 slave dyers were
employed in the textile industry 'and countless women who spun and
carded raw cotton'.

2　The Koran forbids the enslavement of believers, but this rule has never
been faithfully respected. Al Omari (pp. 41–2) reports the sultan of
Bornu's complaints against the sultan of Egypt on this matter (1391).
Mauny (1961: 507) writes that ' . . . the enslavement of Muslims . . .
was current in the medieval Sudan'. Nadel notes that among the Nupe,
'immunity from slave-raids (for the Mohammedans) was never strictly
obeyed – unless the religious qualification was supported by the more
solid one of political protection' (1942: 142–3). 'In Islam, of course,
slavery has a venerable tradition and in Muslim Africa it was widely
practised . . . there is provision in Islamic law, not only for the sale of
non-Moslems into slavery . . . but in addition freemen, under specified

conditions, may pass into slavery. Such action of taking freemen as slaves is termed *mubah*' (Baillie, 1869: 365–6, in Sanneh, 1976b: 60 n.57).

3 *Jihad* [*Gihad*]: 'effort on the path to God . . . ' 'The term is used to describe legal war against unbelievers hostile to Islam . . . ' (Mahibou and Triaud, 1983: 234).

4 Mage shows clearly which side he has taken.

5 Drum of war.

6 Amadu's soldiers: literally, 'disciples'.

7 Cola nut.

8 Pagans.

9 That is, towards 1879–80.

10 Samori.

11 Terms like 'Malinke', which are considered ethnic, also have social significance. Galliéni's remark casts doubt on the interpretation of Y. Person, who described Samori's efforts as 'a *dyula* revolution' – that is, a merchant revolution.

12 These were indeed, therefore, seasonal campaigns, like the wars of capture fought by the political formations devoted to war, and not 'national' types of military campaigns.

13 Unit of account.

14 It must be remembered that Caillié passed himself off as a Muslim.

15 The thesis of Y. Person (1968) (who recognizes neither this division nor the importance of the African market for slaves) is that 'Samori was not a merchant of slaves' and that he waged war only to impose his sovereignty (p. 929). He does, however, admit that this sovereignty fed on slavery: 'It is true', he adds, 'that the trade in slaves had an important place in the economy of his empire, as in that of all the contemporary States. The frequency of wars meant that he had numerous men at his disposal to sell, and, in times of need, he could withdraw others from the cultivating hamlets, to the detriment of agricultural production' (ibid.).

16 Meillassoux, Doucoure and Simagha, 1967.

17 *Kafo* (Arabic): grouping of villages which were allied or submitted to a common authority.

3: Forms of Exploitation

1 In the same conditions of productivity, a free-born couple who did not pay any dues could breed four to five children over a period of twenty years.

2 In Gumbu 4·5 *mude* of sorghum were exchanged for 1 *tama* of 20 cubits, whose market price was estimated at 10 *mude* of sorghum. According to Bazin (1975), among the Maraka of Segu this payment was effected

at the master's discretion.

4: THE INTERNAL MARKET FOR SLAVES

1 On the other hand, *captives* waiting to be sold had to be fed (see Bathily, 1985: 414).

2 Even in the West Indies – where, in order to encourage trade, the 'Code noir' forbade planters to make slaves grow their own food – 'Negro gardens' constantly increased (Jamard, 1981, unpublished).

3 In this respect, Nieboer (1900) correctly observed that agricultural slavery developed where land was available and when the productivity of agricultural labour was low. He deduced from this that in order to establish an exploited labour force, the labour force had to be compelled to stay on the master's land and denied the right to settle freely on vacant land. In contrast, he did not see self-sustenance as organically necessary to the functioning of merchant slavery and as a factor in the low productivity of agricultural labour: he treats this low productivity as given.

4 The above prevents me from adhering to the thesis of Patterson (1979), who, in an article which in other respects is very stimulating, sees slavery as a form of capitalism.

5: TO BUY OR TO BREED?

1 This question 'To buy or to breed?' is raised by Mörner (1980) in a well-documented article on slaves in the New World entitled 'Buy or Breed'.

2 Measure of capacity.

3 Length of woven cotton.

4 Meillassoux, 1981: 102.

5 This value corresponds to the labour-time and effort necessary, in the economic and social conditions of the society of origin, to his formation and subsistence as a living individual of given age and capacity for labour. This corresponds to $K\alpha A$ in our formulation (Part I, Chapter 4).

6 We know that during slavery in the New World, most of the attempts to breed slaves were a failure.

7 It is clear that the slave-owners did not devote the whole of production to the purchase of slaves, but this hypothesis can be used as the basis for a calculation which makes it possible to measure the advantages of merchant over eco-demographic reproduction. It also provides a determinate magnitude in terms of which other data in the economy can be evaluated.

8 m: annual revenue from the sale of commodities produced by the slave;
B: length of the slave's active life;
H: purchase price of the slave (equal to the replacement price);
P: profit $(P = mB - H)$;

annual profit: $\dfrac{mB - H}{\beta}$;

period of amortization: $D = \dfrac{HB}{m}$

rate of profit: $\dfrac{mB}{H}$;

rate of amortization: $\dfrac{m}{H}$;

9 These considerations raise the problem of the price of slaves in terms which are very different from those of Terray (1982b).

10 Raffenel does not specify whether these 'hard-working men' were slaves.

11 In a more intensive form of slavery, that of the West Indies, Pruneau de Pommegorge estimated in his 1789 work that a slave 'earned his head' – that is, his price – in one year. According to the figures given by Frossard (an opponent of slavery) (1789: 357), a slave bought for £1,000 in the West Indies brought £3,000 to £4,000 in returns during the year (KC 40); i.e. an amortization period of three or four months. In the same year, Lamiral (who was in favour of slavery) estimated the amortization period of a slave in Santo Domingo as four or five years. In São Tomé, on the sugar plantations, a slave was amortized in less than three years. (See also Gemery and Hogendorn, 1981: 21.)

12 Number of slaves who could be bought from the annual sale of the commodities produced by a slave, where their subsistence needs and those of their master were covered by their food-producing activities.

13 Number of children a couple could bring to maturity each year during its active life.

14 Simple reproduction (one replacement for each adult individual) implies a rate of eco-demographic reproduction of 0·05.

15 This of course does not refer to luxury women slaves, who formed a distinct market and were sought after more for pleasure than as bearers of children.

16 'In parts of the coast, working conditions resembled Alabama more than Oman' (Cooper, 1981: 281).

17 Et toute la terre retentit du vacarme des pioches Dans l'épaisseur du minerai noir . . .

René Depestre, *Minerai noir*, Présence Africaine)

6: THE DISINTEGRATION OF SLAVERY

1 The demographic models built by Patrick Manning (unpublished) provide original and interesting data on this point.
2 I refer here to the excellent recent works of R. Roberts and M. Klein.
   See also earlier work by D. Bouche (1968); Renault (1972, 1976); Pollet
   and Winter (1971: 253s) and the interesting analysis by Delaunay (1984)
   which appeared after this book had been written.
3 The liver was supposed to be the site of the feelings and moods which
   we locate in the heart.

Conclusions

1 This sort of method leads to the construction of 'modes of production'
   independently of their historical context. This is, possibly, the problem
   with certain attempts which seem to give rise to loglcal combinations
   which are formal rather than real.

Bibliography

Abitbol, M., 1979, *Tombouctou et les Arma*, Maisonneuvre & Larose.

Aguessy, C., 1956, 'Esclavage, colonisation et tradition au Dahomey (sud)', *Présence africaine*, 6: 58–67.

Aguessy, H., 1970, 'Le Dan-Homè au xixᵉ siècle était-il une société esclavagiste?', *Rev. franç. d'Et. pol. afr.*, 50: 71–91.

Akindele, A. and Aguessy, C., 1953, *Contribution à l'Étude de l'histoire de l'ancien royaume de Porto-Novo*, Dakar, IFAN.

Akinola, G. A., 1972, 'Slavery and Slave Revolts in the Sultanate of Zanzibar in the Tenth Century', *Jl of the Hist. Soc. of Nigeria*, 6:215–27.

Al-Bakri [1968], 'Routier de l'Afrique blanche et noire du Nord-Ouest',trad. notes V. Monteil, *B. IFAN*, B, 30, 1: 39–116.

Al-Bekri, see Al-Bakri, El-Bekri.

Alencastro, L.-F. de, 1981, 'La traite négrière et les avatars de la colonisation portugaise au Brésil et en Angola', *Cah. du CRIAR*, 1: 9–76.

Almeida-Topor, H. d', 1984, *Les Amazones*, Paris, Rochevignes.

Al-Omari [1927], *Masàlik el Afsàr*, I: *L'afrique moins l'Egypte* (transl. Gaudefroy-Demombynes), Paris, P. Geuthner.

Alpers, E. A., 1975, *Ivory and Slaves in East Central Africa*, London, Heinemann.

Alpers, E. A., 1983, 'The Story of Swema: Female Vulnerability in 19th Century East Africa', *in* Robertson and Klein, 1983: 185–99.

Amselle, J.-L., 1977, *Les négociants de la savane*, Paris, Anthropos.

Amselle, J.-L., Doumbia, Z., Kuyate, Y., Tabure, M., 1979, 'Littérature orale et idéologie: la geste des Jakite-Sabasni du Ganan (Wasolon-Mali)', *Cah. Et. afr.*, 19 (1–4): 73–6; 381–439.

376

Antoine, R., 1974, 'Adventure d'un jeune négrier français d'après un manuscrit inédit du xviiie siècle', *Notes africaines.*

Arhin, K., n.d., *Peasants in Asante in the Nineteenth Century*, 39 p. mult.

Aristotle [1958], *Economics*, Paris, Libr. Phil. J. Vrin.

Aubin-Sugy, C., 1975, *Economic Growth and Secular Trends in the Pre-Colonial Sudanic Belt*, Ph.D., New York, Columbia U., Faculty of History.

Augé, M., 1969, 'Statut, pouvoir et richesse: relations lignagères, relations de dépendance et rapports de production dans la société alladian', *Cah. d'Etudes afr.*, 9, 3 (35), 1969: 461–81.

Augé, M., 1975, Les faiseurs d'ombres, *in* Meillassoux (ed.), 1975*b*: 455–76.

Austin, M. and Vidal-Naquet, P., 1972, *Economies et sociétés en Grèce ancienne*, Paris, A. Colin.

Aymard, M., 1983, 'Autoconsommation et marchés: Chayanov, Labrousse ou Le Roy-Ladurie?', *Annales*, 38, 6, Nov.–Dec. 1983: 1392–411.

Azevedo, M. J., 1980, 'Precolonial Sara Society in Chad and the Threat of Extinction due to Arab and Muslim Slave Trade, 1870–1917', *Journal of African Studies*, 7, 2: 99–108.

Ba, A.-H. and Daget, J., 1962, *L'Empire peul du Macina* (I), Paris, Mouton & Co.

Ba, A.-H. and Kesteloot, L., 1968, 'Une épopée peule: Silimaka', *L'Homme*, 8, 1: 5–36.

Baduel, C., Meillassoux, C., 1975, 'Modes et codes de la coiffure ouest-africaine', *L'Ethnographie*, n.s., 69 (1975–I): 11–59.

Baer, G., 1967, 'Slavery in 19th-Century Egypt', *Jl of Afr. Hist.*, 8, 3: 417–41.

Balandier, G., 1965, *La vie quotidienne au royaume du Kongo*, Paris, Hachette.

Balde, M.-S., 1975, 'L'esclavage et la guerre sainte au Fuuta-Jalon', *in* Meillassoux (ed.), 1975*b*: 183–220.

Barnet, M. (ed.), 1967, *Esclave à Cuba*, Paris, Gallimard.

Barry, B., 1972, *Le royaume du Waalo*, Paris, Maspero.

Barth, Henry, 1857–8, *Travels and Discoveries in North and Central Africa*, London, Frank Cass [1965], 3 vols.

Bataille, H., 1967, *La part maudite*, Paris, Ed. de Minuit.

Bathily, A., 1975, 'A Discussion of the Traditions of Wagadu', *Bull. IFAN. B.* 37, 1: 1–94.

Bathily, A., 1985, *Guerriers, tributaires et marchands*, doctoral thesis, Etat ès lettres, Dakar, 3 vols.

Bathily, A. and Meillassoux, C., 1976, Lexique soninke (sarakole)-français, Dakar, Centre Linguistique appliquée.

Battuta, Ibn [1968], *Voyages d'Ibn Battûta* (transl. C. Defremery and B.-R. Sanguinetti, Paris, Anthropos, reissue of 1854 edition (preface by V. Monteil), 4 vols.

Bay, E. G., 1983, 'Servitude and Worldly Success in the Palace of Dahomey', *in* Robertson and Klein, 1983: 340–68.

Bazin, J., 1972, 'Commerce et prédation: l'Etat bambara de Segou et ses communautés maraka', *Conference on Manding Studies*, 27 p. mult.

Bazin, J., 1975, 'Guerre et servitude à Ségou', *in* Meillassoux (ed.), 1975*b*: 135–81.

Bazin, J., 1979, 'La production d'un récit historique', *Cah. Et. africaines*, XIX, 1–4: 435–84.

Bazin, J., 1982, 'Etat guerrier et guerres d'Etat', *in* Bazin and Terray (eds), 1982: 319–72.

Bazin, J. and Terray, E. (eds), 1982, *Guerres de lignages et guerres d'Etats en Afrique*, Ed. des Archives Contemporaines.

Becker, C. and Martin, V., 1975, 'Kayor et Baol: Royaumes sénégalais et traite des esclaves au XVIIᵉ siècle', *Revue franç. d'Hist. d'OM*, 62, 226–7; 270–300.

Bedaux, R. M. A. *et al.*, 1978, 'Recherches archéologiques dans le Delta intérieur du Niger', *Paleohistoria*, 20: 91–220.

Bellat, Cap., 1893, *Renseignements historiques sur le Sansanding et le Macina*, Arch. Dakar, 1 G 184.

Benveniste, E., 1969, *Le vocabulaire des institutions indo-européennes*, Ed. de Minuit, 2 vols.

Berlin, I., 1980, 'Time, Space and the Evolution of Afro-American Society on British Mainland, North America', *Amer. Hist. Rev.*, 85, 1: 44–78.

Berlioux, E.-F., 1870, *La traite orientale*, Paris, De Guillaumin.

Bernardi, B., Poni and Triulzi, 1978, *Fonti orali, Antropologia e Storia*, Milan, F. Angeli.

Bernus, E., 1976, 'Les Touaregs et la guerre', communication Séminaire EPHESS, Paris.

Binger, Cap., 1892, *Du Niger au golfe de Guinée*, Paris, Hachette, 2 vols.

Blachère, R. (transl.), 1980, *Le Coran*, Paris, G.-P. Maisonneuve & Larose.

Blanc, R., 1957, *Manuel de recherche démographique en pays sous-développés*, Paris, Service des Statistiques des Territoires d'Outre-Mer.

Bloch, Marc, 1947, 'Comment et pourquoi finit l'esclavage antique', *Annales*, 1, Jan.–Mar. 1947: 30–40. 2, Apr.–Jun. 1947: 161–70.

Bloch, Marc, 1939 [1968], *La société féodale*, Paris, Albin Michel.

Bloch, Marc, 1955, *Les caractères originaux de l'histoire rurale française*, Paris, A. Colin.

Bloch, Marc, 1963, 'Les *colliberti*: étude historique sur la formation de la classe servile', in *Mélanges historiques*, SEVPEN, 1: 385–451.

Bloch, Maurice, 1975, 'Property and the End of Affinity', *in* Bloch, M. (ed.), 1975: 203–28.

Bloch, Maurice (ed.), 1975, *Marxist Analysis and Social Anthropology*, London, Malaby Press, ASA Studies.

Bohannan, P., 1963, *Social Anthropology*, NY, Holt, Rinehart & Winston.

Bonnafé, P., 1975, 'Les formes d'asservissement chez les Kukuya d'Afrique centrale', *in* Meillassoux (ed.), 1975*b*: 529–56.

Bonte, P., 1975, 'Esclavage et relations de dépendance chez les Touaregs Kel Gress', *in* Meillassoux (ed.), 1975*b*: 49–76.

Bosman, G., 1705, Voyage de Guinée (transl. from Dutch), Utrecht.

Botte, R., 1974, 'Processus de formation d'une classe sociale dans une société africaine précapitaliste', *Cah. Et. afr.*, 56, 14/4: 605–26.

Bouche, D., 1968, *Les villages de liberté en Afrique noire française*, Paris, Mouton.

Bourgeot, A., 1975, 'Analyse des rapports de production chez les pasteurs et les agriculteurs de l'Ahaggar', *in* Monod, T. (ed.), 1975: 263–83.

Boutillier, J.-L., 1968, 'Les captifs en AOF (1903–1905)', *Bull. IFAN*, B, 30, 2.

Boutillier, J.-L., 1975, 'Les trois esclaves de Bouna', *in* Meillassoux (ed.), 1975*b*: 253–80.

Bovill, G. W., 1968, *The Golden Trade of the Moors*, London, OUP.

Bowdich, T. E., 1819, *A Mission from Cape Coast Castle to Ashantee*, London.

Bradbury, R. E., 1957, *The Benin Kingdom and the Edo speaking Peoples of South-Western Nigeria*, London, IAI.

Bradbury, R. E., 1967, 'The Kingdom of Benin', *in* Forde and Kaberry, 1967: 1–35.

Brisson J.-P., 1959, *Spartakus*, Paris, Club Français du Livre.

Brun, Th. and Layrac, C., 1979, 'Fragilité de l'ajustement production-consommation en zone soudano-sahélienne', *Cah. Nutr. Diét.*, XIV, 1: 33–9.

Brunet, R., 1981, 'Géographie des Goulag', *L'Espace géographique*, 3: 215–32.

Brunschwig, R., 1960, 'Abd', in *L'Encyclopédie de l'Islam* (2nd French edn), Paris, Brill, Leide & Besson, I: 25–41.

Bucher, H. H., 1979, 'Liberty and Labor: The Origins of Libreville Reconsidered', *Bull. IFAN*, B, 41, 3: 478–96.

Bugner, L., 1976, *L'image du Noir dans l'art occidental*, Paris, Office du Livre, 3 vols.

Burnham, P., 1980, 'Raiders and Traders in Adamawa: Slavery as a Regional System', *in* Watson (ed.), 1980: 43–72.

Burton, R. F., 1864, *A Mission to Glegle, King of Dahomy*, London, 2 vols.

Busnot (Père), 1690 [1925], *Récit d'aventure au Maroc au temps de Louis XIV*,

Paris, Ed. Pierre Roger.

Butler, J. (ed.), 1964, *Boston Univ. Papers on African History* (vol. 1), Boston, Boston U. Press.

Ca da Mosto, A., 1895, *Relation des voyages à la côte occidentale d'Afrique (1455–1457)*, Paris, Leroux.

Cahen, C., 1968, *L'Islam, des origines au début de l'Empire ottoman*, Paris, Bordas.

Caillié, R., 1830 [1965], *Journal d'un voyage à Tembouctou et à Jenné dans l'Afrique centrale*, reprinted Anthropos, 3 vols.

Cairnes, J. E., 1863 [1958], *The Slave Power*, reprinted David & Charles, Newton Abbot.

Camps, G., 1970, 'Recherches sur les origines des cultivateurs noirs du Sahara', *Revue de l'Occident musulman*, 7: 35–45.

Canot, Cap., 1854 [1938], *Vingt années de la vie d'un négrier*, Paris, Mercure de France.

Centre d'Etudes juridiques comparatives (ed.), 1979, *Sacralité, pouvoir et droit en Afrique*, Paris, Ed. CNRS.

Centre de Recherche d'Histoire ancienne (ed.), 1972, *Actes du Colloque 1971 sur l'esclavage*, Paris, Les Belles-Lettres, 'Ann. litt. de l'Univ. de Besançon'.

Centre de Recherche d'Histoire ancienne (ed.), 1976, *Textes, politique, idéologie Cicéron*, Paris, Les Belles-Lettres, 'Ann. litt. de l'Univ. de Besançon'.

Centre de Recherche d'Histoire ancienne (ed.), 1979, *Terre et paysans dépendants dans les sociétés antiques*, Paris, CNRS.

Centre of African Studies (ed.), 1977, 1981, *African Historical Demography*, Univ. of Edinburgh.

Chastanet, M., 1983, 'Les crises de subsistances dans les villages soninke du cercle de Bakel, de 1858 à 1945', *Cah. Et. afr.*, 23 (89–90), 1–2: 5–36.

Chauveau, J.-P., 1978, 'Contribution à la géographie historique de l'or en pays baule (Côte-d'Ivoire)', *J. des Afric.*, 48, 1: 15–70.

Chauveau, J.-P., 1979, *Kokumbo et sa région*, Paris, ORSTOM.

Chauveau, J.-P., 1980, 'Spécialisations écologiques. Etat et réalisation de la valeur par les échanges à longue distance', *Cah. Et. afr.*, 77–8; 161–7.

Chayanov, A. V., 1925 [1966], *The Theory of Peasant Economy*, Homewood, R. D. Irwin, Inc.

Chilver, E. M. and Kaberry, P. M., 1967, 'The Kingdom of Kom in West Cameroon', *in* Forde and Kaberry, 1967: 123–51.

Ch'ü Ts'ung-tsu, *Han Social Structure*, vol. I: *Han Dynasty China*, Seattle, Un. of Washington Press.

Cissoko, S. M., 1968, 'Famines et épidémies à Tombouctou et dans la boucle du Niger du xviᵉ au xviiiᵉ siècle', *Bull. IFAN*, B, 30, 3: 806–21.

Cissoko, S. M., 1969*a*, 'Traits fondamentaux des sociétés du Soudan occidental, du xviiᵉ siècle au début du xixᵉ s.', *Bull. IFAN*, B, 31, 1: 1–30.

Cissoko, S. M., 1969*b*, 'La royauté (*Mansaya*) chez les Mandingues occidentaux d'après leurs traditions orales', *Bull. IFAN*, B, 31, 2: 325–38.

Cissoko, S. M., 1975, *Tombouctou et l'Empire songhay*. Dakar. Nouv. Ed. Afr.

Cissoko, S. M. and Sambou, K., 1974, *Recueil des traditions orales des Mandingues de Gambie et de Casamance*, Niamey, Centre Rég. pour la Trad. or.

CLAD, *Lexique wolof-français*, Dakar, IFAN, 3 vols.

Clarence-Smith, W. G., 1979, 'Slaves, Commoners and Landlords in Bulozi', *Jl of Afr. Hist.*, 20, 2: 219, 234.

Coale, A. J. and Demeny, P., 1966, *Regional Models-life Tables and Tables of Population*, Princeton University Press.

Contamine, P., 1976, 'Guerre et christianisme médiéval', *in* Glénisson J. (ed.), 1976.

Cooper, F., 1977, *Plantation Slavery on the East Coast of Africa*, New Haven, Yale UP.

Cooper, F., 1979, 'The Problems of Slavery in African Studies', *Jl of Afr. Hist.*, 20, 1: 103–25.

Cooper, F., 1981, 'Islam and cultural hegemony', *in* Lovejoy (ed.), 1981: 271–307.

Cooper, J., 1876, *Le continent perdu ou l'esclavage et la traite en Afrique (1875)*, Paris, Hachette.

Coquery, C. (ed.), 1965, *La découverte de l'Afrique*, Paris, Julliard, 'Archives'.

Coquery-Vidrovitch, C., 1971, 'De la traite des esclaves à l'exportation de l'huile de palme et des palmistes au Dahomey, xixᵉ siècle', *in* Meillassoux, C. (ed.), 1971: 107–23.

Cornu, R. and Lagneau, J., 1969, *Hiérarchies et classes sociales*, Paris, A. Colin.

Corro, B., 1975, *L'esclavage dans les Andes*, Mém. de maîtrise ethnologie, Un. de Bordeaux II.

Coser, L. A., 1964, 'The Political Functions of Eunuchism', *Amer. Soc. Rev.*, 29, 6: 880–5.

Coulibaly, T., 1979, 'La Communautée noire d'Algérie', *Peuples noirs, Peuples africains*, 2, 9: 115–23.

Crone, P., 1980, *Slaves on Horses: The Evolution of the Islamic Policy*, London, Cambridge U. Press.

Cuoq, J. M., 1975, *Recueil des sources arabes concernant l'Afrique occidentale du VIIIᵉ au XVIᵉ siècle*, Paris, CNRS.

Curtin, P. D. and Vansina, J., 1964, 'Sources of the xixth Cent. African

Slave-Trade', *Jl of Afr. Hist.*, 2: 185–208.

Curtin, P. D. (ed.), 1966, *Narratives of the West African Slave Trade*, Madison, Un. of Wisconsin Press.

Curtin, P. D., 1967, *Africa Remembered*, Madison, Un. of Wisconsin Press.

Curtin, P. D., 1969, *The Atlantic Slave Trade*, Madison, Un. of Wisconsin Press.

Curtin, P. D., 1975, *Economic Change in Pre-colonial Africa*, Madison, Un. of Wisconsin Press.

Cuvillier, A., 1958, *Manuel de sociologie*, Paris, PUF, 2 vols.

Daaku, K. Y., 1970, *Trade and Politics on the Gold Coast, 1600–1720*, Oxford, Clarendon Press.

Daaku, K. Y., 1971, 'La traite des Noirs et la société africaine', *in Perspective nouvelle sur l'histoire africaine*, Paris, Présence, Africaine: 152–8.

Dalby, D. (ed.), 1970, *Language and History in Africa*, London, F. Cass.

Dalzel, A., 1793, *The History of Dahomey*, London, G. and W. Nicol.

Daubigney, A., 1976, 'Contribution à l'étude de l'esclavagisme: la propriété chez Cicéron', *in Centre de Recherche d'Histoire ancienne*, 1976: 13–72.

Daumas, Lt-Col., E., 1845, *Le Sahara algérien*, Paris, Fortin-Masson.

Daumas, Gen. E., 1857, *Le Grand Désert (suivi du Code de l'esclavage chez les Musulmans)*, Paris, M. Levy Frères.

Daumas, Gen. E., 1858, *Les chevaux du Sahara et les mœurs du désert*, Paris, M. Levy Frères.

Debien, G.: 1961–1967, 'Les origines des esclaves aux Antilles', *Bull. IFAN*, B, 23, 3–4, 1961: 363–87. 25, 1–2, 1963: 1–38. 25, 3–4, 1963: 215–65. 26, 1–2, 1964: 166–211. 26, 3–4, 1964: 601, 675. 27, 3–4, 1965: 755–99. 29, 3–4, 1967: 536–58.

Debien, G., Delafosse, M., Thilmans, G., 1978, 'Journal d'un voyage de traite en Guinée, à Cayenne, aux Antilles fait par Jean Barbot en 1678–1679', *Bull. IFAN*, B, 40, 2: 235–395.

Deherme, P., 1908, *Rapport sur la captivité en Afrique Occidentale*, Archives Dakar, K25.

De Jonghe, E., 1949, *Les formes d'asservissement dans les sociétés indigènes du Congo belge*, Bruxelles, Inst. roy. col. belge.

Delafosse, M., 1912, *Haut-Sénégal – Niger*, Paris, Larose, 3 vols.

Delaunay, D., 1984, *De la captivité à l'exil*, Bondy, ORSTOM.

Delcourt, A., 1952, *La France et les Etablissements français au Sénégal entre 1713 et 1763*, Mémoire IFAN, no. 17, Dakar.

Delobsom, A.-A.-D., 1933, *L'empire du Mogho-Naba*, Paris, Domat-Monchrestien.

Demougeot, A., 1949, 'L'esclavage et l'émancipation des Noirs au Sénégal', *Tropiques*, n.s., 47, 312: 10–17.

Depestre, René, *Minerai noir, Poèmes*, Paris, Présence Africaine.

Dermenghem, E., 1956, *Mahomet et la tradition islamique*, Paris, Seuil.

Derrick, J., 1975, *Africa's Slaves Today*, London, Allen & Unwin.

Deschamps, H., 1971, *Histoire de la traite des Noirs de l'Antiquité a nos jours*, Paris, Fayard.

Devisse, J., 1970, 'La Question d'Audagust', *Tegdaoust I*: 109–57.

Diabaté, M.-M., 1970*a*, *Janjon*, Paris, Présence Africaine.

Diabaté, M.-M., 1970*b*, *Kala Jata*, Bamako, Ed. Populaires, coll. 'Hier'.

Diallo, O., 1947, 'Les *Kore* et les *Simo* au Fouta Dialon', *Notes afr.*, 33: 2–5.

Dieng, A.-A., 1974, *Classes sociales et mode de production féodal en Afrique de l'Ouest*, Dakar, 15 p. mult.

Dieng, A.-A., 1983, *Contribution à l'étude des problèmes philosophiques en Afrique noire*, Paris, Nubia.

Dinafla, *Lexique bambara-français*, Bamako, DINAFLA.

Diop, A.-B., 1981, *La société wolof*, Paris, Karthala.

Diop, A.-S., 1978, 'L'impact de la civilisation manding au Sénégal. La génèse de la royauté gelwar au Siin et au Saalum', *Bull. IFAN*, B, 40, 4: 689–707.

Diop, C. A., 1960, *L'Afrique noire précoloniale*, Paris, Présence Africaine.

Diop, M., 1971–2, *Histoire des classes sociales dans l'Afrique de l'Ouest*, Paris, Maspero, 2 vols.

Dockes, P. and Servet, J.-M., 1980, *Sauvages et ensauvagés*, PU de Lyon.

Dorman, W., 1973, *Serfs, Peasants and Socialists*, Berkeley, Un. of California Press.

Doutressoule, G., 1940, 'Le cheval au Soudan français', *B. IFAN*, B, 2, 3–4: 324–46.

Dubois, F., 1897, *Tombouctou la Mystérieuse*, Paris, Flammarion.

Duby, G., 1973, *Guerriers et paysans*, Paris, Gallimard.

Duby, G., 1981, *Le chevalier, la femme et le prêtre*, Paris, Hachette, 'Pluriel'.

Dumestre, G. (ed.), 1979, *La geste de Ségou*, Paris, A. Colin, 'Les Classiques africains'.

Dumestre, G. and Kesteloot, L. (eds), 1975, *La prise de Dionkoloni*, Paris, A. Colin, 'Classiques africains'.

Dunbar, R. A., 1977, 'Slavery and the Evolution of xixth Century Damagaram', *in* Miers and Kopytoff, 1977: 155–77.

Dupire, M., 1970, *Organisation sociale des Peuls*, Paris, Plon.

Edrisi [1866], *Description de l'Afrique et de l'Espagne* (transl. R. Dozy and M.-J. de Goeje), Leyde, Brill.

Ekholm, K., 1972, *Power and Prestige, the Rise and Fall of the Kongo Kingdom*, Uppsala, Skriv Service.

El-Bekri, A.-O., 19th cent. [1965], *Description de l'Afrique septentrionale* (transl. de Slane), Paris, A. Maisonneuve.

Elwert, G., 1973, *Wirtshaft und Herrshaft von Dahomey*, Munich, Kommission Verlag K. Rinner.

Emmer, P., Mettas, J., Nardin, J.-E. (eds), 1975, 'La traite des Noirs par l'Atlantique: nouvelles approches', special issue, *Rev. franç. d'OM*, 42: 226–7.

Engels, F., 1877–8 [1950], *Anti-Dühring*, Paris, Ed. Sociales.

Engels, F., 1884 [1954], *L'origine de la famille, de la propriété privée et de l'Etat*, Paris, Ed. Sociales.

Engerman, S. L. and Genovese, E. D. (eds), 1975, *Race and Slavery in the Western Hemisphere: Quantitative Studies*, Princeton, Princeton University Press.

Engerman, S. L., 1981, 'L'esclavage aux Etats-Unis et aux Antilles anglaises: quelques comparaisons économiques et démographiques', *in* Mintz S. (ed.), 1981: 223–46.

Es-Sa'di, A. [1964], *Tarikh es-Soudan*, Paris, Leroux.

Ezeanya, S. N., 1967, 'The *osu* System in Igboland', *Jl Relig. in Afr.*, 1, 1: 35–45.

Fabre, M., 1970, *Esclaves et planteurs dans le Sud américain*, Paris, Julliard, 'Archives'.

Fabre, J. D., 1964, 'Some Thoughts on State Foundation in the Western Sudan before the 17th Cent.', *in* J. Butler (ed.), 1964: 17–34.

Fage, J. D., 1969, 'Slavery and the Slave-Trade in the Context of West African History', *Jl of Afr. Hist.*, 10, 3: 393–404.

Fage, J. D., 1974, *State and Subjects in Sub-Saharan African History*, Raymond Dart Lectures, Witwatersrand Univ.

Fage, J. D., 1980, 'Slave and Society in Western Africa, *c.*1445–*c.*1700', *Jl of Afr. Hist.*, 21, 3: 289–310.

Farias, P. F. de M., 1980, 'Model of the World and Categorial Models: The "Enslavable Barbarian" as a Model of Classificatory Label', *Slavery and Abolition*, 1, 2: 115–31.

Fayet, C., 1931, *Esclavage et travail obligatoire. La main-d'œvre volontaire en Afrique*, Paris, Libr. Générale de Droit et de Jurisprudence.

Filipowiak, W., 1979, *Etudes archéologiques sur la capitale médiévale du Mali*, Warsaw, Museum Narodowe w. Szczenie.

Finley, M. I., 1960, *Slavery in Classical Antiquity*, Cambridge, Heffer.

Finley, M., 1969, 'The Idea of Slavery: Critique of David Brion Davis: *The Problem of Slavery in Western Culture*', *in* Foner and Genovese, 1969: 260.

Finley, M. I., 1973, *The Ancient Economy*, Berkeley, Univ. of California Press.

Finley, M. I., 1979, Slavery and the Historians, *Histoire sociale*, 12, 24: 247–61.

Finley, M. I., 1981, *Esclavage antique et idéologie moderne*, Paris, Ed. de Minuit.

Fisher, A. G. B. and Fisher, N. J., 1970, *Slavery and Muslim Society in Africa*, London, Hurst.

Fisher, H. J. and Rowland, V., 1971, 'Firearms in the Central Sudan', *Jl of Afr. Hist.*, 12: 215–39.

Fohlen, Cl., 1975, 'L'esclavage aux Etats-Unis', *Revue franç. d'Hist. d'Outre-mer*, 52: 226–7; 372–83.

Foner, L. and Genovese, E. D., (eds), 1969, *Slavery in the New World*, Englewood Cliffs, NJ, Prentice Hall.

Forde, D., 1951, *The Yoruba Speaking People of South Western Nigeria*, London, Int. Afr. Inst.

Forde, D. and Kaberry, P. M. (eds), 1967, *West African Kingdoms in the 19th century*, London, IAI, OUP.

Fraser, D. and Cole, H. M. (eds), 1972, *African Art and Leadership*, Madison, Un. of Wisconsin Press.

Freyre, G., 1933, *Maîtres et esclaves*, Paris, Gallimard.

Frossard, M., 1789 [1889], *La cause des esclaves nègres et des habitants de la Guinée*, Lyon (micro-ed., Hachette).

Fuglestad, F., 1977, 'Quelques réflexions sur l'histoire et les institutions de l'ancien royaume du Dahomey et de ses voisins', *Bull. IFAN, B.*, 39, 3: 493–517.

Gabriel, J. and Ben-Tovim, G., 1978, 'Marxism and the Concept of Racism', *Economy and Society*, 7, 2: 118–55.

Gaden, H., 1931, *Proverbes et maximes peuls et toucouleurs*, Paris, Inst. d'Ethnologie.

Gallais, J., 1967, *Le delta intérieur du Niger*, Dakar, IFAN, 2 vols.

Galliéni, Ct, 1885, *Voyage au Soudan français*, Paris, Hachette.

Gamble, D. P., 1957, *The Wolof of Senegambia*, London, Int. Afr. Inst.

Garlan, Y., 1982, *Les esclaves en Grèce ancienne*, Paris, Maspero.

Garnsey, P., 1976, 'Peasants in Ancient Roman Society', *Jl of Peasant Studies*, 3, 3: 221–35.

Gaston-Martin, 1948, *Histoire de l'esclavage dans les colonies françaises*, Paris, PUF.

Gautier, A., 1985, *Les sœurs de solitude*, Paris, Ed. Caribéennes.

Gemery, H.-A. and Hogendorn, J. S., 1981, 'La traite des esclaves sur l'Atlantique: essai de modèle économique', *in* S. Mintz (ed.), 1981: 18–45.

Genovese, E. D., 1968, *Economie politique de l'esclavage*, Paris, Maspero.

Genovese, E. D., 1974, *Roll, Jordan, Roll. The World the Slaves Made*, New

York, Pantheon.

Geoffroy de Villeneuve, A., 1814, *De l'Afrique*, Paris, Nepveu, 4 vols.

Gerbeau, H., 1967, 'Un mort-vivant: l'esclavage', *Prés. africaine*, 61, 1: 180–98.

Gerbeau, H., 1970, *Les esclaves noirs*, Paris, A. Balland.

Girard, J., 1969, *Genèse du pouvoir charismatique en Basse-Casamance (Sénégal)*, Dakar, IFAN.

Giraud, M., 1979, *Races et classes en Martinique*, Paris, Anthropos.

Giraud, M. and Jamard, L.-L., 1976, *Les Antillais et le travail*, Paris, Grimsca, MSH.

Gisler, A., 1965, *L'esclavage aux Antilles françaises (XVIIᵉ–XIXᵉ siècle), Contribution au problème de l'esclavage*, Fribourg, Ed. Univ.

Gleave, M. B. and Prothero, R. M., 1971, 'Population Density and Slave Raiding, A Comment', *Jl of Afr. Hist.*, 12, 2: 319–24.

Glélé, M.-A., 1974, *Le Danxome*, Paris, Nubia.

Glénisson, J. (ed.), 1976, *La guerre au Moyen Age*, Paris, Pons.

Gomila, J., 1976, 'Définir la population', *in* Jacquard, 1976: 5–36.

Goody, J. (ed.), 1968, *Literacy in Traditional Society*, Cambridge, CUP.

Goody, J., 1971, *Technology, Tradition and the State in Africa*, London, IAI, OUP.

Goody, J., 1980, 'Slavery in Time and Space', *in* Watson (ed.), 1980: 16–42.

Grace, J., 1975, *Domestic Slavery in West Africa*, London, Frederick Muller Ltd.

Graham, J. D., 1965, 'The Slave-Trade, Depopulation and Human Sacrifice in Benin', *Cah. Et. afr.*, 5 (2), 18: 317–34.

Granderye, Cap., 1947, 'Notes et souvenirs sur l'occupation de Tombouctou', *Rev. Hist. col.*, 1947, 34: 87–131.

Grant, D., 1968, *The Fortunate Slave*, London, OUP.

GROMSCA, 1975, *Reproduction des hiérarchies sociales et action de l'Etat*, Paris, MSH, Ecology et Sciences humaines (mult.).

Groupe universitaire de Recherche inter-Caraïbes, 1969, *Le passage de la société esclavagiste à la société postesclavagiste*, Pointe-à-Pitre.

Gueye, M., 1966, 'La fin de l'esclavage à Saint-Lous et à Gorée en 1848', *Bull. IFAN, B.*, 28, 3–4: 637–56.

Gueye, M., 1965, 'L'affaire Chautemps (avril 1904) et la suppression de l'esclavage de case au Sénégal', *Bull. IFAN, B*, 27, 3–4: 543–59.

Guillaume, E., 1895, *Le Soudan en 1894, la vérité sur Tombouctou. L'esclavage au Soudan*, Paris, Savine.

Guillaume, H., 1974, *Les nomades interrompus*, Niamey, 'Etudes nigériennes', no. 35.

Gutman, H., 1981, 'Familles et groupes de parenté chez les Afro-Américains en esclavage dans les plantations de Good Hope (Car. du S.) 1760–1860', *in* Mintz (ed.), 1981: 141–72.

Hafkin, N. and Bay, E. G., 1976, *Women in Africa*, Stanford, Stanford Univ. Press.

Halphen, L. (ed.), 1964, *Histoire anonyme de la première croisade*, Paris, Soc. d'Ed. Les Belles-Lettres.

Harms, R., 1978, *Competition and Capitalism: the Bobangi Role in Equatorial Africa's Trade Revolution*, Ph.D. Dissertation, Un. of Madison.

Harms, R., 1983, 'Sustaining the System: Trading Towns along the Middle Zaïre', *in* Robertson and Klein (eds), 1983: 95–110.

Harries, P., 1981, 'Slavery, Social Incorporation and Surplus Extraction: the Nature of Free and Unfree Labour in SE Africa', *Jl of Afr. Hist.*, 22, 3: 309–30.

Hecquard, H., 1853, *Voyage sur la Côte et l'intérieur de l'Afrique occidentale*, Paris, Bénard & Cⁱᵉ.

Heers, J., 1981, *Esclaves et domestiques au Moyen Age*, Paris, Fayard.

Héritier, F., 1975, 'Des cauris et des hommes: production d'esclaves et accumulation de cauris chez les Samo (Haute-Volta)', *in* Meillassoux (ed.), 1975b: 477–508.

Herskovits, M. J., 1978, *Dahomey, an Ancient West African Kingdom*, New York, Augustin, 2 vols.

Hindess, B. and Hirst, P. Q., 1975, *Pre-Capitalist Modes of Production*, London, Routledge & Kegan Paul.

Hogendorn, J. S., 1977, 'The Economics of Slave Use on two "Plantations" in the Zaria Emirate of the Sokoto Caliphate', *Int. Jl of Afr. Hist. Stud.*, 10, 3: 369–83.

Hogg, P., 1973, *The African Slave Trade and its Suppression (A Classified Bibliography)*, London, Frank Cass.

Holas, B., 1949, 'A propos de l'étymologie du *komo*', *Notes afr.*, 42: 49.

Hopkins, A. G., 1973, *An Economic History of West Africa*, London, Longman.

Hopkins, K., 1978, *Conquerors and Slaves*, London, CUP.

Horton, R., 1975, 'On the Rationality of Conversion', *Africa*, 45, 3: 219–35. 45, 4: 373–99.

Horton, W. R. G., 1954, 'The Ohu System of Slavery in a Northern Ibo Village', *Africa*, 24, 4: 311–36.

Hunkandrin, L., 1964, 'L'esclavage en Mauritanie', *Ed. dahoméennes*, 3: 31–49.

Hunwick, J. O., 1970, 'The Term Zanj and its Derivatives in West African Chronicles', *in* Dalby (ed.), 1970: 102–8.

Hunwick, J. O., 1973, 'The Mid-Fourteenth-Century Capital of Mali', *J. Afr. Hist.*, XIV, 2: 195–208.

Ibn Khaldun [1852], *Histoire des Berbères*, Algeria.

Idrissi, see: Edrisi.

Igbafe, P. A., 1975, 'Slavery and Emancipation in Benin, 1897–1945', *Jl of Afr. Hist.*, XVI, 3: 409–29.

Imbert, J., Sautel, G. and Boulet-Sautel, M., 1957, *Histoire des institutions et des faits sociaux*, Paris, PUF, 2 vols.

Innes, G., 1974, *Sunjata, Three Mandinka Versions*, London, SOAS.

Isaac, E., 1980, 'Genesis, Judaism and the "Sons of Ham"', *Slavery and Abolition*, 1, 1: 3–17.

Isaacman, B. and A., 1977, 'Slavery and Stratification among the Sena of Mozambique: A Study of the Kaporo System', *in* Miers and Kopytoff (eds), 1977: 105–19.

Isert, P.-E., 1973, *Voyages en Guinée et dans les îles Caraïbes en Amérique*, Paris, Maradan.

Itoh, M., 1985, *La crise mondiale*, Paris, EDI.

Izard, M., 1970, *Introduction à l'histoire du royaume mossi*, Paris, Ouagadougou, Recherches Voltaïques, 2 vols.

Izard, M., 1975, 'Les captifs royaux dans l'ancien Yatenga', *in* Meillassoux (ed.), 1975: 281–97.

Izard, M., 1976, 'Formes d'organisation militaire dans la Haute-Volta de la seconde moitié du XIXᵉ siècle', communication, Séminaire EHESS, Paris.

Jacquard, A. (ed.), 1976, *L'étude des isolats, espoirs et limites*, Paris, INED.

Jacques-Meunie, D., 1947, 'Les oasis de Lektaoua et des Mehamid', *Hesperis*, 3–4: 410–12.

Jacques-Meunie, D., 1958, 'Hiérarchie sociale au Maroc présaharien', *Hesperis*, 3–4, 239–67.

Jacques-Meunie, D., 1961, *Cités anciennes de Mauritanie*, Paris, Klincksieck.

Jamard, J.-L. (n.d.), *Les systèmes socio-économiques antillais, leurs modalités de constitution et de transformation*, Paris, CORDES.

Jamard, J.-L., 1982, 'Le mode de production esclavagiste en Guadeloupe et en Martinique en rapport avec le mouvement de la société française', *Archipelago*, 1: 57–95.

Jaulin, R., 1971, *La mort sara*, Paris, UGE.

Jawara, M., 1976–7, *Monographie du royaume de Jara du XVIᵉ au XVIIIᵉ siècle*, Mémoire, Bamako, Ecole normale supérieure.

Jean Leon l'Africain, 1550/1956, *Description de l'Afrique*, Paris, Adrien-Maisonneuve.

Jewsiewicki, B., 1981, 'The social context of Slavery in Equatorial Africa during the 19th and 20th Centuries', *in* Lovejoy (ed.), 1981: 41–72.

Johnson, M., 1970, 'The Cowrie Currencies of West Africa', *Jl of Afr. Hist.*, 11, 1: 17–49. 11, 3: 331–54.

Johnson, M., 1976, 'The Economic Foundation of an Islamic Theocracy:

The Case of Masina', *Jl of Afr. Hist.*, 17, 4: 481–96.

Johnson, M., 1980, 'Polanyi, Peukert and the Political Economy of Dahomey', *Jl of Afr. Hist.*, 21, 3: 395–9.

Jonckers, D. de, 1981, *Organisation socio-économique des Minianka du Mali*, thesis, Fac. Sc. soc., Univ. Libre de Bruxelles.

Jones, A. and Johnson, M., 1980, 'Slaves from the Windward Coast', *Jl Afr. Studies*, 21, 1: 17–34.

Josefsson, C., 1981, *Kuba Slavery*, unpublished, Göteborg Univ.

Kaba, L., 1981, 'Archers, Musketeers and Mosquitoes: The Moroccan Invasion of the Sudan and the Songhay Resistance (1591–1612)', *Jl of Afr. Hist.*, 22: 457–75.

Kake, I. B., 1969, 'L'aventure des Bukhara (Prétoriens noirs) au Maroc au xviiiᵉ siècle', *Prés. afr.*, 70, 2: 69–74.

Kamissoko, W., 1975, *L'empire du Mali* (transl. Y.-T. Cissé), 1st International Colloquium, Bamako, scoa.

Kâti [1964], *Tarikh el-Fettach* (transl. O. Houdas and M. Delafosse), Paris, E. Leroux.

Kea, R. A., 1971, 'Firearms and Warfare on the Gold and Slave Coast (16th to 19th Cent.)', *Jl Afr. Hist.*, 12: 185–213.

Keim, C. A., 1983, 'Women in Slavery among the Mangbetu, 1800–1910', *in* Robertson and Klein (eds), 1983: 144–60.

Kersaint-Gilly, F. de, 1924, 'Essai sur l'évolution de l'esclavage en Afrique occidentale française. Son dernier stade au Soudan français', *Bull. Com. Et. hist. scient. AOF*, 9: 669–78.

Kesteloot, L. (ed.), 1972, *Da Monzon de Ségou*, Paris, F. Nathan, 4 vols.

Kesteloot, L. (ed.), 1978, 'Le mythe et l'histoire dans la formation de l'Empire de Ségou', *Bull. IFAN*, B, 40, 3: 578–681.

Kimba, I., 1979, *Guerres et sociétés*, thesis, uer Geog., Hist. and Soc. Sc., Paris VIII.

Klein, H. S., 1983, 'African Women in the Atlantic Slave Trade', *in* Robertson and Klein (eds), 1983: 29–38.

Klein, M. A., 1971, 'Slavery, the Slave-Trade and Legitimate Commerce in the Late 19th Cent.', *Et. d'Hist. Afr.*, 2: 5–28.

Klein, M. A., 1972, 'Social and Economic Factors in the Muslim Revolution in Senegambia', *Jl of Afr. Hist.*, 13, 3: 419–41.

Klein, M. A., 1977, 'Servitude among the Wolof and Sereer of Senegambia', *in* Miers and Kopytoff (eds), 1977: 335–63.

Klein, M. A., 1978, 'The Study of Slavery in Africa', *Jl of Afr. Hist.*, 19, 4: 599–610.

Klein, M. A. (n.d.), *From Slave to Metayer in the French Sudan: An Effect at Controlled Social Change*, 22 p. mult. (unpub.).

Klein, M. A., 1983, *Slavery, Forced Labour and French Rule in Colonial Guinea*, Un. of Toronto, 15 p., mult. (unpub.).

Klein, N., 1981, 'The Two Asantes', *in* Lovejoy (ed.), 1981: 149–67.

Klein, N., *Asante Slavery*, mult.

Kodjo, N.-G., 1976, 'Contribution à l'étude des tribus dites serviles du Songaï', *Bull. IFAN*, B, 38, 4: 790–812.

Kohler, J.-M., 1972, *Les migrations des Mosi de l'Ouest*, Paris, ORSTOM, 'Travaux et Documents', no. 18.

Konare Ba, A., 1977, *Sonni Ali Ber*, Niamey, 'Etudes nigériennes'.

Koubbel, L., 1968, 'Histoire de la Vallé du Niger supérieur et moyen du VIIIᵉ au XVIᵉ siècle: quelques réflexions sur le découpage chronologique', *Notes et Doc. voltaïques*, 1, 4: 13–28.

Kouloub, Out el, 1958, *Ramza*, Paris, Gallimard.

Kouroubari, A., 1959, 'Histoire de l'imam Samory', *Bull. IFAN*, B, 21, 3–4: 544–71.

Kula, W., 1970, *Théorie économique du système féodal*, Paris, Mouton.

Labouret, H., 1955, 'Le servage, étape entre l'esclavage et la liberté en Afrique occidentale', *Deutsche Afr. Studien*, 1955: 147–53.

Lacoste, Y., 1966, *Ibn Khaldoun*, Paris, Maspero.

Lacroix, L., 1967, *Les derniers négriers*, Paris, Inter Presse.

Lamiral, D. H., 1789, *L'Affrique et le peuple affriquain, considérés sous tous leurs rapports avec notre commerce et nos colonies*, Paris, Dessenne.

Lanfry, J., 1966, *Gadames*, Algeria.

Lange, D., 1972, 'L'intérieur de l'Afrique occidentale d'après Giovanni Lorenzo Anania (XVIᵉ siècle)', *Cah. d'Hist. mondiale*, 14, 2: 299–351.

Lange, D., 1978, 'Progrès de l'Islam et changement politique au Kanem du XIᵉ au XIIIᵉ siècle: un essai d'interprétation', *Jl of Afr. Hist.*, 19, 4: 495–514.

La Roncière, C. de, 1933, *Nègres et négriers*, Paris, Portiques.

Latour, E. de, 1981, *Une aristocratie coloniale*, thesis, Paris VIII.

Latour, E. de, 1982, 'La Paix destructice', *in* Bazin and Terray (eds), 1982: 235–68.

Laurentin, A., 1960, 'Femmes Nzakara', *in* Paulme (ed.), 1960: 121–72.

Law, R., 1971, 'The Constitutional Trouble of Oyo in the 18th Cent.', *Jl of Afr. Hist.*, 12, 1: 25–44.

Law, R., 1975, 'A West African Cavalry State: The Kingdom of Oyo', *Jl of Afr. Hist.*, 16, 1: 1–16.

Law, R., 1976, 'Horses, Firearms and Political Power in Pre-colonial West Africa', *Past and Present*, 72: 112–32.

Law, R., 1977a, *The Oyö Empire: 1600–1836*, Oxford, Clarendon Press.

Law, R., 1977b, 'Royal Monopoly and Private Enterprise in the Atlantic Trade. The Case of Dahomey', *Jl of Afr. Hist.*, 18, 4: 555–77.

Lefebvre des Noëttes, 1924, *La force animale à travers les âges*, Paris, Berger-Levrault.

Lefebvre des Noëttes, 1931, *L'attelage, le cheval de selle à travers les âges. Contribution à l'histoire de l'esclavage*, Paris, Picard, 2 vols.

Lefebvre des Noëttes, 1932, 'Autour du vaisseau de Boro-Boudan', *La Nature*, 2885: 49–58.

Leff, N. N., 1974, 'Long Term Viability of Slavery in a Backward Closed Economy', *Jl of Interdisciplinary History*, 5: 103–8.

Legassick, M., 1966, 'Firearms, Horses and Samorian Army Organization 1870–1898', *Jl Afr. Hist.*, 7: 95–115.

Le Goff, J., 1965, *La civilisation de l'Occident médiéval*, Paris, Arthaud.

Le Hérissé, 1911, *L'ancien royaume de Dahomey*, Paris, Larose.

Lengellé, M., 1967, *L'esclavage*, Paris, 'Que sais-je?'.

Levtzion, N., 1971, 'A 17th Century Chronicle by Ibn al Makhtar: A Critical Study of *Tarikh al-Fattash*', *Bull. of the SOAS*, 34, 3, 1971: 571–93.

Levtzion, N., 1971, 'Mahmud Kati fut-il l'auteur du *Tarikh al-Fattash?'* *Bull. IFAN*, B, 33, 4: 665–74.

Levtzion, N., 1973, *Ancient Ghana and Mali*, London, Methuen & Co.

Lévy-Bruhl, H., 1931, 'Théorie de l'esclavage', *Revue générale du Droit*, 55, 1931: 1–17.

Leynaud, E. (n.d.) [1961], *Les cadres sociaux de la vie rurale dans la Haute Vallée du Niger*, Paris, BDPA, 2 vols. mult.

Littré, E., 1877 [1959], *Dictionnaire de la langue française*, Gallimard/Hachette, 7 vols.

Lombard, J., 1967, 'The Kingdom of Dahomey', *in* Forde and Kaberry (eds): 70–92.

Louis-Joseph, C., 1976, *Capital marchand, esclavage et sucre aux Antilles françaises, 1635–1848*, unpub. ms.

Lovejoy, P. E., 1978, 'Plantation in the Economy of Sokoto Caliphate', *Jl of Afr. Hist.*, 19, 3: 341–68.

Lovejoy, P. E. (ed.), 1981, *The Ideology of Slavery*, Beverly Hills, Sage.

Lovejoy, P. E., 1981, 'Slavery in the Sokoto Caliphate', *in* Lovejoy (ed.), 1981: 201–43.

Lovejoy, P. E. (ed.), 1983, *Transformation in Slavery*, London, CUP.

Lovejoy, P. E. and Baier, S., 1975, 'The Desert Side Economy of the Central Sudan', *Intl Jl of Afr. Hist. Study*, 8, 4: 551–81.

Loyer, P. G. de, 1660–1715, *in* Roussier, 1935.

Ly, A., 1958, *La compagnie du Sénégal*, Paris, Présence Africaine.

Ly, B., 1967, 'L'honneur dans les sociétés ouolof et toucouleur du Sénégal', *Prés. africaine*, 61, 1: 32–67.

McCall, D. F., 1967, 'The Horse in West African History', *Congrès inter-*

national des Africanistes, Dakar.

McCall, D. F. and Bennett, N. R. (eds), 1971, *Aspects of West African Islam*, Boston.

MacCormack, C. P., 1977, 'Wono: Institutionalized Dependency in Sherbro Descent Group', *in* Miers and Kopytoff (eds): 181–200.

Machiavelli, N., 1571 [1938], *Le Prince*, Paris, Ed. de Cluny.

MacLeod, W. C., 1928, 'Economic Aspects of Indigeneous American Slavery', *Am. Anthrop.*, n.s., 30: 632–50.

MacLeod, W. C., 1929, 'The Origin of the Servile Labor Groups', *Am. Anthrop.*, n.s. 30: 89–113.

McCaskie, T. C., 1980, 'Office, Land and Subjects in the History of the Manwere Fekuo of Kumase', *Jl of Afr. Hist.*, 21, 2: 189–208.

McDougall, E. A., 1980, *The Ijil salt Industry*, Ph.D. Un. of Birmingham.

Magalhaes-Godinho, V., *L'économie de l'Empire portugais aux XVe et XVIe siècles*, Paris, SEVPEN.

Mage, E., 1868, *Voyage dans le Soudan occidental (Sénégambie-Niger)*, Hachette, Paris.

Mahibou, S.-M. and Triaud, J.-L., 1983, *Voilà ce qui est arrivé*, Paris, CNRS.

Malowist, M., 1966, 'Le commerce de l'or et des esclaves au Soudan occidental', *Africana Bull.*, 4: 49–72.

Manning, P., 1969, 'Slaves, Palm-oil and Political Power on the West African Coast: A Historical Hypothesis', *Afr. Hist. Stud.*, 2, 2: 279–88.

Manning, P., 1975, 'Un document sur la fin de l'esclavage au Dahomey (Rapport de l'administrateur Charles, 1904)', *Notes africaines*, 147: 88–91.

Manning, P., 1981, *Slavery, Colonialism and Economic Growth in Dahomey, 1640–1960*, Cambridge, CUP.

Manning, P. (n.d.), *The Enslavement of Africans: A Demographic Model*, 71 p. mult., unpub.

Marchal, F., Rabut, O., *et al.*, 1972, 'La conjoncture démographique: l'Afrique, l'Amérique latine et l'Asie', *Population*, 27, 6: 1076–117.

Markov, W. (ed.), *Etudes africaines*, Leipzig.

Marty, P., 1920–21, *Etudes sur l'Islam et les tribus du Soudan*, Paris, Leroux, 4 vols.

Marx, K. [1964], *Pre-capitalist Economic Formations* (with an introduction by Eric Hobsbawm), London, Lawrence & Wishart.

Marx, K., 1857–1858 [1969], *Fondements de la Critique de l'économie politique*, Paris, Anthropos.

Marx, K., 1867, *Capital*, London, Lawrence & Wishart, 1970.

Marx, K., 1861–1865 [1970], *La guerre civile aux Etats-Unis*, Paris, Union Gén. d'Ed.

Mason, M., 1971, 'Population Density and Slave-raiding. A Reply', *Jl of Afr. Hist.*, 12, 2: 324–7.

Mason, M., 1973, 'Captive and Client Labour in the Economy of the Bida

Emirate', *Jl of Afr. Hist.*, 14, 3: 453–71.

Maugham, R., 1961, *Les esclaves existent toujours*, Paris, Ed. Universitaires.

Mauny, R., 1961, *Tableau gégraphique de l'Ouest africain au Moyen Age*, Mém. IFAN, Dakar.

Mauny, R., 1967, 'Le livre de bord du navire Santa-Maria da Comeiça (1522)', *Bull. IFAN*, B. 29, 34: 512–35.

Maurin, J., 1975, 'Remarques sur la notion de *puer* à l'époque classique', *Bull. de l'Ass. Guillaume-Budé*, 4: 221–30.

Mazillier, 1894, 'Rapport sur la captivité dans les cercles du Soudan', *Archives nationales du Sénégal*, K14.

Mbodj, M., 1978, *Un exemple d'économie coloniale, le Sine-Saloum de 1877 à 1940*, thesis, Paris VIII.

M'Bow, A. M., Ki-Zerbo, J. and Devisse, J., 1965, *La traite négrière du XVIIIe au début du XIXe siècle*, Paris, Hatier.

Meillassoux, C., 1964, *Anthropologie économique des Gouro de Côte-d'Ivoire*, Paris, Mouton.

Meillassoux, C., 1966, 'Plans d'anciennes fortifications (*tata*) en pays malinke', *Jl Soc. Afr.*, 36, 1: 29–43.

Meillassoux, C., 1968, 'Ostentation, destruction, reproduction', *Economies et Sociétés*, II, 4: 760–72.

Meillassoux, C. (ed.), 1971a, *The Development of Indigenous Trade and Markets in West Africa*, Oxford, OUP.

Meillassoux, C., 1971d, 'Le commerce, pré-colonial et le développement de l'esclavage à Gumbu du Sahel (Mali)', *in* Meillassoux (ed.), 1971a: 182–95.

Meillassoux, C., 1971e, 'Review of *Technology, Tradition and the State in Africa* by J. Goody', *Africa*, 41, 4: 331–3.

Meillassoux, C., 1972b, 'L'itinéraire d'Ibn Battuta de Walata à Malli', *Jl of Afr. Hist.*, 13, 3: 389–96.

Meillassoux, C., 1972d, 'Les origines de Gumbu du Sahel', *Bull. IFAN*, B, 34, 2: 268–98.

Meillassoux, C., 1972f, 'Réexamen de l'itinéraire d'Ibn Battuta entre Walata et Malli', *Conference on Manding Studies*, London.

Meillassoux, C., 1972g, 'Où donc était Suleyman? (Réponse à J. O. Hunwick sur l'emplacement de la capitale du Mali)', *Conference on Manding Studies*, London.

Meillassoux, C., 1975a, 'Etat et condition des esclaves à Gumbu (Mali) au XIXe siècle', *in* Meillassoux (ed.), 1975b: 221–52.

Meillassoux, C. (ed.), 1975b, *L'esclavage en Afrique précoloniale*, Paris, Maspero.

Meillassoux, C., 1978a, 'L'interprétation légendaire de l'histoire du Jonkoloni (Mali)', *in* Bernardi *et al.* (eds), 1978: 347–92.

Meillassoux, C. 1978d, 'Correspondence (On Slavery)', *Economy and*

Society, 7, 3: 322–31.

Meillassoux, C., 1979d, 'Historical Modalities of the Exploitation and Overexploitation of Labour', Critique of Anthropology, 4, 13/14: 9–16.

Meillassoux, C., 1979e, 'Le mâle en gésine', Cah. Et. afr., 19, 1–4 (73–76): 353–80.

Meillassoux, C., 1981, Maidens, Meal and Money: Capitalism and the Domestic Economy, Cambridge, CUP.

Meillassoux, C., 1983, 'The Economic Basis of Demographic Reproduction', Journal of Peasant Studies, 11, 1: 50–61.

Meillassoux, C., 1984, 'Habitat e modi di vida', in Spini, A. and S. (eds), 1984: 5–9.

Meillassoux, C. and Niaré, A.-C., 1963, 'Histoire et institutions du Kafo de Bamako', Cah. Et. africaines, 4, 2 (14): 186–226.

Meillassoux, C., Doucoure, L. and Simagha, D., 1967, Légende de la dispersion des Kusa (Epopée Soninké), Dakar, IFAN.

Meillassoux, C. and Silla, A., 1978, 'L'interprétation légendaire de l'histoire du Jonkoloni', in Bernardi, B. et al. (eds), 1978 347–92.

Mercadier, F.-J.-G., 1971, L'esclave de Timimoun, Paris, Ed. France-Empire.

Mettas, J., 1978, Répertoire des expéditions négrières françaises au XVIIIe siècle, Paris, Soc. franç. d'Hist. d'OM.

Meunier, D., 1980, 'Le commerce du sel de Taoudeni', Jl Soc. des Afr., 50, 2: 133–44.

Meyers, A., 1971, 'Slavery in Hausa-Fulani Emirates', in McCall, D. F. and Bennett, N. (eds), 1971.

Michelet, J., 1861, La sorcière, Paris, Bibliothèque Mondiale.

Miers, S. and Kopytoff, I. (eds), 1977, Slavery in Africa, Madison, Un. of Wisconsin Press.

Miller, J. C., 1977, 'Imbangala Lineage Slavery (Angola)', in Miers and Kopytoff, 1977: 205–31.

Miller, J. C., 1977, Slavery: A Teaching Bibliography, Brandeis, Crossroad Press and suppl. in Slavery and Abolition, 1980, 1, 1: 65–110.

Mintz, S. (ed.), 1981, Esclave = Facteur de production, Paris, Dunod.

Molin, Mgr, 1959, Recueil de proverbes bambaras et malinkes, Bamako, Les Presses Missionnaires.

Mollien, Th.-G. [1967], L'Afrique occidentale en 1818, Paris, Calmann-Lévy.

Monier, R., 1947, Manuel élémentaire de droit romain, Paris, Domat-Montchrestien.

Monod, T., 1975 (ed.), Les sociétes pastorales en Afrique tropicale, London, OUP.

Monteil, C., 1902–3, Carnets, unpub. documents, Arch. V. Monteil.

Monteil, C., 1915, Les Khassonké, Paris, E. Leroux.

Monteil, C., 1924 [1977], Les Bambara de Ségou et du Kaarta, Paris, Larose.

Monteil, C., 1927, *Le coton chez les Noirs*, Com. Et. Hist. Sci., AOF, Paris, Larose.

Monteil, C., 1929, *Les empires du Mali*, Paris, Maisonneuve & Larose.

Monteil, C., 1932 [1971], *Une cité soudanaise, Djenné*, Paris, Anthropos.

Monteil, C., 1966, 'Fin de siècle á Médine (1898–1899)', *B. IFAN*, B, 28, 1–2: 82–172.

Monteil, V., 1963, 'Contribution à la sociologie des Peuls: "Fonds Vieillard" de l'IFAN', *Bull. IFAN*, B, 25, 3–4: 351–414.

Monteil, V., 1964, *L'Islam noir*, Paris, Seuil.

Monteil, V., 1967, 'The Wolof Kingdom of Kayor', in Forde and Kaberry (eds), 1967: 260–82.

Monteil, V., 1968a, 'Un cas d'économie ostentatoire: les griots d'Afrique noire', *Economies et Sociétés*, 2, 4: 772–91.

Monteil, V., 1968b, 'Introduction aux voyages d'Ibn Battuta (1325–1353)', *Bull, IFAN*, B, 30, 2: 444–62.

Montrat, M., 1935, 'Notes sur les Malinke du Sankaran', *Outre-mer*, 7: 107–27.

Moraes, N.-I. de, 1978, 'La campagne négrière du *San-Antonio-e-as-Almas* (1670)', *Bull, IFAN*, B, 40, 4: 708–17.

Moraes Farias, P. F. de, 1974, 'Great States Revisited', *Jl of Afr. Hist.*, 15, 3: 479–88.

Moraes Farias, P. F. de, 1980, 'Model of the World and Categorial Models: The "Enslavable Barbarians" as a Mobile Classificatory Label', *Slavery and Abolition*, 1, 2; 115–31.

Mörner, M., 1980, *Buy or Breed*, Bucharest, Int. Congress of Historical Sciences.

Morton-Williams, P., 1967, 'The Yoruba Kingdom of Oyo', in Forde and Kaberry (eds), 1967: 36–69.

Mousnier, J., 1957, *Journal de la traite des Noirs*, Paris, Ed. de Paris.

Mousnier, R., 1969, *Les hiérarchies sociales de 1405 à nos jours*, Paris, PUF.

Munson, P., 1972, 'Archeology and the Prehistoric Origins of the Ghana Empire', *Conf. on Manding Studies*, London, SOAS, 1972.

Nadel, S. F., 1942, *Black Byzantium*, London, OUP.

N'Dyaye, B., 1970, *Les Castes au Mali*, Bamako, Editions Populaires.

N'Diaye, M, (ed.), 1978, 'Histoire de Ségou par Cheik Moussa Kamara', *Bull. IFAN*, 40, 3: 458–88.

Newbury, C. W., 1960, 'Une ancienne enquête sur l'esclavage et la captivité au Dahomey', *Zaïre*, 14, 1: 53–67.

Niane, D. T., 1960, *Soundjata ou l'épopée mandingue*, Paris, Présence Africaine.

Niane, D. T., 1974, 'Histoire et tradition historique du Manding', *Présence africaine*, 89, 1: 59–74.

Nicolas, F. J., 1977, 'L'origine et la signification du mot HARTANI et de ses équivalents', *Notes africaines*, 156: 101–6.

Nieboer, H. J., 1900, *Slavery as an Industrial System*, The Hague, Martinus Nijhoff.

Northrup, D., 1976, 'The compatibility of the Slave and Palm Oil Trades in the Bight of Biafra', *Jl of Afr. Hist.*, 17, 3: 353–64.

Northrup, D., 1981, 'Slavery in a Yoruba Society in the 19th Century', *in* Lovejoy (ed.), 1981: 101–22.

Nwachukwu-Ogedengbe, 1977, 'Slavery in Nineteenth Century Aboh (Nigeria)', *in* Miers and Kopytoff (eds), 1977: 133–52.

Nyendal, D. Van, 1705, 'Lettre', *in* Bosman, 1705: 458.

Obichere, B. I., 1978, 'Women and Slavery in the Kingdom of Dahomey', *Rev. franç. d'Hist. d'OM*, 65, 238: 5–20.

O'Fahey, R. S., 1973, 'Slavery and the Slave-Trade in Dār-Fūr', *Jl of Afr. Hist.*, 14, 1: 29–43.

Olivier de Sardan, J.-P., 1969a, *Les voleurs d'hommes*, Niamey, 'Etudes nigériennes', 25.

Olivier de Sardan, J.-P., 1969b, *Systèmes des relations économiques et sociales chez les Wogo du Niger*, Paris, Inst. d'Ethno.

Olivier de Sardan, J.-P. 1973, 'Personnalité et structures sociales (le cas sonxai)', *in* Colloques internationaux du CNRS, *La notion de personne en Afrique noire*: 421–46.

Olivier de Sardan, J.-P., 1973, 'Esclavage d'échange et captivité familiale chez les Songhay-Zerma', *Jl Soc. des Afr.*, 43, 1: 111–51.

Olivier de Sardan, J.-P., 1975, 'Captifs ruraux et esclaves impériaux du Songhay', *in* Meillassoux (ed.), 1975: 99–134.

Olivier de Sardan, J.-P., 1976, *Quand nos pères étaient captifs*, Paris, Nubia.

Olivier de Sardan, J.-P., 1982, *Concepts et conceptions Songhay-Zarma*, Paris, Nubia.

Olivier de Sardan, J.-P., 1984, *Les sociétés Songhay-Zarma (Niger-Mali)*, Paris, Karthala.

Ortoli, H., 1939, 'Le gage des personnes au Soudan français', *Bull. IFAN*, B, 1, 1: 313–24.

Panoff, M., 1970, 'Du suicide comme moyen de gouvernement', *Les Temps modernes*, 27, 288: 109–30.

Panoff, M., 1979, 'Travailleurs, recruteurs et planteurs dans l'archipel Bismarck de 1885 à 1914', *Jl de la Soc. des Océanistes*, 35, 64: 159–73.

Park, M. [1960], *Travels* (R. Miller, ed.), London, Dent & Sons.

Pasquier, R., 1967, 'A propos de l'émancipation des esclaves au Sénégal en

7

1848', *Rev. franç. d'Hist. d'OM*, 54, 194–7; 188–208.   (V

Patterson, O., 1979, 'On Slavery and Slave Formations', *MLR*, II, 7: 31–67.

Paulme, D., 1940, *L'organisation sociale des Dogon*, Paris, Domat-Mont-chrestien.

Paulme, D. (ed.), 1960, *Femmes d'Afrique noire*, Paris, Mouton.

Peristiany, J. G. (ed.), 1965, *Honour and Shame*, London, Weidenfeld & Nicolson.

Peroz, E., Cap., 1896, *Au Soudan français*, Paris, Calmann-Lévy.

Perrot, C.-H., 1975, 'Les captifs dans le royaume Anyi du Ndenye', *in* Meillassoux, C. (ed.), 1975*b*: 351–88.

Perrot, C. H., 1983, *Les Anyi-Indenye et le pouvoir aux XVIIIᵉ et XIXᵉ siècles*, Abidjan, CEDA.

Person, Y., 1968–75, *Samori, une révolution dyula*, Dakar, IFAN, Mém. no. 80, 3 vols.

Peytraud, L., 1897 [1973], *L'esclavage aux Antilles françaises avant 1789*, Pointe-a-Pitre, Desormeaux.

Piault, M., 1975, 'Captifs du pouvoir et pouvoir des captifs', *in* Meillassoux (ed.), 1975*b*: 321–50.

Piault, M., 1982, 'Le héros et son destin', *Cah. Et. afr*, 87–88, 22, 3–4; 403–40.

Pietri, Cap., 1885, *Les Français au Niger*, Paris, Hachette.

Pipes, D., 1981, *Slave Soldiers and Islam. The Genesis of a Military System*, London, CUP.

Polanyi, K., 1964, 'Sortings and "Ounce Trade" in the West African Slave Trade', *Jl of Afr. Hist.*, 5, 3: 381–94.

Polanyi, K., 1965, *Primitive, Archaic and Modern Economics*, New York, Doubleday, Anchor.

Polanyi, K., 1966, *Dahomey and the Slave-Trade*, Seattle, Un. of Washington Press.

Pollet, E. and Winter, G., 1971, *La société Soninke*, Brussels, Inst. de Sociologie, Ed. de l'Un. de Bruxelles.

Pontie, G., 1973, *Les Guiziga du Cameroun septentrional: l'organisation traditionnelle et sa mise en contestation*, Paris, Mém. ORSTOM, no. 65.

Postma, J., 1972, 'The Dimension of the Dutch Slave Trade from Western Africa', *Jl Afr. Hist.*, 13, 2: 237–48.

Pouillon, J. and Maranda, P. (eds), 1970, *Echanges et communications*, Paris, Mouton.

Pruneau de Pommegorge, 1789, *Description de la Nigritie*, Amsterdam.

Quesne, J.-S., 1819, *Histoire de l'esclavage en Afrique de P.-J. Dumont*, Paris, Pillet Aîné.

Quimby, L. G., 1975, 'History as Identity: The Jaaxanke and the Founding of Tuuba', *Bull. IFAN*, B, 37: 619–45.

Quinn, C. A., 1972, *Mandingo Kingdoms of the Senegambia*, Evanston, Northwestern Un. Press.

Raffenel, A., 1846, *Voyage dans l'Afrique occidentale (1843–1844)*, Paris, Arthus Bertrand.

Randles, W. G. L., 1968, *L'ancien Royaume du Congo des origines à la fin du XIXe siècle*, Paris, Mouton.

Randles, W. G. L., 1975, *L'Empire du Monomotapa du XVe au XIXe siècle*, Paris, Mouton.

Rattray, R. S., 1923, *Ashanti*, Oxford, Clarendon Press.

Rattray, R. S., 1929 [1969], *Ashanti Law and Constitution*, Oxford, Clarendon Press.

Reindorf, C. P., 1895, *The History of Gold Coast and Asante*, Basle.

Renaud, R. (ed.), 1972, *De l'ethnocide*, Paris, UGE, '10× 18'.

Renault, F., 1971, *Lavigerie, l'esclavage africain et l'Europe, 1868–1892*, Paris, E. de Boccard, 2 vols.

Renault, F., 1972, *L'abolition de l'esclavage au Sénégal*, Paris, Soc. franç. d'Hist. d'OM.

Renault, F., 1976, *Libération d'esclaves et nouvelle servitude*, Dakar, NEA.

Retel-Laurentin, A., 1974, *Infécondité en Afrique noire*, Paris, Masson & Cie.

Retel-Laurentin, A., 1979, *Causes de l'infécondité dans la Volta noire*, Paris, PUF, 'INED, Trav. et Doc.', no. 87.

Rey, P.-P., 1971, *Colonialisme, néo-colonialisme et transition au capitalisme*, Paris, Maspero.

Rey, P.-P., 1975, 'L'esclavage lignager chez les Tsangui, les Punu et les Kuni du Congo-Brazzaville', *in* Meillassoux (ed.), 1975b: 509–28.

Rey, P.-P., 1976, *Capitalisme négrier*, Paris, Maspero.

Rey, P.-P. (n.d.), *Les concepts de l'anthropologie économique marxiste*, thesis, Doct. Etat, Univ. R. Descartes.

Rey-Hulman, D., 1975, 'Les dépendants des maîtres tyokossi pendant la période coloniale', *in* Meillassoux (ed.), 1975b: 297–320.

Richard-Molard, J., 1948–9, 'Démographie et structure des sociétés négo-peul parmi les hommes libres et les "serfs" du Fouta Dialon (région de Labé)', *Rev. Géog. humaine et Ethnol.*, 1, 4: 45–51.

Richards, W. A., 1980, 'The Import of Firearms into West Africa in the 18th Century', *Jl of Afr. Hist.*, 21, 1: 43–60.

Richardson, J., 1854, *Narrative of a Mission to Central Africa*, London, 2 vols.

Riesman, P., 1974, *Société et liberté chez les Peul Djelgôbé de Haute-Volta*, Paris, Mouton.

Rizvi, M. S. S. A., 1967, ' "Zenj": its First Known Use in Arabic Literature', *Azania*, 2: 200–1.

Roberts, R., n.d., *Production and Reproduction in Warrior States: Segu Bambara and Segu Tukulor*, 22 p. mult.

Roberts, R., 1978, *The Maraka and the Economy of the Middle Niger Valley*, Ph. D. Dept. of History, Un. of Toronto.

Roberts, R., 1980a, *Multiplier Effect in the Ecologically Specialized Trade of Pre-colonial West Africa*, Centre for African Studies, Dalhousie Univ.

Roberts, R., 1980b, 'Long-distance Trades and Production: Sinsanni in the 19th Cent.', *Jl of Afr. Hist.*, 21, 2: 169–88.

Roberts, R., 1980c, 'The Emergence of a Grain Market in Bamako, 1883–1908', *Rev. canadienne des Et. afr.* 14, 1: 55–81.

Roberts, R., 1984, *Warriors and Merchants*, Dept of History, Stanford Un.

Roberts, R. and Klein, M. A., 1980, 'The Banamba Slave Exodus of 1905 and the Decline of Slavery in Western Sudan', *Jl of African Hist.*, 21, 3: 375–94.

Robertson, C. C., 1983, 'Post-Proclamation Slavery in Accra: A Female Affair?', *in* Robertson and Klein (eds), 1983: 220–42.

Robertson, C. C. and Klein, M. A. (eds), 1983, *Women and Slavery in Africa*, Madison, Un. of Wisconsin Press.

Robertson, G. A. (1819), *Notes on Africa*, London, Sherwood, Neely & Joves.

Roche, D., 1973, *Ordres et classes*, Paris, Mouton.

Rodinson, M., 1966, *Islam et capitalisme*, Paris, Seuil.

Rodney, W., 1966, 'African Slavery and Other Forms of Social Oppression on Upper Guinea Coast in the Contact of the Atlantic Slave Trade', *Jl Afr. Hist.*, 7: 431–43.

Rodney, W., 1969, 'Gold and Slaves on the Gold Coast', *Trans. Hist. Soc. Ghana*, 10: 13–38.

Ronen, D., 1971, 'On the African Role in the Transatlantic Slave Trade in Dahomey', *Cah. Et. afr.*, 11, 1 (41): 5–13.

Rouch, J., 1953, *Contribution à l'histoire des Songhay*, Dakar, IFAN.

Roussier, P., 1935, *L'établissement d'Issinie (1628–1702)*, Paris.

Ruyle, E. E., 1973, 'Slavery, Surplus, and Stratification of the Nothern Coast', *Cur. Anthropology*, 14, 5, Dec. 1973: 603–32.

Ryan, T. C. I., 1975, 'The Economics of Human Sacrifice', *Afr. Econ. Hist. Rev.*, 2, 2, Fall 1975: 1–9.

Ryders, A. F. C., 1969, *Benin and the Europeans, 1485–1897*, London.

Saint-Père, J.-H., 1925, *Les Sarakollé du Guidimakha*, Paris, Larose.

Salifou, A., 1971, *Le Damagaram ou le sultanat de Zinder au XIXe siècle*, Niamey, 'Etudes nigériennes', no. 27.

Samb, A., 1980, 'L'Islam et l'esclavage', *Notes africaines*, Dakar, 168: 93–7.

Samuel, M., 1977, *Le prolétariat africain noir en France*, Paris, Maspero.

Sanneh, L. O., 1976a, 'Slavery, Islam and the Jakhanke People of West Africa', *Africa*, 46, 1: 80–97.

Sanneh, L. O., 1976b, 'The Origin of Clericalism in West African Islam', *Jl of Afr. Hist.*, XVII, I: 49–72.

Saraiva, A. J., 1967, 'Le P. Antonio Vieira, s.j., et la question de l'esclavage des Noirs au xviie siècle', *Annales, Et. Soc. Civ.*, 22, Nov.–Dec.: 1289–309.

Sauvageot, S., 1965, *Contribution à l'histoire du royaume bambara de Ségou – XVIIIe et XIXe siècles*, Paris, Fac. des Lettres, Sorbonne.

Schnakenbourg, C., 1980, *La crise du système esclavagiste 1835–1847*, Paris, L'Harmattan.

Schoelcher, V., 1880, *L'esclavage au Sénégal en 1880*, Paris, Librairie Centrale des Publications Populaires.

Schoelcher, V., 1948, *Esclavage et colonisation*, Paris, PUF.

Servet, J.-M., 1981, *Genèse des formes et pratiques monétaires*, thesis, Doct. d'Etat et Sc. éco., Université Lyon II.

Seydou, C., 1972, *Sillâmaka et Poullôri*, Paris, A. Colin.

Shui Hu, 1974, *Les 108 brigands du Liang Shan*, Paris, Signes, 2 vols.

Sidibe, M., 1935, 'Tableau de la vie indigène au Soudan et dans la boucle du Niger (du xviiie à nos jours)', *L'Educ. afric.*, 24, 89: 3–26.

Silberbauer, G. B. and Kuper, A. J., 1966, 'Kalagari Masters and Bushmen Serfs: Some Observations', *Afr. Stud.*, 25, 4: 171–9.

Siran, J.-L., 1980, 'Emergence et dissolution des principautés guerrières Vouté (Cameroun)', *Jl Soc. des Afric.*, 50, 1: 25–58.

Sissoko, K., 1975, 'La prise de Dionkoloni', *in* Dumestre and Kesteloot (eds), 1975.

Skertchly, J. A., 1874, *Dahomey as it is*, London.

Skinner, E. P., 1964, *The Mossi of the Upper Volta*, Berkeley, Stanford Un. Press.

Smaldone, J. P., 1972, 'Firearms in the Central Sudan: A Revolution', *Jl of African History*, 13: 591–607.

Smith, M. G., 1954, 'Slavery and Emancipation in Two Societies', *Social and Econ. Stud*, 3, 3–4: 239–90.

Smith, M. G., 1967, 'A Hausa Kingdom: Maradi under Dan Bashore, 1854–1875', *in* Forde and Kaberry, 1967: 93–122.

Smith, R., 1967, 'Yoruba Armaments', *Jl Afr. Hist.*, 8: 96–8.

Snelgrave, W., 1734, *A New Account of Some Parts of Guinea and the Slave Trade*, London, James, John and Paul Knapton.

Sow, A. I. (ed.), 1971, *Dictionnaire élémentaire fulfulde-français*, Niamey, CRDTO.

Spini, A. and S. (eds), 1984, 'I Bozo del Niger: Insediaments e Architettura', *Storia della Citta*, 25, 132 p.

Stavenhagen, R., 1969, *Les classes sociales dans les sociétés agraires*, Paris, Anthropos.

Stein, R., 1978, 'Measuring the French Slave Trade', *Jl of African History*, XIX, 4: 515–22.

Strobel, M., 1983, 'Slavery and Reproductive Labor in Mombasa', *in* Robertson and Klein, 1983: 111–29.

Suret-Canale, J., 1964a, 'Contexte et conséquences sociales de la traite africaine', *Présence africaine*, no. 50: 142–3.

Suret-Canale, J., 1964b, *L'Afrique noire, l'ère coloniale 1900–1945*, Paris, Ed. Sociales.

Suret-Canale, J., 1969, 'Les origines ethniques des anciens captifs du Fouta Djalon', *Notes afr.*, 123: 91–2.

Sy, M.-O., 'Le Dahomey, gouvernement, administration', *Acta Ethnographica* (Budapest), XII, 3–4: 333–65.

Sy, M. O., 1965, 'Le Dahomey, le coup d'Etat de 1818', *Folia Orientalia*, VI: 205–38.

Talhami, G. H., 1977, 'The Zanj Rebellion Reconsidered', *Int. Jl of Afr. Hist. Studies*, 10, 3: 443–61.

Tandeter, E., 1981, 'Forced and Free Labour in Late Colonial Potosi (Bolivia)', *Past and Present*, 93: 98–136.

Tardits, C., 1970, 'Femmes à crédit', *in* Pouillon and Maranda (eds), 1970: 382–90.

Tardits, C., 1973, 'Parenté et pouvoir politique chez les Bamoum', *L'Homme*, XIII, 1–2: 37–49.

Tardits, C., 1980a, *Le royaume bamoum*, Paris, A. Colin.

Tardits, C., 1980b, 'Roi divin', *Encyclopedia Universalis*, Paris.

Tautain, Dr L., 1884, 'Notes sur les castes chez les Mandingues et chez les Bamanas', *Rev. d'Ethnographie*, III: 343s.

Tembera, T., 1978, 'Biton Kulibali ka masala', *in* Kesteloot (ed.), 1978.

TEF: Tarikh el-Fettach [1964], Adrien Maisonneuve (see Kâti).

Teixera da Motta, A., 1969, 'Un document nouveau pour l'histoire des Peuls au Sénégal pendant les xve et xvie siècles', *Bol. Cult. da Guiné Portuguesa*, 96.

Teixera da Mota, A. and Mauny, R., 1978, 'Livre de l'armement du navire *São Miguel* de l'île de São Tomé au Bénin (1522)', *Bull. IFAN*, 40, B, 1, 1978: 68–86.

TEN (Tedzkiret en-Nisiān) [1966] (transl. O. Houdas), Paris, A. Maisonneuve.

TES: Tarikh es-Sudan [1964], A. Maisonneuve (see Es-Sa'di).

Terray, E., 1974, 'Long-Distance Exchange and the Formation of the

State', *Economy and Society*, 3, 3: 315–45.

Terray, E., 1975*a*, 'Class and Class Consciousness in the Abron Kingdom of Gyaman', *in* Bloch (ed.), 1975: 85–136.

Terray, E., 1975*b*, 'La captivité dans le royaume abron du Gyaman', *in* Meillassoux (ed.), 1975*b*.

Terray, E., 1976, 'Contribution à une étude sur l'armée asante', *Cah. Et. afr.*, 61–62, XVI (1–2): 297–356.

Terray, E., 1982*a*, 'Nature et fonction de la guerre dans le monde akan', *in* Bazin and Terray (eds), 1982: 375–422.

Terray, E., 1982*b*, 'Réflexions sur la formation du prix des esclaves à l'intérieur de l'Afrique de l'Ouest précoloniale', *Journal des Africanistes*, 52, 1–2: 119–44.

Terray, E., 1983, 'Gold Production, Slave Labour and State Intervention in Pre-colonial Akan Societies', *Research in Economic Anthropology*, 5: 95–129.

Thapar, R., 1980, 'State Formation in Early India', *Int. Soc. Sci. J.*, XXX, I, 4: 655–69.

Thapar, R., 1984, *From Lineage to State*, Bombay, OUP.

Thilmans, G., 1976, 'La relation de François de Paris (1682–1683)', *B. IFAN*, B, 38, 1, Jan. 1976: 1–51.

Thilmans, G., Descamps, C. and Khayat, B., 1980, *Protohistoire du Sénégal*, I: *Les sites mégalithiques*, Dakar, IFAN, Mem. no. 91.

Thorner, A., 1982, 'Semi-Feudalism or Capitalism', *in* 'Caste et classe en Asie du Sud', special issue, *Purusārtha*, 6: 19–72.

Thornton, J., 1979, *The Kingdom of Kongo in the Era of Civil Wars, 1641–1718*, Ph.D. dissertation, Berkeley, Univ. of California.

Tiendrebeogo, 1963, 'Histoire traditionnelle des Mossi de Ouagadougou', *Jl Soc. Afric.*, 33, 1963: 11.

Toledano, E. R., 1981, 'Slave Dealers, Women, Pregnancy and Abortion', *Slavery and Abolition*, 2, 1: 53–68.

Traore Ray Autra, M., 1979, 'Les unités de mesure dans l'ancienne société mandingue de Guinée', *Notes afr.*, 163: 63–5.

Triaud, J.-L., 1981, 'L'Islam en Afrique de l'Ouest', *Colloque de la Société pour l'avancement des études islamiques*, Paris, 27–28 Mar. 1981.

Trimingham, J. S., 1962, *A History of Islam in West Africa*, London, OUP.

Triulzi, A., 1981, *Salt, Gold and Legitimacy*, Istituto Un. Orientale.

Tuden, A., 1958, 'Ila Slavery', *Hum. Prob. Brit. Cent. Afr.*, 24: 68–78.

Tymowski, M., 1974*a*, 'La ville et la campagne au Soudan occidental du XIV^c au XVI^c siècle', *Acta Poloniae Historica*, 29: 51–79.

Tymowski, M., 1974*b*, *Le développement et la régression chez les peuples de la boucle du Niger à l'époque précoloniale*, Warsaw, Wydawnictwa Universytetu Warszawskiego.

Unesco (ed.), 1979, *The African Slave-Trade from the 15th to the 19th Century*, Paris, Unesco.

Valensi, L., 1967, 'Esclaves chrétiens et esclaves noirs à Tunis au xviii^c siècle', *Annales (ESC)*, 22: 1267–88.

Van Dantzig, A., 1975, 'Effects of the Atlantic Slave on Some West African Societies', *Revue franç. de l'Hist. d'OM*, 62, 226–7; 252–69.

Vansina, J., 1961, 'De la tradition orale', *Annales*, no. 36, Tervuren.

Vansina, J., 1975, 'Kuba Chronology Revisited', *Paideuma*, 21: 134–50.

Vercoutter, J., 1976, 'L'iconographie du Noir dans l'Egypte ancienne des origines à la xxv^c dynastie', *in* Bugner, L., 1976, I: 33–88.

Verlinden, C., 1955, *L'esclavage dans l'Europe médiévale*, Bruges.

Verlinden, Ch., 1966, 'Esclavage noir en France méridionale et courants de traite en Afrique', *Annales du Midi*, 78, 77–78; 335–43.

Vidal-Naquet, P., 1965, 'Economie et société dans la Grèce ancienne: l'œuvre de Moses I. Finley', *Archives européennes de Sociologie*, 6: 111–48.

Vidal-Naquet, P., 1967, 'Les esclaves grecs étaient-ils une classe?', *Raison présente*, 6: 103–12.

Villamarin, J. A. and J. E., 1975, *Indian Labor in Mainland Colonial Spanish America*, Newark, Un. of Delaware, Latin America Studies Program, Mon. no. 1.

Vissière, I. and J.-L., 1982, *La traite des Noirs du siècle des Lumières*, Paris, A.-M. Métailié.

Walckenaer, C.-A., 1842, *Collection des relations de voyages par mer et par terre en différentes parties de l'Afrique depuis 1400 jusque' à nos jours*, Paris, 21 vols.

Wansbrough, J., 1970, 'Africa and the Arab Geographs', *in* Dalby, D. (ed.), 1970: 89–101.

Watson, J. L. (ed.), 1980, *Asian and African Systems of Slavery*, Oxford, Blackwell.

Weil, P. M., 1970, 'Mandinka Fertility, Islam, and Integration in a Plural Society', *American Anthropological Ass.*, San Diego, 19–22 November.

White, L. A., 1969, *The Science of Culture*, New York, Farrar, Straus & Giroux.

Wilks, I., 1967, 'Ashanti Government', *in* Forde and Kaberry, 1967: 206–38.

Wilks, I., 1971, 'Asante Policy towards the Hausa Trade in the 19th Century', *in* Meillassoux (ed.), 1971: 124–44.

Williams, E., 1944, *Capitalism and Slavery*, NY, Capricorn Books.

Wismes, A. de, 1973, *La vie quotidienne dans les ports aux XVIIe et XVIIIe siècles*, Paris, Hachette.

Wright, M., 1983, 'Bwanikwa: Consciousness and Protest among Slave Women in Central Africa', *in* Robertson and Klein, 1983: 246–67.

Zeys, E., 1900, 'Esclavage et guerre sainte. Consultation adressée aux gens du Touat par un érudit nègre, cadi de Timboctou au xviie siècle', *Bull. Réunion Et. algér.*, 2: 125–151; 166–89.

Index of Proper Names

405

Subject Index

abduction, 20, 31, 103, 143
abolition, 314–16
abortion, 82, 134, 135
absolutism, 177, 182, 196, 245;
  aristocratic, 185
adelphic succession, 296
adolescents, 153–4, 160, 214, 269
adoption, 12, 30, 301
adultery, 136
affinity, 30, 31, 33, 100,1 102, 107, 146,
  180, 191, 194–6
agamy, 328
age set, 128, 225
alien, 25, 26, 28–34, 35–9, 40, 67, 75,
  99, 102, 103, 105, 106, 115, 146–7,
  151, 195, 244, 256, 325, 327, 332 (see
  also extraneousness)
alienability, 9, 124, 125, 208, 213, 285,
  291, 317
alienation, 11, 108, 112, 127–9, 193, 245,
  319
alliance, 69, 102–5, 146
alms, 247
amalgam, 33, 109
Amazon, 194
anceocracy, 187; feminine, 193
ancestor, 147, 173, 182, 223, 246
ancillary, 19, 103, 172, 185, 197, 313
apparatus, 231
arbitrary decisions (of master), 118,
  122, 125, 136–7
arbitration, 32, 70, 113, 152, 243–6

aristocracy, 54, 66, 72, 83, 105, 116,
  140, 148, 162, 165, 170, 171, 180,
  182–6, 191, 197–200, 207, 214–16, 219,
  220, 222, 223, 226, 228, 231, 235,
  243, 249, 251, 327; dynastic, 818;
  military, 54, 505; Muslim, 52, 264;
  slaving, 215; warrior, 49, 57, 63, 241
aristocrats, 136, 167, 169, 173, 188, 189,
  190, 194, 201, 205, 211, 213, 215, 219,
  234–5, 243, 246, 318
army, 46, 48, 51, 71, 73, 78, 152, 158,
  160, 164, 169, 187, 191, 204, 218, 266,
  318; colonial, 265, 272, 275;
  numbers in the, 165–8; permanent,
  167, 174, 201, 205; army police, 234
  (see also soldier–slave)
art, 251
artisan, 206, 214, 222, 234 (see also
  craft); of caste, 286
avuncular, 122, 132, 134, 176, 326

ban, 259
band, 58, 70, 71, 76, 144, 147, 152–3,
  156, 218, 228, 276, 328
barter, 14
bastard, 27, 32, 136
bestiality, 74
birth, 23, 28, 101, 107, 122–5, 127, 134,
  136, 138, 149–50, 173, 193, 197, 225,
  241, 194, 330; fictitious, 108
booty, 20, 45, 59, 94, 119, 148, 151,
  159, 164, 168, 169, 216, 222, 225,

414